G000242827

COLIN TAYLOR, retired associate professor in the Department of Geographical Sciences and Planning at the University of Queensland, has held town-planning positions in Victoria, Tasmania and Scotland, and has given conference papers and talks on planning and transportation all over the world. He has also produced articles and broadcasts on the fascination of railways.

In the last 30 years he has taken more than 6000 rail journeys in Australia and overseas, covering some 603,000km (375,000 miles). He compiles the biennial World Speed Review for *Railway Gazette International* and is also the author of *Great Rail Non-Journeys of Australia*, *Steel Roads of Australia* and *Traincatcher*.

Australia by Rail
Fourth edition: November 2000

Publisher
Trailblazer Publications
The Old Manse, Tower Rd, Hindhead, Surrey, GU26 6SU, UK
Fax (+44) 01428-607571
info@trailblazer-guides.com
www.trailblazer-guides.com

British Library Cataloguing in Publication Data
A catalogue record for this book is available from the British Library

ISBN 1-873756-40-2

Maps © Trailblazer 2000
Photographs © as follows and reproduced by permission of the copyright holders.
Queensland Rail: cover photograph and photographs opposite p32 and p224 (top);
Roy Sinclair: photograph of author on p1; Bryn Thomas: opposite p33 (top), p64
(top left), pp96-97 and pp128-129; Venice-Simplon Orient-Express: opposite p33
(bottom); RN Schroeder: opposite p64 (bottom left, top right, bottom right);
Countrylink: opposite p64 (middle right); South Australian Tourism Commission:
opposite p160 (top), p193 and p256 (bottom); Tourism Queensland: opposite p160
(bottom) and p256; Western Australian Tourism Commission, Ethel Davies: opposite p161; Skyrail: opposite p225; The Ipswich Workshops: opposite p257

Editor: Anna Jacomb-Hood
Series editor: Patricia Major
Typesetting: Margaret Jones
Layout: Anna Jacomb-Hood
Cartography: Nick Hill
Index: Jane Thomas

Every effort has been made by the author and publisher to ensure that the
information contained herein is as accurate and up to date as possible. However,
they are unable to accept responsibility for any inconvenience, loss or injury sustained by anyone as a result of the advice and information given in this guide.

Printed on chlorine-free paper from farmed forests by
Star Standard (☎ +65-8613866), Singapore

AUSTRALIA
BY RAIL

COLIN TAYLOR

TRAILBLAZER PUBLICATIONS

Acknowledgements

Marvin Saltzman of California, author of the famous *Eurail Guide Annual*, encouraged the first edition of this book. Since then I have had support and assistance in every possible way from the management and staff of all the rail operators in Australia (and at all levels from chief executives to passenger attendants, drivers, guards and even porters – yes, there's not many of that breed left!), from Metro Monorail and Light Rail in Sydney, from Skyrail Pty Ltd of Cairns, and from individuals and travellers too numerous to mention even if I remembered all their names.

Special mention must be made of Mike Kent, long-time friend and travel companion now a Queensland engine driver, of Bob Schroeder for reviewing the text of the previous edition and correcting errors and whose photographs appear on p64, and of John Morley, John Atkin, Cathy Fuller, Roger Stanton and Margot Logan, who made so many things possible. The personal interest and encouragement of Hilary Bradt, publisher of the earlier editions, who has experienced some of Australia's best train trips is also greatly appreciated. My thanks also to Bryn Thomas for taking on the task of publishing and to Anna Jacomb-Hood for her painstaking and meticulous work in editing the text.

Finally, without the patient tolerance of my wife Barbara, the guide could never have been produced in the first place, let alone run to five editions (including one in German).

A request

The author and publisher have tried to ensure that this guide is as accurate and up to date as possible. However, things change: prices rise, rail services are extended or cut back, hotels open and close. If you notice any omissions or changes that should be included in the next edition of this book, please write to Colin Taylor at Trailblazer (address on p2). A free copy of the next edition will be sent to persons making a significant contribution.

Front cover: The Savannahlander – stopping for a break.

CONTENTS

TIMETABLES

INTRODUCTION

By the scale of European countries, Australia is vast. Imagine the whole northern half of Africa, a great desert with population centres mostly on the edges. That is something like Australia. And travel in much of Australia is not unlike a journey on the African continent – the same timeless bush, the same enervating heat. In a car the distances and glare of the sky induce drowsiness. The unsealed gravel roads of the outback are like the laterite roads of the African savannah, slippery when wet, loose when dry, ridged like corrugated iron and infested with road trains – thundering great lorries hauling multiple trailers at breakneck speed. These are frightening to meet and more lethal than the snakes and crocodiles you will rarely see. Travelling by road you may reach your destination hot, tired and thirsty, hating both the bush and the concrete jungles of the city. Visitors can find Australia's road rules confusing and the unwary motorist can easily fall foul of the law. If a sign says 'Next Petrol 300km' you can be sure that when you run out of fuel and wander into the bush you will easily get lost.

It is better to see Australia by rail. Australia's railways offer a unique way of travelling round the country. You may not always get there more quickly but you will get there more safely and have time to relax, enjoy the scenery, and converse with Australians and tourists from all over the world, while sitting in comfort without the constraining bonds of a seat belt. Overseas visitors can make use of the excellent-value Austrailpass or the passes and fare concessions offered by the country's railway systems, which residents can also use to explore the country.

And Australia is worth exploring because it is a land of contrasts. Not only is there a world of difference between the wheat fields of Victoria and the sugar plantations of Queensland, or the dry red desert of the interior and the torrential downpours of the coastal ranges; there is a great contrast between the fastest and newest trains and some you may find on the lesser-known branch lines.

You can penetrate the remote outback in air-conditioned comfort on trains like the Spirit of the Outback or The Ghan and travel through Crocodile Dundee country on the Gulflander or Savannahlander. The world's fastest rack railway, the Perisher Skitube, will take you to the slopes of Mt Blue Cow in the Snowy Mountains or you can cross the famous Harbour Bridge by train in the heart of Sydney. By train you can also see examples of almost every type of Australian landscape – from the dense rainforests of tropical Queensland to the unbelievable emptiness of the Nullarbor Plain, the deep canyons of the Blue Mountains and the rocky crags of the outback ranges.

Options range from planned itineraries through package tours to doing it your own way. As well as giving essential details about the principal and other popular train services, *Australia by Rail* offers ideas not found in official publications or ordinary travel literature. This should assist both those who stick to the main lines and those who like to wander off the beaten track. And you can!

IMPORTANT NOTES

Train schedules

As with all guide books it is necessary to explain some general principles and issue a few words of caution to the intending traveller. First of all, before commencing any journey, double check the departure and arrival times given in this book or in any timetable, as they are subject to change without prior notice. Changes will usually be minor and have little effect on most of the trips described in this book but Australia is not as well served by rail networks as Europe, for example, and you would not want to miss the only train of the day. Most interstate and long-distance trains run regularly, though not necessarily every day of the year, but other trains may not operate on public holidays such as Christmas Day, Good Friday and Anzac Day (25 April). Train schedules are particularly liable to change at weekends and during holiday periods (see p105), eg the Queenslander does not run between mid-December and mid-March, but additional Sunlanders usually operate in December and January. Schedules should also be checked during Australian long weekend holidays, which vary from state to state.

Eastern Summer Time applies between late October and March in Victoria, New South Wales and South Australia. This affects the times of trains to or from the other states, eg interstate trains will arrive in or leave Queensland one hour earlier. Schedules to and from Western Australia are less likely to be altered but arrivals at and departures from Adelaide to and from the west should always be checked. There is a 30-minute time-zone change between the Eastern states and South Australia, and one of 90 minutes out in the Nullarbor. Usually the train conductor will tell you when to alter your watch.

No publication which includes railway (or any other) timetables can hope to remain up-to-date. Not even those published by the railways

---

Goods and Services Tax

July 1, 2000, marked the introduction of a Goods and Services Tax (GST) in Australia. Unless stated otherwise, all prices quoted in this book are pre-GST. The full effects of the new tax and associated changes are still unclear, but it is wise to assume that fares, accommodation and meal costs, admission charges, and almost anything else for which a price is given in this book may be increased by around 10 per cent.

themselves! As an official in one major railway booking office said to me 'We'd be the last to know!' There are regular travellers who will swear that railway timetables should properly be classed as works of fiction; that their main use is 'to show how late the train is' is a well-known saying. The fact of life is that trains can be and often need to be rescheduled for all sorts of reasons which might or might not be understood if explained at the time to the unfortunate travellers. This is not peculiar to the railways of Australia; it is a worldwide phenomenon.

Most Australian rail services as well as bus and ferry schedules are summarised in the Thomas Cook *Overseas Timetable*; this is published bi-monthly. Timetables given in this book are extracts only and do not show complete schedules on most lines. In particular, the times given for any round trips may not reflect all the departure times from either the base city or the destination city. On a particular route there may be later departure times from the base city and earlier departure times from the destination city than are shown, none of which would be applicable to a one-day round trip, but which might be useful if an overnight stay were contemplated. Where it is stated that services are frequent, this means at least once an hour during normal daylight hours or between the time limits indicated.

Up-to-date information on changes and local timetables can usually be obtained free of charge at major railway stations and rail travel centres. A small charge is made for V/line and Metropolitan timetables in Victoria. Timetable information is increasingly becoming available on the Internet (see p25) but it is best to double check.

Timetables

All departure, arrival or other times in this book are based on the 24-hour clock. A departure at 1.10pm is shown as 13.10; midnight is 24.00. Time between midnight and 1am is shown as 00.01 to 00.59. This corresponds to the practice used in most railway timetables (eg in Europe) and in the timetables published by Thomas Cook, though railways in Australia mostly tend to use 'am' and 'pm'.

The numbers appearing at the start of each timetable (other than itineraries) are the relevant Thomas Cook numbers (*Overseas Timetable*) and are prefixed by a 'C'. This enables the traveller to make a preliminary check before making a booking. It does not obviate the need for a final check before actually going to the station. Where Cook's tables do not cover all the places or trains referred to, the word 'local' is used instead of table numbers. There are also some references to Cook's tables in the text using the same format. Lowercase letters after times or place names, eg 10.35g, refer to explanatory footnotes which follow each table.

Where arrival or departure times vary on some days by less than five minutes from the normal, the differences are not always shown in the tables so as to save space and simplify the presentation. In such cases the departure times given will always be the earliest, so that you do not miss your train.

Bus and coach services

Details of bus and coach services are given only where they connect otherwise isolated railheads or provide the only service to destinations of interest which are within reasonable distance of a railway. The Thomas Cook timetable gives details of bus and ferry services.

General

This book does not list hotels/restaurants for all the places described, nor does it provide a comprehensive guide to Australia generally. This would merely duplicate information available in more general guides, such as the Lonely Planet series. Lonely Planet's *Australia* is an extremely comprehensive volume and well worth the price. Another good buy is Thomas Cook's *Australia* in the Independent Traveller's series.

This book, however, provides enough information to keep the average visitor from going wrong, as well as offering a few tips on where to stay or eat. These are restricted to such establishments as are handy to railway stations or which have been personally sampled by the writer or recommended by others. This is no guarantee that things will not have changed or that other establishments might not better suit the traveller.

Fares

Fares quoted in this guide are correct to the time of going to press. Rail Australia warns that 'all fares as well as timetables are subject to alteration without notice'. This is, of course, also true for all other prices in this book.

 Warning – conditional or restricted stopping services (†)
Most interstate trains as well as many long-distance intrastate trains do not carry passengers between, or may not stop at, all intermediate stations for which times are given in the timetable. Many are conditional stops, where the train stops only on prior request and confirmed bookings. Some are restricted stops, either for picking up only or setting down only; yet others may be both conditional and restricted. Where '(†)' follows the name of a stopping place in this guide, it means there are some restrictions of this kind. These are mostly explained but conditions may vary and intending passengers should always enquire before attempting to travel to or from these places.

Getting to Australia

It is assumed you will be coming to Australia the most likely way: by air. Airlines may be contacted direct or through your local travel agent who is usually able to offer discounted fares. Special package deals and inclusive tours abound and prices vary according to season, route taken and demand. Travellers should beware of bogus tour operators: stick to known firms with a sound reputation or ones recommended by other travellers, and **always** take out travel insurance.

It is often possible to arrange to fly into Australia at one place and leave from another. This extends the range of options for working out a personal rail itinerary within Australia. Travellers from Western Europe have another option in that air fares via Asia and air fares via America are not greatly different so that round the world fares or packages are available often at little more than the price of an ordinary return.

From some countries, especially Britain, there are as many ways of flying to Australia as there are of skinning the proverbial cat. Often an indirect and seemingly expensive route can prove the best bargain.

Flight Centre, a Queensland-based firm which has offices in Britain, Canada, the USA, South Africa and New Zealand, can book flights as well as rail travel on Queensland Rail (QR).

MAKING A BOOKING IN THE UK AND IRELAND

From London, flights to Australia are offered by many airlines, for example Air New Zealand via Auckland or LA, Alitalia via Milan, Cathay Pacific via Hong Kong, Egypt Air via Cairo, Garuda via Denpasar or Jakarta, KLM via Amsterdam, Lauda Air via Vienna, Malaysia Airlines via Kuala Lumpur, Olympic via Athens, Royal Brunei, Singapore Airlines, Thai via Bangkok and United via New York and LA, apart from the direct flights by the obvious airlines of Qantas and British Airways. At the time of writing Virgin is poised to enter the Australian market, while charter airline Britannia is likely to offer increased services. On the writer's last visit to Britain, the best deal was with Japan Air Lines via Osaka (outward) and Tokyo (homeward) – inclusive of an overnight hotel stop each way; return fares can be as low as £440.

● **Austravel** (☎ 020-7734 7755 or 0870 055 0245), 50 Conduit St, London W1; branches also in Bristol (☎ 0117-927 7425, 🖹 0117-927

6494), Edinburgh (☎ 0131-226 1000, 🖹 0131-226 4000), Manchester (☎ 0161-832 2445, 🖹 0161-832 7473) and other cities. Flights to Sydney, Adelaide, Brisbane, Cairns, Melbourne and Perth from £469.

● **Bridge the World** (☎ 020-7734 7447, 🖹 020-7734 6455, 🖳 sales@bridge-the-world.co.uk, www.bridgetheworld.com), 4 Regent Place, Regent St, London W1R 5FB, offers return flights, round the world fares, a visa/ETA service and packages on The Ghan, Indian Pacific and the Great South Pacific Express.

● **Kuoni Travel** (☎ 01306-744296, 🖹 01306-741099, 🖳 australia.sales@kuoni.co.uk, www.kuoni.co.uk), Kuoni House, Dorking, Surrey RH5 4AZ, offers packages on The Ghan, Indian Pacific and the Great South Pacific Express.

● **Qantas Holidays** (☎ 0990 673464, 🖹 020-8748 7505), Sovereign House, 361 King St, Hammersmith, London W6 9NA. Books flights, accommodation etc and has tours on The Ghan, Indian Pacific, Queenslander, and the Great South Pacific Express. Visas/ETAs are arranged free of charge for people booking tours through Qantas Holidays.

● **STA Travel** has many branches in Britain including: 117 Euston Rd, London NW1 2SX (☎ 020-7465 0484); 38 Store St, London WC1 E7BZ (☎ 020-7580 7733); 86 Old Brompton Rd, London SW7 3LQ (☎ 020-7581 4132); 11 Goodge St, London W1P 1FE (☎ 020-7436 7779); 25 Queens Rd, Bristol (☎ 0117-929 4399, 🖹 0117-929 4791); 75 Deansgate, Manchester (☎ 0161-839 7838); 38 Sidney St, Cambridge (☎ 01223-366966); 38/9 North St, Brighton (☎ 01273-728282); 36 George St, Oxford (☎ 01865-792800); 88 Vicar Lane, Leeds (☎ 0113-244 9212); 184 Byres Rd, Glasgow (☎ 0141-338 6000, 🖹 0141-338 6022). A student travel centre which specialises in student and independent travellers.

● **Trailfinders** has branches in London at 194 Kensington High St, W8 7RG (☎ 020-7938 3939), 42-50 Earls Court Rd, W8 6FT (☎ 020-7938 3366) and 1 Threadneedle St, EC2R 8JX (☎ 020-7628 7628). Other branches are at: 22-24 The Priory, Queensway, Birmingham B4 6BS (☎ 0121-236 1234); 48 Corn St, Bristol BS1 1HQ (☎ 0117-929 9000); 254-284 Sauchiehall St, Glasgow G2 3EH (☎ 0141-353 2224); 58 Deansgate, Manchester M3 2FF (☎ 0161-839 6969); 7-9 Ridley Place, Newcastle-upon-Tyne NE1 8JQ (☎ 0191-261 2345).

Trailfinders offers return fares, round the world fares (such as London–Brisbane–Sydney–London), a visa/ETA service and a package on the Great South Pacific Express.

Rail passes and tickets
Leisurail (☎ 0870-750 0222 or ☎ 0870 750 0246 for a brochure, 🖹 0870 750 0333), PO Box 113, Peterborough, Cambridgeshire PE3 8HY, is Rail Australia's agent in the UK; a 14-day Austrailpass costs £290, 21 days

£375 and 30 days £450. An 8-day (for travel within six months) Austrail Flexipass costs £240, 15 days £345, 22 days £485 and 29 days £630. Leisurail can also book tickets for many train journeys and for all classes.

From Ireland

● **Australia Travel Centre** (☎ 01-804 7188, 🖹 01-873 3163, 💻 info@abbeytravel.ie), 43 Middle Abbey St, Dublin 1. Books flights and arranges ETAs.

● **Trailfinders** (☎ 01-677 7888, 🖹 01-677 8492), 4/5 Dawson St, Dublin 2. Flights from Dublin to Cairns, Sydney or Perth start from Irish Punts 659 excluding taxes.

● **Usit** (☎ 01-679 8833, 🖹 01-602 1617, 💻 www.usitworld.com), 19-21 Aston Quay, O'Connell Bridge, Dublin 2. Books flights and arranges ETAs.

MAKING A BOOKING IN CONTINENTAL EUROPE

From Austria

See Germany (Britz Australia) for details of the Rail Australia agent.

From Belgium

● **Boundless Adventures** (☎ 02-426 40 30, 🖹 02-426 03 60, 💻 boundless.adventures@joker.be), ave Verdilaan 23/15, 1083 Brussels.

From Denmark

● **Benns Rejser A/S** (☎ 9742 5000, 🖹 9740 6565), Noerregade 51, Holstebro, DK 7500; also Frederiksberg Alle 18-20, 1820 Frederiksberg C, Copenhagen (☎ 3355 7511, 🖹 3355 7500, 💻 bh@benns.com, www.bennsrejser.de). Books flights and is a Rail Australia agent.

From Finland

● **AKTIV Resor** (☎ 9-602 900, 🖹 9-602 398, 💻 sales@aktiv-resor.fi, www.aktiv-resor.fi), Lonnrotinkatu 35, 00180 Helsinki. Books flights and is a Rail Australia agent.

● **OY Finnsov Tours Ltd** (☎ 09-694 2011/2511, 🖹 09-694 5534, 💻 webmaster@finnsov.fi, 💻 www.finnsov.fi), Eerikinkatu 3, 00100 Helsinki.

● **STA Travel** (☎ 09-818 3491, 🖹 09-818 3293), Mikonkatu 2D, 2nd Floor, 00100 Helsinki. Books flights.

From France

● **Australie Tours** (☎ 01 53 70 23 47, 🖹 01 51 70 26 46, 💻 australe@worldnet.net), 129 rue Lauriston, Paris 75116. Rail Australia agent.

From Germany

● **Britz Australia** (☎ 89-7257 9550, 🖹 89-725 4516, 💻 astrid.somer@britz.com), Plinganserstr 12, 81369 Munich. Rail Australia agent (also for Austria and Switzerland).

● **STA Travel** has many branches in Germany some of which include: Renzelstrasse 16, 20146 Hamburg (☎ 040-450 38400); Nassestrasse 11, 53113 Bonn (☎ 0228-225579); Goethestrasse 73, 10625 Berlin (☎ 030-311 0950); Bockenheimer Landstrasse 133, 60325 Frankfurt/Main (☎ 069-703035); L14.11, 68161 Mannheim (☎ 0621-10074); Zuelpicher Strasse 178, 50937 Cologne (☎ 0221-442011); Haupstrasse 139, 69117 Heidelberg (☎ 06221-23528); Zwinger 6, 97070 Wuerzburg (☎ 0931-52176).

From the Netherlands
● **Incento BV** (☎ 035-695 5111, ▤ 035-695 5155, ⌨ info@incento.nl), Stationweg 40, 1404 Ap Bussum (PO Box 1067, 1400 BB Bussum). Rail Australia agent.

From Sweden
● **Benns Resor AB** (☎ 031-774 0025, ▤ 031-774 0228, se@ausnz.org), Kastellgatan 17, S-40233, Gothenburg, and Roslagsgatan 35-37, 113 54 Stockholm (☎ 08-442 9880, ▤ 08-673 5708). Books flights and is a Rail Australia agent.
● **STA Travel** (☎ 046-13 72 05, ▤ 046-13 43 66), Kiliansgatan 17, 5-223 51 Lund and also at Uppsala (☎ 018-601000, ▤ 018-6001001, St Olofsgatan 11).

From Switzerland
See Germany (Britz Australia) for details of the Rail Australia agent.
● **SSR Travel** (part of STA Travel) has many branches in Switzerland some of which include: Steinenberg 19, 4001 Basle (☎ 61-284 90 60, ▤ 61-284 90 66); Falkenplatz 9, 3012 Bern (☎ 31-302 03 12, ▤ 31-302 39 93); rue de Lausanne 35, 1700 Fribourg (☎ 26-322 61 62, ▤ 26-322 64 68); rue Vignier 3, 1205 Geneva (☎ 22-329 77 33/4, ▤ 22-329 50 62); blvd de Grancy 20, 1006 Lausanne (☎ 21-617 56 27, ▤ 21-616 50 77); Stadelhofestrasse 22, 8001 Zurich (☎ 1-260 7050, 1-266 7056).

MAKING A BOOKING IN NORTH AMERICA

From the USA
● **ATS Tours** (☎ 310-643-0044, tollfree ☎ 800-423-2880, ▤ 310-643-0032, ⌨ rgieschen@atstours.com), Suite 325/2381 Rosecrans Avenue, El Segundo, California 90245. Rail Australia agent and arranges all aspects of travel to Australia.
● **Swain Australia Tours** (☎ 610-896-9595, ▤ 610-896-9592), Corporate Headquarters, 6 West Lancaster Ave, Ardmore, PA 19003. Books flights, accommodation etc and is a Rail Australia agent.
● **STA** (☎ 415-391-8407), 51 Grant Ave, San Francisco CA 94108. Other branches include: 297 Newbury St, Boston, MA 02115 (☎ 617-266-6014); 411 Santa Monica Blvd, Santa Monica, CA 90401 (☎ 310-394-

5126); 10 Downing St (6th Avenue and Bleecker), New York, NY 10014 (☎ 212-627-3111, 🖹 212-627-3387); 429 South Dearborn St, Chicago, Il 60605 (☎ 312-786-9050) and 4341 University Way NE, Seattle, WA 98105 (☎ 206-633-5000). Discount flights for student and youth travel.
● **Council Travel** (☎ 1-800-226-8624 or ☎ 212-822-2700, 🖳 www.coun-ciltravel.com), 205 E 42nd St, New York, NY 10017. Cut-price student and youth flights; many more branches across America.

From Canada

● **Goway Travel** (☎ 416-322-1034, 🖹 416-322-1109, 🖳 www.goway.com), 3284 Yonge St (Suite 300), Toronto, Ontario M4N 3M7; also at Suite 1050, 1200 West 73rd Avenue, Vancouver, BC V6P 6G5 (☎ 604-264-8088, 604-267-2111). Rail Australia agent and arranges all aspects of travel to Australia.
● **Adventure Centre/Westcan Treks** has several branches in Canada: 25 Bellair St, Toronto, Ontario M5R 3L3 (☎ 416-922 7584, 🖹 416-922-8136, 🖳 toronto@theadventurecentre.com); 2911 West 4th Avenue, Vancouver BC V6K 1R3 (☎ 604-734-1066, 🖳 vancouver@westcantreks.com); 8412 109th St, Edmonton, Alberta T6G 1E2 (☎ 780-439-0024, 🖳 edmonton@westcantreks.com) and 336 14th St NW, Calgary, Alberta T2N 1Z7 (☎ 403-283-6115, 🖳 calgary@westcantreks.com). Books flights.
● **Marlin Travel** (☎ 416-979-9300, 🖹 416-979-0087), Eaton Centre, 218 Yonge St, Toronto M5B 2H6. Marlin has branches all over Canada and can arrange rail travel and book flights.

MAKING A BOOKING IN AUSTRALASIA

From Australia
See pp23-5.

From New Zealand
● **Intercity Management Ltd (Rail Auckland)** (☎ 09-379 8372, 🖹 09-379 8371, freecall ☎ 0800 801060), Union House, Level 4, Corner of Quay and Commerce Sts, Auckland. Rail Australia agent.
● **Tranz Rail Ltd** (☎ 03-372 8209, 🖹 03-372 8507), Clarence St, Addington, Christchurch. Rail Australia agent.

MAKING A BOOKING IN SOUTH AFRICA

● **Go Australia** (☎ 011-289 8112, 🖹 011-787 3800, 🖳 cdland@traveldirections.co.za, 🖳 www.go-australia.co.za), Holiday House, 158-160 Hendrik Verwoerd Drive, Randburg 2125 (PO Box 2140); also at Suite 901, Musgrave Centre, Musgrave Rd, Berea, Durban 4001 (PO Box 51182), (☎ 031-201 6061, 🖹 031-201 7809) and 2nd Floor, Olivetti House, 17 Lower Long St, Cape Town 8000 (☎ 021-419 9382, 🖹 021-419 5208). Rail Australia agent and can book flights etc.

MAKING A BOOKING IN ASIA

From Japan

● **Humannetwork (Toyo World/Sunworld Tours)** (☎ 03-3498 7636, 🗎 03-3498 5403, 🖳 sales@sunworldtours.co.jp, www.sunworldtours.co.jp), 7th Floor, DPM Building, 5-50-6 Jingumae, Shibuya-ku, Tokyo 150-0001. Rail Australia agent and books flights.

● **Travel Plaza International** (☎ 03-3284 7303, 🗎 03-3284 7390), JTB Bldg, 3rd Floor, 1-6-4 Maranouchi, Chiyoda-ku, Tokyo 100-8264 ; also at NV Tomioka Bldg 6F, 2-1-9 Tomioka, Koto-ku, Tokyo 136-8531 (☎ 03-3820 8011, 🗎 03-3820 8035), and Jutakukinyukoko-Sumitomoseimei Bldg, 4-5-20 Minamihonmachi, Chuo-ku, Osaka 541-0054 (☎ 06-6449 1478, 🗎 06-6449 1424); 4-6-18 Meieki, Nakamura-ku, Nagoya City, Aichi, 450-0002 (☎ 05-2563 6966, 🗎 05-2571 0431). Rail Australia agent and books flights.

From Hong Kong

● **Westminster Travel Ltd (New Asian Dreams Holidays)** (☎ 2369 5051, 🗎 2723 3746), 16th Floor, Oriental Centre, 67 Chatham Rd, Tsimshatsui, Kowloon. Rail Australia agent and books flights.

From Korea

● **Seoul Travel** (☎ 2-755 9696, 🗎 2-753 9076), 5th Floor, Jaeneung Bldg, 1-KA Ulji-Ro, 192-11 Jung-ku, Seoul. Rail Australia agent and books flights.

From Singapore

● **Ken-Air Tours Pty Ltd** (☎ 333 8308, 🗎 339 0321), 3 Temasek Boulevard, No 03-043/045 Suntec City Mall, Singapore 038983. Rail Australia agent and books flights.

Before you leave

WHEN TO GO

Choose to come whatever time of year suits you! Compared with much of Europe and North America, Australia is warm. In spring and autumn (seasons which are not as clearly distinguished as in much of Europe and North America), the climate is equable and there are no special problems of transport, holidays, or anything else to cause unusual difficulties for the visitor. But if you are from a really cold climate, you will find Australian summers (November to March) rather hot, especially in the north. Conversely if used to warmer climes you may find Tasmania and the south of Victoria rather cool in the winter (June to August); see also the temperature chart on p106.

PASSPORTS AND VISAS

All visitors need a passport valid for at least six months; visitors from everywhere except New Zealand also need a visa/Electronic Travel Authority (ETA). A tourist ETA is free but a charge is made for a business ETA; both allow multiple entry, are valid for 12 months or the length of your passport and permit a stay of up to three months.

Working holiday visas are also available for anyone with a valid UK, Irish, Dutch, Canadian, Korean, Maltese or Japanese passport who is between 18 and 30 years old. Applications must be made in your home country and a charge is made.

For further details about all kinds of visas and ETAs contact the Australian embassy, high commission or consular office in your country (see the list on p20) or check ⌨ www.immigov.gov.au. Alternatively ask your travel agent, tour operator or airline, though agents may charge a fee for the service.

WHAT TO BRING

For summer wear, open-neck shirts and shorts are comfortable and acceptable for all but formal occasions. In winter, overcoats, scarves or gloves are rarely seen but in all seasons a mackintosh is advisable.

Also you should always bring or obtain a hat as the Australian sun is strong: our skies are blue and skin cancer, not to mention sunburn, is something to be reckoned with. Ensure you have a tube of sun-blocking cream, particularly if you come in the summer months.

A roll-on stick or small spray can of 'Rid', or similar insect repellent, is useful especially if getting off the train and staying in bush country.

For anyone planning to travel overnight sitting up in a train, or for any long journey, it is wise to bring or acquire on arrival an inflatable neck pillow.

HEALTH

No special requirements for health apply. Injections and vaccinations are not required. Tap water is universally drinkable.

Telephone and fax numbers
Within Australia, telephone and fax numbers begin with a zero, eg 02-1111 1111. When dialling from overseas, the zero must be replaced by the country code (61). This does not apply to numbers beginning 1800 or 13; the former are freecall numbers within Australia only and the latter are calls charged at local rates. Neither can be dialled from outside Australia.

❏ Embassies and consulates

Belgium
Australian Embassy
Guimard Centre
rue Guimard 6-8
1040 Brussels
☎ 286 050, ▤ 230 6802

Canada
Australian High Commission
Suite 710, 50 O'Connor St
Ottawa, Ontario K1P 6L2
☎ 613-236-0841, ▤ 613-236-4376
(Consulate offices in Toronto and
  Vancouver)

Finland
Australian Consulate
Museokatu 25B
FIN-00100 Helsinki
☎ 09-447233, ▤ 09-440916

France
Australian Embassy
4 rue Jean Rey
75724 Paris, Cedex 15
☎ 01 40 59 33 00
▤ 01 40 59 33 10

Germany
Australian Embassy
Philip Johnson House, 6th Floor
Freidrichstrasse 2000
10117 Berlin
☎ 8800 880, ▤ 8800 88310
(Consulate office in
  Frankfurt/Main)

Ireland
Australian Embassy
2nd Floor, Fitzwilton House
Wilton Terrace, Dublin 2
☎ 01-676 1517, ▤ 01-678 5185

Italy
Australian Embassy
Via Alessandria 215, Rome 00198
☎ 85 2721, ▤ 8527 2300
(Consulate office in Milan)

Japan
Australian Embassy
2-1-14 Mita
Minato-ku, Tokyo 108-8361
☎ 03-5232 4111, ▤ 03-5232 4057
(Consulate offices in Osaka,
  Nagoya, Sapporo, Sendai and
  Fukuoka)

The Netherlands
Australian Embassy
Carnegielaan 12
2517 KH The Hague
☎ 070-310 8200, ▤ 070-310 7863

New Zealand
Australian High Commission
72-78 Hobson St
Thorndon, Wellington
☎ 04-473 6411, ▤ 04-498 7103
(Consulate office in Auckland)

South Africa
Australian High Commission
292 Orient St (corner of
Schoeman St), Arcadia
Pretoria 0083
☎ 12-342 3781, ▤ 12-342 8442
(Also in Cape Town and
  Johannesburg)

UK
Australian High Commission
Australia House, The Strand
London WC2B 4LA
☎ 0891 6000333, info 10am-12
  noon only ☎ 020-7887 5107,
  ▤ 020-7465 8218

USA
Australian Embassy
1601 Massachusetts Ave NW
Washington DC 20036-2273
☎ 202-797-3000
▤ 202-797-3100
(Consulate offices in Los Angeles,
  New York, San Francisco and
  Atlanta)

MONEY

Money can be carried as travellers' cheques but credit cards are acceptable nearly everywhere. Banknotes should be changed into Australian dollars as other currencies are acceptable only in banks, currency exchange agencies or the most expensive hotels.

TOURIST INFORMATION

Offices of the Australian Tourist Commission (see p22) have a variety of brochures which provide general information about the country, such as where to stay and what to see.

The Commission also has representative offices in Cyprus, India (New Delhi), Indonesia (Jakarta), Malaysia (Kuala Lumpur), South Africa (Johannesburg), Sweden (Stockholm) and Thailand (Bangkok). Alternatively check out the Commission's website at www.australia.com.

The respective states also have tourism offices in many countries. Australian Tourist Commission offices should be able to provide contact details for these.

Rail travel in Australia

OBTAINING INFORMATION

Before you arrive

Rail Australia is the name of the organisation, based in Adelaide, which co-ordinates the marketing of the principal Australian railway services overseas; there are sales agents in Canada, China (Hong Kong), Denmark, Finland, France, Germany, Japan, Korea, New Zealand, Singapore, South Africa, Sweden, the Netherlands, the UK and the USA. Your travel agent should be able to obtain information from these agents or you can contact them direct through the companies listed as being Rail Australia agents in the Making a booking section (pp13-18).

The Australian section of the Thomas Cook *Overseas Timetable*, obtainable from bookshops around the world (including Australia), provides the closest thing to an up-to-date Australia-wide rail timetable. Thomas Cook also publishes an Independent Travellers' guide, *Australia*, obtainable in the UK from bookshops, Thomas Cook shops or direct from Thomas Cook Publishing, PO Box 227, Peterborough PE3 6PU.

In Australia

Few travel agencies in Australia have information on rail travel and most are unenthusiastic about finding it for you unless a rail trip is part of a

---

❏ **Australian Tourist Commission offices**

Australia
Level 4, 80 William St
Woolloomooloo, NSW 2000
☎ 02-9360 1111, 🖷 02-9331 6469

China
Room 1101, Shanghai Bund
International Bldg
99 Huang Pu Rd
Shanghai 200080
☎ 21-6307 7055, 🖷 21-6037 0069

Germany
Neue Mainzer Strasse 22
D 60311 Frankfurt/Main
☎ 069-274 0060, 🖷 069-274 0640

Hong Kong
Central Plaza Suite 1501
18 Harbour Rd, Wanchai
☎ 2802 7700, 🖷 2802 8211

Japan
Australian Business Centre
New Otani Garden Court Bldg,
  28th Floor
4-1 Kioi-cho, Chiyoda-ku
Tokyo 102-0094
☎ 03-5214 0720, 🖷 03-5214 0719

OCAT Bldg, 4th Floor
1-4-1 Minato-machi
Naniwa-ku
Osaka 556-0017
☎ 06-6635 3291, 🖷 06-6635 3297

Korea
Suite 801, Hotel President
188-3 Ulchiro 1-ka
Chung-ku, Seoul 100-191
☎ 02-753 6455, 🖷 02-779 8929

New Zealand
Level 13, 44-48 Emily Place
Auckland 1
☎ 09-379 9594 🖷 09-307 3117

Singapore
101 Thomson Rd
26-05 United Square
Singapore 307591
☎ 265 2554, 🖷 253 8421

Taiwan
Suite 2208, Level 22
333 Keelung Rd, Sec 1 Taipei
☎ 02-2757 7188
🖷 02-2757 6483

UK
Gemini House
10-18 Putney Hill
London SW15 6AA
☎ 020-8780 2229 🖷 020-8780 1496
☎ 0906-863 3235 (for brochures)

USA
2049 Century Park East, Suite 1920
Los Angeles, CA 90067
☎ 310-229-4870
🖷 310-552-1215

---

package tour they are promoting. State tourist offices sometimes have branches in the capital cities of the other states; these are useful places to obtain general information, particularly about accommodation and tours, but not details about rail services or fares as such.

Each of the state rail authorities and the privately-owned railways publishes their own timetables, usually in the form of individual leaflets or booklets covering particular regions; these are mostly free of charge. Suburban timetables are published separately and leaflets or booklets for particular lines can be obtained at most railway stations on those routes.

Rail Australia publishes a summary sheet of major interstate, New South Wales and Queensland Rail (QR) services. Queensland Rail publishes regularly-updated individual timetable and fare sheets for all interstate and other major long-distance services, as well as for their own trains. A composite Traveltrain services sheet gives summary timetables for Queensland coastal and major inland services showing connections. Copies of these publications can be obtained only at QR travel centres (see p24).

Residents of Australia should have little difficulty starting out on a tour by rail, since they will know, or can easily find out, where the railway station is and can telephone for information and to make bookings, provided, that is, they can get through in the first place. Railway enquiry numbers, like so many other telephone enquiry services, tend increasingly to be engaged and to put the caller in a holding queue listening to music or advertising blurb until, frustrated, they give up. This is all part of the general trend to economise by cutting staff numbers which is endemic to societies that have allowed so-called economic rationalism to take the place of commonsense and until people rise up and complain forcefully about it, it is something we all just have to put up with. If at first you cannot get through, just try again.

RAIL TRAVEL CENTRES AND BOOKING OFFICES

Each Australian mainland state capital has an information and reservation office at its main railway terminal. There are also rail travel centres in central city locations and at some suburban, metropolitan or provincial stations. These offices can book hotels, tours etc as well of course as rail travel. The list which follows should cover most needs.

Australian Capital Territory
Countrylink Travel and Booking Centre (☎ 02-6249 8159 or ☎ 132 232), Railway station, Canberra.

 Timetable warning
Railway timetables have long confused many people. Australia has a wonderful variety for the timetable collector, full of information of fascination to historians, geographers and students of language, law, or philosophy, but not necessarily giving easy, ready to read information about what people want to know – how to get from A to B.

Even knowing when the train may leave or may reach your destination, can also be a problem. Different systems have been known to quote different times for the same interstate train and even publish the different times in their timetables. Often the information is out of date or wrong. The computerised train information and booking systems of the different systems are largely incompatible, just like the track in days gone by.

In short, check carefully.

New South Wales
Countrylink Rail Travel Centre (enquiries and bookings ☎ 132 232, 🖹 02-9224 4513), City Booking Office, Transport House, 11-31 York St, Sydney NSW 2000; also at the main booking office, Sydney Central Station, Railway Square, and at the underground stations for Town Hall, on George St, and Wynyard, on York St (near the rail travel centre).

Northern Territory
Booking Office (☎ 132 147), Railway Station (off George Crescent), Alice Springs.

Queensland
Brisbane Travel Centre (☎ 132 232 or ☎ 07-3235 2941, 🖹 07-3235 2940), Ground Floor, 305 Edward St (at Central Station), GPO Box 1429, Brisbane, Queensland 4001. Also **Roma St Travel Centre** (☎ 07-3235 3291, 🖹 07-3235 1902), Brisbane Transit Centre, Roma St and at the **Gold Coast**, Robina Travel Centre (☎ 07-5562 0539, 🖹 07-5562 0493).

In **Cairns**, at Cairns railway station, Bunda St, (☎ 07-4036 0234, 🖹 07-4036 9216. In **Townsville** at Townsville Railway Station (☎ 07-4772 8546, 🖹 07-4772 8467), Flinders St, and at **Rockhampton** railway station, (☎ 07-4932 0234, 🖹 07-4932 0627); within Queensland phone ☎ 132 232 to be put through to the nearest QR travel centre.

South Australia
Great Southern Railway (☎ 132 147, 🖹 08-8213 4419), Keswick Rail passenger terminal, Keswick, SA 5035.

Tasmania
Tasmanian Travel Centre (☎ 03-6232 0211, 🖹 03-6224 0289), 80 Elizabeth St, Hobart, Tas 7000. There are no mainline railways in Tasmania but bookings through Rail Australia can be made on ☎ 132 147.

Victoria
V/Line Travel (☎ 1800 811 452, 🖹 03-9619 2465 or for general information ☎ 136 196), Spencer St station, opposite Transport House at the western end of Collins St. For **Countrylink** services (Melbourne–Sydney) phone ☎ 132 232.
West Coast Railway (☎ 03-5221 8966) at Geelong railway station.
Hoys Coaches (Rail Division) (☎ 03-5831 2880 or 136 196), at Shepparton station.
Great Southern Railway (bookings ☎ 132 147), Melbourne Office, Level 18, 535 Bourke St, Melbourne, Victoria 3000.

Western Australia
Interstate Booking Office Westrail Centre (☎ 131 053 or ☎ 1800 099 150, 🖹 08-9326 2619), East Perth, WA 6000 (GPO S1422); also

at **Westrail Travel Centre** (☎ 09-9326 2690, ▤ 09-9326 2063), City rail-way station, Wellington St, Perth. For details of Great Southern services phone ☎ 132 147.

RESERVATIONS

As far as possible, key bookings should be made before you leave home, through your travel agent or direct through one of the companies listed on pp13-18.

Knowing about alternative routes and services can, however, be fruit-ful for the tourist who has been unable, or chose not, to make prior reser-vations and arrives in Australia to find some of the popular 'named' trains have been fully booked weeks in advance. Sleeping accommodation is particularly hard to find on trains in the Eastern states at short notice dur-ing December and January, the Australian summer holiday months, but trains can be fully booked at other times such as the beginning and end of school holidays and just before holiday weekends (pp105-107). September/October tends to be the busiest period on the TransAustralian route whilst the northbound Ghan and Queenslander can be heavily booked in the southern winter months (June, July, August).

 Useful websites
Railways as well as coach lines in Australia are now increasingly mak-ing use of the Internet. At the time of writing this medium offers far from complete coverage and with some systems the information can be posi-tively misleading. Email addresses are given where available. The following websites may be useful:
Countrylink trains and coaches: www.countrylink.nsw.gov.au (can be quite misleading if used for route planning)
Queensland Transport Information: www.transinfo.qld.gov.au
Sydney Public Transport: www.sydneytransport.net.au
CityRail, NSW: www.cityrail.nsw.gov.au
Transadelaide (suburban transport): www.transadelaide.sa.gov.au
Transperth (suburban transport): www.transperth.wa.gov.au
Victoria public transport: www.victrip.vic.gov.au
V/line Passenger (trains and coaches): www.vline.vic.gov.au
Bayside Trains (Melbourne): www.baysidetrains.com.au
Hillside Trains (Melbourne): www.hillsidetrains.com.au
Great Southern Railway: www.gsr.com.au
Puffing Billy Railway (Victoria): www.pbr.org.au
West Coast Rail (Victoria): www.wcr.com.au
Westrail country train services: www.westrail.wa.gov.au
Zig Zag Railway (NSW): www.ozemail.com.au/~harburg/zzr.htm
Skitube, Snowy Mountains: www.perisherblue.com.au/skitube
Orient-Express Trains and Cruises: www.orient-expresstrains.com
Queensland Rail: http://qroti.bit.net.au

You may have heard the standard Aussie assurance that 'she'll be right, mate'. If you haven't, you will! The railways will try hard to help the visitor in difficulty but it is not sensible to leave everything to chance. Long-distance trains will often not stop at an intermediate station unless a booking has been made and some will not accept unbooked passengers in any case. Reservation at least 10 days in advance is almost essential if you have a tight schedule and want to be sure of travelling on the best-known trains over the main routes. Three months in advance is a fairly safe bet for almost any booking, though not guaranteed.

It can, however, be difficult actually to book. Almost all Australian long-distance trains and all the railway-operated buses, require advance booking and **do not take standing passengers**. But there are restrictions on booking, sometimes it can be a year in advance, sometimes six months, sometimes not more than a month or not more than a week and sometimes on the day of travel only. Restrictions particularly apply for journeys between intermediate stations. Acceptable advance periods vary from as much as 600 days for a long journey, such as Alice Springs to Sydney, to only one day in advance or even the day of travel for a short trip like Brisbane to Nambour on the QR Tilt Train; seven days is the maximum advance-booking period for most journeys between intermediate stations on Great Southern Railway trains.

There are no seat reservation fees on Australian railways and seats and berths on the principal trains may usually be reserved up to a year or more in advance, but fees are charged for late cancellations of paid-for bookings. In extreme cases, no fare refund may be made. Advance booking is essential on the main long-distance trains; passengers cannot simply walk up and expect to board as the train arrives as they might do in Europe.

FARES

Rail fares in Australia are mostly based on single point-to-point journeys. Return tickets, if issued, are normally twice the single fare. Single and return tickets (where available) on long-distance trains are normally valid for up to 12 months.

Concessionary fares are available for pensioners and some senior citizens, students and children (see below). In Victoria, special Business Cards in the form of multi-trip transferable tickets are obtainable by individuals, companies and partnerships between certain locations. Various

---

❏ **Fares**
Fares quoted in this guide are correct at the time of going to press. Rail Australia warns that 'all fares as well as timetables are subject to alteration without notice'.

discounted promotional fares are also offered and on some suburban systems off-peak and weekend fares may be available. The cheap day return and monthly return tickets familiar to rail passengers in the UK are not a feature of the Australian rail fare structure.

Except for special tickets like the Austrailpass, children aged under 16 (under 15 in Victoria) are entitled to discounted fares, generally half the normal adult fare. Children aged under 4 travel free unless occupying a separate seat on interstate trains or occupying a sleeping berth. Tertiary students, pensioners and senior citizens who can produce evidence of their status, such as a pensioner or senior citizen card, can travel at reduced fares (half the normal fare in NSW and Queensland). Students wishing to benefit from the reduced fare must produce an International Student Identification Card (ISIC), especially for interstate travel. Other discounted fares, varying from 10 to 40 per cent off the normal, are available on some routes and some trains at various times of the year: details on application to the relevant system.

There are restrictions on the length of time allowed for a break of journey on a through ticket; in New South Wales a break of more than 12 hours and in Queensland four hours involves the fare being the sum of the fares for each sector.

A surcharge of between $35 and $114 per night per person is made for a sleeping berth.

You can obtain full information on ticket prices from most railway stations and from rail travel centres. Some specimen fares are given in the section describing the trains (pp38-59).

CLASSES

Most Australian trains, other than suburban and interurban services, have both first-class and economy seating, though it is sometimes hard to tell the difference. For the budget-conscious traveller the economy seating in XPT and Explorer carriages (Sydney to NSW north coast, Tablelands, Dubbo, Brisbane, Melbourne and Canberra) is not noticeably different from first class – seats in the latter recline further. Western Australia's Australind and Prospector (Perth–Bunbury and Kalgoorlie) have one class only and there are no different classes if you travel on any of the remaining 'mixed' trains in outback Queensland (p55) or on the Spirit of Capricorn, the Gulflander, Savannahlander or Kuranda Scenic Railway. There are no first-class seats as such on Great Southern or QR trains

---

❑ **Prices in this book – Australian dollars**
Note that all prices quoted in this book are given in Australian dollars unless otherwise indicated. The current exchange rate is Australian $1 to US$0.58 or UK£0.38. For up-to-the-minute rates visit **www.xe.net/currency**.

(except on the latter's Tilt Train, p52), where first-class fares are inclusive of berths and in some cases, meals.

All sleeping berths in New South Wales require a first-class ticket. In addition to first-class sleeping berths, most Queensland long-distance trains have economy berths which are not unlike the first-class couchettes of some European trains, three to a cabin but all one sex except when occupied by a family.

On The Ghan (Melbourne or Sydney–Adelaide–Alice Springs) and the Indian Pacific (Sydney–Adelaide–Perth) there is a holiday class with twinette berths similar to first class but more compact. Holders of economy-class tickets, including the Australpass, can upgrade to holiday class on payment of a fare adjustment. These two trains, as well as the Overland, Sunlander, Queenslander, Spirit of the Tropics and Spirit of the Outback (Brisbane–Townsville and Cairns, and Brisbane–Longreach) also have very comfortable economy seating and carry shower compartments for sitting passengers.

Rail passes

THE AUSTRAILPASS

This pass is available only to visitors from overseas (including Australian passport holders living abroad and having a valid return air ticket to the country of residence). It allows unlimited economy-class travel on all government-owned or franchised rail systems in Australia, including railway-operated or railway-contracted coach services and suburban trains in Sydney, Melbourne, Brisbane and Newcastle, but not Adelaide or Perth – although there is some confusion here between what the pass states and what some systems maintain. The pass is valid on the franchised rail services in Victoria (West Coast Railway, Hoys, Bayside Trains and Hillside Trains) and on the Great Southern Railway.

The Australpass can be purchased from Rail Australia agents (see pp13-18 and p21) around the world.

In Australia the pass can be purchased from Great Southern Railway at Keswick terminal, Adelaide, from the main Countrylink and QR rail travel centres, and from V/line Travel and the Rail Australia offices in Melbourne and at Spencer St station, Melbourne; it can be bought only by residents of countries where there is no Rail Australia agent or by visitors who have been unable to obtain one before arrival in Australia. The applicant must produce a passport and outbound flight tickets. However, it is strongly recommended that this pass is purchased before arriving because the one you want may not be in stock.

Use of the pass must begin within six months of the date of issue (12 months when issued in New Zealand) and be completed by midnight on the last day of validity (but see below re the Flexipass). The pass must be presented with your passport at the departure station of the initial journey for validation. No refund is payable after use commences.

There are two kinds of pass: the normal Austrailpass for consecutive days of travel and the Austrail Flexipass for those wishing to select a set number of days within a longer period (six months). This is ideal for people wishing to visit Australia and travel between places by train but not every day or couple of days.

With the Austrail Flexipass, a day is counted as a period of up to 24 hours from the scheduled departure time of the train on which that day's journey commences. For example, an overnight trip between Melbourne and Adelaide starting one evening and finishing the following morning would count as only one day of use – provided there was no other rail travel using the pass on either of the two days. This also applies to the last day of use, when, for example, the pass would be valid for a journey commencing in Longreach at 07.00 and finishing in Brisbane at 06.30 the next morning.

It is unfortunate that a recent policy change has led to the First Class Austrailpass being discontinued. The Austrailpass and Austrail Flexipass now cover economy travel only, and according to current public advertising cannot be upgraded to first class except where no economy sleeping or sitting accommodation is available.

The reason for this curious and seemingly counter-productive situation is unclear but the non-availability of first-class seating (other than with a sleeping berth) on most long-distance trains, coupled with changed marketing philosophies may be among the reasons. The implications do not appear to have been fully considered. The curious restriction on

---

❏ **Prices for Austrailpasses in Australian dollars:**

Austrailpass	Economy	Austrail Flexipass	Economy
14 days	$575	8 days	$475
21 days	$705	15 days	$650
30 days	$900	22 days	$915
		29 days	$1250

Notes
● A 7-day extension for the Austrailpass costs $300.
● The 8-day Flexipass is **not valid** for travel between Adelaide and Perth or between Adelaide and Alice Springs.
● These passes cover seat reservations but not ancillary charges such as sleeping berths and meals. There is no reduction in price for children, students or pensioners.
● It is no longer possible to buy a first-class Austrailpass or Flexipass.

> **Sample savings with an Australailpass**
>
> An itinerary of 14 days travelling from Sydney to Cairns and back, then across to Perth and returning via Melbourne would, by paying normal fares, cost $1370 economy as against $575 with an Australailpass.
>
> Using economy or holiday-class sleepers where available for overnight journeys only and economy seats otherwise, the totals would be $2196 as against $1403 with the Australailpass. Full first class, including meals where these are part of the fare, would cost $3575, or $2780 using the Australailpass and upgrading if permitted (see p29).

---

upgrading seems to be a hangover from the time when there was a clear choice between first-class and budget passes. If followed to the letter it makes it all but impossible to reserve first-class berths in advance on any train without paying the full first-class fare for that journey, since economy berths and seats are usually among the last to be filled. The visitor wishing to follow a pre-planned itinerary may therefore – unless the policy is soon changed – have to be content with economy travel throughout or pay full first-class fare for any sector where the extra comfort and amenities of first class are desired.

However, an Australailpass economy booking can be upgraded to holiday class on The Ghan and Indian Pacific subject to payment of the fare difference, including berth charges. It is also possible that, despite the stated restriction, upgrading to first class would not be refused on any train if berths are available and booking is sought a few days before travel. The best advice is, ask. Few railway systems in the world turn down the chance to take in more money when they can!

The Australailpass and Flexipass are still bargains compared to paying normal fares. They allow a fairly leisurely to extremely leisurely exploration of at least the main Australian rail routes, but also enable the visitor to pack in a tremendous variety if full advantage is taken of overnight journeys. Much greater savings were possible with the first-class Australailpass even though, as with all such passes worldwide, berth charges and meals were additional. However, the example in the box above (which is based on Itinerary 1, p66) is sufficient to show that substantial savings are possible; in this simple case up to 58 per cent.

OTHER PASSES

The following passes can be purchased by both visitors and Australians in the states concerned.

New South Wales

Countrylink offers a one calendar month **Discovery Pass** for $249. This is available from the rail travel centre and Countrylink's central reservation office in Sydney and from other main stations in New South Wales (NSW). The pass covers all trains and state-rail-operated buses in NSW except the Brisbane route north of Kyogle; Sydney to Tweed Heads, Grafton, Taree, Newcastle, Wollongong, Nowra, Cooma, Albury, Griffith, Broken Hill, Bourke, Lightning Ridge, Bathurst, Tamworth and many smaller centres shown on maps included in free Countrylink timetables or other leaflets. It is also valid for XPT services and Sydney suburban trains but not for interstate travel, except to Canberra. The cost of sleeping berths and meals is not included and the pass covers economy travel only.

There is another special kind of ticket, rather misleadingly called a pass; this is the **East Coast Discovery Pass**. It is simply a one-way economy-class ticket at a special fare which can be used at any time (subject to the usual reservation restrictions) once only, but allowing breaks of journey, within a period of six months. It is available for Sydney to Brisbane or Surfers Paradise or vice versa, or Sydney to Melbourne or vice versa ($76), Melbourne to Brisbane or Surfers Paradise or vice versa ($152), Sydney to Cairns via Surfers Paradise or Brisbane or vice versa ($199), or Melbourne to Cairns or vice versa, again by either of the two routes ($275).

CityRail in Sydney offers various passes and special tickets within the Sydney and Newcastle areas. For details contact CityRail on ☎ 131 500 or call at any major CityRail station.

Victoria

The **V/line Victoria Pass** is a first-class pass which costs $130 for 14 days; half price for persons aged under 15 or holders of an ISIC. A seven-day version ($75) is also available but only to holders of overseas passports.

Passes are obtainable from V/line Travel (see p24), YHA Travel (205 King St) and at Spencer St and Flinders St stations in Melbourne; also at Geelong, Ballarat and Bendigo railway stations. The pass covers all rail and coach services operated by V/line Passenger, West Coast Railway and Hoys Coaches within Victoria (Melbourne to Albury/Wodonga, Shepparton, Sale, Bairnsdale, Geelong, Warrnambool, Ballarat, Bendigo, Echuca, Cobram, Mildura, Swan Hill and many smaller towns); it is not valid on Melbourne metropolitan trains, bus or tram systems, for which separate daily and other passes at very reasonable rates are available, or on Countrylink or Great Southern Railway trains.

Queensland

The Sunshine Rail Pass is, at the time of writing, expected to be replaced by a **Flexipass** allowing 8, 15, 22 or 29 days of economy travel on QR Traveltrains in a period of six months, with half price for children. It will be available from QR travel centres at both Roma St and Central station, in Brisbane, and from Surfers Paradise, Rockhampton, Townsville, Cairns and other main railway stations in Queensland.

Restrictions on interstate travel
It is important to note that state rail passes do not overlap or even meet. The NSW rail pass is valid only as far south as Albury and as far north as Kyogle or Tweed Heads. Although the Victoria Pass extends to Albury the two cannot be used together for a Sydney–Melbourne journey, unless of course you break it at the border when no-one else has the need or the business to know. The Victoria Pass is not valid on through trains which are now operated exclusively by Countrylink of NSW. Nor can you use a NSW Discovery Pass to travel between New South Wales and Brisbane, even by offering to pay the fare difference north from Kyogle. You have to pay the whole fare or break the journey at Kyogle (or Tweed Heads on the Countrylink coach), involving an overnight wait.

The Flexipass will cover all Traveltrain rail services in Queensland, including Brisbane to Toowoomba, Charleville, Longreach, Mount Isa, Rockhampton, Townsville, Cairns and many smaller places.

It will also be valid for the Kuranda Scenic Railway, the Gulflander, the Savannahlander, and coach services operated by or on behalf of QR (Charleville to Cunnamulla and Quilpie, Longreach to Winton, and some shorter runs), but not for the standard-gauge trains to the NSW border operated by Countrylink. It may be upgraded to first class for specific journeys where surcharges will also apply for sleeping berths. Economy sleeping berths are available at normal supplementary charges. The pass will cover connecting Citytrain services in the Brisbane area on the days of travel. Until this new pass is available, the **Sunshine Rail Pass**, valid for consecutive days only, can be purchased.

McCafferty's/Queensland Rail Road/Rail Pass is an unusual but valuable pass which can be purchased from all QR travel centres and McCafferty's coach terminals. It provides unlimited economy-class sitting car travel on all Traveltrain services in Queensland except the Kuranda Scenic Railway and on all McCafferty's express coach services through-out Queensland. It is not available for Citytrain services or any part of an interstate journey (eg on Countrylink).

It is a flexipass covering 10 days of travel within 60 ($269) or 20 days within 90 ($349), a day counting as 24 hours or part thereof from the start of a journey. Travel by both train and coach is not permitted in one day.

Western Australia
Westrail Southern Discovery Pass is a one-class pass costing $119 for 28 days. Like the NSW East Coast Discovery ticket this is not a pass in

(**Opposite**) The **Spirit of the Outback** (see p53) winds its way through the Drummond Range in the outback of central Queensland.

Luggage
The passenger luggage allowance on Australian trains is 50kg (not counting hand luggage) with a maximum of two bags per person, neither over 25kg. A heavy tag may be required on some trains for items over 20kg. Luggage may be checked in at major railway stations usually not less than half an hour before train departure. Such luggage will be placed in the baggage car and is not accessible during the journey, nor may it be possible to retrieve at small intermediate stations. It will also be difficult or impossible to retrieve should you decide to change your destination en route. Sitting and sleeping cars on long-distance trains have ample space for luggage at the end of the carriage or in the compartments. Luggage may be left at stations either in lockers or depositories. Charges for this vary from $2 or more to nil at smaller stations where you arrange it with the station master (if you can find one).

the normal sense. Travel is restricted to the Westrail Southern Circle Route in one direction only, clockwise or anticlockwise, so it covers Perth–Bunbury–Margaret River–Augusta–Pemberton–Albany–Esperance –Kalgoorlie–Merredin– Perth (coaches and trains). It is not valid for the special Wildflower coach tours, for the Transperth suburban rail system, or on the Indian Pacific.

Major routes and services

TRAVELLING THE NETWORK

Australia's vastness and diversity cannot be covered in just a few days. Be prepared for long distances from one major city to another – in fact from almost anywhere to anywhere else. From Brisbane northwards up the Queensland coast to Cairns is as far as from Paris to Naples; from Melbourne to Perth is further than from London to Moscow, while a rail journey from Brisbane to Perth is further and takes longer than one from New York to Los Angeles.

To explore the whole rail network of Australia – or rather those parts of it served by regular passenger trains – would take a minimum of 50 days' almost non-stop travel. Even then you would not cover the privately-operated preserved and narrow-gauge lines either on the mainland or in Tasmania, or the Normanton railway in the *Crocodile Dundee* gulf country of the far north.

(**Opposite**) **Top**: The observation car of the Great South Pacific Express (GSPE). **Bottom**: Every attention to detail in the State cabin on the GSPE (see p44).

The main routes join the cities of Sydney, Melbourne, Brisbane, Adelaide and Perth. As far as passenger trains are concerned there is only one route between Brisbane and Sydney, two between Sydney and Adelaide, one of which is via Melbourne, and one between Adelaide and Perth. The only other line which can reasonably be classified as a main route is the North Coast line from Brisbane up to Cairns. On only two of these routes is there a train service every day of the week, between Brisbane, Sydney and Melbourne. The major services, along with trains on these and other routes, are described on pp37-59 and comprise the following:

● The Brisbane XPT and Great South Pacific Express between Brisbane and Sydney
● The Olympic Spirit and Southern Cross between Sydney and Melbourne
● The Indian Pacific and Ghan between Sydney and Adelaide
● The Overland and Ghan between Melbourne and Adelaide
● The Indian Pacific between Adelaide and Perth
● The Queenslander, Sunlander and Great South Pacific Express between Brisbane and Cairns.

In Part 5 these and other routes are described as the traveller might see them.

SCENIC ROUTES

In Thomas Cook's *European Timetable* a list is given of the most scenic rail journeys in Europe, based largely on research by the late John Price, former managing editor of Cook's Timetables. Scenic appreciation is partly an individual matter but not entirely so; there is a consensus about what is attractive, as evidenced by calendars, picture postcards, colour slide sales and the facts of where people go, where they stay and what they gasp about and take photographs of. My list (pp36-37) of the most scenically interesting or unusual routes served by regular (and in some cases irregular) passenger services may help tourists plan an itinerary if scenery is what they most seek.

Timetable changes and bus substitutions in recent years in nearly all states have deprived rail travellers of much potentially attractive or dramatic scenery or confined it to periods of travelling in darkness, but sometimes because of late running, diversions or special excursions, there is a chance to discover and enjoy otherwise hidden panoramas.

The Thomas Cook European scenic rail list includes information on the type of scenery found on each route, ie coastal, forest, gorge, lake, mountain or river, or a combination of any or all of these. This has not been attempted for Australia because the scenery is in many ways so different. The sheer overwhelming nothingness of the Nullarbor, for example, does not fall into any of the foregoing categories, yet it cannot by any criterion be omitted. It has its own unique attraction.

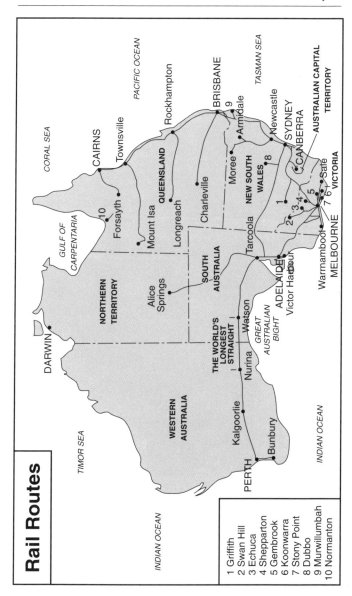

Rail Routes

1 Griffith
2 Swan Hill
3 Echuca
4 Shepparton
5 Gembrook
6 Koonwarra
7 Stony Point
8 Dubbo
9 Murwillumbah
10 Normanton

Coastal scenery is rare on the railways of Australia. In terms of conventional scenic values, it might be said that the routes through the Great Dividing Range, combining mountain, forest, gorge and sometimes river scenery are the most attractive but how do you classify the wonderful sedgeland around Cromarty in Queensland with its teeming flocks of Burdekin ducks, brolgas and other birdlife?

The eye of the beholder will determine what appeals. The suggested list can only offer ideas. Some scenic areas are hard to access, involving long journeys away from population centres, but others are virtually on the doorstep of a city. It should be noted that the scenic sections in suburban Sydney – North Sydney to Wynyard, the Illawarra route south of Waterfall, and the Blue Mountains (Penrith–Lithgow) – are readily accessible and can easily be included in almost any itinerary focused on or including the Greater Sydney area.

An asterisk (*) indicates a route on which no scheduled services operate but for which special excursions might be advertised.

Scenic sections	Rail route	Page
New South Wales		
Penrith–Lithgow	Blue Mountains	p175
Lithgow–Mudgee	Mudgee line*	p177
Manildra–Parkes	Main Western	p179
Bungendore–Queanbeyan	Canberra branch	p219
Queanbeyan–Cooma	Michelago tourist railway*	p258
Sutherland–Cronulla	Illawarra line	p129
Waterfall–Wollongong	CityRail south coast line	p220
Unanderra–Nowra	CityRail south coast line	p136
Unanderra–Robertson	Cockatoo Run (3801 Ltd)	p255
Wynyard–North Sydney	NSW North Shore	p128
Cowan–Gosford	Central Coast	p220
Willow Tree–Muswellbrook	Main North line	p222
Tamworth–Armidale	Main North line	p224
Gloucester–Taree	North Coast line	p226
Nambucca Heads–Glenreagh	North Coast line	p226
Glenreagh–Dorrigo	Preserved railway*	p255
Lismore–Murwillumbah	Murwillumbah branch	p227
Kyogle–Tamrookum (Qld)	North Coast line	p228
Victoria		
Ballan–Bacchus Marsh	Western line (Ballarat)	p202
Gisborne–Malmsbury	Bendigo line	p206
Ringwood–Belgrave	Hillside trains (Met)	p209
Belgrave–Gembrook	Emerald Railway Tourist Board	p209

The trains

INTRODUCTION

There is great variety in Australia's passenger trains: the Tangara suburban trains of Sydney are among the most modern in the world and the Great South Pacific Express ranks with the Venice-Simplon-Orient-Express as the epitome of luxury travel. Other long-distance passenger trains are among the world's finest, with accommodation and service unmatched anywhere by normal scheduled services; air conditioned, with quality catering, lounge bars, entertainment and staff whose function is to make your journey not only enjoyable but memorable. The best have luxurious twinette sleeping compartments with showers – they even have doonas (duvets) on the bed. They also carry motor cars.

By contrast, there are almost forgotten branch lines where the traveller can share the dust-laden breeze and searing afternoon heat with flies and nameless biting insects as the train rolls uncertainly along what railwaymen call 'two wires in the grass'. Up and down the railway goes, winding among the rocks of dry creek beds, into gorges, across trestle bridges, through timeless country that could have been the film-set for *Crocodile Dundee* and where nothing ever hurries except the occasional kangaroo or galah disturbed by the passing train, finally to reach some outback one-horse one-pub town. Such is a trip on the Savannahlander (Cairns to Forsayth) which takes four days there and back, including night stops.

All interstate trains require seat or berth reservations. Most of them, as well as many long-distance intrastate trains, do not carry passengers between, or may not stop at, all intermediate stations for which times are given in the timetable. Many are conditional stops, where the train stops only on prior request and confirmed bookings. Some are restricted stops, either for picking up only or setting down only; yet others may be both conditional and restricted. Where '(†)' follows the name of a stopping place in this guide, it means there are some restrictions of this kind. These are mostly explained but conditions may vary and intending passengers should always enquire before attempting to travel to or from these places.

As a general principle it can be expected that a long-distance train will not take passengers from its city of origin to somewhere in the suburbs, but may well pick passengers up from suburban stations to go a longer distance, or set them down there on a return journey.

All interstate and most other long-distance trains have catering of some sort, though not always for the entire journey; with a few exceptions non-smoking is the rule (as it is on all coaches and internal airline services and in most public buildings). Credit cards are usually accepted for meal payments exceeding $10.

Motor vehicles may be carried on the Queenslander (Brisbane–Townsville and Cairns), the Spirit of the Outback (Brisbane–Longreach), the Gulflander (Normanton–Croydon), and trains between Adelaide and Melbourne, Sydney, Alice Springs and Perth.

Guide dogs for the blind may be carried on all services. Facilities for the disabled otherwise vary and should be checked before starting a journey.

INTERSTATE TRAINS

The Indian Pacific – Cruise Ship of the Desert

The Indian Pacific (Sydney–Adelaide–Perth and vice versa) departs Sydney westbound on Mondays and Thursdays at 14.55 and Adelaide a

Train names

It has long been a practice for railways to give their best trains individual names. Many started as nicknames: Britain's Flying Scotsman being one of the first and most famous. Thus it is not surprising that railways in Australia have their share of these too.

The legendary Ghan is Australia's oldest named train. It is now very different from the old narrow-gauge train which first acquired the appellation Afghan Express and which took 33¹/₂ hours – when it was on time – to cover the 869km from Marree near Lake Eyre to Alice Springs at 26km/h overall with 20 intermediate stops, some of nearly an hour. The Ghan derives its name from the Afghan drivers of the camel trains who pioneered this south-north trade route.

Visitors may well wonder when they hear about the Fish and Chips. These are two separate trains, the Fish named after John Heron, a driver they called The Big Fish when the business commuter train he drove down from the Blue Mountains in the 1860s was hauled by a single driving wheel Beyer Peacock steam locomotive. A semi-fast train which followed later naturally became The Chips and both names have been officially recognised and survive to this day in the timetable. At one stage these trains even had a headboard. Later another train on the same line, calling at the smaller stations they missed, was called the Heron, and yet another in the Sydney area, the Gull.

The famous Tea and Sugar (just The Sugar to rail workers) served the isolated camps on the TransNullarbor route from when the line was under construction until just a few years ago. This unique travelling supermarket was open at each major stop – a major stop in this context being a railway settlement of perhaps no more than half a dozen houses. It included a butcher's shop and a community-services car which at Christmas brought Santa Claus himself.

Leaping Lena or The Tin Hare are unofficial names for the Normanton–Croydon Gulflander, which itself was originally a nickname to match Queensland's other 'lander' trains: Inlander, Sunlander, Westlander and Midlander.

A contest was held to find names for the Brisbane and Murwillumbah XPT trains when these replaced the popular overnight dining and sleeping-car trains north from Sydney, but nobody won and nothing better than Brisbane XPT and Murwillumbah XPT has emerged. Some disrespectful names such as The Masochist for the overnight version were frivolously suggested but understandably not taken up by State Rail. At least the message was brought home that the new trains had to have sleeping cars; this amenity was restored a few years later.

The Melbourne XPTs which replaced the Intercapital Daylight and overnight Southern Aurora have been named the Olympic Spirit and Southern Cross but the names appear neither in the public timetables nor on the trains themselves. Like the TGV of France, an XPT is an XPT is an XPT. Individuality is not evident.

day later at 18.30; it departs East Perth eastbound on Mondays and Fridays at 10.55 and Adelaide two days later at 07.45. A 68¹/₂hr transcontinental trip, of 4348km, the longest in Australia with three nights on the train. The journey is aptly advertised as 'An adventure that spans Australia'.

> **Civilised travel**
> There is no better way to experience the diversity and the great size of this stunning country, than first-hand on the Indian Pacific. There's something particularly civilised and comforting about this form of travel. The sound of the wheels on the rails, with the train's gentle rocking never fails to send me to sleep. And the ability to meet other travellers over an afternoon gin and tonic – and dining – this has an appeal all of its own.
>
> **Natasha Genat**

The Indian (Australian railway people always shorten names) stops at Lithgow (†), Bathurst (†), Blayney (†), Orange East Fork (†), Parkes, Condobolin (†), Ivanhoe (†), Menindee (†), Broken Hill, Peterborough (†), Gladstone (†), Adelaide, Coonamia (†), Port Augusta, Pimba (†), Kingoonya (†), Tarcoola, Cook, Loongana (†), Rawlinna (†), Kalgoorlie, Southern Cross (†), Merredin (†), and Northam (†). Travel just between Sydney and Lithgow, or between Northam and Perth, in either direction is not permitted.

The train has first-class roomettes (single sleepers with toilet); twinettes (double sleepers with toilet and shower); a few family sleepers (interconnecting twinettes); one luxury bedroom/drawing-room compartment which will sleep three and a suite for disabled passengers. Holiday-class sleepers (twin) are also available plus economy sitting cars with reclining seats.

The Indian has a 48-seat restaurant car, the Queen Adelaide restaurant, and a lounge bar car for first-class passengers with complimentary 24-hour tea and coffee service. The Matilda restaurant offers holiday-class passengers main courses ordered at the counter, with a quality self-serve salad bar. A bar and buffet service is also available for coach-class passengers.

Video films are shown in the Matilda lounge car and at overhead display units in coach class. There are separate smoking capsules in the first and holiday-class lounge/club cars while sit-up passengers in economy have a smoking lounge in the adjoining brake van.

First-class sleeping cabins have seats with armrests converting into beds, a visitor's seat, wash basin and toilet, wardrobe, reading lights, venetian blinds, luggage rack and an electric razor socket (note that Australia uses 240 volt AC current). Complimentary toilet packs are provided and there is a conductor call button. A wake-up cup of tea or coffee is brought to your cabin in the morning. Holiday-class sleepers are less spacious, consisting virtually of two berths (upper and lower) in the space of a first-class roomette. Economy sitting cars and all sleeping cars have showers at the end of each carriage; first-class twinettes have showers in each sleeping compartment.

Meals for passengers travelling first-class are paid for when booking. A special effort is made to incorporate Australian native bush foods in the menus. Breakfast consists of fruit juices, cereal or fresh fruit, scrambled or fried eggs or savoury omelette with bacon and sausages, toast and coffee or tea; lunch may include pumpkin and bush honey yoghurt soup followed by lamb and lemon myrtle pie or bushman's platter, whilst a typical dinner menu might offer onion soup or wattleseed linguini and smoked chicken entrée, grilled kangaroo fillet with native pepperleaf and bush tomato chutney, macadamia and bush honey tart, tea or coffee and handmade chocolates. More familiar dishes – not without that special touch – include lamb cutlets, beef fillet, snapper or Tasmanian salmon, traditional apple pie and warm fruit pudding.

Local fine quality wines are available with lunch and dinner and in the lounge and club cars, as well as beer, spirits and soft drinks. Timetables indicating approximate times of stopping and passing places en route are available, while booklets, cassettes and videos of the journey and a wide variety of souvenirs, from postcards at $1 to polo shirts with the train's motif at $45, are obtainable to order.

The normal first-class fare (Sydney–Perth), with berth and meals included, is $1350, holiday class (berth included) $888, coach class $424. The Indian carries motor vehicles between Sydney, Adelaide and Perth. Charges vary from $220 (Perth–Adelaide) to $650 (Sydney–Perth) for an accompanied vehicle up to 5.5m long. Charges for unaccompanied or longer vehicles are higher. The prices westbound are dearer than eastbound.

The Ghan

On Sunday 4 August 1929 the first steam-hauled Ghan passenger train pulled out of Adelaide for the town of Stuart in the Red Centre (now Alice Springs). The old Ghan was notorious for being held up by flooding in the many creeks. The modern Ghan, introduced in 1980, follows a different route after leaving Port Augusta which, though not immune from flood-

 For that special occasion
For passengers really wishing to indulge themselves or for that special occasion, Great Southern Railway has a de luxe private carriage, the Chairman's Car, which can be attached to the Indian Pacific, The Ghan or the Overland. This has two de luxe and two first-class twin cabins, a lounge area, dining room and self-contained kitchen, though occupants may if preferred take meals in the train's restaurant at no extra cost. One-way hire per sector ranges from $2400 Melbourne–Adelaide to $7500 Adelaide–Perth, with return journey costs proportionately cheaper at around 10 to 15 per cent more than a one-way fare. With a full party of eight people the costs would compare quite favourably with normal first-class fares on a two-way trip.

ing, ensures a faster journey and greater reliability. Like its predecessor it has become a legend and in 1991 won the Australian Tourist Industry Association's award for the Best Tourist Transportation service.

The new Ghan now runs twice weekly year-round from Melbourne or Sydney via Adelaide to Alice Springs and back with two nights on board each way except Alice Springs to Melbourne which takes one night. It leaves Melbourne at 22.30 on Wednesdays, Sydney at 13.10 on Sundays and Adelaide at 15.00 on Thursdays and Mondays, returning from Alice Springs at 13.00 on Tuesdays for Melbourne arriving at 21.00 on Wednesdays, and on Fridays for Sydney arriving at 09.15 on Sundays.

The extension to Sydney is recent and has an interesting pedigree. In 1983 a new train, named The Alice, with its headboard 'The Alice to Wonderland' ran from Sydney via Broken Hill and Port Pirie to Alice Springs to let people explore the scenic wonderland of central Australia. For various reasons, including disagreement between rival managements and lack of vigorous promotion it was withdrawn at the end of 1988. The Alice took 45 hours from Sydney, a journey which after its withdrawal took over 50 hours with train changes in Melbourne and Adelaide. The journey time for the new Ghan is practically the same as the Alice, but includes the 400km diversion to Adelaide in its route.

Intermediate stations are (from Alice Springs), Manguri (†), Tarcoola, Port Augusta, Coonamia (†), Adelaide, then Broken Hill, Parkes, Lithgow (†) to Sydney and Bordertown (†), Dimboola (†), Horsham (†), Ararat (†) and North Shore Geelong (†) to Melbourne. Booking from Melbourne to Geelong can be made only on the day before travel, but travel from Geelong to Melbourne only is not permitted.

The Ghan is a far cry from the primitive travel standards of the pioneer days. It has comfortable first-class twinette and roomette sleepers, a de luxe suite as on the Indian Pacific, also holiday-class sleepers and economy recliner seats. These last could well be called first class on other railway systems, being 59cm wide, in 2+1 formation (two seats one side of the aisle and one the other), with a generous 1.17-metre pitch (the technical term for the spacing between the front of one seat and the front of the one behind it). For first-class passengers there is the Stuart Restaurant with silver service and tantalising dishes like venison and juniper pie, baked barramundi or roast Scotch fillet, while economy and holiday passengers have a separate family-style restaurant (the Matilda) serving excellent freshly-prepared food at reasonable prices.

Lounge cars, including a smoking capsule, are available in both first and holiday class. Video films, showers and a ladies' retiring room are available in the economy and holiday cars, while first-class passengers have showers in their compartment or at the end of the coach. Toilet packs are provided for sleeping-car passengers, and booklets about The Ghan and souvenirs featuring The Ghan motif, a black camel on a reddish-brown background, can be purchased from the bar.

The normal first-class fare (Adelaide–Alice Springs), berth and meals included, is $574, holiday class (berth included) $374, coach class $182.

The Ghan carries motor vehicles between Sydney, Melbourne or Adelaide and Alice Springs, prices varying from $190 Alice–Adelaide to $580 Sydney–Alice.

The Overland

This service recently celebrated its 100th anniversary, although it had different names in its early years and followed another route until very recently. For many years an overnight train noted for its comfort, the Overland now runs four days a week between Adelaide and Melbourne on the standard-gauge line opened in 1995; 834km in 9½ hours westbound, 10½ hours eastbound. The overnight service departs Melbourne at 21.30, whilst the eastbound run is now by day, leaving Adelaide at 09.00. Intermediate stations are Geelong North Shore (†), then Ararat, Horsham, Dimboola, Bordertown and Murray Bridge.

The train carries first-class roomette and twinette sleepers. Twinettes have en suite shower and toilet, roomettes have toilet and washbasin with

---

❑ **Prices in this book – Australian dollars**
Note that all prices quoted in this book are given in Australian dollars unless otherwise indicated. The current exchange rate is Australian $1 to US$0.58 or UK£0.38. For up-to-the minute rates of exchange visit **www.xe.net/currency**.

showers at the end of the carriage. The first-class fare includes full break-fast or lunch in the Kookaburra Club Car, in which other meals, wines and drinks are also available.

Economy seats recline, have individual footrests and reading lights and video entertainment. They are two abreast and can swivel to make a foursome. Meals and drinks are available in the buffet car and there is a separate smoking area.

Motor vehicles are conveyed Melbourne–Adelaide and vice versa. The Overland connects at Adelaide with the Indian Pacific. The normal first-class fare (Melbourne–Adelaide), including meal, is $199, coach class $64; an accompanied vehicle costs $100.

The Great South Pacific Express

Newly introduced in 1999, the Great South Pacific Express (Australia's Orient-Express) is a joint venture between the Orient-Express Trains and Cruises company and Queensland Rail (QR). Built at QR's Townsville workshops, the train recreates the opulence and charm of the luxury trains of the 19th century while taking full advantage of the technical achievements appropriate to the 21st century. Both internally and externally it displays richness in design, quality in construction, attentiveness to detail and perfection in finish.

Although not a heritage train in the true sense, it has the feel of one. Its striking external appearance, based on a 1903 Queensland Rail carriage, more than matches that of its sister trains the Venice Simplon-Orient-Express and the Eastern and Oriental Express of South-east Asia. This, together with features such as leadlight clerestory windows, quality wood panelling, marble bar top, custom-made brass fittings and general interior decor, realise QR Chief Executive Vince O'Rourke's vision of 'the world's most beautiful train'.

A recent television programme dubbed it 'the Five-Star Rattler'; five star it certainly is but rattler is unkind. The ride is generally smooth, with only the occasional jerk as a change in speed puts a momentary stress on couplings (common to many passenger trains) but rattles there are not. For a heavy 20-coach train on narrow-gauge track it is remarkably stable in running even at speed, although the average is well below the safe maximum permitted line speed.

The GSPE (as it is known) follows a leisurely schedule and passengers are pampered from the moment of boarding. In the words of the promotional literature the train 'lays every claim to being the most unashamedly romantic hotel on wheels in the Southern hemisphere'; it is also the most expensive.

The train comprises twin cabins of three grades of increasing luxury; Pullman, State and Commissioners, each en suite with a shower, private safe, desk and chair, as well as two restaurants, piano lounge, boutique shop and open-sided observation car. Maps, information sheets, stationery, toilet accessories and spring water are in each cabin and an attendant is on 24-hour call at the press of a button.

Fares include accommodation, table d'hôte gourmet lunch and dinner (the à la carte menu is extra) and entertainment. Breakfast and afternoon tea are served in your own cabin at whatever time you choose. Quality wines, spirits and liqueurs are available at prices comparable to those expected for a five-star hotel and the bar stays open as long as anyone wants. Between Brisbane and Cairns a Barrier Reef excursion by helicopter or seaplane to a private pontoon is included and the Kuranda sector includes a trip on the Skyrail rainforest cable car to or from the Caravonica check-in north of Cairns. It is altogether an experience of a lifetime for all who can afford it – and a surprising number do.

The train operates to a more or less regular timetable between Sydney, Brisbane, Proserpine, Cairns and Kuranda. Unique among Australian passenger trains, the wheel bogies are exchanged at Brisbane to accommodate the rail-gauge difference between Queensland and New South Wales.

The scheduled departures are twice monthly ex-Brisbane for Sydney on Fridays and ex-Sydney on Saturdays. From Brisbane to North

❏ **Table 1 Great South Pacific Express**
Sydney–Brisbane–Proserpine–Kuranda and vice versa

dep Sydney	15.05	dep Kuranda	17.30b
arr Brisbane	13.00ac	arr Proserpine	08.30d
dep Brisbane	10.50	dep Proserpine	16.30
arr Proserpine	08.30c	arr Brisbane	14.40c
dep Proserpine	16.30	dep Brisbane	13.50a
arr Kuranda	11.40c	arr Sydney	11.30c

Notes
Days of running as advertised.
a One hour earlier during Eastern Summer Time
b Boarding time; overnight stop in Kuranda
c Next day
d Two days later; two-hour break, 14.00 to 16.00, at El Arish the previous day

Queensland they are mostly once per week with days of departure varying but mostly on a Monday. Southbound from Cairns the departures are mostly every Wednesday.

Fares vary from $1370 Brisbane–Sydney or vice versa per person in a twin-share Pullman cabin to $5780 per person for the combined Sydney–Brisbane and Brisbane–Kuranda runs in the Commissioner's Suite, with its double bed. Brisbane–Kuranda in a twin-share Pullman costs $2500, State $3190, Commissioner's $4140.

There are no deductions for the Austrailpass or QR Traveltrain Pass but there is 10 per cent reduction for two consecutive sectors (Sydney–Brisbane plus Brisbane–Cairns) or for a return booking on the one ticket and a 20 per cent reduction for children aged 11 or under accompanied by an adult.

For bookings or further information contact Orient-Express Trains and Cruises (☎ 07-3247 6595, ▤ 07-3247 6565 or for freecall reservations ☎ 1800 000 395).

The Olympic Spirit

This XPT service (Melbourne–Sydney and vice versa) replaced the Intercapital Daylight Express which was withdrawn in 1991. The 962km is covered in approximately 10½ hours, departing Melbourne 08.30 and Sydney 07.43, calling at Benalla, Wangaratta, Albury, Henty, Wagga Wagga, Junee, Cootamundra, Harden, Yass Junction, Goulburn, Moss Vale, Campbelltown (†) and Strathfield (†), connecting southbound with the Overland or The Ghan to Adelaide. The XPT is a sleek, modern diesel train based on the British InterCity 125 HST. It carries a take-away buffet including bar. A payphone is available (phonecard or credit card). Countrylink coach connections from Albury, Wagga Wagga and

Cootamundra serve places in northern Victoria and southern New South Wales formerly connected by train. The normal Melbourne–Sydney first-class fare is $145, economy $104.

The Southern Cross

The night-time counterpart of the Olympic Spirit is also an XPT; it offers limited first-class sleeping accommodation (18 berths in twinette compartments) as well as first-class and economy seating. There is a take-away buffet with a restricted bar service. The service operates Melbourne–Sydney and vice versa daily, departing Melbourne at 19.45 and Sydney at 20.43. The northbound service connects at Strathfield with the Murwillumbah XPT. The normal fares are the same as for the Olympic Spirit; a first-class berth costs $95 extra.

Brisbane XPT

A sitting-car service Sydney–Brisbane daily which departs at 16.24 for the overnight service, with a daylight return departing at 07.30, 990km in 14^1/$_4$ hours. The night service carries one 18-berth sleeping car consisting of first-class twinette compartments with a bathroom (toilet and shower) cubicle for each two twinettes. On the day service this car is available as first-class three-seat compartment stock. There is first-class and economy seating with a take-away buffet (at seat refreshments are available for the aged or infirm) and limited bar service (light beer only and no spirits). A breakfast voucher for sleeping-car passengers gives a choice of juice or yoghurt plus muffin or croissant and tea or coffee.

A payphone is available as on all XPT trains. The seating, in common with all XPT services, is in 2+2 formation in both first-class and econo-

---

The land of the Southern Cross

Mariners of old navigated by the stars. Visitors from the Northern hemisphere will not see familiar constellations such as the Great Bear, or Plough as it was generally known in England, in Australian skies. You may discern Orion's belt pointing to Sirius low down on the horizon as in the north, but in Australia look out instead for the Southern Cross. It is identified by the Pointers, two 1st magnitude stars, Alpha and Beta Centauri, in the constellation Centaurus. If you take an imaginary line at 90° to a line joining the Pointers and another line projected from the longest axis of the Southern Cross, then where these lines meet is the South Celestial Pole, due south. Taking your direction from the Southern Cross you may find your way and perhaps feel something of the spirit of Australia.

The Southern Cross is an Australian icon. From the Eureka Stockade of 1854, the adoption of the Australian Flag in 1903, the Antarctic exploration ship of 1898 to the aeroplane in which Charles Kingsford Smith crossed the Pacific in 1928 and the Atlantic in 1930; it has symbolised Australia. It has even given its name to a place in Western Australia and to the XPT night train between Sydney and Melbourne.

my and although Countrylink boasts that it is based on top European designs some passengers find it uncomfortable on long journeys, such as this and the Murwillumbah services. The normal fares (Sydney–Brisbane) are the same as for the Southern Cross Melbourne–Sydney.

The service calls at Strathfield (†), Hornsby (†), Gosford (†), Wyong (†), Broadmeadow, Maitland, Dungog, Taree, Kendall (†), Wauchope, Kempsey, Macksville (†), Nambucca Heads (†), Urunga (†), Sawtell (†), Coffs Harbour, Grafton, Casino and Kyogle. The day train (southbound) calls unconditionally at Macksville and additionally at Wingham and Gloucester. Countrylink coach connections operate to NSW North Coast centres and the Gold Coast.

Murwillumbah XPT

This train is identical to the Brisbane XPT, running Sydney–Murwillumbah, wholly within NSW but with coach connections to Queensland. Departing Sydney daily at 07.15, returning from Murwillumbah nightly at 21.50, it covers the 935km in 13 hours 20 minutes, calling at Strathfield (†), Hornsby (†), Gosford (†), Wyong (†), Broadmeadow, Maitland, Dungog, Taree, Kendall (†), Wauchope, Kempsey, Macksville, Nambucca Heads (†), Urunga (†), Sawtell (†), Coffs Harbour, Grafton, Casino, Lismore, Byron Bay and Mullumbimby. The northbound (day service) calls unconditionally at Macksville and additionally at Gloucester and Wingham. Countrylink coach connections to Coolangatta, Gold Coast, Helensvale, Beenleigh and Brisbane to and from Murwillumbah.

The normal first-class fare (Sydney–Murwillumbah) is $135, economy $98; a first-class berth costs $95 extra.

Grafton XPT

The third daily XPT train on the NSW North Coast Line, with similar facilities, leaves Sydney at 11.35 and Grafton at 06.30, 695km in 10½ hours. The service calls at all the above stations plus Eungai (†). The normal first-class fare (Sydney–Grafton) is $113, economy $81.

OTHER LONG-DISTANCE TRAINS

Except where stated, the following trains are air conditioned and require seat reservations.

New South Wales

The **Northern Tablelands Xplorer** goes daily from Sydney to Armidale (579km) and vice versa and Sydney to Moree (666km) and vice versa. It departs Sydney at 09.35, Moree at 08.20 and Armidale at 09.00, with journey times varying from eight to nine hours. Intermediate stops are at Strathfield (†), Hornsby (†), Gosford (†), Wyong (†), Broadmeadow, Maitland, Singleton, Muswellbrook, Aberdeen (†), Scone, Murrurundi

(†), Willow Tree (†), Quirindi and Werris Creek, where the train divides. The Armidale portion then calls at all stations to Armidale (Tamworth, Kootingal, Walcha Road and Uralla), while the Moree portion calls at Gunnedah, Boggabri, Narrabri, and Bellata (†).

The Xplorer is somewhat similar to the XPT and is well suited to the shorter runs to which it is assigned. It offers first-class and economy seating with a buffet bar. Countrylink has bus connections to Burren Junction, Inverell and Tenterfield. The normal first-class fare (Sydney–Armidale) is $105, to Moree $113, economy to Armidale is $75, to Moree $81.

The **Central West XPT** is a daily express linking Sydney with Lithgow, Bathurst, Blayney, Orange, Stuart Town, Wellington, Geurie and Dubbo (462km), with conditional stops at Strathfield, Parramatta, Blacktown, Penrith, Katoomba, Rydal and Tarana. The service departs Sydney at 07.10 and Dubbo at 14.10; the journey time is 6½ hours. The train has first and economy-class seating as well as a buffet bar. There are numerous coach connections for this route. The normal first-class fare (Sydney–Dubbo) is $86, economy $62.

Countrylink Griffith and **Broken Hill** services – to fulfil an election promise to restore regional services provided by the former Riverina Express and Silver City Comet two new loco-hauled weekly trains were introduced in 1996 but withdrawn early in 2000. The latest arrangements are that an Xplorer service leaves Sydney at 08.15 on Saturdays via East Hills, calling at Campbelltown, Moss Vale, Goulburn, Yass Junction, Cootamundra, Junee, Coolamon, Narranderra and Leeton, arriving in Griffith at 17.30, 652km in 9¼ hours. Returning from Griffith at 08.00 on Sundays, calling additionally at Harden but stopping at Campbelltown only to set down. The first-class fare (Sydney–Griffith) is $113, economy $81. On board the train is referred to as the Riverina Express.

The Broken Hill train had a broken journey, commencing from Sydney on a Tuesday and running to Orange, there to remain overnight. The following afternoon it continued to Broken Hill shortly after the arrival of the Central West XPT from Sydney, making it quicker to take the XPT from Sydney that morning! For the time being there is no Countrylink Broken Hill train but passengers are booked on the Indian Pacific or The Ghan at Countrylink fares and the trains stop on request additionally at Eubalong West and Darnick. The NSW Explorer pass is valid. The normal adult fare is $110 economy only (first class or holiday class Sydney–Broken Hill with sleeper is available at normal Great Southern Railway fares). Refreshments are available on all Griffith and Broken Hill services.

The **Canberra Xplorer**, Sydney to Goulburn and Canberra, is a thrice-daily return service, departing Sydney at 07.05, 11.44 and 18.14, and Canberra at 06.45, 12.15 and 17.15, 327km in just over four hours. All trains call regularly at Moss Vale, Goulburn, Tarago, Bungendore and

Queanbeyan and conditionally at Strathfield, Campbelltown, Mittagong, Bowral and Bundanoon.

It is a diesel trainset which has first-class and economy seating and a takeaway buffet/bar. The 12.15 from Canberra connects with railway-contracted bus services from Cooma, Bombala, Bega and Eden in the southern highlands of New South Wales. In the outward directions similar connections are made from either or both of the two earliest trains from Sydney. The first-class fare (Sydney–Canberra) is $63, economy $45.

Endeavour is a generic name given to diesel railcar sets operating on the outer urban sections of the Sydney CityRail network; Dapto–Nowra, Campbelltown–Goulburn, and Newcastle to Maitland, Dungog, Scone and Muswellbrook. Economy class has surprisingly comfortable air-conditioned carriages with 3+2 seating and schedules connect with CityRail electric trains to and from Sydney. Seat reservations are not required and there is no catering.

Queensland

The **Sunlander**, which replaced the former Sunshine Express as the QR flagship in June 1953, follows the Queensland north-coast route 1673km from Brisbane through Rockhampton and Townsville to Cairns. It runs three days a week (Tuesday, Thursday and Saturday from Brisbane and Monday, Thursday and Saturday from Cairns) and takes just under 32 hours northbound and a little longer southbound.

The service departs at 08.25 from Brisbane, 08.00 from Cairns, calling at Caboolture (†), Nambour (†), Gympie North, Maryborough West, Bundaberg, Miriam Vale, Gladstone, Mount Larcom, Rockhampton, St Lawrence, Carmila, Sarina, Mackay, Proserpine, Bowen, Home Hill, Ayr, Giru, Townsville, Ingham, Cardwell, Tully, Innisfail, Babinda and Gordonvale, as well as some other places on request.

Accommodation includes first-class roomette and twinette and economy three-berth sleeping cars as well as economy sitting cars, with a 24-seat restaurant car plus an annexe of 16 extra seats in the adjoining lounge car for use if required. Macrossan's lounge is for first-class passengers only but the Tropics club car is open to all. Meals are not as elaborate as on the QR premier service, The Queenslander (see below), either in choice or quality but there is still a wide range, from snacks and fork dishes for a few dollars in the buffet lounge cars to table d'hôte two- or three-course meals or à la carte in the dining car. The dining and buffet services are not available during periods of night travel. A public telephone is available in one of the cars. There is no car-carrying facility.

The normal first-class fare (Brisbane–Cairns), including berth, is $263, economy $142 (with berth $35 extra).

The **Queenslander**, every Sunday from Brisbane to Cairns, returning on Tuesdays, ousted the Sunlander as the QR flagship from its inception in 1986. It departs Brisbane at 08.25, Cairns at 08.00; a 1680km journey in approximately 31½ hours with one night aboard. The train carries first-class sleeping-car passengers between Brisbane and the north Queensland stations of Mackay, Proserpine, Ayr, Townsville, Ingham, Tully, Innisfail and Cairns. It also picks up northbound and sets down southbound at Caboolture, Nambour, Gympie North, Maryborough West, Bundaberg, Gladstone and Rockhampton. Motor vehicles may be carried between Brisbane and Townsville or Cairns.

The accommodation comprises roomettes with toilet and wash basin, twinette sleepers (without toilet), the Coral Cay Restaurant, Daintree piano lounge (named after the World Heritage Greater Daintree National Park) and the Canecutters bar. Showers and toilets are at the end of every sleeping car and passengers have their own cabin key. Special fares (first class plus a supplement which is payable by all passengers including rail-passholders) include berths, meals, self-serve tea and coffee, happy hour cocktail voucher, complimentary toilet and stationery packs and an information brochure about the train and the places through which it passes.

The Queenslander also carries economy sitting-car passengers for whom a separate club car is provided, offering fork-type dishes such as spaghetti bolognaise and chicken à la king with pasta, as well as meat pies, sandwiches, and drinks including wine by the glass. Economy passengers may also book to or from most stations without the distance restriction applying to first class.

In the Coral Cay Restaurant breakfasts include tropical fruit, cereals, fruit juice, coffee or tea, bacon, eggs, omelette, croissant or toast with marmalade, jam, honey or vegemite (a favourite Australian savoury spread). Favourite main dishes served include chicken and shitake-mushroom terrine with smoked salmon rose, ham cornette and garden salad, seafood platter of crab or Moreton Bay Bug, banana prawns, oysters and salad, lamb in filo pastry, prime fillet of beef or porterhouse steaks, with desserts such as Black Forest gateau, and strawberry ice with fresh mango coulis.

The bar serves various cocktails and quality vintage wines or wines by the glass, in addition to the usual range of drinks. The Queenslander is

---

Warning – conditional or restricted stopping services (†)

Most interstate trains as well as many long-distance intrastate trains do not carry passengers between, or may not stop at, all intermediate stations for which times are given in the timetable. Many are conditional stops, where the train stops only on prior request and confirmed bookings. Some are restricted stops, either for picking up only or setting down only; yet others may be both conditional and restricted. Where '(†)' follows the name of a stopping place in this guide, it means there are some restrictions of this kind. These are mostly explained but conditions may vary and intending passengers should always enquire before attempting to travel to or from these places.

claimed to be Australia's top luxury train and is as far as normal first-class service is concerned (ie not counting the Great South Pacific Express). QR is the only rail system in the world to have received the Royal Doulton Award for excellence in service and cuisine, in recognition of the standards achieved on the Queenslander. The normal first-class fare (Brisbane–Cairns), including berth and meals, is $459, economy seat $142; an accompanied motor vehicle costs $170.

The Queenslander is a travel experience not to be missed, even though the supplementary fare (including meals and sleeping berth) may cost a third as much as your Austrailpass. After all, even going by ordinary train you would still need to eat and sleep, and you could spend just as much money sitting in a lonely motel room for the day and a half it takes you to travel through entrancing scenery in comfort and style!

The **Spirit of the Tropics** was introduced in July 1992 as a mid-week service, then known unofficially as the Whitsunday Queenslander, linking Brisbane with Mackay, Proserpine (gateway to the Whitsunday Islands) and Townsville. It follows a different schedule to that of the Sunlander or Queenslander, affording views of parts of the Sunshine route not otherwise seen in daylight.

It departs Brisbane at 18.55 on Wednesdays and Sundays returning from Townsville at 08.00 on Tuesdays and Fridays; 1333km in 22½ to 23 hours. It calls at the same stations as the Sunlander as far as Townsville, carrying first-class roomette and twinette sleepers and economy sitting and sleeping cars, a grill/buffet restaurant car with a small lounge area and a club car. The latter was originally a travelling disco bar called the Club Loco, the world's only disco on rails, with videos and all-night dancing but this proved too rowdy for some passengers and crew and has been sus-pended. Showers are at the end of most cars. The normal first-class fare (Brisbane–Townsville), including berth, is $235, economy $124, with berth $35 extra.

The **Tilt Train** is an air-conditioned all-electric express service between Brisbane and Rockhampton, covering 639km in seven hours, and is Australia's fastest service (and holder of the word speed record for narrow-gauge trains). It departs Brisbane at 10.30 daily except Saturdays, (07.40 daily from Rockhampton) and calls at Caboolture (†), Landsborough (†), Nambour, Cooroy, Gympie North, Maryborough West, Howard (†), Bundaberg, Miriam Vale (†), Gladstone and Mount Larcom (†), with connecting coach to Gympie, Maryborough and Hervey Bay.

The train has first-class and economy seating with a take-away buffet and an at-seat service. Baby change, wheelchair, phone and fax facilities are available; video and audio entertainment with headphones, as on an airline, are also provided. First class (called business class) is airline style including meals with a complimentary glass of wine or beer at lunch or dinner, also complimentary tea, coffee, juice, spring water and newspapers.

On Mondays to Fridays there is an additional service from Bundaberg, departing at 05.00, with a return service from Brisbane at 17.00. The return service also runs on Sundays and continues to Rockhampton on Sundays and Fridays. The normal business-class fare (Brisbane–Rockhampton), including meal, is $152, economy $70.

The **Spirit of Capricorn** is an air-conditioned electric service which replaces the Tilt Train northbound on Saturdays, departing Brisbane at 07.30, arriving Rockhampton at 17.00. Economy-fare passengers get first-class contoured seating (2+1 layout throughout) with individual reading lights and background music (not all the time!). Refreshments and drinks are served at your seat from trolleys brought round at regular intervals. The fares are the same as for the Tilt Train economy class.

The **Spirit of the Outback** is a loco-hauled through-train which travels twice weekly between Brisbane and Longreach, 'Gateway to the Outback', in central Queensland. It departs Brisbane (Roma St) at 18.25 on Tuesdays and Fridays and Longreach at 07.00 on Thursdays and Sundays; a 1325km journey in 24½ hours outward and 23½ hours homeward. The train carries first and economy sleepers and economy sitting cars, with the

 High tea on the Spirit of the Outback
Between Barcaldine and Longreach high tea is served in the Tuckerbox Restaurant of the Spirit of the Outback, the arrival time in Longreach being rather early for dinner. This is rare in railway catering nowadays, but is reminiscent of pre-war days in the north of England where dinner was the midday meal, followed later by high tea and then supper. The Spirit of the Outback high tea, however, is unlikely to include succulent York Ham or other typical English tucker, although the menu does offer Muttaburra Pie – beef pie in a sea of mushy peas – and hot scones with jam and cream as afters – the typical Devonshire (cream) tea known all over Britain and Australia.

TUCKERBOX RESTAURANT
❖ 1ST SITTING ❖

🚃 TRAVELTRAIN

Welcome to the Tuckerbox Restaurant. Prior to your sitting an announcement will be made. Passengers are advised this ticket is not transferable to other sittings, and you are required to present this card on entry to the restaurant.

SPIRIT OF THE OUTBACK

QLD · AUSTRALIA

🍵 HIGH TEA

Tucker Box restaurant-car, the Stockman's Bar (for sleeping-car passengers only) and the Captain Starlight club car for all passengers. A public telephone is available.

The service calls at Caboolture, Nambour, Cooroy, Gympie North, Maryborough West, Bundaberg, Miriam Vale, Gladstone, Rockhampton and 15 other stations between there and Longreach, the major stops being at Blackwater, Emerald, Alpha, Jericho, Barcaldine and Ilfracombe. A QR-contracted road coach connects at Longreach for Winton (a two-hour trip).

The normal first-class fare (Brisbane–Longreach), including berth, is $235, economy $134, with berth $35 extra. Meals can be included for sleeping-berth passengers at $16 Brisbane to Rockhampton, $48 Brisbane to Longreach, $38 Longreach to Brisbane. Accompanied motor vehicles are carried between Brisbane and Longreach for $150.

The **Inlander** goes from Townsville to Mount Isa and vice versa; 977km in 20½ hours outbound, 19 hours return. The service runs on Sundays and Wednesdays from Townsville, departing at 18.00, returning on Mondays and Fridays from Mount Isa, departing at 18.00, serving Mingela, Charters Towers, Pentland, Torrens Creek, Hughenden, Richmond, Julia Creek, Cloncurry and Duchess, as well as many smaller intermediate stations on request. The train has first and economy sleepers, economy coach cars and a dining car/lounge with at-seat service, ordered from the counter.

The normal first-class fare (Townsville–Mount Isa) is $175 including berth, economy $84, with berth $35 extra.

The **Westlander** is another similar train, linking Brisbane with Charleville in western Queensland, from where QR coach connections serve Cooladdi, Cheepie, Quilpie, Wyandra and Cunnamulla. The service operates on Tuesdays and Thursdays leaving Brisbane at 19.20, returning from the west on Wednesdays and Fridays at 18.15; the 777km overnight journey takes 16½ hours. Intermediate stations are Corinda (†), Ipswich (†), Rosewood (†), Toowoomba, Dalby, Chinchilla, Roma, Mitchell, Morven and numerous smaller places west of the Citytrain terminus of Rosewood, on request. The train has first and economy sleepers plus economy-class seating, with a grill buffet/diner (order at counter for at-seat service).

The normal first-class fare (Brisbane–Charleville) is $157 including berth, economy $68, with berth $35 extra.

The **Gulflander** is a unique rail-motor service on the remote Normanton Railway in North Queensland's Gulf Country; details are given on p89.

The **Savannahlander** is a two-car rail-motor set linking Cairns, Mareeba, Mount Surprise and Forsayth in the rangeland country of north

Queensland. Introduced first in 1995 running only between Mount Surprise and Forsayth, it replaced the former 'last great train ride', the Forsayth 'mixed', train 7A90, which ran all the way (see p88). Trains run every Wednesday from Cairns at 06.30, on Friday from Forsayth at 07.45, calling at Freshwater (†), Redlynch (†), Stoney Creek (†), Barron Falls (†), Kuranda (†), Koah, Mareeba, Dimbulah, Lappa, Almaden, Mount Surprise and Einasleigh. There is an overnight-stop outbound at Almaden with a bus to Chillagoe and inbound at Mount Surprise.

The service includes commentary, wayside stops at places of interest and limited on-board refreshments. The normal fare (Cairns–Forsayth) is $85; the return coach fare for the Chillagoe diversion, if required, is $17 extra.

The **Yaraka Mixed** and the **Hughenden–Winton goods** trains are the last remnants of a dwindling number of unofficially named non-air-conditioned long-distance Queensland trains. These trains are discussed on p267 but, along with the Gulflander and Savannahlander, are ones which should be experienced rather than described. They are not for the faint-hearted but a journey on any of them will, as Scottish poet McGonagall would have said, 'be remembered for a very long time'!

Victoria

In Victoria the appellation InterCity was adopted by V/line for its principal country expresses which are air-conditioned, usually of three or more coaches and diesel hauled, with first and economy-class seats.

There have been changes in the last ten years when trains on some former intercity routes have been replaced by buses and the remainder have been privatised. Services between Melbourne and the regional destinations of Shepparton, Swan Hill, Bendigo, Sale and Warrnambool have in fact increased and improved in the last three years. On the Bendigo route former loco-hauled trains have mostly been replaced by Sprinter diesel rail-cars which can operate singly or in multiple-unit formation. These are economy class only but the major intercity loco-hauled services have first-class seating as well and most carry a buffet. Although not specifically referred to now as InterCity the trains listed below are the remaining services outside the metropolitan area.

The **Northerner** is the name attached to V/line intercity trains between Melbourne and Swan Hill, the timetable for which varies with the day of the week. The train runs daily and takes an average of four hours to cover the 345km route. On Sundays it leaves Swan Hill at 16.40 and on other days at 07.10, whilst from Melbourne the departure times are 16.37 on Fridays, 17.50 Saturdays, 17.30 Sundays and 17.42 Mondays to Thursdays, probably the most complicated train service in Australia for the number of trains involved.

All Northerner trains call at Kyneton, Castlemaine, Bendigo, Eaglehawk, Dingee, Pyramid and Kerang; while the Friday and Sunday trains also call at St Albans (†), Sunbury (except Friday northbound) and Woodend. Additionally the northbound Sunday train calls to take up only at Footscray, while the southbound trains on Friday and Sunday call to set down only at Sunshine. V/line coaches connect with trains to serve Mildura, a 2 hour 40 minute journey from Swan Hill.

The first-class fare (Melbourne–Swan Hill) is $60.80, $43.40 economy. The train carries first-class and economy seats and a licensed buffet; if you want an egg and bacon roll for breakfast go to the buffet soon after leaving Swan Hill!

The popular **Vinelander** overnight sleeping-car train between Melbourne and Mildura in north-western Victoria was withdrawn in 1993. Moves are afoot to restore a rail service but up to the time of writing this night train has been replaced only by a bus (but see pp79-80).

The **Goulburn Valley Limited** links Shepparton with Melbourne, leaving Shepparton at 07.10, arriving Melbourne 09.25, returning at 18.15, arriving 20.30, Mondays to Fridays (times differ at weekends); the train calls at Broadmeadows (†), Seymour, Nagambie, Murchison East and Mooroopna. This is matched by a Melbourne-based service leaving at 09.05 and returning from Shepparton at 14.55.

Accommodation and facilities are similar to V/line intercity trains, but the buffet is unlicensed. Tea and coffee are complimentary and conductors will arrange taxis to meet trains on request. Coach connections serve Cobram and Griffith from Shepparton and Echuca from Murchison East. The economy fare (Melbourne–Shepparton) is $23.30, off-peak saver return $32.60, first-class single $32.60.

Echuca is also served by direct train, usually a Sprinter via Bendigo on Fridays and Sundays, calling at various stations up to Bendigo, then Elmore and Rochester. A useful summary of V/line rail and coach services between Melbourne and Echuca is given in the V/line North timetable booklet, but the number of direct train services may improve so enquiry is recommended. The first-class fare (Melbourne–Echuca) is $34.10 (if available), economy $26.90.

Victorian attitudes to alcohol
Drinks on trains have a curious history in Victoria; for several years the intercity trains served only light beer and cooler, a local effervescent wine/cordial mix popular with some young people. Even the Vinelander served no wine in the days before its withdrawal but some time in the last three years there has been an improvement, the wowser influence has declined, wine as well as beer are once more available to thirsty travellers on V/line passenger's main intercity trains, including what was once the Albury Express.

The **Gippslander** is the principal day service linking Melbourne (Spencer St) and Sale in eastern Victoria. It departs Melbourne at 07.47 returning from Sale at 13.40, Mondays to Fridays, with later times at weekends (C 9029), covering 206km in 2 hours 40 minutes and calling at Flinders St (†), Caulfield (†), Dandenong (†), Pakenham, Warragul, Moe, Morwell, Traralgon and Rosedale.

The train is air-conditioned and non-smoking with first-class (2+2) layout) and economy (2+3) seating and a buffet service. V/line coaches connect to Bairnsdale and other places in East Gippsland and over the border into New South Wales. There are additional trains at other times, up to nine a day between Melbourne and Traralgon, but not all with the same facilities. The first-class fare (Melbourne–Sale) is $37.60, $26.90 economy.

Twin City Limited is the name of the morning V/line Albury to Melbourne train which returns in the evening, but there is little to distinguish it from other trains on this run. There are three weekday intercity trains each way between Melbourne and Albury, two on Saturdays and Sundays, all with first and economy seating and a buffet. The 307km journey takes an average of 3 hours 45 minutes, calling at Broadmeadows (†), Seymour and various stations between Seymour and Albury always including Euroa, Benalla and Wangaratta. The first and economy-class seating is similar to the Gippslander and there is a buffet; the buffet has traditionally been dry since the days of the Albury Express, sometimes dubbed the travelling 'pub with no beer', and V/line make the unusual boast in their promotional literature that 'Most services are alcohol free'.

The first-class fare (Melbourne–Albury) is $54.40 first, $38.90 economy. Countrylink XPT trains also serve Benalla, Wangaratta and Albury, adding two more daily trains each way, but V/line tickets are not accepted.

The **West Coaster** is the name given to a fully licensed dining car (formerly part of the Southern Aurora Sydney–Melbourne express) which is provided for special bookings with steam haulage on the West Coast Railway (WCR) between Melbourne and Warrnambool (see also p262). The normal services on this route, jointly run by V/line and the privately-owned WCR, carry exceptionally comfortable and roomy first-class plus economy seating (including some compartments) and a buffet car. Unlike the West Coaster, this is dry, but on alternate Saturdays the morning outward service from Melbourne, returning from Warrnambool at 13.05 carries the dining car and accepts individual bookings. Otherwise reservations are not required and the Austrailpass is honoured.

As with most country trains in Victoria, the service at weekends differs markedly from that on normal weekdays (a Victorian Sunday has long perpetuated some of the characteristics of the era so named in Britain). There are three services each way on weekdays, two outward and three return on Saturdays, and only one each way in the evening on Sundays.

The morning Saturday service is steam-hauled, leaving Melbourne Spencer St at 08.43, returning from Warrnambool at 17.05, the only regularly timetabled steam-hauled mainline passenger train in Australia. The 267km journey takes just over three hours, calling at Geelong, Winchelsea, Colac, Camperdown and Terang. Tickets between Geelong and Melbourne are interchangeable with V/line Passenger and WCR accept Austrailpass.

Some trains call additionally at Birregurra whilst Sunday trains call additionally at Werribee (to take up westbound and set down eastbound) and the last weekday return train from Warrnambool at 17.35 calls to set down at North Geelong, Corio, Lara and Werribee, reaching Melbourne at 21.00. Connecting coaches serve Port Fairy, Portland and other places on the Victorian west coast, and Mount Gambier in South Australia.

The first-class fare (Melbourne–Warrnambool) is $47.80, economy $34.20.

South Australia

Regional services in South Australia, comprising the **Silver City Limited** (Adelaide–Broken Hill and vice versa), the **Iron Triangle Limited** (Adelaide–Whyalla and vice versa) and the **Blue Lake** (Adelaide–Mount Gambier and vice versa) were all suspended in 1991 and, despite much local agitation, independent inquiry, solemn agreement and careful estimates of replacement costs, they remain victims of misplaced government economic policy. With the standardisation of the Adelaide–Melbourne route, Mount Gambier in particular, on the 1600mm broad-gauge system, has been isolated. At the time of writing, and for the foreseeable future, buses appear to be the only alternative for places in South Australia not served by the interstate trains of Great Southern.

An exception recently introduced is a privately-run tour train which has brought back a rail service by refurbished Bluebird rail-cars to the famous Barossa Valley north-east of Adelaide. This is the **Barossa Wine Train**, which operates a day tour to Tanunda leaving Adelaide thrice weekly (Tuesday, Thursday and Sunday) at 08.50, arriving at 17.20 on the return. The 70.5km journey takes $1\frac{1}{2}$ hours each way, with over five hours at Tanunda; fares start from $55 return. A coach tour of famous wineries and a lunch can be included for a total cost of $85. The Austrailpass is not valid on the Barossa Wine Train. For further details and bookings contact ☎ 08-8212 7888, ▤ 08-8231 5771 or ▢ info@barossawinetrain.com.au.

Western Australia

The **Prospector** goes from Perth to Kalgoorlie and vice versa; 655km normally in $7\frac{1}{2}$ to 8 hours (the schedule differs almost every day). It runs daily in both directions with an extra run each way on Mondays, Wednesdays and Fridays. There are 16 intermediate stops, all only on

> **Meals on wheels**
> A word about railway catering, especially eating on trains. Sometimes you will have to indulge; there is nowhere else to find sustenance without taking your own (which though not exactly prohibited is frowned upon). Generally Australian railway food is good, some of it excellent. You can get tasty hot snacks reasonably cheaply on trains like the XPT or Xplorer, and on all Queensland long-distance trains. V/line's intercity trains have rather more limited fare but there is no need to starve. Main meals in dining cars cost no more, often less, than they would in a comparable restaurant (one with sit-down service, not a pub counter lunch). Trains like The Ghan, the Indian Pacific and the Queenslander border on gourmet-style food whilst a mixed grill or steak and eggs breakfast on the Inlander will sustain you for most of the day! Not all Australians really consume chunks of steak or chops with egg for their daybreak meal, but travelling on some long-distance trains you would certainly think they did.
>
> Less extravagant is the humble Railway Pie (meat and gravy, served piping hot, with or without tomato sauce), which has recently made a comeback and is a very tasty, inexpensive form of sustenance for the hungry, even if a trifle messy to consume.

request but usually including Midland, Northam, Kellerberrin, Merredin and Southern Cross. Only one-class reclining seats are available; meals and refreshments as ordered are served at every seat. The service connects at Kalgoorlie with Westrail buses to and from Esperance. The fare (Perth–Kalgoorlie) is $49.30.

In Western Australia there is the **Avon Link** (East Perth–Northam), a commuter version of the Prospector, and the sleek, modern little **Australind**. This narrow-gauge train zips along at a steady 80km/h through the wild flowers of the Western Australian coastal plain from Perth to the historic little town of Bunbury. It leaves Perth City main station at 09.30 and 17.45, Bunbury at 06.00 and 14.40; the journey time is 2¼ hours and trains call at up to 10 intermediate stations provided bookings have been made. A buffet service is available on the train, and a courtesy bus from the rail terminal to the city centre in Bunbury is provided except on Sundays and public holidays. The fare (Perth–Bunbury) is $18.

SUBURBAN AND INTERURBAN TRAINS

Tedious though many suburban rail journeys can be, the train is clearly superior to driving a car or riding a bus in the rush hour. Within all the state capitals there are suburban rail services giving access to the city centre and other points of interest.

By tram, on the oldest passenger rail line in Australia, you can go down to Port Melbourne where the ships used to bring the migrants under the Assisted Passage Scheme. You can go across Sydney Harbour bridge by train and look out at the hot, congested streams of frustrated motorists on the adjoining road; they also have to pay a toll that is more than your train fare and will take longer to reach their city destinations than you will on the state-of-the-art double-deck Tangara trains of Sydney's CityRail network. You can go by rail to the Olympic Stadium, up into the Blue Mountains, down to the beach at Cronulla or to the Royal National Park at Sutherland just south of Botany Bay.

Suburban and interurban trains in Australia vary tremendously. **Sydney** has some ultra-modern suburban trains (the Tangara), continuing the pioneering spirit which gave it the honour of being the first city in the world to have double-deck suburban electric multiple-unit (EMU) trains. CityRail's Interurban EMU trains are also double deck, air conditioned and have toilets.

Melbourne too has some modern suburban sets and a version of the Tangara has recently been given trials. The Melbourne Met system has been privatised but under very strict operating conditions, which apply also to the privatised intercity network.

Operators in Melbourne are Hillside Trains (Epping, Hurstbridge, Lilydale, Belgrave, Alamein and Glen Waverley routes), Bayside Trains (Upfield, Broadmeadows, St Albans, Williamstown, Werribee, Frankston, Cranbourne and Pakenham routes) as well as Yarra, Swanston and City Circle trams and Met buses. The City Circle tram is free.

A Passengers' Charter ensures that service levels will be maintained, fares will not increase above the rate of inflation, concessions will continue, tickets will be valid on all modes and performance and punctuality will be monitored, with incentives and penalties applied. And more! In some circumstances passengers can actually be compensated, eg by ticket extension following bad punctuality. Australia has not yet adopted the Japanese practice of refunding fares when express trains are late. This would be an expensive matter in the wet season, when lateness may be measured in hours or even days rather than minutes. But the Victorian idea may be a start in the right direction. The first signs are that it is working well.

Brisbane's Interurban (IMU) sets serving the Gold Coast hinterland boast toilet and rest-room accommodation, as well as luggage racks, not normally found on suburban trains, and are capable of speeds up to 140km/h.

Most **Perth** suburban services run every 15 minutes even at weekends. **Canberra** has an intensive bus service but no suburban rail.

No Australian suburban trains, so far, have any first-class accommodation or buffet service as you might find in European cities like Frankfurt or Bonn or in Greater London.

Suburban rail services operate usually at least every half-hour during daytime and at least hourly in the late evening and on Sundays but this varies between cities; between central city stations in Sydney the frequency is often every few minutes. Some ideas and itinerary suggestions are given in Part 4 to help the visitor make the most of even one day in each capital. They assume a start from the main station, but remember that suburban locations are often very convenient to reach and often offer cheaper accommodation.

Tour and itinerary options

INTRODUCTION

Before considering how to make the most effective use of whatever passes or tickets you have, it would be helpful to read the preceding section on the trains (pp37-61), if you have not already done so.

On any itinerary based on a consecutive pass, much of your time will be spent on quality trains, which will become your travelling hotel. You will need to take enough clean clothes and money to last most of the time because the itineraries allow for only limited time for shopping or bank transactions after leaving your starting point.

If you have a flexipass, not only will you have more time to look around at places you reach, you will be able to do your banking and have your laundry attended to. You can plan your own excursions from selected bases, leaving your heavy luggage at a hotel to be called for later. You need not always rent a hotel room for this: it is usually possible to come to some arrangement with the management. Luggage can also be left at railway station depositories and laundry can be left at laundries where it belongs. Remember to keep a note of where you've left everything: it is annoying to have to make a special trip back somewhere just to collect a suitcase or a couple of shirts you had forgotten about.

Whatever you do, watch the days of the week! Saturday afternoons and Sundays must be counted as dead periods for attending to these necessities. Even in Sydney on a Sunday it is almost impossible to obtain cash unless you have a card with pin number and can find the right autobank. American Express and Thomas Cook offices are useful in an emergency but you will find them only in the larger cities. It is easy to forget the day of the week when travelling on long-distance trains like the Indian Pacific. Time-zone changes are enough to contend with as it is.

The additional comfort of a sleeping berth (not covered by rail passes) is not prohibitively expensive. A twin-berth sleeper on an interstate train costs up to 30 per cent less than the price of a double room in a first-class (four-star) hotel in a city such as Melbourne. For the single traveller the difference is even greater. Although the train cannot offer quite the luxury or spaciousness of the hotel it is still, with air-conditioning, private toilet and shower, an attractive proposition for the traveller wishing to use limited time to the best advantage.

By spending some of your nights sleeping comfortably on a train you can wake up in a new place every day with new things to see and do. You will not only save money and cover more of the country, but have opportunities to meet, talk and relax with people far more than in a lonely suite in a big city hotel. Depending on where you want to start and finish your tour, you can visit all the mainland state capitals of Australia; Perth, Adelaide, Melbourne, Sydney and Brisbane in less than three weeks and you can include a side trip to Cairns or Alice Springs as well.

Getting to Alice Springs by train is simple, thanks to the augmented Ghan service from both Sydney and Melbourne (C 9034, 9035). However, travelling to the Alice by train from the west involves changing at Tarcoola or Port Augusta or Port Pirie at inconvenient times and with no sensible connections, or simply going on to Adelaide to wait for The Ghan there. Table 2 below shows how inconvenient such a journey can be.

PLANNING A 14-DAY ITINERARY

Yes! Despite such time-consuming non-connections as those in Table 2 below, you can actually travel right round the country by train in only two weeks. But if you want to make the most of an Austrailpass in a limited time it is imperative that you make advance reservations for all the trains

---

❏ **Table 2**
Perth–Tarcoola–Alice Springs (C 9034)

Perth dep	Monday 10.55	Friday 10.55
Tarcoola arr	Tuesday 18.12a	Saturday 17.54a
Tarcoola dep	Friday 00.30	Tuesday 00.30
Alice Springs arr	Friday 10.00b	Tuesday 10.00b

Alice Springs–Tarcoola–Perth (C 9034)

Alice Springs dep	Friday 13.00	Tuesday 13.00
Tarcoola arr	Friday 23.25	Tuesday 23.25
Tarcoola dep	Saturday 05.11	Wednesday 04.52
Perth arr	Sunday 09.30	Thursday 09.30

Notes
All trains have catering and sleeping accommodation.
a Option of continuing from Tarcoola to Port Augusta, arriving around midnight, or to Adelaide arriving 06.05 the next day with over a day free in Adelaide before The Ghan's departure at 15.00 on Monday or Thursday.
b One hour earlier during Eastern Summer Time (end October to mid-March). For other possibilities of a journey break in Tarcoola see pp77-78.

on which you will need them. Your first decisions must therefore be the cities at which your rail tour will begin and end.

In planning your itinerary it is important to realise, in case you had overlooked earlier comparisons, that Australia is nearly as big as the United States of America and three-quarters the size of Europe. Texas would fit into a corner of Queensland – and does! It is in fact the name of a little town on a former freight branch (the trains used to carry a passenger van) in Queensland's south-west.

In the old days a trans-Australian journey by rail was not for the faint-hearted. Breaks of gauge, changes of train, intense heat, dust and flies made it something to be contemplated with misgiving and remembered with mingled horror and amazement. Many are the tales that have been told and the books that have been written. As recently as 1970 it was still not possible to go from Sydney to Perth without four changes of train – at Melbourne, Adelaide, Port Pirie and Kalgoorlie.

It still takes three days to cross the whole continent. The return trip takes six days if you start from Perth, seven if you start from Sydney, and this without spending much more time at the other end than it takes for the train to be turned around, cleaned and reprovisioned (5 hours in Sydney, just over 24 in Perth). It is therefore sensible, if you have only a 14-day Australpass, to plan your arrival at one port and your departure from another. This can often be arranged easily when making your airline bookings. Many international flights regularly serve Perth, Sydney, Melbourne and Brisbane. Sydney is the base with the greatest concentration of rail as well as external air routes, but starting your rail trip in Perth and finishing in the east or starting in Queensland (some airlines serve Cairns as well as Brisbane) and finishing in the west can give better options for the holder of a short-term Australpass. Also, many airline package deals to and from Australia allow one or more internal flights without extra charge. This sort of concession could be useful for bridging some of the gaps in the rail network such as Perth–Darwin–Cairns or for travelling direct between Canberra and Melbourne without having either to change trains at Goulburn or use the bus between Canberra and somewhere further along the main south line.

A boon to travellers is the Austrail Flexipass, introduced in recent years. It's ideal for those who wish to spin out a tour by spending several days, perhaps a week or more, in one place before going on to another.

The basic triangle

With almost any itinerary at all, some retracing of route is necessary because there is no real rail network in the sense of a web of intersecting routes as in Europe. Basically, Australia has a fundamental triangle of passenger main lines – Adelaide, Sydney, Melbourne. Every other route, however long or short, is a dead-end system branching from this triangle,

❏ **Table 3**
**Sydney–Melbourne–Adelaide–Sydney and vice versa
(C 9020, 9026 and 9035)**

	Daily		Daily		Sun	Mon/Thu
Sydney	07.43		20.43	Sydney	13.10	14.55
					Mon	Tue/Fri
Melbourne	18.15		07.00	Adelaide	12.50	16.50
	ExTue/Wed/Sat		Wed		ExTue/Wed/Sat	Wed
Melbourne	21.30		22.30	Adelaide	09.00	10.15
	ExWed/Thu/Sun		Thu			
Adelaide	07.40		10.10	Melbourne	20.10	21.00
	Sat		Wed/Sun		Daily	Daily
Adelaide	10.10		07.45	Melbourne	08.30	19.45
	Sun		Thu/Mon			
Sydney	09.15		09.15	Sydney	19.13	06.25

Notes
All trains have refreshments, must be booked, and have sleeping accommodation on overnight journeys.
Ex means except ie ExTue/Wed/Sat means Except Tuesdays, Wednesdays and Saturdays.

with here and there a minor loop on one of the branches. A 14-day Austrailpass, wherever you start, will still allow you to visit all the capital cities, but you may well wish to include places like Cairns and Alice Springs as well, or instead.

To give some idea of the time-scale of things, the basic south-eastern capital-city triangle takes a minimum of 2 days 4½ hours (anti-clockwise from Sydney starting on a Monday or Thursday) to 3½ days (starting from Melbourne anti-clockwise on a Monday or Friday or clockwise on a Sunday or Wednesday). This is shown in Table 3 above; the summary table of interstate trains on the basic south-eastern triangle.

Alice Springs is a three-day round trip from Adelaide (more from Sydney or Melbourne) whilst Cairns is a five-day round trip from Sydney. You can just go from Perth to Cairns and back, or vice versa in 14 days, but you would not have much more than a night there or anywhere in between.

On many interstate trips you will cross time zones, which may vary with the season. Summer time operates in the eastern states except Queensland. As a general rule, travelling west between the eastern states

---

(**Opposite**) **Top left**: The Tilt train at Roma St. **Top right**: The XPT at Roma St. **Middle left**: The Gulflander. **Middle right**: Countrylink Xplorer. **Bottom left**: The Ghan at Keswick Station. **Bottom right**: The Spirit of the Outback at Emerald.

and South Australia, you put watches back 30 minutes and between South and Western Australia back 90 minutes; forward in the other direction. Be careful at Broken Hill, which is in New South Wales but observes South Australian time. The train conductor will clear up any doubts for you and in fact west of Adelaide the train operates on its own sweet time, so you need not worry unless you need to telephone somebody.

SOME 14-DAY ITINERARIES

On p70 of this book are some ideas on how to make the best use of the Austrailpass if you are staying for a month or more, but if you are limited to an ultra-short stay the most you can pack into it in the way of rail travel is set out in the following four itineraries. These 14-day packages are essentially quick reconnaissance tours – seeing on the move. Most visitors would probably prefer to spread these itineraries over a longer period, which can now readily be done by obtaining an Austrail Flexipass covering 14 days of travel spread over up to six months, but if you are really pushed you can see an astonishing amount of the country in a very short time and at little cost.

It is not difficult in 14 days to visit **all** the mainland state capital cities as well as the national capital of Canberra, as Itinerary 1 (p66) shows. You can spend a day or more in each capital city and still have time for side trips or variations to your itinerary. But be warned. These 14-day maximum mileage itineraries are not for geriatrics or the faint-hearted, though if they are followed you will have something to talk about for years afterwards – and few people will believe you did it all by train!

These itineraries cover mainly capital cities, but capital cities are not what everyone wants to see. To many visitors, an Australian trip would not be fulfilled without seeing romantic places like the 'Town called Alice' or the railway station at Kuranda. It is possible to vary any itinerary to fit in a trip either to the 'red centre' or to tropical north Queensland. Caution! If you insist on staying for a night in the middle of the Nullarbor, climbing to the top of Ayers Rock or scuba-diving off the Barrier Reef, you are not going to manage it with a 14-day rail pass. But you can come close to such achievements if you take, say, a 21-day Flexipass and plan your itinerary carefully, following the advice given in this book.

More economic and interesting use can be made of the 14-day Austrailpass if you start your journey on one side of Australia and finish it on the other. After all, you may feel that one crossing of the Nullarbor in a 14-day tour is sufficient (though many travellers find it

(**Opposite**) **Top**: The Daintree lounge on the Queenslander (see p50). **Bottom**: Facilities on trains are generally modern and good; pictured here is a toilet and baby-change room on the Gold Coast Interurban (IMU) Express (see p60).

❑ **Itinerary 1**
Sydney–Cairns–Brisbane–Sydney–Perth–Adelaide–Melbourne

Day	Place	Time	Remarks
Day 1 Friday	dep Sydney	16.24a	Brisbane XPT (a)
Day 2 Saturday	arr Brisbane #	06.35a	1½ hours free (a)
	dep Brisbane	08.25b	Sunlander (b)
Day 3 Sunday	arr Cairns	16.20	night-stop
Day 4 Monday	dep Cairns	08.00	Sunlander
Day 5 Tuesday	arr Brisbane	16.10	night-stop
Day 6 Wednesday	dep Brisbane #	07.30	Brisbane XPT
	arr Sydney	21.51	night-stop
Day 7 Thursday	dep Sydney	14.55	Indian Pacific
Day 8 Friday	en route: Broken Hill to Spencer Gulf		
Day 9 Saturday	en route: Nullarbor Plain and Kalgoorlie		
Day 10 Sunday	arr Perth	09.30	night-stop
Day 11 Monday	dep Perth	10.55	Indian Pacific
Day 12 Tuesday	en route: the Nullarbor Plain		
Day 13 Wednesday	arr Adelaide (c)	06.05	four hours free (c)
	dep Adelaide	10.15	The Ghan
	arr Melbourne	21.00	night-stop
Day 14 Thursday	dep Melbourne	08.30	Olympic Spirit
	arr Sydney	19.13	

Notes

One hour earlier during Eastern Summer Time.

a If you are unable to book a sleeper and are not keen to sit up all night, an option is to take the Murwillumbah XPT, dep Sydney 07.15, change to coach at Murwillumbah to arrive in Brisbane at 22.50 for a night-stop. The bus journey could be reduced by taking the Countrylink coach to Robina or Beenleigh for a QR train to Brisbane, but the connections are poor and Brisbane would not be reached until almost midnight. For details of this option see Itinerary 4 (p69).

b An alternative is to depart Brisbane at 10.30 on the Tilt Train, changing en route to the Sunlander; see p83.

c An alternative is to break the journey for a few hours at Tarcoola instead of the four-hour early morning wait in Adelaide, arriving in Tarcoola at 17.54 and leaving on The Ghan at 23.30, but this can only be booked seven days in advance. See pp77-78 for full details.

draws them back again and again – the writer is one); itineraries 2, 3 and 4 allow such variation, two starting in Perth and finishing on the east and one going in the other direction. All three include Alice Springs, while two also include north Queensland.

The recent extension of The Ghan to Melbourne and an additional weekly service to Sydney (reinstating a former direct Sydney–Alice Springs train called The Alice) doubles the service to and from Alice Springs, allowing a three- or four-day stay there. Itinerary 4 is an example, though the gain is offset by the omission of north Queensland from this itinerary.

However, a three-day wait in one place takes rather a large slice of your time with only a 14-day Austrailpass; the Flexipass would be a better investment if this is your choice.

Note that an Austrailpass does **not** cover air or boat trips, nor are discounts on other transport offered to Austrailpass holders as in Europe.

Itinerary 1 (see p66)

With a 14-day Austrailpass and travelling to north Queensland, South Australia, Western Australia and Victoria, this itinerary involves night-stops in Cairns, Brisbane, Sydney, Perth and Melbourne with eight nights on trains; sleeping berths are available on all the night trains. The maximum continuous time away from base is seven days.

The itinerary (see p66) commences on a Friday from Sydney but it can also be based on Melbourne (commencing as Day 14 and ending as

---

❏ **Itinerary 2**
Perth–Adelaide–Alice Springs–Melbourne–Sydney–Gold Coast
Brisbane–Cairns

Day	Place	Time	Remarks
Day 1 Friday	dep Perth	10.55	Indian Pacific
Day 2 Saturday	en route: the Nullarbor plain		
Day 3 Sunday	arr Adelaide	06.05	night-stop
Day 4 Monday	dep Adelaide	15.00	The Ghan
Day 5 Tuesday	arr Alice Springs	10.00#	three hours free
	dep Alice Springs	13.00	The Ghan (e)
Day 6 Wednesday	arr Adelaide	09.00	one hour free
	dep Adelaide	10.15	The Ghan (e)
	arr Melbourne	21.00	two-night stopover
Day 8 Friday	dep Melbourne	08.30	Olympic Spirit
	arr Sydney	19.13	two-night stopover
Day 10 Sunday	dep Sydney	07.15	Murwillumbah XPT
	arr Murwillumbah	21.00	change to bus
	dep Murwillumbah	21.15	Countrylink coach
	arr Gold Coast (f)	22.15#	night-stop
Day 11 Monday	dep Gold Coast (f)	14.38g	QR coach connection
	arr Nerang	15.04g	change to train
	dep Nerang	15.23g	QR Interurban electric
	arr Brisbane	16.26g	night-stop
Day 12 Tuesday	dep Brisbane	08.30b	Sunlander
Day 13 Wednesday	arr Cairns	19.30	night-stop
Day 14 Thursday	Kuranda Scenic Railway day excursion (see p237)		

Notes

e Book through from Alice Springs to Melbourne and check heavy luggage through if not wanted on board or at Adelaide.

f Surfers Paradise (Beach Rd bus station)

g Other connections to Brisbane at least hourly throughout the day

See Itinerary 1, p66, for details of the other relevant notes.

Day 13), Brisbane (commencing as Day 6 and ending as Day 5) or commencing in Perth as on Day 11, ending as on Day 10.

There would be no point using a Flexipass for Itinerary 1, unless it was to spend several days in one or more of the places where an overnight stop is indicated. It should be carefully noted that not all the trains run every day of the week so that, for example, if you decided to spend two extra days in Cairns on a Flexipass, there would not be a train south on the Wednesday. Waiting until the next one, on Thursday, would mean missing the Indian Pacific at Sydney – where the next one would not be until the following Monday. If you are happy to spend a whole week in any of the night-stop cities, then the Flexipass would be fine, since you would still be leaving each place on the same day of the week as indicated in the itinerary.

Itinerary 2 (see p67)
Starting in Perth on a Friday and ending in Cairns with five nights on trains and briefly visiting all the eastern state capital cities plus Alice

---

❑ **Itinerary 3**
Cairns (Kuranda)–Brisbane–Sydney–Alice Springs–Adelaide–Perth

Day	Place	Time	Remarks
Day 1 Monday	Kuranda Scenic Railway day excursion from Cairns (for details see p249)		
Day 2 Tuesday	dep Cairns	08.00	The Queenslander
Day 3 Wednesday	arr Brisbane	15.10	two-night stopover
Day 5 Friday	dep Brisbane #	07.30	Brisbane XPT
	arr Sydney	21.51	two-night stopover
Day 7 Sunday	dep Sydney	13.10	The Ghan (h)
Day 8 Monday	arr Adelaide	12.50	two hours free
	dep Adelaide	15.00	The Ghan (h)
Day 9 Tuesday	arr Alice Springs	10.00#	three hours free
	dep Alice Springs	13.00	The Ghan
Day 10 Wednesday	arr Adelaide	09.00	one hour free
	dep Adelaide	10.15	The Ghan
	arr Murray Bridge	12.14	night-stop
Day 11 Thursday	dep Murray Bridge	07.55	The Ghan
	arr Adelaide	10.10	night-stop
Day 12 Friday	dep Adelaide	18.30	Indian Pacific
Day 13 Saturday	en route: The Nullarbor and Kalgoorlie (i)		
Day 14 Sunday	arr Perth	09.30i	

Notes
h Book through to Alice Springs from Sydney and check heavy luggage through if not wanted on board or at Adelaide.
i Option of a night-stop at Kalgoorlie on the Saturday, arriving at 19.20, departing Sunday at 14.00 on the Prospector, arriving in Perth at 21.55.
For other notes see Itinerary 1, p66.

Springs before ending the tour in north Queensland. Night-stops are in Adelaide, Melbourne (2), Sydney (2), Gold Coast, Brisbane and Cairns.

Itinerary 3 (see p68)
Starting from Cairns, this itinerary includes travel on Australia's three top trains (excluding the privately-owned Great South Pacific Express).

With a 14-day Austrailpass, the itinerary includes visits to all the state capital cities except Melbourne, then to Alice Springs before ending the tour in Perth. There are six nights on trains, with night-stops in Brisbane (2), Sydney (2), Murray Bridge and Adelaide.

Itinerary 4 (see below)
Starting in Perth on a Friday and ending in Brisbane, visiting Adelaide, Alice Springs, Sydney, Canberra and Melbourne with ample time to visit Uluru (Ayers Rock). Six nights are on trains; sleeping berths are available.

❏ **Itinerary 4**
Perth–Adelaide–Alice Springs–Sydney–Canberra–Melbourne–
Sydney–Brisbane

Day	Place	Time	Remarks
Day 1 Friday	dep Perth	10.55	Indian Pacific
Day 2 Saturday	en route: the Nullarbor Plain		
Day 3 Sunday	arr Adelaide	06.05	two-night stopover
Day 4 Monday	dep Adelaide	15.00	The Ghan
Day 5 Tuesday	arr Alice Springs	10.00#	three-night stopover (j)
Day 8 Friday	dep Alice Springs	13.00	The Ghan (k)
Day 9 Saturday	arr Adelaide	07.40f	1½ hours free
	dep Adelaide	10.10	The Ghan (k)
Day 10 Sunday	arr Sydney	09.15	night-stop
Day 11 Monday	dep Sydney	07.05	Canberra Xplorer
	arr Canberra	11.15	six hours free
	dep Canberra	17.15	Canberra Xplorer
	arr Moss Vale	19.34	2½ hours free
	dep Moss Vale	22.31	Southern Cross XPT
Day 12 Tuesday	arr Melbourne	07.00	night-stop
Day 13 Wednesday	dep Melbourne	08.30	Olympic Spirit XPT
	arr Sydney	19.13	night-stop
Day 14 Thursday	dep Sydney	07.15	Murwillumbah XPT
	arr Murwillumbah	21.00	change to bus
	dep Murwillumbah	21.20	Countrylink coach
	arr Robina	22.05#	change to train
	dep Robina	22.47#	QR Interurban electric
	arr Brisbane	23.54#	two-night stopover

Notes
j Option of one or more night-stops at Yulara (for Ayers Rock).
k Book through to Sydney; check -in any heavy luggage not needed till then.
For other notes see Itinerary I, p66.

ITINERARIES FOR A ONE-MONTH AUSTRAILPASS

Assuming that amongst other things you will want to spend a day or two in most, if not all, capital cities; to cross the Nullarbor, visit the Red Centre, north Queensland and the Barrier Reef, and other places of scenic, cultural, or historic interest, even if only to say you have been there – the following outline itinerary (Itinerary 5) allows a full day or more in most major centres and a return to base part way through for laundry or other domestic purposes. Three successive nights are allowed in Sydney; this gives your hotel a chance to deal with all your laundry for the previous week and a half.

Some readers of the first edition of this guide protested that this itinerary was too exhausting. It is a revised and updated version of an itinerary first published in *Great Rail Non-Journeys of Australia*. It packs in about the maximum it is reasonably possible to achieve in a short time. Certainly it is not for the faint hearted. It might be classed as moderate to intensive, but for those who seek a more leisurely month on the railways of Australia, the answer is to omit some parts or select the Flexipass.

The itinerary is capable of many variations, some of which are examined on pp75-91. However, the actual days of travel, ie day of the week, for some of the principal journeys cannot be altered without disrupting the schedule.

Itinerary 5 (see p71)

A one-month Austrailpass itinerary based on Sydney, starting on a Sunday with a return to base just over halfway through. The itinerary could also be based on Melbourne by starting on a Monday or based on any other city at which an overnight stop is indicated. Many variations and side trips are possible.

With the 30-day Austrailpass there are nine additional full days free in the above itinerary. If no rail travel at all is done on these days, then the 30-day pass would be partially wasted, but other journeys could be made on these days, even if only local trips where the pass is valid, such as in Melbourne, Sydney and Brisbane.

Itinerary 6 (see pp72-73)

This is an example of an intensified 30-day itinerary, showing how the 30-day pass could be used more fully, while still allowing R & R days in key cities between longer journeys.

The 29-day version of the Flexipass would be needed for this itinerary.

PRE-PLANNED PACKAGES

Most of the railway systems offer pre-planned package tours. These vary from half-day trips to excursions lasting anything up to a fortnight. The thing to watch if planning to use such packages is whether the rail fare is

❏ **Itinerary 5**
Sydney–Alice Springs–Adelaide–Perth–Melbourne–Sydney–
Brisbane–Cairns–Brisbane–Sydney

Travel day			Place	Time	Remarks
(a)	**(b)**				
1	1	Sunday	dep Sydney	13.10	The Ghan (a)
3	2	Tuesday	arr Alice Springs	10.00b	three hours free
	3		dep Alice Springs	13.00	The Ghan (a)
4	3	Wednesday	arr Adelaide	09.00	two-night stopover
6	4	Friday	dep Adelaide	18.30	Indian Pacific
8	5	Sunday	arr Perth	09.30	night-stop
9	6	Monday	dep Perth	10.55	The Indian Pacific
11	7	Wednesday	arr Adelaide	06.05	three hours free
	8		dep Adelaide	10.15	The Ghan
			arr Melbourne	21.00	five-night stopover
16	9	Monday	dep Melbourne	08.30	Olympic Spirit XPT
			arr Sydney	19.13	three-night stopover
19	10	Thursday	dep Sydney	07.15	Murwillumbah XPT
			arr Murwillumbah	21.00	change to bus
			dep Murwillumbah	21.30	Countrylink coach
			arr Robina	22.05b	change to train
			dep Robina	22.47b	QR Interurban electric
			arr Brisbane	23.54b	three-night stopover
22	11	Sunday	dep Brisbane	08.25c	Queenslander
23	12	Monday	arr Cairns	16.20	three-night stopover
26	13	Thursday	dep Cairns	08.00	The Sunlander
27	14	Friday	arr Brisbane	16.10	two-night stopover
29	15	Sunday	dep Brisbane	07.30b	Brisbane XPT
			arr Sydney	21.51	night-stop

Notes
Travel day numbers refer to (a) Consecutive pass use (b) Flexipass (15-day) use.
Requirements: 30-day Austrailpass $900, with one day in hand or 15-day
Flexipass $685, with no days in hand.
a Book through to Alice Springs from Sydney and check heavy luggage
through if not wanted on board or at Adelaide.
b One hour earlier during Eastern Summer Time (end October to mid-March)
c A later departure from Brisbane is possible by taking the Tilt Train (dep
10.30) to Bundaberg, Gladstone or Rockhampton; see Itinerary 6 (p72).

included. There is no point in taking a trip which includes the train fare if
you already have a pass or ticket which covers the same journey.

QR have recently introduced various all-inclusive packages which
should interest those visitors not using one of the rail passes. These range
from two-night packages at a little over $200 per person to a 16- or 19-
day 'see it all' tour at $2700 or more. Options include rail/cruise/air tours
and cover the Gold Coast, Sunshine Coast, Capricorn Coast, the Barrier

❏ **Itinerary 6 Sydney–Katoomba–Alice Springs–Adelaide–Kalgoorlie–Perth–Melbourne–Sydney–Byron Bay–Gold Coast–Brisbane**

Travel day (a)(b)			Place	Time	Remarks
1	1	Saturday	dep Sydney	10.02	CityRail interurban
			arr Katoomba	11.58	night-stop
2	2	Sunday	dep Katoomba	10.09	CityRail interurban (a)
			arr Sydney	11.53	one hour free (a)
			dep Sydney	13.10	The Ghan (a)
3	3	Monday	arr Adelaide	12.50	two-hour break
			dep Adelaide	15.00	The Ghan
4	4	Tuesday	arr Alice Springs	10.00b	three hours free
			dep Alice Springs	13.00	The Ghan
5	5	Wednesday	arr Adelaide	09.00	two-night stopover
7	6	Friday	dep Adelaide	18.30	Indian Pacific
8	7	Saturday	arr Kalgoorlie	19.05	night-stop
9	8	Sunday	dep Kalgoorlie	14.00	The Prospector
			arr Perth	21.55	night-stop
10	9	Monday	dep Perth	10.55	The Indian Pacific
11	10	Tuesday	en route Kalgoorlie and the Nullarbor		
12	11	Wednesday	arr Adelaide	06.05c	four hours free (c)
			dep Adelaide	10.15	The Ghan
			arr Melbourne	21.00	four-night stopover
15	12	Saturday	West Coaster steam train or Puffing Billy (d)		
16	13	Sunday	dep Melbourne	12.30	V/line
			arr Echuca	15.45	1½ hours free
			dep Echuca	17.20	V/line
			arr Bendigo	18.35	change trains
			dep Bendigo	18.50	The Northerner
			arr Melbourne	20.47	night-stop
17	14	Monday	dep Melbourne	08.30	Olympic Spirit XPT
			arr Moss Vale	17.15	night-stop
18	15	Tuesday	dep Moss Vale	08.54	Canberra Xplorer
			arr Canberra	11.15	six hours free
			dep Canberra	17.15	Canberra Xplorer
			arr Sydney	21.26	night-stop
19	16	Wednesday	dep Sydney	07.15	Murwillumbah XPT (e)
			arr Byron Bay	20.00	night-stop (e)
20	17	Thursday	dep Byron Bay	20.00	Murwillumbah XPT (e)
			arr Murwillumbah	21.00	change to bus
			dep Murwillumbah	21.15	Countrylink coach
			arr Gold Coast (f)	22.15b	night-stop
21	18	Friday	dep Gold Coast (f)	15.08g	QR Trainlink bus
			arr Nerang	15.36g	change to train
			dep Nerang	15.51g	Interurban electric
			arr Brisbane	16.56g	two-night stopover
23	19	Sunday	dep Brisbane	10.30	Tilt Train
			arr Gladstone	16.24	one hour free
			dep Gladstone	17.52	Queenslander

❏ **Itinerary 6 cont'd**
Cairns (Kuranda)–Brisbane–Sydney

Travel day (a)(b)	Place	Time	Remarks
24 20 Monday	arr Cairns	16.20	night-stop
25 21 Tuesday	dep Cairns	09.30	Kuranda Tourist Train
	arr Kuranda	11.10	four hours free (h)
	dep Kuranda	15.30	Kuranda Tourist Train
	arr Cairns	17.10	two-night stopover (h)
27 22 Thursday	dep Cairns	08.00	The Sunlander
28 23 Friday	arr Brisbane	16.10	two-night stopover
30 24 Sunday	dep Brisbane	07.30b	Brisbane XPT
	arr Sydney	21.51	night-stop

The 30-day consecutive Australpass ($950) allows no days in hand.
The 29-day Austrail Flexipass ($1250) allows five days in hand.

Notes
Travel day numbers refer to (a) Consecutive pass use (b) Flexipass use
a The following alternative allows more time in the Blue Mountains, but notice must be given to GSR by phone on ☎ 132 147 (not at a railway station or on any other number) 24 hours in advance of travel.

Day 2 Sunday	dep Katoomba	13.58	CityRail interurban
	arr Lithgow	14.45	change trains
	dep Lithgow	16.10	The Ghan

b One hour earlier during Eastern Summer Time (end October to mid-March)
c An option is to change from the Indian Pacific to The Ghan at Tarcoola instead of Adelaide, arrive in Tarcoola at 18.12 on Tuesdays, depart at 23.30; see pp77-78 for further details.
d The West Coaster is covered by the Australpass; the Puffing Billy is not. Both are usually steam hauled and thus of interest to rail enthusiasts. The Puffing Billy route is more scenic; the West Coaster offers more comfortable accommodation. These are only two of the many options for side trips when in the Melbourne area.
e If a longer break in Sydney is desired take the Murwillumbah XPT a day later and omit the night-stop at Byron Bay or at the Gold Coast.
f Surfers Paradise bus depot, Beach Rd.
g Other connections to Brisbane at least hourly throughout the day.
h An alternative is for a one night-stop in Kuranda, departing at 14.00 or 15.30 the next day, arriving in Cairns at 15.40 or 17.10 as above. This is within the validity of the Australpass but uses one of the spare days on the Flexipass.

Reef, Fraser Island, Yeppoon, Daintree rainforest and the outback. A series of Tilt Train Short Breaks are also offered based on Rockhampton, ranging from afternoon tours to nearby heritage features, caves and sanctuaries to four-night packages visiting Great Keppell Island. Prices range from $42 to $399 per person, not including rail fare ex-Brisbane.

Countrylink and Queensland Rail probably offer the widest variety of package tours and most of them either do not include the rail fare to the place on which the tour is based or if they do, there is the option of paying a lower price which does not include it. This assumes you make your own way to the tour starting point, whether by rail using a pass you hold or by some method of your own devising.

State Rail Day-A-Way Tours

Some all-in Day-a-Way tours operated by CityRail in NSW include coach and ferry with lunch or other refreshments en route; the rail fare is deducted from the inclusive price if you have a rail pass. The tours start and finish at Sydney Central. Itineraries include parts of the South Coast, the Blue Mountains, Hunter Valley, The Riverboat Postman covering the Hawkesbury River and one to Old Sydney Town, a recreated historic settlement near Gosford. Local enquiry is necessary. Longer Countrylink holiday tours are also offered.

In Victoria, V/line offer numerous short rail escapes which include accommodation and guided sightseeing. Places included are Albury, Bairnsdale, Ballarat, Bendigo, Castlemaine, Daylesford, Echuca, Mildura and Swan Hill. Hoys Coaches offer various day tours from Melbourne by train and coach to the Goulburn Valley area, visiting places such as the old country town of Murchison, a yabby (fresh-water crayfish) farm, WWII camps, the SPC canned fruit factory, and Shepparton Equestrian Centre with its Andalusian horses. For prices, times and bookings phone ☎ 03-5831 2880.

For those tourists with a week or more to spend in Western Australia, Westrail's famous wildflower tours are a good way to see the amazing colours of the desert flora. Tours are usually held between August and October and last a week, but rail passes are not valid. Details from Westrail Travel Centre (see p25) or East Perth Terminal station.

To list all possible tours would be beyond the scope of this or almost any guide book. Places and itineraries vary from time to time. It is best to ask at the travel centres in the main railway stations. The examples below illustrate the range on offer. These are NSW State Rail and Queensland tours which effectively start and finish at railway stations, from which you are picked up and to which you are returned when the tour ends. The prices quoted are per person for twin-share accommodation.

● Getabout Tours (☎ 07-4939 4888 or ☎ 1800 675785) three-night Capricorn Palms Holiday Village, Great Keppell Island, Queensland; $176 plus the train fare to Rockhampton.

❏ **Prices in this book – Australian dollars**
Note that all prices quoted in this book are given in Australian dollars unless otherwise indicated. The current exchange rate is Australian $1 to US$0.58 or UK£0.38. For up-to-the-minute rates visit **www.xe.net/currency**.

● Getabout Tours three-night package at Rydges Capricorn International resort, Rockhampton; $240 plus the train fare to Rockhampton.
● Countrylink Grafton and National Park six-night tour, northern NSW; $349 plus the train fare to Grafton (see p24 for contact details.)
● Countrylink Byron Bay and Wilderness six-night tour, NSW; $450 plus the train fare to Byron Bay.
● Queensland Rail Lawn Hill, Undara, Mount Isa and Gulfland 11-night tour, north Queensland, including train en route; $1700 plus train fare to Mount Isa for commencement and from Cairns at tour end. (See p24 for contact details)
● An interesting pre-planned itinerary is advertised by QR for a Townsville to Cairns trip via Mount Isa, the Gulf and Savannah country, including rail travel on the Gulflander and Savannahlander trains and possibly including a visit to Undara Lava Tubes. A modified version of this is presented in Itinerary 7 below.

PLANNING YOUR OWN ITINERARY

Although this guide suggests several pre-planned itineraries many people prefer to plan their own itinerary. But even the most detailed, such as some in this guide, can be varied to get the utmost value from Austrail or

---

❏ **Itinerary 7**
Townsville to Cairns via Gulf and Savannahland

Travel day		Place	Time	Remarks
1	Sunday	dep Townsville	18.00	Inlander
2	Monday	arr Cloncurry (a)	10.37	night-stop
3	Tuesday	dep Cloncurry (a)	11.00	Coral Coaches
		arr Normanton	16.20	night-stop
4	Wednesday	dep Normanton	08.30	Gulflander
		arr Croydon	12.30	night-stop
5	Thursday	dep Croydon	10.00	Coral Coaches
		arr Georgetown	12.15	lunch break
		dep Georgetown	13.30	Forsayth Coaches
		arr Forsayth	14.15	night-stop
6	Friday	dep Forsayth	07.45	Savannahlander
		arr Mount Surprise	13.00	night-stop (b)
7	Saturday	dep Mount Surprise	08.15	Savannahlander
		arr Cairns	16.40	

Notes
a Option of continuing to Mount Isa arriving at 14.25, departing 18.00, return arriving in Cloncurry at 21.26 for a night-stop, or a night-stop in Mount Isa, departing Tuesday at 09.00 by Normanton coach via Cloncurry.
b Option of changing to Coral Coach at Mount Surprise, departing at 13.20, arriving in Cairns at 18.00 for a night-stop and to connect with the Saturday Sunlander.

other passes. However, a few comments may help if you decide to work out your own salvation, plus a word or two of warning where appropriate.

Your starting point will be where you intend to land in Australia (or where you live if already here), and your finishing point will be determined likewise. Most probably you will have already decided where you want to go and what you want to see. If your aim is to cover as much of the country as you can by train then an Austrailpass is the best basis if you are eligible for it. Otherwise, a combination of Victorian, New South Wales and Queensland passes will enable you to cover all the eastern half of the country. Should your interests be mainly in one state, then the passes for that state are your best answer.

You have already seen something of what you can do in as little as 14 days and been warned on what is and is not possible within a limited time. Part 3 describes the history of the Australian rail network, while Part 4 deals with getting between the capital cities and suggests things to do and see in each of them, especially using the local rail services. It also describes various day trips and other excursions you can make from these major centres where you might be based including important advice on how to make sure of getting back when you have intercity or interstate trains to catch, or when your ticket is about to expire. The routes are described in detail in Part 5.

Even if you are determined to make your own plans it will do no harm to have a look at the outlined itineraries first (see pp65-73). Any itinerary may be varied to suit the individual. If none of the itineraries suggested suits your taste the section headed Itinerary variations and side trips (pp76-91) highlights some of the options which are possible. Although there are not too many different ways you can go between the major cities – in fact keeping exclusively to trains there is usually only one – there are still branch routes which you can follow by breaking a journey some place en route and making that a temporary base for an excursion. The features and places on all routes are described, section by section, in the last part of this guide. This should provide further guidance on the options available when devising an itinerary of your own. The possibilities are many. Subject to the kind of ticket you have and the time of day or night you are willing to embark or disembark, there is a great variety of places you can visit during your tour.

ITINERARY VARIATIONS AND SIDE TRIPS

From Sydney

In the section on Sydney (see pp126-138) various day or two-day trips from Sydney are outlined: the South Coast, Southern Highlands including Canberra, Blue Mountains, Central West, Central Coast and Newcastle and its hinterland. Longer excursions or diversions from an itinerary which includes a break in Sydney might be to the Riverina area based on Griffith, to the Western Plains (Dubbo or Broken Hill) or to the Northern Tablelands and New England (Tamworth, Armidale and Moree). Route maps and descriptions are given later.

Neither Griffith, Broken Hill or the Tablelands can be covered in a day excursion. Not only is a night-stop required; a base nearer to the area is a sensible starting point. For Griffith, where there is only one train a week, Junee on the main Sydney–Melbourne route or Cootamundra would be good bases. For access to the Tablelands, Hamilton near Newcastle, or Maitland would be a good base. The trains run daily.

● **Sydney westwards** The Indian Pacific and Ghan interstate trains on the western route from Sydney start in the early afternoon and return in the morning. This allows an optional morning start or evening finish to an interstate journey by using one of the frequent interurban trains to break the journey at Lithgow in the Blue Mountains. Going west on the Indian Pacific there is also the option of taking the XPT to break the journey for several hours further west, at Bathurst, Blayney or Orange.

Note that to join the Indian Pacific to continue west it is necessary to go to Orange East Fork, 1.8km from Orange main station, from where it leaves at 21.00.

● **Broken Hill night-stop options** The full range of options for a break of journey in Broken Hill are set out in Table 4, p78. They involve either waiting between two successive calls of the Indian Pacific or Ghan (one or three days for trains going in the same direction, two days if you are taking a there and back trip from Adelaide, or at least one day if going there and back from Sydney). The outback train of Countrylink increased the options as it allowed a full day at the Hill but it is currently suspended. The only other options are aircraft or bus.

● **West of Broken Hill** Beyond Broken Hill there are no opportunities for side trips or substantial variations to an itinerary since there is only the twice-weekly Indian Pacific and Ghan (once weekly to and from Sydney and once weekly to or from Melbourne) to choose from. Even west of Kalgoorlie the addition of the Prospector adds nothing to the prospects of a deviation, only to the number of trains available. Side trips from Adelaide and Perth are discussed on pp162-165 and pp166-170. The only other deviations possible anywhere west of Broken Hill are private and preserved railways such as the Pichi Richi which are described in Part 6 (pp268-271).

Even with only the Indian Pacific and The Ghan running west from Adelaide as far as Tarcoola there is the interesting possibility of breaking the journey there, as suggested in the footnotes to Itinerary 6 (pp72-73). Such a break would only reasonably be made coming from the west. The

❏ **Table 4**
Sydney–Broken Hill–Adelaide and vice versa (C 9020)

	Mon/Thu	Tue	Wed	Sun	Daily
dep Sydney	14.55a	17.10#	07.10	13.10a	07.10f
arr Orange		21.11#	11.56x		
dep Orange	21.11b		12.35#	19.14a	11.56f
arr Broken Hill	08.30de		21.10c#	04.43cd	22.30c
dep Broken Hill	10.00c			05.50	
arr Adelaide (Keswick)	16.50			12.50	

	Wed/Sun	Thu	Sat	Daily
dep Adelaide (Keswick)	07.45		10.10	
arr Broken Hill	14.45c		17.00c	
dep Broken Hill	17.00ae	20.40c#	17.55ae	04.00cg
arr Orange	03.15bd	05.51d#	03.30d	15.55
arr Sydney	09.15	11.33#	09.15	20.48

Notes
All trains in this table are air-conditioned, have refreshment facilities and
require reservations.
Suspended (see p49); enquiry recommended.
a Sleeping accommodation is available
b Orange East Fork station
c Central Standard Time
d Next day
e Eastern Standard Time
f Bus connection (nine-hour journey) from XPT train at Dubbo
g Bus connection (nine-hour journey) to XPT train at Dubbo
x Change trains

calling times at Tarcoola westbound are rather too early in the morning.
Changing from the eastbound Indian arriving in Tarcoola at about 18.12
on Tuesdays gives a break of over four hours. The Melbourne Ghan
should leave Tarcoola at around 23.30 the same day for Adelaide (up to
one hour later during Eastern Summer Time). Changing from the Friday
Indian from the west which arrives at Tarcoola on Saturday is not an
option unless you plan several days' stay in the desert: the Sydney Ghan
has already left and the only option is to wait until the next eastbound
Indian comes along three days later.

For any break at all at Tarcoola it is essential not only to book the connecting trains but to make arrangements with *Wilgena Hotel* (☎ 08-8672
2042), which is about 200m from the station.

● **Between Adelaide and Melbourne** It is sensible to arrange your
itinerary so that whichever route you take between Sydney and Adelaide
you come back by a different one. The choice, apart from coach links, is
via Broken Hill (as on the Indian and Ghan) or via Melbourne. The

Overland and The Ghan between Melbourne and Adelaide offer only overnight travel westbound but offer a daylight run from Adelaide.

Ararat is a centre from which to explore Victoria's Grampians, Pyrenees and Central Highlands. It is reached in late afternoon on the eastbound Ghan and Overland. The only other options for travelling to or from Ararat are via the westbound trains at times varying from 00.52 to 02.10. Tourists wishing to see this part of Victoria, with its many attractions, might therefore consider the V/line bus, there being three services a day (two on Saturdays and Sundays), all connecting with V/line trains at Ballarat and serving also Great Western, Stawell, Murtoa, Horsham and Dimboola, most of which are also request stops for eastbound trains (C 9035, 9090a).

From Melbourne

One- or two-day trips based on Melbourne, outlined on pp144-149, include Port Phillip Bay, Gippsland area, Warrnambool and the south-west coast, Ballarat, Bendigo, Swan Hill and Echuca.

A diversion of two days or more to the Gippsland area could include a trip by connecting the V/line bus from Sale to **Bairnsdale** (approximately one hour, C 9029). Bairnsdale is the main gateway to the coastal lakes of eastern Victoria. Paynesville on Lake Victoria (10km from Bairnsdale) and Lakes Entrance (35km) are specially popular resorts, the latter adjoining Victoria's Ninety Mile Beach. At **Nowa Nowa**, north of Lakes Entrance is the largest timber trestle bridge in the Southern hemisphere, on the freight-only Orbost branch of the railway, now closed to traffic altogether. Tenders for franchisees to operate a restored passenger train service to Bairnsdale are currently in the pipeline.

Ballarat, a historic mining centre 119km west of Melbourne, is a convenient day trip from Melbourne and also worth an overnight stay (see also p148). Ballarat trains take on average around 90 minutes, running approximately every two hours (C 9031). The single (economy class) fare to Ballarat is $13.80; first class $19.40 is available on only one or two trains.

Swan Hill, north of Bendigo at the confluence of the Marraboor river and the Murray, is worth a visit but cannot be reached by train on a day trip. Details of the train service are given in Table 12 (p148); features of the route are described on pp204-207.

If you have time to spare in Victoria it would be a pity to miss a trip to **Mildura**, a city of flowers and vines on the banks of the Murray near historic Wentworth where the Murray and the Darling meet. Mildura is capital of Sunraysia district, noted for its wide streets with a profusion of flowers in the centre strips, its wineries and dried fruits, Hattah Lakes National Park, and the Mildura working-men's club with, in the 1970s, the longest bar in the world. For several years the only regular train to Mildura was the Vinelander, a pleasant sleeping and sitting-car train with buffet, which left Melbourne's Spencer St nightly, Saturdays excepted, to arrive in Sunraysia's capital at breakfast next day. The trains on that line now go only as far as Ballarat. Now there is only a daily bus connection from the train at Swan Hill but restoration of a train service is currently under consideration.

An interesting variation on any itinerary is to take a V/line bus from Mildura to Broken Hill, a useful shortcut if five hours on a bus does not appal you, especially after having to reach Mildura by bus in the first place. A unique geological feature, the Walls of China, at the ancient bed of Lake Mungo, is accessible by day coach tour from Mildura.

You can still enjoy a night and most of a day in Mildura or two nights and a day and a half if you leave Melbourne on a Saturday at 17.50 or Friday at 16.37, returning to Swan Hill by bus leaving at 13.45 on Sunday. Otherwise, a Mildura trip on current schedules, with any useful time there at all, means going all the way by bus or leaving for the return by the 04.20 coach to Swan Hill, which operates daily except Friday and Sunday (C 9032). Mildura is the kind of place where you will want to linger.

Melbourne to Sydney

If it is fruit harvest time you might like a diversion to **Shepparton** in Victoria's fertile Goulburn Valley to try their luscious pears. There are direct trains from Melbourne but you will need to change trains at Seymour if travelling on a Melbourne–Albury train or at Benalla, then Seymour, if on the XPT from interstate. You will have time to spare at Seymour before going on to Shepparton.

If continuing north the same day a trip to the Goulburn Valley will still bring you back to Melbourne in time for the Southern Cross XPT for Sydney, but you can change instead at Seymour and take the intercity north to Benalla, Wangaratta, or Albury. Stop for dinner, then join the train for Sydney afterwards.

Between Melbourne and Sydney there is a choice between day and night trains, both running daily. Any itinerary which includes a day or more in either capital city therefore allows the option of a break of journey in north-east Victoria or southern New South Wales.

If leaving Sydney on the daylight train, for example, you could break your journey at Cootamundra, Junee, or Wagga Wagga. Or, if you preferred, carry on to Albury and stay there beside the River Murray for the night. In the morning you could then, if a compulsive early riser, board the V/line intercity at 06.30 (07.45 on Sundays) or wait for the 12.15 (weekdays only). You can break the journey again at Chiltern, Wangaratta or Benalla but watch your times if intending to catch the Overland or Ghan to Adelaide that same night. The last connection from Chiltern is at 16.26; from Wangaratta and Benalla at 16.54 and 17.19 respectively; one hour later from all three on Sunday (C 9028).

Northbound, a Melbourne departure at 08.30 on the XPT would allow a break at Benalla or Wangaratta or both, with plenty of time to reach Albury for a night-stop or in time to catch the XPT sleeper to Sydney from there at 22.53. In either direction the timetables favour journey breaks for periods of a few hours in places between Melbourne and Albury. Between Albury and Sydney the scheduling and less frequent service necessitate a 24-hour break unless you like catching or leaving trains in the middle of the night.

● **A Riverina diversion to Griffith** Junee has been suggested as a base for an excursion to Griffith in the Riverina district of NSW (see p77). Table 5 below shows the train service options. Countrylink buses serve Griffith daily from Wagga Wagga and Cootamundra and Hoys Coaches of Victoria connect with trains at Shepparton but times of nearly all these services are unattractive. The footnote to Table 5 shows those that can be made in daytime.

The Countrylink train allows the option of either an overnight or full week stay in Griffith, but Countrylink coach services run daily. Hoys Coaches have a connecting service to their Melbourne train at Shepparton and Countrylink have coach connections also from Cootamundra, albeit at somewhat unattractive hours.

Sydney to Brisbane

Assuming a daylight start from Sydney refreshed and ready for the road (the railroad of course) you have the opportunity of starting north much earlier than the 16.24 departure time of the Brisbane XPT suggested in Itinerary 1 (see p66). The Tablelands Xplorer at 09.35 or the morning Grafton XPT at 11.35, or one of the numerous, fast, double-deck, air-conditioned electric

❏ **Table 5** Riverina links from Junee (C 9026)			
Connection:		Daily	Saturday
Melbourne	dep	08.30	08.30
Junee	arr	13.14	13.14
Sydney	dep	07.43	08.15
Junee	arr	13.21	14.45
Junee	dep		14.45
Griffith	arr	17.18a	17.30
		Sunday	Daily
Griffith	dep	08.00	09.40b
Junee	arr	10.36	
Junee	dep	10.36	13.16
Sydney	arr	17.12	19.13
Connection:			
Junee	dep	13.23	13.23
Melbourne	arr	18.15	18.15

Notes
All trains have first-class and economy seating and there is a buffet service.
Passengers from Melbourne change at Junee.
a Connection by bus, changing from train at Wagga Wagga, dep 14.40, instead of Junee.
b Connection by bus, changing to train at Wagga Wagga, arr 12.20, instead of Junee.

interurban trains north from Sydney will give you time to visit all sorts of places en route.

If you are exploring the area north of Sydney, up as far as Newcastle or even Maitland and you are going further north overnight the same day, there is no need to go back to Sydney because the Brisbane XPT calls at Hornsby at 16.56, Gosford at 17.41, Broadmeadow at 18.45 and Maitland at 19.09. There are later trains from Sydney to the Central Coast and Newcastle if you intend a longer break by staying overnight.

If intending to travel south from Sydney the day you are exploring the NSW Central Coast (as the area up to Newcastle is called) your deadline times to return for the Southern Cross Melbourne XPT on weekdays are 18.02 from Newcastle, 18.12 from Broadmeadow, 19.02 from Wyong, 19.17 from Gosford and 19.41 from Hawkesbury River. Weekend and holiday times from north of Hawkesbury River are up to 35 minutes earlier. These connections all involve changing at Strathfield to the Melbourne train. If you have left your luggage at Sydney and not booked it on the XPT you will have to leave the Central Coast earlier but times vary at weekends so local enquiry is recommended.

Another option for the northbound traveller is to take the Murwillumbah or Grafton XPT during daytime to Dungog, Gloucester or even Taree. From there a seat or berth on the Brisbane XPT can be taken overnight; the overnight train must be picked up at Dungog at 19.55. From Gloucester it is necessary to leave at 17.22, returning to pick up the northbound XPT at Dungog. For the overnight Melbourne XPT departure deadline you must return to Sydney by local connecting trains from Dungog at 15.00 Mondays to Fridays or at 15.07 on Saturdays. On Sundays the XPT from Dungog at 13.12 or from Gloucester at 12.15 is the only return connection.

Options are also possible travelling south from Queensland if you have a day in hand. Break your journey at a northern NSW town such as Casino, Grafton or Coffs Harbour, and continue south the next day.

Whilst Itinerary 6 (pp72-73) envisions a night-stop in Byron Bay followed by rail and bus connections via the Gold Coast to Brisbane, determined rail addicts can forgo the night-stop and avoid the bus by returning on the XPT to Grafton, then taking the Brisbane XPT north. A night-stop in Grafton or even Byron Bay as well could be included within the time available, the deadline being Sunday morning in Brisbane. Even with only a couple of hours in Byron Bay you have time to walk to the beach and back, or have a good meal, or enjoy the nightlife with the locals at the swinging bar lounge (the *Railway Friendly Bar*, ☎ 02-6685 7662) – which now occupies most of the former station refreshment and waiting rooms. This should steel you for the tedious midnight wait you may later endure at Grafton for your connection north to Brisbane at two o'clock in the morning.

The sensible alternative to a Byron Bay–Grafton–Brisbane overnight journey is to continue on the train to **Murwillumbah**, railhead for Queensland's Gold Coast, and from thence by connecting Countrylink coach to the Gold Coast for a night-stop en route, as shown in the suggested itineraries (see pp66-73). Alternatively take the coach direct to the QR railhead at Robina.

Table 6 (p84) summarises some alternatives for northbound journeys. The options southbound are in effect similar but at easier times of day, ie not involving middle of the night transfers.

In Queensland

Side trips and day excursions from Brisbane are discussed on pp155-160.

On a journey from New South Wales to north Queensland you do not need to spend a night on the Gold Coast or in a Brisbane hotel as suggested in Itineraries 5 and 6 (pp70-73). Budget-conscious travellers wishing to make the train their travelling hotel can leave Brisbane the day they arrive from the south, whether the Sunlander runs that day or not, by taking the Tilt Train up to **Rockhampton** and spending a day or more there before continuing northwards. Alternatively, the Sunlander or other northbound train can be picked up, if running that day, at Rockhampton or even earlier at Bundaberg or Gladstone.

With an Austrailpass or QR Flexipass you can break the journey at many centres north of Brisbane. Inland excursions are possible, offering a marked contrast to the scenery of the North Coast line.

There are several long rail trips in Queensland, taking at least two days out and back from the coastal centres of Brisbane, Rockhampton, Townsville or Cairns. To cover the whole system would need a long holiday. With a greater passenger route length than any other Australian state and sometimes only once-weekly trains a minimum of 50 days of virtual non-stop travelling would have to be set aside to cover all possible QR routes where passenger trains or mixed freight and passenger trains still run.

● **The real outback** Whilst the experience of crossing the Nullarbor by train gives a vivid impression of the vast expanse of near nothingness that is a feature of inland Australia, and you can understand the remoteness and heat experienced by workers in the railway camps along the track, this is not really the true outback of the cattle and sheep stations, or of the tiny towns with their dusty roads and pubs with verandahs. To see these you have to leave the main routes (but not necessarily the air-conditioned trains) and you have to allow plenty of time. Most such journeys are in Queensland, the only state which still has rail services solely to small inland settlements. This is not to say there are not some delightful small towns to come upon in other states, but you will see these usually on your way through to somewhere else and if the place attracts your attention you can break your journey there, depending on the time. Rather than present

❏ **Table 6**
Sydney to Grafton, the Pacific Coast of northern NSW, the Gold Coast and Brisbane – northbound options (C 9015, 9017 plus local)

dep	Sydney	07.15a	11.35a	16.24a
arr	Grafton City	17.08	22.00	02.13
arr	Casino	18.33		03.31b
dep	Casino	18.35		03.50c
arr	Byron Bay	20.00		05.34c
arr	Murwillumbah	21.00b		06.32c
dep	Murwillumbah	21.15c		
arr	Surfers Paradise	22.15f		06.43f
dep	Murwillumbah	21.20c		
arr	Tweed Heads	21.36		05.57c
arr	Robina	22.05f		
dep	Robina	22.47d		
arr	Brisbane Roma St	23.54f		06.35
dep	Murwillumbah	21.50a		07.50c
dep	Byron Bay	22.43		
arr	Casino	00.04		09.53d
dep	Casino	00.08		10.12a
arr	Grafton City	01.44e		11.44
dep	Grafton City	02.13		
dep	Casino	03.31		
arr	Brisbane	06.35f		

Notes
All trains in this table are air-conditioned and all except the QR Robina–Brisbane services require reservations.
a XPT train with buffet.
b Change to Countrylink bus.
c Air-conditioned Countrylink bus (State Rail operated)
d Change to train.
e Change trains.
f One hour earlier during Eastern Summer Time.

an itinerary (which might well cover two months or more), the following is a summary of rail safaris from major Queensland centres, leaving the traveller to select one or more as time and inclination dictate.

The base cities for these outback safaris are Brisbane, Rockhampton, Townsville and Cairns. With all of them the climbing of the ranges – the northern spurs of the Great Dividing Range – is always of scenic interest, though unfortunately done at night by some of the main air-conditioned trains. Once beyond the ranges, the countryside becomes fairly flat, semi-bushland, brigalow scrub, with occasional hills and rocky outcrops, numerous small creeks, dry for most of the year, but with here and there a deep ravine and, on the Mount Isa line, a major bridge over the Burdekin River. Soil gives way to sand and the bush to flat plains the further you travel west. On some routes the rails may be very lightweight, reducing speed to 40km/h or less. The towns bask in the hot glare of the sun and the locals seek the cool shade of the verandah or bar. Some will sit on the station platform for hours and it is a good idea to wave to them. The arrival of the train, perhaps only once a week, is still something of an event.

Exploring Queensland by rail offers glimpses of the coast, of cities, canefields, rainforest, wetlands, mighty rivers, ranges and seemingly endless vistas of bush and the red dust of the outback. The adventurous could try the four-day round trip by the Savannahlander on the former Etheridge Railway to Forsayth and back.

Looking at the options in order from Brisbane, getting 'a little further north' if not 'each year', as the popular Queensland song has it, then each trip, the first and nearest is out west from Brisbane up the ranges to Toowoomba, then across the Darling Downs through Dalby, Chinchilla, Miles and Roma to Charleville. The return trip takes 2½ days including two nights on the train and allows over six hours at Charleville, with the option of a there-and-back coach trip to the even more remote settlement of Cunnamulla or Quilpie instead of waiting in Charleville. The journey could alternatively be broken at Mitchell or Morven. Notes on these places accompany the route maps which follow. If a longer stay is desired, the next train back is either two or five days later than the one you came on.

The next major stop on the North Coast line from which outback excursions may be made is Rockhampton. A diversion from Rockhampton into central Queensland or from Townsville inland to Mount Isa (see below) will easily fill two days or more with experiences of rural and outback Australia many tourists never see and which you are unlikely to forget quickly. At Rockhampton the Spirit of the Outback, which starts its journey in Brisbane, follows the route of the old Midlander Mail as far as Longreach. Two full days from Rockhampton are needed, with a night-stop at Longreach or anywhere else en route that takes your fancy. Emerald, Barcaldine and Ilfracombe are places full of interest and the route description will provide further suggestions. The journey in each direction is entirely in daylight. There is a coach connection to Winton but this is only a viable option if you wait for a later train back to Rockhampton, either three or four days depending which train you came on.

Townsville, headquarters of the former Great Northern Railway, is the home station for Queensland's oldest 'lander' train, the Inlander which, like its Charleville and Longreach cousins, runs twice weekly. As far as time to spend in the west is concerned there is a choice with this service: the Sunday train from Townsville returns the next day from Mount Isa, whereas the Wednesday train remains there a whole day, returning on the Friday.

❏ **Table 7**
Townsville–Ingham

| Townsville | dep | Mon:08.50 | | Wed:08.50 | Fri:08.50 | Sun:08.50 |
| Ingham | arr | Mon:10.30 | | Wed:10.38 | Fri:10.38 | Sun:10.30 |

Ingham–Townsville

| Ingham | dep | Mon:13.16 | Tue:13.00 | Thu:13.16 | Sat:13.16 |
| Townsville | arr | Mon:15.20 | Tue:14.45 | Thu:15.20 | Sat:15.20 |

Notes
All trains have refreshment facilities. Booking is recommended.

Among places of interest en route are Charters Towers, Hughenden Richmond, Julia Creek and Cloncurry. See route description and maps 47-49 on pp247-249. At Hughenden there is a connection of sorts by goods train with a carriage attached for passenger use (possibly), to Winton. Enquiry at QR Townsville station is essential before seriously considering undertaking this diversion.

● **Between Townsville and Cairns** A pleasant day trip or two-day trip from Townsville is possible to **Ingham** (see route description p234). Table 7 above shows the times, which allow 2¹/₂ hours or just over a day (or more) for the trip.

Approaching Cairns from the south there are opportunities for a break of journey at **Tully** or further north at Innisfail, Babinda or Gordonvale, even though there are only four trains weekly each way.

The options comprise (a) breaking the journey north before reaching Cairns, (b) breaking the journey on the way back south or (c) making Cairns your base and doing an out-and-back trip, normally two-day but varying from a possible brief hour or so at Tully on a Monday from Cairns to as long as you wish. Table 8 (p87) illustrates these options.

● **From Cairns** Even a brief night-stop in Cairns is enough to see the nightlife and experience the warm extrovert feeling of the tropics. But Cairns is a useful base for local trips, by train, coach, launch, or hired car. A day trip to one of the islands on the Great Barrier Reef is easily under-taken from Cairns if you have a whole day there. Full-day coach tours are available to Atherton Tableland with its crater lakes, orchid gardens and waterfalls; or to Cape Tribulation and Mossman gorge. At historic **Port Douglas** the Ballyhooley Express (see p263), if operating, runs through canefields towards **Mossman** and at **Gordonvale** the Mulgrave Rambler (see p266) offers a similar yet more accessible adventure, although at the time of writing it runs on special occasions or not at all.

Best known of all outback trains is the Gulflander railcar on the still isolated Normanton–Croydon branch, the only difficulty being in finding

❏ **Table 8**
Cairns–Tully–Cairns options

Cairns	dep	Mon:08.00	Tue:08.00	Thu:08.00	Sat:08.00
Gordonvale	arr	Mon:08.38		Thu:08.38	Sat:08.38
Babinda	arr	Mon:09.22		Thu:09.22	Sat:09.22
Innisfail	arr	Mon:10.00	Tue:09.54	Thu:10.00	Sat:10.00
Tully	arr	Mon:11.13	Tue:11.07	Thu:11.13	Sat:11.13
Tully	dep	Mon:12.35	Wed:12.35	Fri:12.35	Sun:12.35
Innisfail	dep	Mon:13.50	Wed:13.50	Fri:13.50	Sun:13.50
Babinda	dep		Wed:14.30	Fri:14.30	Sun:14.30
Gordonvale	dep		Wed:15.18	Fri:15.18	Sun:15.18
Cairns	arr	Mon:16.20	Wed:16.20	Fri:16.20	Sun:16.20

Notes
All trains have refreshment facilities. Booking is recommended.

a way to reach it in the first place. Cairns is the nearest mainline station and obvious starting point, although Townsville offers a useful entry to Gulf Country via Cloncurry or Mount Isa (see Itinerary 7, p75).

More accessible, and still unforgettable, is the now world-famous Kuranda Scenic Railway based on Cairns. This has become one of Australia's most popular train rides and not without reason. The line twists and turns through a series of five chain curves, through tunnels and across creeks, along the sides of gorges and almost under a waterfall, for its 33km ascent of the range to the plant-festooned station of the 'village in the rainforest', **Kuranda** in north Queensland.

● **The Rainforest Skyrail** Although there are daily trains (two daily except on Saturday) between Cairns and Kuranda (C 9007) there are also many private coach tours which allow outward or return travel by train. There is also the option of taking the recently-opened 7.5km Skyrail Rainforest aerial cableway from the Caravonica Lakes terminal, two minutes from Smithfield shopping centre and 11km from Cairns city centre. Winner in the Major Tourist Attractions category of the 1999 National Tourism Awards, the Skyrail is a breathtaking experience, with tremendous views over the rainforest of the ranges and over the Barron Gorge. Even in heavy rain you are among the clouds just above the tree canopy and you may see the Barron Falls in flood. There are two intermediate stations en route, Barron Falls and Red Peak, where passengers can leave their gondola car and follow a boardwalk in the rainforest. Rangers are on hand as guides.

The Skyrail fare is $23 single, $39 return, or $49 return including transfers to and from hotels. Skyrail/Scenic Railway combined return bookings may also be made for $56 including transfers; children pay half the relevant fare. Passengers on the Great South Pacific Express, starting or terminating in Cairns, join or leave the train at Kuranda using the Skyrail from or to Cairns. Individual passengers should note that only hand luggage similar to cabin baggage on an aircraft may be taken aboard Skyrail, so leave your heavy stuff at your hotel or the railway station in Cairns or Kuranda. Kuranda terminal adjoins the railway station.

For more details and to make a booking phone ☎ 07-4038 1555 or fax 🖹 07-4038 1888. The local Sunbus (☎ 07-4057 7411) has an hourly service past Caravonica terminal. While waiting for a return bus there is time to visit the adjoining Tjapukai Aboriginal centre and experience something of the culture of Australia's first custodians.

● **Atherton Tableland** An alternative to a night-stop in Cairns or Kuranda is to go up to the Atherton Tableland. Take the Kuranda Scenic Railway to have a quick look around Kuranda, then catch the bus (not covered by rail passes) to Mareeba, Atherton, Herberton or even Ravenshoe, stay the night and be back in Cairns next day.

Close to **Ravenshoe**, the former end of the Atherton railway (and where a private railway now operates – see p266), are Millstream Falls, the widest waterfall in Australia, and dense Eucalypt forests. The Atherton Tableland is one of the oldest land masses in the world. Its many attractions include a giant curtain fig tree and the tranquil crater lakes of Eacham and Barrine, all about 15km east of Atherton. Private coach tours visit these features. While in the area, do your best to urge restoration of full rail services to this scenic paradise!

● **Gulf Country and the Etheridge Railway** Probably the nearest places on the railway to the real Gulf Country of *Crocodile Dundee* fame are **Mount Surprise**, **Einasleigh** and **Forsayth** in Etheridge shire, and **Croydon** and **Normanton** in the shire of Carpentaria. The last two are isolated from the rest of the system, while the others are near the end of a long inland branch from Mareeba. This long journey is unique. Until early 1995 a weekly freight train carrying passenger cars, called 'The Last Great Train Ride', covered the whole route. When this was withdrawn a railcar operated a reduced service over the isolated section between Mount Surprise and Forsayth but a through service from Cairns has since been reinstated as the Savannahlander. Up and down the line goes, here curving along the side of a gorge, there descending to the creek bed and meandering among the boulders. It passes through timeless country where you just let it all happen.

On this journey there is no dining car, but the co-driver has an Esky (portable ice box) loaded with limited supplies of essentials like drinking water, soft drinks, potato crisps and beer, available on request at moderate prices. There are also lengthy stops at places where pies, cake, sandwiches and other foodstuffs and drinks can be obtained.

● **The Normanton–Croydon Railway** This completely isolated 152km branch of Queensland Rail is now well-known and frequented by many tourists other than rail enthusiasts. The once-weekly regular passenger service (sometimes with non-passenger wagons attached) is by the Gulflander railmotor. It also carries motor vehicles. The current timetable is given in Table 9 below.

If you want to ride the Savannahlander as well as the Gulflander on the Normanton Railway, various coach firms operate services offering some form of connection; these are summarised in Table 10 (p90). The table shows that to use both trains in both directions would take 18 days. Six days would cover the Gulflander alone. Take the Karumba coach straight out to Normanton on a Monday, leaving Cairns at 06.45 to reach Normanton at 17.15 the same day, returning from there at 07.55 on Fridays and reaching Cairns at 18.00. This allows a return trip on the Gulflander with a night in Croydon. From Croydon, a coach connection to Forsayth on Thursdays is an alternative to a Normanton return by train, substituting a train trip from Forsayth to Mount Surprise on the Friday, then continuing by train or transferring to the bus for the remainder of the journey to Cairns.

Whilst none of the options is perfect Table 10 (p90) shows there is a variety of possibilities. Changing from train to bus at Mount Surprise on a return journey saves a day and allows a connection the following day with the Sunlander to Brisbane, a useful saving in time if you are running short. Among other options are to take in part of the Gulflander trip with a package tour, or fly to Normanton, take the train to Croydon and back, then fly back to Cairns. Either way, you will need the best part of a week. Hiring a car in Cairns might be quicker, but Croydon is over 563km from Cairns and much of the road is rough!

Combining the Gulflander in one direction with the Savannahlander experience is a most attractive option in which you start from Townsville with the train to Cloncurry and bus to Normanton; this option was outlined in Itinerary 7 on p75.

To check on connecting coaches and accommodation, to make bookings or obtain up-to-the-minute information phone Cairns QR travel centre (☎ 07-4036 0234) or Normanton station (☎ 07-4745 1391).

● **The Unforgettable Adventure** Those who venture this far into Gulf country know they are experiencing something unique as the elderly dri-

---

❏ **Table 9**
Normanton–Croydon and vice versa (The Gulflander C 9010)

	Wednesday		Thursday
dep Normanton	08.30	dep Croydon	08.30
arr Croydon	12.30	arr Normanton	12.30

❏ **Table 10**
Rail and bus connections – Savannahlander and Gulflander (C 9009, 9010, 9070)

	Mon Bus	Mon Bus	Wed Bus	Thu	Thu Bus	Thu Bus	Wed
Cairns		06.45	06.45			06.45	06.30
Mareeba		07.55	07.55			07.55	09.25 Thu
Mt Surprise		11.55	11.55			11.55	12.15
Forsayth	10.00				10.00		17.45
Georgetown		10.45	13.30	13.30		10.45	13.30
Croydon		15.15	15.15	08.30		15.15	
Normanton		17.15	17.15	12.30		17.15	

	Mon Bus	Tue Bus	Wed	Thu Bus	Thu Bus	Fri	Fri Bus	Sat
Normanton		07.55	08.30	07.55			07.55	
Croydon		10.00	12.30	10.00			10.00	
Georgetown		13.30	12.15		12.15	13.30		12.15
Forsayth	14.15				14.15	07.45		
Mt Surprise		13.20		13.20		13.00	13.20	08.15
Mareeba		17.00		17.00			17.00	16.00
Cairns		18.00		18.00			18.00	18.40

Notes
The Cairns–Forsayth train includes a night-stop (at your own expense) at Almaden or Chillagoe outbound and at Mount Surprise on the return.

ving railcar with its little front bogie and large single rear axle rattles along with its trailer car over the kinky track, brushing aside grass and small trees on its four-hour dash between Croydon, once a thriving gold rush town with its own suburban rail service, and Normanton with its magnificent heritage railway station building.

No two trips on the Gulflander are ever the same. Blackbull is one regular stop, for refreshments, but the train may stop anywhere: just ask the driver if you see something interesting. The trip is one you will never forget. One tourist told the driver 'Thanks for the wonderful ride. It's taken all the kinks out of my back'.

Useful bus connections and extensions
Since the railways in Victoria and New South Wales operate or charter
bus services covering some routes no longer served by rail and to other
places worth visiting and within reasonable distance of a railway station, it
may be useful to list some of these.

Road coaches owned or contracted by State Rail can extend the range of
places you can visit in New South Wales (and some go into Victoria). Maps
and timetables can be obtained at railway stations. The places listed in
Appendix D (p277) are served by bus from the stations named.

Australia probably has the longest feeder bus connection in the world,
according to Thomas Cook, the well-known timetable publishers and authorities on world rail. This was introduced when State Rail of NSW replaced the
historic Silver City Comet (the first air-conditioned train in the Southern hemisphere) with a bus. Leaving Broken Hill in the middle of the night, the bus
offers a nine-hour trip to connect with the Central West XPT at Dubbo which
then takes only 6½ hours to reach Sydney (see Table 4 p78).

Although V/line abandoned many of its former passenger rail routes,
Austrailpass- and Victoria Pass-holders may use the bus services listed in
Appendix D (p277) which augment or extend the rail service on major routes.

Queensland Rail does not operate bus services to anything like the extent
seen in New South Wales or Victoria. The few rail-contracted bus services that
exist simply replace trains on some of the remote branch lines (Cunnamulla
and Quilpie from Charleville, Winton from Longreach and Toogoolawah from
Ipswich) or link new stations on the outskirts of some towns with the older stations in the central area (as at Gympie and Maryborough).

There are no railway bus services linking Queensland railheads, but private buses, particularly McCafferty's (see under Rail Passes p32) offer some
useful cross-country connections; to list all these would, however, be beyond
the scope of this book. Many of them make poor connections or connections
at unreasonable times of day. Those listed in Appendix D (p277) are those that
might just prove useful to a traveller with an Austrail Flexipass, QR Flexipass
or QR/McCafferty's Pass who is willing to endure some hours in a bus to go
from one remote destination to somewhere equally obscure.

PART 2: AUSTRALIA

Facts about the country

GEOGRAPHY

Australia is the sixth largest country in the world and a continent in its own right. Approximately 4000km from east to west and 3200km north to south it has a total land area of 7.68 million square kilometres but a population density of less than three persons per square kilometre. Most of these live on or near the south and eastern seaboard from Cairns in north Queensland round to the Spencer Gulf in South Australia.

The continent is bounded on the west by the Indian Ocean, on the north by the Timor and Arafura seas and the Torres Strait, on the east by the Coral Sea and the Tasman Sea, both being part of the South Pacific Ocean, and on the south by the Southern Ocean.

The mainland comprises the states of New South Wales (NSW), Victoria, Queensland, South Australia (SA), Western Australia (WA), Northern Territory (NT) and Australian Capital Territory (ACT). Tasmania is the island state, separated from the south coast of Victoria by Bass Strait.

There are many other islands of which the most significant are Bathurst and Melville to the north, Groote Eylandt and Mornington Island in the Gulf of Carpentaria, Fraser Island on the east coast, King and Flinders islands in the Bass Strait and Kangaroo Island off the coast of South Australia. The coastline on the whole appears smooth on a map; only some parts near the Kimberlys in the north-west and Arnhem Land in the north show the kind of fractal pattern that might have been noted by Mandelbrot or other exponents of chaos theory. The main indentations in the coastline are the Great Australian Bight and Spencer Gulf in the south and the Gulf of Carpentaria in the north.

Mountainous areas are generally confined to the coastal regions. The Great Dividing Range extends 3500km from Cape York, at the tip of northern Queensland, down through the state (Queensland) and New South Wales to near Ballarat in Victoria, its highest point being Mt Kosciusko at 2228m. Other mountainous areas include Victoria's Grampians and Pyrenees, the Mt Lofty and Flinders ranges east of Adelaide, the extreme south-west, the Pilbara and Kimberly regions of the north-west and Kakadu and Arnhem Land in Northern Territory. Tasmania is almost wholly mountainous.

The interior of the continent is mostly low lying, broken only by a few ranges, such as the MacDonnell Ranges, and strange monoliths such as Uluru (Ayers Rock) in the Red Centre. The interior is also largely stony or sandy desert: the Simpson desert, Great Victoria desert (not in Victoria), the Great Sandy desert and the Nullarbor Plain. Travelling in a straight line from Ceduna on the South Australian Bight to the coast at the Eighty Mile Beach near Broome on the north-west coast, if such a journey were possible, would be through nothing but desert for the whole 1900km, the only signs of human occupation being the TransAustralian Railway near Maralinga and a few barely motorable desert tracks.

There are many lakes but the largest, Lake Eyre, is rarely full of water. Rivers draining into this area tend to lose their waters in the sands of the desert, except at times of exceptional heavy rain and flood, and many inland lakes are usually seen as nothing more than salt pans. The extensive, many branched rivers of the 'Channel country' the Georgina, Diamantina, Thompson River and Cooper Creek which start in the north, never reach the sea. The Murray is Australia's greatest river; with its tributaries the Darling, the Lachlan and the Murrumbidgee, its catchment extends through most of Victoria and NSW north and west of the Dividing Range, as well as most of western Queensland south of the Tropic of Capricorn. By comparison with the Murray, the famous Snowy River is a trickle, especially since much of its water has been diverted for hydroelectric power.

CLIMATE

Australia extends from latitude 10 to 44 south. The northern third of the country is therefore within the tropics. The hottest months are December and January, while winter is in July and August, but in the north the seasonal distinction is more between dry (winter) and wet seasons; Darwin is in the monsoon belt. Christmas dinner to many Australians is a barbecue in the garden beside the pool.

Although temperatures may fall below freezing point snow is rare except in the Snowy Mountains of NSW and the High Country of Victoria where skiing is popular in season, yet snow is not unknown even in Queensland. It can be bitterly cold in Southern Tasmania or Canberra (normal range 1° to 28°C) or in the interior of the continent at night, but visitors from Europe tend to find Australia warm. It is not unknown for a newly-arrived migrant in Tasmania from northern Europe to go for a swim in August, something few Australians would contemplate other than in a heated pool.

The climate is usually not extreme in populated places. Sydney's temperature normally ranges between 8° and 26°C, Alice Springs between 4° and 37°C, while Cairns enjoys a fairly general warmth of 18° to 32°C and

Darwin a couple of degrees higher. Cloncurry in Queensland holds the record for the hottest temperature in Australia of 53.1°C in January 1889. Marble Bar in WA holds the record for the hottest sustained temperature, over 37.8°C (100°F) for 160 days, while Wyndham, also in WA, sweltered for 333 consecutive days in 1946 with temperatures at or above 32.2°C (90°F).

The Darwin area and north Queensland have the highest average rainfall. Tully (p235) has the reputation of being Australia's wettest city, while Mt Bellenden Ker in the ranges south of Cairns, recorded over 11,000mm of rain in 1979, 960mm (38 inches) being in one period of 24 hours. By contrast, there is a country song of which the words assert that 'the rain never falls in the dusty Diamantina' and it must seem like that until it does, and then they complain of floods.

Cyclones are a fairly regular occurrence in the wet season. Cyclone Tracey devastated Darwin in 1974 and early in 2000 Cyclone Steve cost millions of dollars in damage by a most unusual circling of the north attacking Queensland, the Northern Territory and Western Australia in succession, each time retreating out to sea only to re-form. Tornados are comparatively rare but can occur with little or no warning. Severe winds during electrical storms are more frequent. In the dry season enervating heat can be experienced in the outback, but also in the cities and often quite unexpectedly. In a city such as Melbourne the temperature can rise quite a number of degrees in the middle of the night with a wind change from cool southerly to hot blasts from the interior. Bush fires in the dry season are a regular hazard. Timetables for steam trains usually show a footnote 'does not run on days of total fire ban' and on some lines special speed restrictions are imposed when temperatures are high.

Recounting that in the summer of 1939, 368 people died from a heatwave that hit the southern states, the Readers Digest *Book of Australian Facts* asserts that Australia is 'one of the least comfortable continents in the world' but most residents including Australians by adoption would tend to disagree.

However, visitors should beware of the sun. Queensland proudly boasts of being' the sunshine state': it is also the skin-cancer capital of the world. Always wear a hat outdoors, use sunscreen (locally bought) liberally on exposed flesh and you should have a good day.

THE ENVIRONMENT

Flora and fauna

Since the early observations of botanist Joseph Banks who accompanied Captain Cook, it has been well known that Australia has a rich, diverse and unusual range of plant and animal life. The gum tree and the kangaroo are now known worldwide but there are thousands more – the colourful and often noisy birds, the marine life and the unbelievable curiosities like the duck-billed platypus, an egg-laying mammal.

Although a visitor can spend weeks in Australia without seeing a kangaroo, let alone a platypus, unless at a wildlife sanctuary, one would have to be both blind and deaf not to become aware that the flora and fauna are different from that found in most other countries.

A walk through a suburban park or down a street can be disturbed by a crowd of noisy galahs or the raucous laughter of a kookaburra, while underfoot the leaves scattered on the footpath are of unfamiliar shape and colour and apparently being shed from trees irrespective of the season; the distinction between deciduous and evergreen trees is blurred. Flowers seem to bloom throughout the year. These are among the differences a migrant notices in the first few months but a short-term visitor who spends time only between four-star hotels in the main cities will miss many of the natural wonders of Australia. Worth looking out for are the following:

● **Birds and beasts** The black and white magpie is widespread; its tuneful call is heard especially in the early morning but its habit of swooping down to attack people approaching too close to its nest in spring does not endear it to postmen.

The kookaburra's call is unmistakable. Once known as the laughing jackass the kookie is a well-loved and easily recognised member of the kingfisher family, at home in the suburbs as well as the bush.

The parrot family is widely represented. Flocks of pink and grey galahs swoop above suburban gardens, while screeching white cockatoos disturb the morning calm. Unbelievably colourful lorikeets (bright red, blue, green and yellow like something painted) and rosellas can be seen feeding on the blossoms which adorn many garden shrubs.

In the bush you may hear the curious call of the whipbird – a faint whimper followed by the sound of a lash but you would be hard put to see one, or to recognise it if you did. More likely sounds in the bush will be the shrill chorus of cicadas or the variety of barks, gulps, grunts and rattling sounds produced by the different species of frogs.

The lyrebird and the golden bowerbird are worth looking out for, the Dandenongs east of Melbourne being a favoured habitat of the former and Lamington National Park on the Queensland/NSW border of the latter. The less-colourful satin bowerbird with its nest strewn with blue lures to attract the female (anything from blue feathers to blue felt-pen tops) may well be among the bush features visible on a trip on Queensland's Savannahlander (see p54 and pp249-253 for the route description).

Larger birds such as the wedge-tailed eagle can be seen on a trip across the Nullarbor, while on lines in western Queensland and NSW emus are a common sight, usually running away from the train. As the song says of Old Man Emu 'I can't fly, I'm telling you, but I'll run the pants off a kangaroo'. In similar places you should see mobs of roos, perhaps standing up looking towards the train, then bounding away when they conclude it not to be friendly. Travelling by road, kangaroos and their smaller cousin the wallaby are more often seen dead at the roadside than moving around. In zoos and managed sanctuaries you can feed roos and wallabies; you can on QR's Savannahlander excursion too.

One of the smallest of the roo tribe is the little pademelon. These may be seen hopping around like rabbits up at O'Reilly's (see p153) in Lamington National Park, a day excursion by road from Brisbane.

Koalas are another distinctive Australian marsupial. Cuddly-looking like a teddy bear they are shy creatures whose environment is very much threatened. Koalas' diet is very limited since they can only eat the leaves of a few of the 700 species of Eucalypt.

● **Trees and flowers** Eucalypts vary tremendously, particularly in the bark. The visitor will soon discern the difference between a scribbly gum, a paperbark, a bloodwood and a ghost gum. Gum species often have confusing names, like peppermint (nothing to do with the herb) or mountain ash (as different from the rowan tree as can ever be imagined). Tasmanian blue gums rival the redwoods of North America for sheer size, as do the jarrah trees of south-west Australia.

The coolabah, famed in song, is a rather undistinguished tree common in the northern bush. Various species of acacia, known as wattles, are widespread, many being noted for their colourful blooms. In fact, most Australian trees at one time or another have noticeable blossoms. The colourful jacaranda, an attractive feature of many built-up environments, is, however, an introduced species.

Wild flowers also abound but, if wandering in the bush, beware of picking flowers; many are poisonous, like the snakes and spiders, and many have sharp prickles. Even the dead leaves of some plants can give a painful sting. Beware the Gympie Tree: it stings like a nettle only ten times worse.

But in spite of the dangers, you are safer in the bush than on the roads of the city.

Ecology

The word 'ecology' (the relationship between living organisms and their environment) first appeared in 1873 and it was perhaps not until then that people began to realise that their own activities could and did change the environment: changes were not due just to nature. Ecology

---

(**Opposite**) **Top**: Tjanpi (spinifex), one of the world's hardiest grasses, and Kurkara (desert oak) which survives because of its ability to conserve water. **Bottom**: Western grey kangaroos at Anglesea golf course near Geelong, Victoria.

and the environment are inextricably linked with the history of human settlement.

Arthur Holmes, in his classic *Principles of Physical Geology* (1944, pp15-16) asserts that, 'Man himself has been one of the most prodigal of the organic agents of destruction', citing experience in Africa and America as evidence. Recent controversy in Queensland over tree clearing shows that many are still unaware that 'Forests break the force of rain...they regularise the actual rainfall' and that 'reckless removal of forests may imperil the prosperity of whole communities.'

The dangers are startlingly evident in Australia today, with fears of the whole Murray basin being ruined by increased salinity, one result of deforestation and overcultivation in areas of low annual rainfall. There is also no doubt that the environment has been substantially altered in many parts of Australia over the years of recorded human activity. The continuing process of degradation can be seen from the train on the plains of the outback, in the bush, among the ranges and even on the coast.

HISTORY

In the absence of written records little is known about Australia's earliest inhabitants. Archaeological excavation, mainly by wind and rain, reveal that ritual burial was practised 15,000 years before the construction of the Egyptian Pyramids and that chipped stone implements were used to prepare food from animal carcasses. Rock paintings depict hunting and other scenes, including pictures of animals now extinct.

The Aborigines probably had a better understanding of ecology than modern Europeans. Their way of life involved moving from place to place, burning the bush in one area, taking its fruits, then moving on and allowing regeneration. The Aboriginal relationship to the land is something quite alien to societies brought up on the concept of private ownership. The principle that the land belongs to the tribe, however, is common to many cultures. The Aboriginal concept goes further: the land and the people are as one:

'Listen carefully this, you can hear me.
I'm telling you because earth just like mother
and father or brother of you.
That tree same thing.'
(*Story about Feeling*, Bill Neidje, Magabala Books 1989)

(**Opposite**) **Top**: Uluru (Ayers Rock) is 441km and almost six hours by coach from Alice Springs, the final stop on The Ghan. **Bottom**: Kata Tjuta (The Olgas), about 30km west of Uluru.

Another Aboriginal philosopher and writer, Kevin Gilbert, expressed the same theme. The first and last verses of his poem *Earth* read:

'Of the earth am I
The breath that nurtured all the young
Of earth; with earth to earth again I fly
With every thought I thought and song I sung
Was earth and earth in all its bounty
Gave to me and mine a wise increase.

'The learned came; and said gods had I none
No politics nor sovereign embassy
Their learned ignorance served as a pass
For pioneers to kill the god in me.'

(*Race Memories*, in *Because a White Man will Never Do it*, 1973
Reprinted by permission of Harper Collins, Publishers)

Australian Aboriginal society has the world's longest continuous cultural history. Although a few European explorers saw and may have set foot on parts of the coast from the early 1600s, the year 1770 marked what must have been to the then inhabitants the beginning of the end of dreamtime and the start of nightmare time. Captain James Cook reported that the locals wanted nothing more than that the strangers go away.

But they did not, except temporarily. They came back and claimed the land for Britain: named it New South Wales and regarded the whole continent as *Terra Nullius* under British law (Land with No People). Aborigines did not count in any census until 1967: Section 127 of the Constitution of 1901 stipulated that 'Aboriginal natives shall not be counted'.

The history since European settlement has been well covered in many books and from different points of view. Several are suggested in Appendix A (p274). Following is a very brief outline:

The selection of Australia as a suitable place for convicts followed Britain's loss of the American colonies. The First Fleet which sailed into Botany Bay, Sydney in 1788 carried 750 convicts, forerunners of over 168,000 before transportation was abolished 80 years later. Settlers including freed convicts, seeking a living out of the land, broke the delicate balance between the original people and nature.

The invaders cut down trees and introduced feral and domestic animals which competed with the native fauna for food and water. Hungry Aborigines might spear cattle and sheep for food. This brought savage reprisals. It is now well known that Tasmanian aborigines were systematically wiped out through a series of punitive actions which culminated in an official drive to collect and resettle the remaining natives on an offshore island where they died. What is less well known is that it was official policy for many years after that to dilute the Aboriginal race by gradual assimilation into white society. A hundred years after the invasion, untainted Aboriginal society had become largely confined to Arnhem Land and small pockets in the interior.

Australia became a nation in the eyes of the rest of the world in 1901 with Federation. In an astonishing repudiation of its history, a bill was passed by the parliament restricting immigration of non-whites. Known as the White Australia Policy, this remained in force until 1972. The non-white Australians who had been custodians of the land for thousands of years were never consulted on the matter.

Land rights remain a contentious issue. The *terra nullius* legal fiction was finally laid to rest by the High Court Mabo decision of 1992. A Native Title Act was passed by the Federal Government in 1993, following Mabo, which recognised Aboriginal land rights to a very limited extent. Even this was bitterly opposed by vested interests, most notably the mining and farm lobbies. Some years later the High Court Wik decision confirmed that native title could exist even where pastoral leases had been granted. The Federal government responded by amending the Native Title Act so as to remove or water down the limited land rights already won by Aboriginal people.

Argument continues and until some of these questions are settled, true 'reconciliation' between Aboriginal people and later settlers may remain unresolved. Discussion continues on subjects like the 'stolen generation' where, over several generations, children of Aboriginal mothers were taken to be brought up in what to them was an alien society. Though many still believe it to have been a well-intentioned policy at the time, documentary evidence shows it was far from benign, at best born of ignorance and now generally recognised as a tragic blunder. But expressing sorrow for what happened in the past seems difficult for some today.

AUSTRALIAN SOCIETY TODAY

Australia is a multicultural society; ethnic groups abound. Melbourne is said to be have a larger Greek population than Athens. Italian migrants are dominant in parts of the Riverina of NSW. In Brisbane's Fortitude Valley the street signs are in Chinese; Chinese were among the earliest settlers of the non-Aboriginal groups. More recently Vietnamese have formed communities of their own, though not in ghettos but mingling with their neighbours. Racism is evident but mainly subdued in spite of the degree of support in 1999 for the short-lived political party, One Nation, with its perceived racial policies, since denied.

The theme 'We are Australian' and the idea of mateship are what most Australians aspire to, but inequalities in the treatment of different groups continue and fuel the misunderstandings and ignorance which so often cloud issues.

All Australian residents aged over 18 are allowed a vote and voting is compulsory. Elections are held all too frequently in the view of some, since there are three levels of government, federal, state and local. The main political parties are (in alphabetical order) Labor, Liberal, and National. Minor parties include the Democrats, the Greens and the remnants of One Nation, which is in the process of registering a new name. Independents are significant in the political arena, sometimes holding the balance of power in a parliament.

There is a Senate as well as a House of Representatives, with the governor-general representing the queen. There is popular support for a republic but distrust of politicians, an Australian tradition, led to the failure of a 1999 referendum on the subject.

Each state has its own government and a parliament, though not all have a senate. Local authorities generally devolve their power from state governments but are elected by the residents of their areas.

The distribution, and separation, of powers between federal, state and local governments, between government and judiciary, and the financial arrangements between them, while to some extent enshrined in the constitution, are matters of constant debate. Keen argument existed over the introduction of a new taxation system, ostensibly beneficial to the states but which included a Goods and Services Tax. Though welcomed by big business and the well-to-do, this is unpopular with the general public.

Practical information for the traveller

This section is not meant to be a comprehensive guide to Australia; providing general practical information would merely duplicate what is available in guides such as Lonely Planet's *Australia* which is an extremely comprehensive volume and well worth the price. Another good buy is Thomas Cook's *Australia* in the Independent Traveller series. *Australia by Rail* does, however, provide enough essential information to keep the average visitor from going wrong, as well as offering tips on places to stay and eat.

ARRIVING IN AUSTRALIA

Most airports – certainly the main international ones – have bus services which convey passengers to city hotels and railway stations at fairly reasonable prices and usually with a fairly frequent service; buses conveniently wait outside the baggage collection areas at airports. There are always taxis as well; these offer a door-to-door service and are generally quicker but cost twice as much (or sometimes considerably more). Sydney is the only city with an airport-to-city rail link, opened May 2000, but one

❏ **Airport links**

The following is a summary of the airport links currently available:

● **Adelaide** A transit minibus leaves every half-hour to and from the city, hourly at weekends and on public holidays; a 7km journey, calling at hotels and the Great Southern rail terminal at Keswick. For further details phone ☎ 08-8381 5311.

● **Brisbane** Coachtrans buses leave on the hour and half-hour from Brisbane transit centre (☎ 07-3236 1000; Roma St station) and hotels in the city centre, and after the arrival of flights from the airport; a 35- to 40-minute journey to/from both the domestic and the international terminals; fare $5.40. An airport rail link connecting to the Citytrain network is due to open in May 2001.

● **Cairns** An airport shuttle bus to the city (7km, $7 for an adult) departs following the arrival of flights and calls at hotels en route as well as at the railway station in the city centre. For further details phone ☎ 07-4031 3555.

● **Melbourne** Skybus (☎ 03-9335 2811) leaves half hourly for Spencer St station; allow up to one hour for the 23km journey.

● **Perth** The Feature Tours bus calls at hotels and East Perth station en route to the city centre. Allow 45 minutes from boarding the bus for the 13km journey; the bus meets all arrivals. Phone ☎ 08-9479 4804 for fares and further information.

● **Sydney** Kingsford Smith airport bus leaves every 30 minutes between 06.00 and 20.00; allow half an hour for the 11km journey. The bus calls at Central railway station and city hotels. The airport rail link, with stations at the domestic and international terminals, connects directly to Central and to the Campbelltown and Illawarra lines at Wolli Creek; the adult fare is $9 single, $12 return to Central and rail passholders pay a station access fee of up to $6.80.

   Darwin and **Hobart**, although served by some international flights, are excluded from this summary since neither is on or near any railway system. Details of local transport can be obtained from the relevant airlines.

is due to open in Brisbane in May 2001. For details of services in the main cities see the box above.

Cairns has a $7 tax for all international arrivals and departures; all arrivals in Sydney are subject to a $3.40 noise tax. A departure tax of $30 is payable for all international flights.

GETTING AROUND

The major cities are all connected by regular flights by the major carriers, Ansett and Qantas; Virgin Blue and Impulse are newcomers in 2000. Smaller operators serve regional routes, mostly based on services to the nearest state capital though with some useful interstate links, eg Broken Hill to Adelaide.

All major towns have bus services, though with development at a generally low density compared to European cities the coverage is not always good and large areas, particularly of newer suburbs may have no public transport. Suburban train services operate in Sydney, Melbourne, Brisbane, Adelaide and Perth and ferries are an essential complement to other public transport in Sydney and Brisbane. Taxis are plentiful in all but the smaller towns and car hire is similarly available.

ACCOMMODATION AND EATING OUT

There are hotels, motels, hostels and camp or caravan sites almost everywhere, ranging from luxury (five-star) hotels in the major cities and international resorts to the country pub, bed and breakfast and backpacker hostel; prices vary accordingly.

Tourist offices supply free brochures like *What's on in Our Town* with lists of hotels and restaurants. Railway travel centres provide similar information, and the Australian Hotels' Association is another source; a list of their state head office phone numbers is given in the box. The NSW Hotels' Association issues a leaflet *Pubstay* listing hotels (mostly budget ones) throughout NSW. The Yellow Pages telephone directory, which can be consulted at any

> ❑ **Australian Hotels' Association (AHA) offices**
>
> AHA offices are combined with the relevant state organisation, thus Queensland Hotels Association (QHA) is the same as AHA Queensland.
>
> | | |
> |---|---|
> | Australian Capital Territory | ☎ 02-6273 4007 |
> | New South Wales | ☎ 02-9281 6922 |
> | Victoria | ☎ 03-9822 0900 |
> | Queensland | ☎ 07-3221 6999 |
> | South Australia | ☎ 08-8232 4525 |
> | Western Australia | ☎ 08-9321 7701 |
> | Northern Territory | ☎ 08-8981 3650 |
> | Tasmania | ☎ 03-6278 1930 |

post office and may still be found in some telephone boxes, lists all the places to stay and eat in whatever town you happen to be.

Some hostels are operated by the Youth Hostel Association (YHA) or are privately run. For details of YHA hostels in Australia contact the YHA in your own country or the Australian YHA (☎ 02-9565 1699, 🖨 02-9565 1325, 🖳 yha@yha.org.au, www.yha.com.au), PO Box 314, Camperdown, NSW 1450.

The two main chains of privately-owned hostels are VIP Backpackers Resorts of Australia (VIP-BRA; 🖳 backpack@backpackers.com.au, www.backpackers.com.au) and NOMADS Backpackers International (🖳 info@nomads-back packers.com, www.nomads-backpackers.com).

> ❑ **Prices in this book – Australian dollars**
> Note that all prices quoted in this book are given in Australian dollars unless otherwise indicated. The current exchange rate is Australian $1 to US$0.58 or UK£0.38. For up-to-the-minute rates visit **www.xe.net/currency**.

Prices in backpacker-type hostels range from $12 (dorm bed) to $50 (single, en suite). Rooms in budget hotels range from about $20 with shared facilities up to $60 for en suite, air-conditioning, fridge and TV. Medium-range hotels and motels (one-star to three-star) may vary in price from $30 to $120, some including breakfast, some not.

Rooms in pubs and country hotels will always have a washbasin but less likely en suite facilities. A motel in Australia almost invariably provides a fridge, tea-making facilities, en suite and TV. Motels with a three-star classification are also likely to have private (en suite) facilities; this is not necessarily so with hotels with a one- or two-star classification.

Suggestions for places to stay in the main cities, some of which are taken from lists supplied by motoring/tourist organisations but chosen because they are near railway stations, are listed in Part 4 under Where to stay; prices quoted are, unless specified, for a single room. Twin/double rooms generally cost the same or little more, unless breakfast is included.

Flag Choice has a wide range of accommodation throughout Australia and also operates a Flag Hotel Pass which must be bought prior to arrival in Australia. For further information ask your travel agent or contact Flag Choice direct at ✉ reservations@flagchoice.com.au or ✉ www.flagchoice.com.au.

Flag Hotels are usually three or four star, in a slightly higher price range than the hotel prices quoted above. Four- and five-star hotels, such as the Hilton, range from $160 to $280 for a single room to over $1000 for an executive suite.

Note that the star rating awarded by motoring or government organisations is based on facilities and thus is not necessarily commensurate with quality. The absence of a rating in no way indicates a low standard of amenities or service. Surly or indifferent service can be encountered in a four-star hotel while friendly hosts may go out of their way to look after your needs in a country town pub with no classification at all.

Meal prices and the quality of food in restaurants also vary tremendously. Unlike hotels, capital city eateries are often no dearer than those in smaller towns. It is possible to obtain a satisfying counter meal in a pub for less than $5 and main courses in restaurants range from $7 to $25; a Townsville quayside open-air restaurant offers monster steaks and

---

Goods and Services Tax

July 1, 2000, marked the introduction of a Goods and Services Tax (GST) in Australia. Unless stated otherwise, all prices quoted in this book are pre-GST. The full effects of the new tax and associated changes are still unclear, but it is wise to assume that fares, accommodation and meal costs, admission charges, and almost anything else for which a price is given in this book may be increased by around 10 per cent.

seafood platters for under $15 and a dozen fresh oysters for $7 (p234). Even in a Queensland Rail dining car a three-course dinner costs only $16.80; there are separate courses and snack meals for less. If you pay more than that anywhere you are either exceedingly well-heeled or you have picked the wrong place. Always look out for a price list at the door before being committed.

TIME

Australia has three time zones; Western Standard Time (WST) in Western Australia is GMT +8; Central Standard Time (CST) in South Australia and Northern Territory is GMT +9½, and Eastern Standard Time (EST) in New South Wales, Australian Capital Territory, Victoria, Queensland and Tasmania is GMT +10.

Daylight saving operates in South Australia (CST +1), but not Northern Territory, and in the eastern states (EST +1) except Queensland, from the last Sunday in October (the first Sunday in Tasmania) to the last Sunday in March. Broken Hill, NSW, adopts South Australian time.

POST AND TELECOMMUNICATIONS

Post offices are generally open from 9am to 5pm, Monday to Friday, though some are open at the weekend, particularly Saturday mornings. Branches within major shopping complexes may also be open on Sundays. Local letters and cards cost 45c. Parcel, express post and other special services are available.

Poste restante services are available throughout Australia; check ▢ www.auspost.com.au for a list of locations.

Telephone kiosks are found in most population centres. Some take coins (minimum 40c); others need phonecards which can be purchased locally. It is increasingly common to find coin-operated machines out of order so it is useful to carry a mobile phone.

The mobile phone network is being converted to digital, but there is difficulty in some rural areas where the analogue system has still to be effectively replaced.

ELECTRICITY

Electricity supply is at 240v and three-pin plugs of an unusual design are used. Adaptors for British and North American plugs are available from most good hardware shops.

BANKS AND MONEY MATTERS

There are banking and exchange facilities at Thomas Cook and American Express offices in major cities, as well as at banks themselves. Banks are usually open from 09.30 to 16.00 and most have an ATM with 24-hour access. There are autobanks at the main railway stations in most capital cities though they are not all easy to find; just ask. At all major stations there is a counter for enquiries about facilities needed by the traveller. Most credit cards are acceptable for rail bookings at major stations, and for meals or other refreshments on

❏ Exchange rates		
USA	$1	A$1.71
Canada	$1	A$1.15
Europe	Euro 1	A$1.55
UK	£1	A$2.47
New Zealand	$1	A$0.78
Japan	¥100	A$1.57
Hong Kong	$1	A$0.21

For up-to-the-minute exchange rates visit **www.xe.net/currency**.

most major train services, usually subject to a $10 minimum. Countrylink of NSW does not, however, accept Amex or Diners Club cards. Taxis usually add a surcharge for credit card use.

The Australian currency is the Australian dollar, consisting of 100 cents. Notes are issued in $5, $10, $20, $50 and $100 denominations and coins are 5c, 10c, 20c and 50c. Prices in odd numbers of cents are rounded to the nearest 5.

TIPPING

Tipping in Australia is optional; it is occasionally practised in restaurants (and in dining cars), less often – if ever – in bars, rarely in sleeping cars, and almost never in taxi cabs – where it is customary to sit next to the driver and engage in friendly conversation. A genuine 'thanks, mate' will be more appreciated than a tip, which is regarded as patronising or even insulting. Remember, the Australian ethic is that everyone is as good as you, and you as good as they provided you don't commit the unforgivable sin of comparing Australia unfavourably with your own country!

HOLIDAY PERIODS

Public holidays

Many firms close or operate with skeleton staff between Christmas and New Year, and January is a holiday month when some businesses are closed for two or more weeks. The following are Australia-wide public holidays:

● **1 January** New Year's Day
● **26 January** Australia Day (commemorating the 1st Fleet arrival in 1788)
● **March/April** (dates vary) Good Friday, Easter Saturday, Sunday and Monday plus Easter Tuesday in Tasmania
● **25 April** Anzac Day (commemorates the troop landings at Gallipoli, Turkey, 1915)
● **25 and 26 December** Christmas Day and Boxing Day

❏ **Temperature/rainfall chart**

	Jan	Feb	Mar	Apr	May	Jun	Jul	Aug	Sep	Oct	Nov	Dec
Adelaide												
max °C	29	29	26	22	19	16	15	16	19	22	25	27
min °C	17	17	15	12	10	8	7	8	9	11	14	15
rainfall (mm)	21	11	25	38	58	79	82	69	62	43	29	29
Alice Springs												
max °C	37	35	33	28	23	20	20	22	27	31	34	35
min °C	21	21	17	13	8	5	4	6	10	15	18	20
rainfall (mm)	36	42	34	13	21	15	15	11	9	20	25	36
Brisbane												
max °C	29	29	28	26	23	21	21	22	24	26	27	29
min °C	21	21	20	17	14	11	9	10	12	16	18	20
rainfall (mm)	160	173	140	89	98	70	62	41	33	93	96	126
Cairns												
max °C	32	32	31	29	28	26	26	26	28	29	31	31
min °C	24	24	23	22	20	18	17	17	19	21	22	23
rainfall (mm)	406	433	423	196	99	49	30	27	35	40	89	177
Canberra												
max °C	28	27	24	20	15	12	11	13	16	19	22	26
min °C	13	13	11	7	3	1	0	1	3	6	9	11
rainfall (mm)	62	55	53	50	49	39	42	46	51	66	64	53
Melbourne												
max °C	26	26	24	20	17	14	13	15	17	20	22	24
min °C	14	14	13	11	9	7	6	7	8	9	11	13
rainfall (mm)	49	47	52	58	57	50	48	51	59	68	60	60
Perth												
max °C	32	32	29	25	21	19	18	18	20	22	25	29
min °C	17	17	16	13	10	9	8	8	9	10	13	15
rainfall (mm)	7	16	15	42	106	174	163	118	70	47	27	12
Sydney												
max °C	26	26	25	22	19	17	16	18	20	22	24	25
min °C	19	19	17	15	11	9	8	9	11	13	16	17
rainfall (mm)	104	117	133	126	121	131	99	80	70	77	83	79

Other public holidays vary from state to state as follows:
- **14 February** Regatta Day (Tasmania)
- **1st Monday in March** Labour Day (WA), Eight Hours Day (Tasmania)
- **2nd Monday in March** Labour Day (Victoria)
- **1st Monday in May**   May Day (Northern Territory), Labour Day (Queensland)
- **1st Monday in June** Foundation Day (WA)
- **2nd Monday in June** Queen's Birthday (all except Western Australia)

- **1st Monday in August** Bank Holiday (ACT, NSW), Picnic Day (Northern Territory)
- **Last Monday in September** Queen's Birthday (WA)
- **1st Monday in October** Labour Day (ACT, NSW, South Australia)
- **1st Tuesday in November** Melbourne Cup Day; this annual horse race is recognised and honoured throughout the country and watched on every available TV set. It is a public holiday in Melbourne.
- **Last Tuesday in December** Proclamation Day (South Australia)

There are numerous regional and local events which attract much attention and may affect transport or disrupt other normal activities. These include such varied events as the Sydney to Hobart Yacht Race (end of year), Sydney Gay & Lesbian Mardi Gras (February), Darwin Beer Can Regatta (August), Birdsville Races in Queensland (August/September, p242), Henley-on-Todd Regatta (p189) and the Australian Country Music Festival in Tamworth, New South Wales (p224).

School holidays

School holidays vary from state to state. Most schools have two weeks' holiday around Easter, two further weeks some time between the last week in June and the third week in July, two more between mid- and late September and the first week in October and the main summer holiday is from just after the middle of December to about the end of January. Private schools generally have up to an extra week in most holiday periods. University vacations are longer. Trains are more crowded at these times thus it is particularly important to book early.

CULTURE AND LEISURE ACTIVITIES

Despite a popular belief overseas that Australians spend most of their spare time in the pub playing 'two up' there is a wide variety of leisure activities to which Australians are devoted. Cricket of course is one of them, whether watching it on TV, going to see a match or participating as the legendary bloke who 'scored a hundred in the backyard at mum's'. Football is also a popular game, though not English soccer or American gridiron. Australia has its own strange Aussie rules football (a development of Gaelic football) while rugby, both Union and League, is popular too.

Swimming, surfing and other activities connected with water are also popular: they even have a boat race at Alice Springs in the dry centre of the continent (see p189). When the Melbourne Cup horse race is on, almost everything else stops. In some places they even race cockroaches or cane toads (and bet on them – gambling is widespread).

Cinemas and theatres have many devotees. Ballet and opera are also popular; the Sydney Opera House is not just a monument and operas and concerts are even performed on occasion in the outback by visiting artistes. An evening spent drinking and socialising in the pub is still common but drink-driving laws have tended to dampen enthusiasm somewhat. Watching television at home (and playing computer games) are popular with old and young alike. Many favourite British and American TV series are just as popular here.

There are commercial and national channels to choose from. The ABC is Australia's free-from-advertising (except of their own programmes and products) radio and TV channel. Listen to Macca's Sunday Morning ABC broadcast *Australia All Over* for a potpourri of real Australiana.

The history of the railways

INTRODUCTION

One of the earliest of all Australian lines and the first to carry passengers was probably unique; with timber rails laid on the ground, the passengers in open trucks and the motive power supplied by unfortunate convicts spurred on by whips, the 8km (5 mile) Tasman Peninsula railway linked Taranna and Oakwood, carrying warders and visitors to the infamous prison of Port Arthur. Very little of this rail route can still be seen but other early lines remain, many of which are still in use. Another of the earliest, and the first loco-hauled public railway, was the Melbourne and Hobson's Bay railway of 1854. Running from Flinders St to Sandridge (as Port Melbourne was then known) it has after a gauge change become the Port Melbourne light rail branch of Melbourne's extensive tramway network.

The system has developed gradually since 1827 when the first coal wagonway was constructed near Newcastle – reminiscent of the early wagonways of England's Tyneside which heralded the start of modern railways a century earlier. New lines are still being planned and constructed as older lines are abandoned, but there has never been a national plan. Most of the first railways were spur lines penetrating inland from the coast, tapping areas of primary produce – wheat, wool and minerals, but taking general freight and passengers too. Most were not connected and there was no uniform gauge.

THE PROBLEM OF DIFFERENT RAIL GAUGES

Rail gauge differences have plagued railways the world over but few countries have suffered more than Australia where, for most of its railway history, long-distance passengers had to transfer from one train to another, often in the middle of the night. Historians have described the rivalries and parochial mentalities which produced this proliferation of gauges. There were sound reasons for different states choosing the gauges they did but some decisions, in retrospect, were unforgivable.

Early days

The story of how they failed to cooperate reads like fiction. The seeds of confusion were sown in the early administration arrangements of the new colonies. Some rail routes began as private ventures, but it was not long before governments took over. The governments of New South Wales (NSW), Victoria and South Australia settled on a uniform gauge before construction commenced but the stubbornness of their engineers led them subsequently to disregard this arrangement.

Historian Geoffrey Blainey recounts the role of one of the key figures, an Irish engineer called Shields, who rejected advice that standard gauge should be adopted, maintaining that the Irish 1600mm-gauge was superior. So it was, in a way, but not enough to make much difference. When New South Wales, following Shields' advice, planned its first lines on the Irish gauge, Victoria decided to follow suit and so did South Australia. These Irishmen certainly have the gift of the blarney! They promptly went ahead. This was in the early 1850s. But by the time they had started Shields had resigned and another engineer took his place who made it his first duty to convince the NSW government that the original plan to build standard gauge was the right one. It should have been easy to resolve differences before things went too far but as politicians postured construction went on, and the longer it went on the less chance there was of putting it right.

Expansion

Things were further complicated from the 1860s when railway construction began in Western Australia and Queensland. It was popularly believed that narrow-gauge railways were cheaper to construct, so with vast distances to cover, these two colonial governments opted for the 1067mm (3ft 6in) narrow gauge. South Australia also opted for new lines on this gauge.

The first railway in Queensland opened in 1865. Extending 35km, it linked Ipswich to Grandchester (then Bigge's Camp). Ten years later another spur had commenced at Rockhampton. Railways gradually penetrated the interior, moving inland from the ports to tap the resources of the hinterland and by 1895 there were seven completely unconnected systems focusing on Brisbane, Rockhampton, Mackay, Townsville, Cairns, Normanton and Cooktown. By 1925 the east-coast branches were linked but the Normanton Railway is still isolated.

Differences remain

New South Wales, from Sydney west to Broken Hill, south to Albury and Canberra, north to the Tablelands and coast and up to Queensland, uses standard gauge (1435mm or 4ft 8½in). The systems in Victoria, radiating north, east and west from Melbourne, are mostly of the broader Irish gauge (1600mm or 5ft 3in) though some have been converted to standard gauge, leaving several branches quite isolated. Victoria had until recently the largest Irish-gauge system in the world.

The main passenger lines of South and central Australia are now all standard gauge but most of the rest of South Australia has different gauges. South Australia has almost the only world example of triple-gauge track; combined 1067, 1435 and 1600mm with four parallel rails. This may still be seen at Gladstone where sidings of three gauges combined remained in use well into the 1980s.

Queensland, from Brisbane north and west retains the narrower 1067mm-gauge giving it the first and largest mainline network in the world at a narrower than standard (less than 1435mm) gauge. In international railway parlance this is sometimes called colonial gauge, a name best not used in Australia; Queensland gauge is preferable. Queensland also has a sugar-cane rail network of 600mm gauge and the private Comalco line at Weipa in the far north is standard gauge. Western Australia has both narrow and standard gauge with some sections combined. Of its two main passenger trains one runs on 1435mm track between Perth and Kalgoorlie and the other on 1067mm track between Perth and Bunbury. Tasmania has 1067mm gauge.

Years of inconvenience

It is easy to picture the havoc this has caused for interstate trains. Before 1917 there was no TransAustralia railway linking east and west. There was a great gap across the dry, sparsely populated semi-desert country between Port Augusta in South Australia and Kalgoorlie in the west. The missing link was completed on 17 October 1917 when construction teams, working simultaneously from each end as they did in the USA in 1869, met at Ooldea on the eastern edge of the Nullarbor. Even so, gauge differences in the state rail systems prevented through running.

In the early days gauge differences meant as many as four changes of train on a journey from Brisbane to Perth. Not until 1930 was a Brisbane to Sydney journey possible without a change of train. The older inland link where standard and Queensland gauge met at Wallangarra was eclipsed when the standard-gauge route from Kyogle in NSW crossed the ranges by the dramatic Border Loop spiral, an engineering feat which reveals the difficulties of the terrain.

The standard gauge was not extended to Melbourne until 1962 when a new single line was built alongside the Victorian broad-gauge line to Albury; Perth had to wait until 1970 and Adelaide until 1983. It was not until 23 February 1970 that a new train, appropriately named the Indian Pacific from the oceans bordering Australia on the west and east, and using the newly standardised Broken Hill to Port Pirie line, marked the end of the former train changes that had so inconvenienced long-distance passengers. The train was welcomed by a crowd of 10,000 as it burst through the welcoming banners at East Perth terminal four days later.

Standardisation at last – in part

Since 1995 the gauge problem has been overcome on all the main interstate routes. Brisbane in Queensland, Sydney in NSW, Melbourne in Victoria,

Adelaide in South Australia, Perth in Western Australia and Alice Springs in the Northern Territory are all now linked by the standard-gauge network, yet the Great South Pacific Express running between Cairns and Sydney requires a bogie exchange in Brisbane. Surprisingly, the Spanish Patentes Talgo wheelset-adjustment principle has never been adopted in Australia.

Ironically, the last of the interstate lines to be standardised was Australia's oldest, the Overland rail route from Adelaide to Melbourne. In 1887, 14 years before Federation, the first interstate train in Australia was introduced, appropriately named the Intercolonial Express. In 1901 the now despised adjective colonial was dropped and the name was changed to Melbourne Express. This in turn gave way in 1936 to the present name the Overland.

Route changes

The route between Adelaide and Melbourne has changed in the last ten years. When it was decided to convert to standard gauge, the old route between Melbourne and Ararat via Ballarat was dismissed in favour of a more level but longer route via North Geelong and Maroona. There has never been a time without a passenger service between Melbourne and Adelaide since 1887 except for a short period in 1995 when the necessary changes to the various sections of track were made to achieve a complete standard-gauge link. Rumours about the future of the Overland have been rife since well before that time.

Following standardisation, few trains were left serving the older route via Ballarat which, apart from its historical role as the interstate link was the main western line of Victoria, serving Ballarat and places west to Serviceton on the South Australian border. Since no thought was apparently given to retaining the broad gauge, combined or alongside the new track, except in the Adelaide and Melbourne suburban areas, Victorian intrastate passenger trains had to be withdrawn west of Ararat where the different gauges now meet. The line south from Ararat to Hamilton and Portland was converted to standard gauge as were some smaller branches, but the result has been the isolation of some sections of the broad-gauge networks in both Victoria and South Australia.

The Wimmera Ltd linking Melbourne and Dimboola through Ballarat and Ararat has been replaced by a bus. So also has the Vinelander night service between Melbourne and Mildura and all other passenger trains on the historic Geelong–Ballarat line have gone also. On this route there used to be a delightful old stone station building at Lal Lal, halfway between Geelong and Ballarat. The standard-gauge route between Geelong and Ararat via Cressy has disused stations with equally quaint names – Nerrin Nerrin, Pura Pura and Vite Vite, the last two sounding like some sort of health drink. (Double-barrelled place names are of Aboriginal origin.)

The Geelong–Ballarat line was part of the route on which, in 1867, the then duke of Edinburgh, Prince Alfred, was so impressed with the train's speed. He travelled from Bendigo to Ballarat via Melbourne and Geelong in just over four hours at an average of 75km/h. As an interesting indication of progress, the same trip would have taken about the same time in 1996 (before the Geelong–Ballarat trains were withdrawn) except that it would miss the connection in Melbourne by three minutes! Connectivity, not only in terms of track gauge but of timetabling, has never been a strong point with Australian railways but they are not alone in this.

The only V/line train services west from Melbourne are now to Ballarat though the south-west route to Warrnambool via Geelong remains, operated by West Coast Railway of Geelong.

RATIONALISATION AND LINE CLOSURES

Failure to think nationally and develop a true railway network, acknowledged repeatedly throughout Australian railway history, has always been submerged under the stronger forces of state autonomy, interstate rivalry and the vested interests of competing modes.

The inability to think nationally

In spite of the vision of lateral thinkers like Sir Harold Clapp, who reported on standardisation in 1944 and stated that any effective national plan had to be 'accompanied by unification of railway thinking and planning', little has been done to follow his advice. Extension of the railway from Alice Springs to Darwin was enshrined in what was called the Northern Territory Acceptance Act of the Australian parliament in 1907; the territory still waits. Sir Harold envisioned a more rational connection from Bourke in the far west of NSW through Queensland, tapping areas of primary produce and connecting Darwin more directly to the eastern seaboard at Sydney.

More recently a Brisbane engineer, Dr Ken Davidson, has conceived an inner circle route linking Melbourne to the Northern Territory through NSW and Queensland, affording closer links with the more developed areas of the east coast. A grant for a pre-feasibility study has been given by the federal government to a consortium led by entrepreneur Everald Compton interested in pursuing this as a high-speed route. Another grant has been given towards the Alice–Darwin connection, while almost at the same time governments have allowed existing lines to deteriorate through lack of funding and services to dwindle.

Economic rationalism

Economic rationalism became a popular catchword among politicians in the 1970s when a spate of rail closures took place. Just as there was no national thinking or planning when the network was constructed there was no national thinking or logic to the process called rationalisation. It ignored historical, social and other factors including future potential, instead adopting narrow financial criteria often based on the assumption that inefficient practices evident in some areas would continue. The policy of spending money on a route or service earmarked for closure, well known to observers of economic rationalism in railway and other fields the world over, was secretly pursued and is far from dead.

Line closures and service reductions

Extensive closures of secondary routes took place in the early 1970s and again in the early 1980s. Between 1970 and 1985 trains were withdrawn from over 50 branch lines and 15 cross-country links or potential links between main routes were severed. Further closures between 1988 and 1994 left a basic national network which was little more than one long curving spine with a series of dead-end branches.

Long-distance passenger train kilometres within the NSW system were reduced by 46 per cent between September 1988 and May 1990, the number of actual trains being slashed from 207 to 98 per week, most being replaced by buses. This, however, was exceptional and some services (to the NSW Northern Tablelands, Broken Hill and the Riverina) have at least been partially restored and more are promised by the current NSW Government. As some governments have opted out of rail management and operation, private enterprise has taken over with mixed results. There have been years of neglect to make up. Current evidence suggests that the tide is turning, but slowly.

ELECTRIFICATION AND MODERNISATION

Pre-electrification

Steam traction reigned supreme on Australian railways until dieselisation of all the major systems between 1950 and 1971, though coal trains in the Newcastle area used steam until 1973. The South Maitland Railway continued with it even longer but steam is now confined mainly to tourist specials and various private or preserved railways. In a category of its own is the West Coast Railway of Victoria which operates a regular Saturday mainline steam-hauled passenger service.

As in other parts of the world, dieselisation was rushed through when there were steam locomotives capable of many years of useful life. So good were some, like the C38 class of New South Wales of which No 3801 has become an institution, that they remained in regular use up to 15 years after serious dieselisation began.

The process starts

Electrification was for many years confined to metropolitan networks, such as that of Melbourne, where it began in 1919, and Sydney, from

1926. It spread to Victoria's Gippsland line east from Dandenong in 1954, when the new Gippslander train first ran, electrically hauled as far as Warragul. Electrification was extended to Moe in 1955 and Traralgon in 1956. In 1987, in contradiction of world trends, the line beyond Warragul was de-electrified, the reason (excuse?) being a decline in non-passenger traffic, the closure of the line beyond Bairnsdale and the cost of replacing ageing electric locomotives.

In 1957 the New South Wales electrified suburban system was extended to the Blue Mountains, in 1960 north to Gosford, in 1986 south to Wollongong and in 1984 the interurban route to Newcastle was electrified. These developments resulted in a substantial saving in average journey times on all interurban routes.

Queensland joins the bandwagon

Although preliminary work was started in Brisbane in 1950, other priorities along with funding cutbacks and changes of government delayed electrification of Brisbane's suburban network until almost the end of 1979, after the Whitlam federal government for the first time offered states subsidies for approved public transport projects. The Brisbane suburban system was steadily electrified and extended and electrification of the North Coast mainline and coalfield routes soon followed.

Queensland's mainline electrification programme of the 1980s increased the proportion of routes electrified from less than one per cent (55km) in 1980 to nearly 17 per cent (1699km) of the QR system by 1990. Substantial speed up of trains resulted, with express freight schedules equalling former passenger speeds and passenger journeys being cut by several hours on North Coast services. The last diesel-hauled suburban service ran in Brisbane 20 years to the day after the first electric.

Perth is the most recent Australian capital to electrify its suburban network. In the 1970s one report recommended closing the system altogether (typical of similar reports of that time elsewhere) and in fact the Fremantle line was closed in 1979, the trains being replaced by 'banana buses' as the articulated vehicles were called. A change of government responded to public pressure and trains were restored. Increased patronage led to electrification and the entire 65km network, plus a new 29km line to the northern suburbs, was served by frequent and interconnecting services by March 1993.

Modernisation

Suburban and mainline trains in all states have been gradually modernised. Air conditioning has become almost universal. The Tangara electric cars of Sydney's CityRail, introduced in 1988 are among the most up-to-date in design and won the 1990 Engineering Excellence Award of Australia. Brisbane's IMU (Interurban Multiple Unit) trains on the Gold Coast line are a match for any in the world, while on the main line north to Rockhampton QR now operates Australia's first tilting train sets which are the world's fastest trains on narrow gauge.

FACTS AND FIGURES

Australia's rail network totals about 40,000 kilometres. The main components, excluding privately-run preserved railways such as the Emerald Tourist (Puffing Billy) Railway in Victoria, NSW's ZigZag, South Australia's SteamRanger and Pichi Pichi Railway, comprise:

- Queensland Rail   9458km
- New South Wales   7469km
- South Australia   5385km
- Western Australia   5139km
- Victoria   4952km
- Queensland sugar-cane railways   4150km
- Broken Hill Pty Ltd railways   1006km

There has been an overall reduction of more than 10 per cent since the end of 1980, all states except Queensland sharing this decrease. At that time Australia's total rail network consisted of some 45,455 route kilometres of six different gauges, owned and operated by six governments and nearly 50 private organisations. These ranged from giant industrial firms like Hammersley Iron and Broken Hill Proprietary Ltd to small preservation societies such as the Van Dieman Light Railway Society of Tasmania. Passenger services of some kind then operated regularly on 51.6 per cent or 23,450 route kilometres and occasionally on a few other sections, serving 2,335 stations, of which 676 were in the city and suburban areas of the mainland state capitals and almost half of all were in Queensland.

Now, 20 years later, there are as many or more operators but some very significant changes, not all for the better. Many passenger services have been reduced or withdrawn completely. Some which were operated jointly by two or more railways are now run by a single entity. This has an obvious management benefit but there is a downside. For example, the Sydney–Melbourne trains were formerly managed jointly by NSW State Rail and Victorian Railways. Now under exclusive Countrylink management V/line tickets are not accepted, even for journeys entirely within Victoria. Some of this may be remedied in time. Any major change in a long-established system is prone to teething problems and the Victorian government has gone to great lengths to ensure compatibility between privatised rail systems under its overall control.

The current management picture

The management picture is basically as follows but may well change during the life of this edition. In NSW, Countrylink and CityRail together form the passenger arm of NSW State Railways while in Queensland,

Queensland Rail (QR) operates all train services, the passenger group comprising Traveltrain and Citytrain. In Victoria, West Coast Railway took over Victoria's south-west route and Hoys Coaches took over the Shepparton route in 1993. In 1999 the rest of V/line passed into private hands, though the name V/line passenger was retained.

On 1 November 1997 Great Southern Railway, owned by Serco Asia Pacific Ltd, took over operation of the three passenger services then operated by Australian National, namely the Indian Pacific, the Overland and The Ghan. Prior to the takeover, service on all three had been gradually allowed to deteriorate through lack of government interest and funding, in spite of the efforts of management and a dedicated troop of railway workers. The Overland in particular had shrunk from one of Australia's longest trains to only a few carriages and had almost ceased running altogether.

Westrail still operates the mainline services and the Transperth suburban network in Western Australia, but privatisation is in the wings.

THE PUBLIC FACE OF THE SYSTEM TODAY

The Australian railway scene is one of contrasts, loved by many but hated by others. Much depends on which journey you undertake. Modern trains and advanced train control systems come side by side with the station master in a white pith helmet ringing a bell for the 'right away' at a country station.

Most Australian trains and all interstate trains are air-conditioned. In fact, Australia had the first air-conditioned trains in the Southern hemisphere. It was also among the first with double-deck suburban electric trains and the first (if not the only) country to provide on-train shower cubicles as part of the ordinary facilities for passengers on long-distance trains holding only economy-class tickets.

Australia is also among world leaders with solar-powered signalling, locotrol and electric traction. Heavy mineral trains rival any in the world while the leading long-distance passenger trains offer a standard of luxury rarely found elsewhere except on special cruise trains designed for the most affluent travellers.

Train speeds

Impressions and reputations do not always accord with facts. For years Spain had the reputation, at least in British eyes, of having the slowest trains in the world. In fact, since 1993 Spain has been way ahead of Britain in the speed league.

The first Australian trains were much faster, as well as more comfortable, than stagecoaches on the dusty corrugated roads, but there seemed to be a process of stagnation for much of the 20th century, so much so that one guidebook of the period described Australian passenger trains as

'lamentable'. It is true that as recently as 1980 one passenger train aver-
aged 11.2km/h (seven miles an hour)! From Thangool where it started it
took nearly 16 hours to cover 178km to its terminus at Rockhampton.
Seven of those hours it spent at Biloela, the first stop on the line, where it
shunted wagons or perhaps just rested to gain strength for the harrowing
journey ahead. In reality of course it was a goods train with a passenger
van.

Long waits, rather than slow running speed, still characterise much of
Australian rail travel even on the main lines. Yet Australia is one of fewer
than two dozen countries worldwide which has earned a place in the
Railway Gazette 'Roll of Honour' of trains with a start to stop speed
between any two stations of over 120km/h. It also holds the world speed
record for narrow gauge – rails less than 1430mm (4ft 8½in) apart – at
210km/h (130.5 mph) achieved by Queensland's Tilt Train on Sunday 23
May 1999.

No Australian trains travel as fast as British or European expresses,
nor are the rail networks anything like the intricate pattern of routes found
in Europe, where there can be many different ways of going between one
place and another; Australian express trains are mostly only about half to
two-thirds as fast as their counterparts in Europe.

Records

Australian railways boast several records and near records, together
with some world 'firsts'. Best known is the famous 'long straight', the
longest straight line of railway in the world, 478 kilometres across the
Nullarbor Plain between Ooldea, South Australia, and Nurina in Western
Australia. Here passengers can cruise in air-conditioned comfort at a steady
100km/h all day, looking out at the brown circle of the far horizon all around.

Apart from the famous 'long straight' there are other sections of straight track
rivalling the longest anywhere. Between Nyngan and Bourke in the far west of
New South Wales is a straight of 187km, probably the third longest in the world.
By contrast, some of the most tortuous sections of track exist, such as in the
Drummond Range west of Bogantungan in central Queensland where trains go
into snake-like contortions to negotiate the succession of 80 to 120m (four to six
chain) reverse curves by which the line overcomes the difficult terrain.

The widest passenger rail vehicles in the world are those operating on the
Perisher Skitube railway (see p259), an incline rack system of eight kilometres,
taking skiers and others up from Bullocks Flat in Perisher Valley to Blue Cow
in the Snowy Mountains of New South Wales. This is the fastest rack railway
in the world and one of only two funicular railways in Australia. The other, the
Katoomba Scenic Railway (see p257) in the Blue Mountains west of Sydney,
is of an unusual 1219mm (4 ft) gauge, is cable operated, and has the steepest
incline of any railway in the world, a gradient of 128 per cent – steeper than 1
in 1 – at its maximum. This excludes fairground roller-coaster type railways,
enclosed mine railways and the unique enclosed capsule 'tramway' in
Saarinen's famous Gateway Arch in St Louis, USA.

Sharp curves and stiff gradients on many routes contribute to Australia's generally slow average speeds. The vintage tourist train from Cairns to Kuranda in the far north of Queensland takes 90 minutes to go 33km (20 miles) but when you see where and how it goes it is no more surprising than the fact that mountain railways in the world are even slower. For example, the Jungfrau railway in Switzerland takes almost an hour to go barely ten kilometres.

Slowness of travel, however, is not a problem with highly scenic routes, whilst longer journeys take on the nature of a cruise.

Frequency of service

Except in suburban, most outer-urban and some interurban areas (such as Newcastle–Sydney–Wollongong and Melbourne–Geelong), Australian train services are nowhere near as frequent as would be expected in Britain, most countries of Europe, or Japan.

For almost all the long-distance routes, including some interstate routes, the frequency is less than one train a day in each direction. For many routes there are no more than two per day. Exceptions are the routes from Rockhampton to Brisbane, Grafton to Sydney and Sydney to Canberra and Junee, Albury to Melbourne and Melbourne to Sale, Bendigo, Ballarat and Warrnambool. Between Junee and Griffith in NSW, Kuranda and Forsayth and Normanton and Croydon in Queensland the frequencies are one train a week in each direction. So it can become very important not to miss a train.

Trends and the future

FRAGMENTATION

Although it is now possible to travel on standard gauge from Brisbane to Perth the same 'State Rights' mentality and inability to think in terms of the 'best interests of the railways or of Australia as a whole', so bemoaned by Sir Harold Clapp in 1945, persists, affecting train scheduling, wagon pooling, ticket validity, computerised booking, concession travel for pensioners and railway staff and many other things.

Even within individual states, railway functions are being increasingly divided, one body responsible for track, another for stations or signalling, and under a misguided National Competition Policy any number of players can be in the game of running trains, using the same track. The potential for confusion and inefficiency is obvious, as any two young boys with a toy train set between them would know. In spite of this the best traditions of railways are largely maintained. There is still pride among rail workers: the philosophy of 'the mail must go through' tends to prevail even against strikes over genuine grievances.

TRAFFIC AND ATTITUDES

Traffic

Freight, or more accurately mineral traffic, is what brings the money in and passengers tend to take second place, except in urban areas. In describing the kind of traffic railways should seek, it has been said (and some Australian rail managements would endorse this view) that 'if it breathes, forget it'.

The potential for tourist traffic on cane railways in Queensland has recently been ignored by the sugar-mill owners, with the near demise of exciting rail experiences such as the Mulgrave Rambler at Gordonvale and Ballyhooley Express at Mossman.

Attitudes

Attitudes change little. In the early days of railway development, revenue-minded managements shuddered with horror at the thought of wasting revenue space on things like toilets, let alone dining or sleeping cars! They still do.

Although freight and minerals are the mainstay of most rail systems worldwide, and mineral traffic is the raison d'être of most Australian lines built in the last few decades the systems of most countries including Australia are continuing to provide high-quality passenger services and investing in new track and rolling stock. In the last ten years over 500km of new lines have been built, mostly in Queensland. New trains have been introduced on almost every system, though many other lines have been closed and services withdrawn.

Economics are not the only consideration. Throughout the whole history of Australian railway development, decisions have been made on political grounds, sometimes wrongly and unjustifiably to serve electoral purposes, but often rightly as representing the triumph of popular demand and genuine need over narrow accounting. The one time 'common carrier' principle has been replaced by 'community service obligation', recognised to some extent by all governments, however much they may require their railways to be commercially activated.

Apart from in Queensland, railways have abandoned stock trains and the carrying of small parcels and mail is now rare. Passengers may be considered a loss-making proposition yet some new lines have been built or former routes re-opened solely for this traffic. In the 1990s the Queensland government rebuilt the Beenleigh–Gold Coast line which had been closed in 1964. In 1998 the Emerald Railway Tourist Board restored the long-closed Emerald–Gembrook narrow-gauge line solely for use by the Puffing Billy tourist train in Victoria's Dandenongs.

Railways in Australia still excite the imagination. In outback areas almost the whole town comes out to greet the once- or twice-weekly arrival. When new services are introduced, like QR's Tilt train (the longest distance all-electric service in Australia), local suburban dwellers stand in their gardens to wave, schoolchildren come out of their classrooms in droves (presumably with official approval as an educational experience) and guards of honour, brass bands, or cocktail parties may bid farewell or greet the train at major stations.

When the famous LNER Flying Scotsman engine number 4472 visited Australia its route was lined by scores of photographers and train-gazers at every vantage point and its tour had to be extended to nearly a year so that it could be seen everywhere – from Brisbane to Perth, from Melbourne to Alice Springs. Similar enthusiasm greets veteran steam locomotive 3801 of New South Wales whenever it appears on a special excursion. Who does not thrill to the sight of a mighty iron beast pouring forth smoke and steam, hissing and pounding its way along the steel road, or to the rhythm of railway wheels and the exhilaration of speed in the safe cocoon of a railway carriage through cityscape and landscape, relaxed in a comfortable seat or sipping a cool drink?

Even the phenomenon of trains reclaiming passenger patronage from short-haul airlines, observable in Europe in the last two decades, has lately been noted in Australia with the advent of Queensland's Tilt Train.

THE FUTURE?

So what of the future for the railways of Australia? No-one knows. Considerations of energy, the environment and social need may well outweigh – and should outweigh – the dismal deliberations of the pseudo-economic rationalists who have so long been influencing government thinking, who would have most of the rail system shut down, who would replace most freight trains by thundering multi-trucks and all the non-urban passenger trains by buses or nothing at all.

They will tell you that most passengers on long-distance trains are pensioners and others heavily subsidised. Many are, but there are children too, mothers with young ones, tourists and even business travellers. What matters more is that people travel by rail because they want to. They like it. Aircraft may be quicker, bus travel cheaper, the car more convenient at the start and end of the journey but there is nothing else quite like the train where you eat, talk, stroll around, play cards, sleep and enjoy the travel experience so eloquently expressed by Ludovic Kennedy in his anthology *A Book of Railway Journeys* (see overleaf).

A 1991 Industry Commission report on the railways, if heeded, would have spelt the demise of all but suburban passenger trains. It offered little more than pious platitudes for the future of rail freight. But micro-economics and financial accountability, important in their place, do not determine events. There are other factors at work. Not only is public opinion a shaper of policy, there are intrinsic technical advantages in the rail mode. The railway is 'not bound for the museum for the same reason that the stage coach landed there', to quote the US Interstate Commerce Commission of 1970. Steel wheel on narrow rail has far less rolling friction than rubber on tarmac, takes less energy to move a given mass, can go faster and obtain its momentum from electricity. With no need for individual steering rail has an unquestionable advantage in safety.

Couple this inherent superiority with tradition and public concern, compare the trends worldwide, the swings back and forth, where Amtrak is renewing services on former abandoned routes and where even in car-oriented Los Angeles they have voted millions for railway development. 'Man has yet to invent an overland passenger mode of transport with the train's unique combination of speed, safety, comfort, dependability and economy' said the US Commission. They might well have added, 'or a more efficient mass mover of freight or produce'.

'Travelling by rail is relaxing, uncomplicated', said a Victorian railway advertisement, ironically just at the time they were substituting buses for trains on some of their routes.

Queensland Railways' promotion has included a television jingle 'Take it easy, take a train' and a clever billboard advertisement aimed at the motoring commuter: 'For relief of stress, take two a day', the illustration being not of pills but a Brisbane suburban electric train.

In *A Book of Railway Journeys*, Ludovic Kennedy praised rail travel even further, not specifically in Australia: 'One is transported in comfort, even style, to the wild places of the earth ... one can move around ... strike up a conversation, read, sleep, snore, make love'. That may not be easy nowadays with few compartment carriages and no sleeping cars on some overnight trains but there's no harm in trying.

Intercapital connections

For those who wish to base their tour on the capital cities the following alphabetically-arranged list summarises the train services between them. This section then tells you how to use the local trains and gives suggestions on what to see. This should enable visitors to devise itineraries to taste.

Notes

Some of the connections to and from Canberra marked 'via Goulburn' involve a long wait there. Where this occurs, marked with a hash sign (#) below, pass holders have the option of changing later in the day at Moss Vale or Campbelltown instead. There are also some alternative connections between Canberra and the south and west using Countrylink road coaches. These and other bus services operated by the railways are not included in this table.

A change of train is required at the places named 'via' on each route.

Note that in summer time (late October to early March) times at Brisbane are an hour different and should be checked locally.

From Adelaide:

to **Brisbane**   dep 07.45 Wednesday and Sunday via Sydney
        arr 06.35 two days later
        dep 09.00 excluding Tuesday, Wednesday and Saturday
          via Melbourne and Sydney; arr 06.35 three days later
        dep 10.10 Saturday via Sydney; arr 06.35 two days later
        dep 10.15 Wednesday via Melbourne and Sydney
          arr 06.35 three days later
to **Canberra**   dep 07.45 Wednesday and Sunday via Sydney
        arr 15.50 next day
        dep 09.00 excluding Tuesday, Wednesday and Saturday
          via Melbourne and Goulburn#, arr 22.21 next day
        dep 10.10 Saturday via Sydney, arr 15.50 next day
        dep 10.15 Wednesday via Melbourne and Goulburn#
          arr 22.21 next day
to **Melbourne** dep 09.00 excluding Tuesday, Wednesday and Saturday,
          arr 20.10
        dep 10.15 Wednesday, arr 21.05

From Adelaide (cont'd):

to **Perth**	dep 18.30 Tuesday and Friday, arr 09.30 two days later
to **Sydney**	dep 07.45 Wednesday and Sunday, arr 09.15 next day
	dep 09.00 excluding Tuesday, Wednesday and Saturday via Melbourne, arr 19.13 next day
	dep 10.10 Saturday, arr 0915 next day
	dep 10.15 Wednesday via Melbourne, arr 19.13 next day

From Brisbane:

to **Adelaide**	dep 07.30 excluding Monday, Tuesday and Friday via Sydney and Melbourne, arr 07.40 two days later
	dep 07.30 Tuesday via Sydney and Melbourne, arr 10.10 two days later
	dep 07.30 Saturday via Sydney, arr 12.50 two days later
	dep 07.30 Wednesday and Sunday via Sydney, arr 16.50 two days later
to **Canberra**	dep 07.30 daily via Sydney; arr 11.15 next day
to **Melbourne**	dep 07.30 daily via Sydney; arr 18.15 next day
to **Perth**	dep 07.30 Wednesday and Sunday via Sydney; arr 09.30 four days later
to **Sydney**	dep 07.30 daily, arr 21.51

From Canberra:

to **Adelaide**	dep 06.45 excluding Tuesday, Wednesday and Saturday via Goulburn and Melbourne, arr 07.40 next day
	dep 06.45 Wednesday via Goulburn and Melbourne, arr 10.10 next day
	dep 06.45 Sunday via Sydney, arr 12.50 next day
	dep 06.45 Monday and Thursday via Sydney, arr 16.50 next day
to **Brisbane**	dep 12.15 daily via Strathfield, arr 06.35 next day
to **Melbourne**	dep 06.45 daily via Goulburn, arr 18.15
	dep 17.15 daily via Goulburn#, arr 07.00 next day
to **Perth**	dep 06.45 Monday and Thursday via Sydney, or via Goulburn, Melbourne and Adelaide, arr 09.30 three days later
to **Sydney**	dep 06.45 daily, arr 10.55
	dep 12.15 daily, arr 16.24
	dep 17.15 daily, arr 21.26

From Melbourne:

to **Adelaide**	dep 21.30 excluding Tuesday, Wednesday and Saturday, arr 07.40 next day
	dep 22.30 Wednesday, arr 10.10 next day
to **Brisbane**	dep 19.45 daily via Sydney, arr 06.35 two days later

From Melbourne (cont'd):

to **Canberra**   dep 08.30 daily via Goulburn#, arr 22.21
                  dep 19.45 daily via Goulburn#, arr 11.15 next day
to **Perth**   dep 21.30 Monday and Thursday via Adelaide, arr 09.30
                  three days later
to **Sydney**   dep 08.30 daily, arr 19.13
                  dep 19.45 daily, arr 06.25 next day

From Perth:

to **Adelaide** dep 10.55 Monday and Friday, arr 06.05 two days later
to **Brisbane** dep 10.55 Monday and Friday via Sydney, arr 06.35 four
                 days later
to **Canberra** dep 10.55 Monday and Friday via Sydney, arr 15.50
                 three days later

Station locations

In all Australian state capital cities there is more than one railway station. Unless otherwise stated in tables and itineraries in this book, trains arrive and depart from the main interstate stations, which are as follows:

Sydney: Central station (also called Sydney Terminal).

Melbourne: Spencer St station.

Brisbane: Roma St station (also called Brisbane Transit Centre) should not be confused with Brisbane Central station.

Adelaide: GSR Terminal, Keswick, is 3.5km from the city centre and ten minutes walk from a suburban station of the same name, from which there is a local service roughly every half-hour to the central city station in North Terrace.

Perth: East Perth Terminal station, West Parade, East Perth, is just over 1.7km from City station. Adjoins the suburban station of East Perth, from which there is a frequent service to City station in the town centre.

Canberra: The railway station is at Kingston, about 5km from the city centre at Civic or the bus station at Jolimont. Local bus services and taxis are available, while Countrylink coaches to destinations like Cooma and Yass connect with trains.

At **Port Pirie** in South Australia, **Bunbury** in Western Australia and **Gympie**, **Maryborough**, **Mackay** and **Bowen** in Queensland, new stations have been built which are anything up to 8km out of town.

At **Mackay** and **New Bowen** passengers are left to their own devices (taxi or a lift from someone with a private car), whilst at **Port Pirie** (Coonamia station), **Maryborough West** and **Gympie North** the railways provide a coach or taxi.

Orange East Fork station, used by the Indian Pacific and The Ghan, is 1.8km from the main Orange station in the town centre. There is no public transport between the two, so if alighting at Orange East Fork from a Great Southern train it would be worth asking the train manager to arrange something (such as a taxi) before arrival (you might be offered a lift in a railway van).

From Perth: cont'd
to **Melbourne**   dep 10.55 Monday via Adelaide, arr 21.05 two days later
                     dep 10.55 Friday via Adelaide, arr 20.10 two days later
to **Sydney**   dep 10.55 Monday and Friday, arr 09.15 three days later

From Sydney:
to **Adelaide**   dep 07.43 excluding Tuesday, Wednesday and Saturday
                     via Melbourne, arr 07.40 next day
                     dep 07.43 Wednesday via Melbourne, arr 10.10 next day
                     dep 13.10 Sunday, arr 12.50 next day
                     dep 14.55 Monday and Thursday, arr 16.50 next day
to **Brisbane**   dep 16.24 daily, arr 06.35 next day
to **Canberra**   dep 07.05 daily, arr 11.15
                     dep 11.44 daily, arr 15.50
                     dep 18.14 daily, arr 22.21.
to **Melbourne**   dep 07.43 daily, arr 18.15.
                     dep 20.43 daily, arr 07.00 next day.
to **Perth**   dep 14.55 Monday and Thursday, arr 09.30 three days
                     later

Sydney

ORIENTATION

Australia's largest city has enough to keep you sightseeing for days.
Sydney's extensive suburban railway system can take you to many of the
principal attractions and right into the heart of the city. **St James**, **Town
Hall** and **Wynyard** are the best stations for the central business district,
but the main terminal itself is close to Chinatown.

Two useful places to obtain information are Travellers Information
Service (☎ 02-9281 9366) in Sydney Coach Terminal, outside Central sta-
tion, and Sydney Visitors Centre (☎ 02-9255 1788), 106 George St, The
Rocks (open 09.00-18.00). There are also information kiosks at Martin
Place, Town Hall and Circular Quay, open daily 09.00-17.00.

> **Goods and Services Tax (GST)**
> July 1, 2000, marked the introduction of a Goods and Services Tax
> (GST) in Australia. Unless stated otherwise, all prices quoted in this
> book are pre-GST. The full effects of the new tax and associated changes are
> still unclear, but it is wise to assume that fares, accommodation and meal costs,
> admission charges, and almost anything else for which a price is given in this
> book may be increased by around 10 per cent.

WHAT TO SEE AND DO

Around St James and Circular Quay stations

You can enjoy panoramic 360° views of the city, the harbour and the Pacific Ocean from the top of the tallest building in Australia, the 305m-high AMP Tower at Centrepoint shopping centre opposite City Centre monorail station. It features a revolving restaurant. Access to the tower observation deck costs $10. **St James** station is close by on CityRail.

A fine collection of traditional and modern, Australian and European art may be seen at the Art Gallery of New South Wales (in The Domain), open daily; take Art Gallery Rd from nearby St James station. You can carry on from there into the Royal Botanic Gardens, open daily until sunset, and see the lush tropical plants and exotic trees including cuttings from the world's oldest-known species, the Wollemi Pine, recently discovered in Wollemi National Park near the Blue Mountains.

North of the gardens at Bennelong Point is the famous Opera House; guided tours (one hour) are offered daily. **Circular Quay** station is nearby and is convenient for a walking tour around The Rocks, the oldest part of Sydney and well supplied with quality eating places. The Museum of Contemporary Art, George St, and the Museum of Sydney, on the corner of Bridge St and Philip St, are both within walking distance of Circular Quay station, from where you can also take a harbour cruise, a ferry to one of the many coves or to Manly for Marineland or the beach; alternatively take a hydrofoil to Taronga Park Zoo. Coach tours also depart from here. Sydney buses run an Explorer bus to 20 places of interest; you can hop on and off where you like.

Around Museum and Martin Place stations

From **Museum** station it is easy to get to the ANZAC War Memorial in Hyde Park where they change the guard every Thursday at 13.30, and also to the Australian Museum (on the corner of William and College Sts), open Tuesday to Saturday from 10.00 and Sunday and Monday from 12.00, for Australia's largest natural history collection and a display of Aboriginal artefacts and relics.

Should the revolving meal turn you 'crook', **Martin Place** station is next to Sydney Hospital. It also adjoins the mall of that name, where you can listen to a free lunchtime concert, and is convenient for visiting the NSW State Library and seeing Parliament House.

Around Town Hall station

Town Hall station adjoins Sydney Town Hall, which features a magnificent pipe organ and rich internal decoration. Underground at Town Hall is also an extensive shopping and restaurant area. There are many hotels between here and Sydney Central. Town Hall is close to Pitt St Mall and many shops and cinemas. It is also the best place to transfer to the Metro monorail circuit which is a must for every Sydney visitor. Park Plaza monorail station is one block east.

The Metro Monorail and Metro Light Rail

The **monorail** will take you over Darling Harbour across Pyrmont Bridge to the Australian National Maritime Museum (Harbourside station) and the Convention Centre (Convention station). At the city end of the bridge is the Sydney Aquarium (Darling Park station) where you can stroll through underwater tunnels past live sharks and other denizens of the sea.

The Metro monorail (formerly Darling Harbour monorail, see p258) is operated jointly with the Metro light rail, part of the CGEA Transport group Europe's leading private operator of 'public' transport. First commissioned in 1988, the monorail is an elevated straddle-type system powered by sheathed conductor rails below the running plate.

There are seven stations; the total circuit is 3.5km, the speed between stops is 33km/h, the service frequency is three to five minutes and it operates 365 days of the year mostly from 07.00 to 22.00 (to midnight Thursdays to Saturdays). The adult fare is $3 but day passes and multi-trip Metrocards are also available.

One attractive feature of the monorail, apart from seeing much of the city centre from treetop level, is that it connects with the **Metro light rail** at two places; Convention and Haymarket. The latter is the station for the Powerhouse Museum (see p259) arguably Sydney's best, the Sydney Entertainment Centre and Paddy's markets. Haymarket is also next door to Chinatown and the Metro light rail goes from there past Capitol Square, handy for the Capitol theatre, George St cinemas and Bridie O'Reilly's Irish Pub, and on to Central, offering a perfect connection with CityRail and Countrylink trains.

In the other direction the Metro light rail serves Star City casino, Sydney fish market and Wentworth Park, home of renowned greyhound races. The 3.7km Metro light rail was opened in 1997 and operates every 8 to 15 minutes, 24 hours a day. A 3.1km extension to Glebe, Rozelle Bay and Lilyfield is under construction and future plans include a city centre loop and a further westward extension to the suburb of Leichardt. Current adult fares are $2 to $4 depending on the fare zones you travel through; various day and weekly passes available.

Rail tours

With even a half day in Sydney, several interesting rail tours can be made. You can go over the Sydney Harbour bridge and see the commuters on their daily rat race. Take the round trip via Hornsby and Strathfield (85 to

(**Opposite**) **Top**: Bondi beach, Sydney, a 20-minute walk from Bondi Junction station. **Bottom**: Melbourne skyline with Flinders St station visible in the foreground (see p139).

> **Rail tickets for the suburban area**
> Sydney's CityRail offers day or longer period travel passes, day rovers and other special tickets covering parts of the suburban system. There is also a SydneyPass giving unlimited travel on regular buses, ferries and central CityRail, including the Sydney and Bondi & Bay Explorer buses and the Airport Express bus.
>   The pass also covers Sydney Harbour cruises, the Manly ferry and the RiverCat to Parramatta (which passes the Olympic site) but does not cover the Olympic Park trains. The fare is $85 for an adult (child $45, family $215) for three days within one week; component parts can be purchased separately and five- and seven-day SydneyPasses are also available.

105 minutes, C 9014 and local timetables) but go first on the City railway to Circular Quay (eight minutes) to view Sydney Harbour and the Opera House. You can go on to colourful Kings Cross or to Bondi junction (seven and ten minutes), though the latter might prove a disappointment if you are expecting Bondi beach. Bondi Junction has a mall, with plenty of interesting shops, market stalls and restaurants. Bondi beach, with many more restaurants, is but a short bus ride or a 20-minute walk from the station. If you want to go all the way to a beach in the Sydney area by train, take the Cronulla service (47 minutes); you may find it full of bronzed, golden-haired kids out for a day of sunshine and surf.

En route to Cronulla, the Sydney–Wollongong rail route skirts Sydney airport at Sydenham and passes close to the famous Botany Bay. Rail buffs will note the XPT depot at Tempe. The route then skirts the first of Australia's national parks, the Royal, just south of Sutherland (27 minutes, C 9014). A branch to the park ranger's office, where the traveller is in the heart of the 'bush', has closed but has been reopened as a tramway (see p239). You can spend a whole day exploring the park's walking tracks and enjoying its excellent views.

Olympic Park is just beyond Strathfield in Sydney's inner western suburbs. The junction station for the Olympic Sprint shuttle service is Lidcombe but there are direct services from Central at peak periods. Further west of Sydney, Parramatta is packed full of Australian history. See the birthplace of Batman. No, not the Gotham City 'caped crusader' but the surveyor who went over Bass Strait from Launceston in Tasmania (not accompanied by Robin), and on the banks of the River Yarra in Victoria said 'Here is the place for a city' and thus founded Melbourne. Within walking distance of Parramatta station (25 minutes from Central) you can also find the 1802 Lennox bridge, the old Government House, the

---

(**Opposite**) Now almost a symbol of the city of Melbourne (see p140), *Ophelia*, the striking statue by Deborah Halpern, stands outside the Southgate Complex across the Yarra River from Flinders St Station.

remains of Australia's first observatory and other historic buildings maintained by the National Trust.

In a day tour of the Sydney area by rail you could start at Central station, visit Town Hall or Wynyard for the shopping centre, then Circular Quay for the harbour and Opera House, go over Harbour bridge to Milsons Point (for Luna Park amusement centre); then back to Central for the train to Cronulla for a spell at the beach before returning to the city centre for dinner. Or you could go at night to Kings Cross, noted for its colourful (some would say 'off-colour') goings on that might broadly be categorised as 'alternative lifestyles'. Lonely Planet's *Australia* guidebook describes the Cross as 'a cocktail of strip joints, prostitution, crime and drugs, shaken and stirred with a handful of classy restaurants, designer cafes, international hotels and backpacker hostels'. If that is your scene

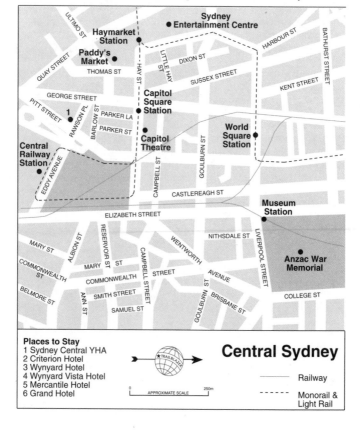

Places to Stay
1 Sydney Central YHA
2 Criterion Hotel
3 Wynyard Hotel
4 Wynyard Vista Hotel
5 Mercantile Hotel
6 Grand Hotel

Central Sydney

Railway

Monorail & Light Rail

APPROXIMATE SCALE
0 ____ 250m

you can certainly have a good time and find budget-priced accommodation but unless you are the partying type you may find it too noisy.

An alternative (or another day's choice) might take you to Campbelltown new town (49 minutes via East Hills), Parramatta (23 to 30 minutes) for its history, Richmond (80 minutes) to see the air base or just for a quiet suburban retreat (a good place to stay), or to Warwick Farm (45 to 50 minutes) for the races if they are on.

WHERE TO STAY

Budget/mid-range

Two hostels worth trying are the 532-bed *Sydney Central YHA* (☎ 02-9281 9111, 📠 02-9281 9199, 🖥 sydcentral@yhansw.org.au), 11 Rawson

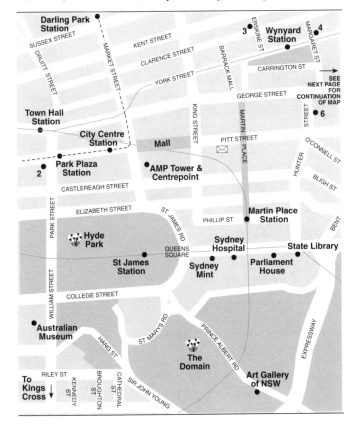

Place (opposite Central station) and *Original Backpackers* (☎ 02-9356 3232), 162 Victoria St, a short walk north from Kings Cross station.

Hotels where you should expect to pay around $50 include: *Criterion* (☎ 02-9264 3093), corner of Pitt and Park Sts (Town Hall station) and *Wynyard Hotel* (☎ 02-9299 1330), which is near Wynyard station. If you prefer to be further out, try *Pymble Hotel* (☎ 02-9144 1039), 1134 Pacific Highway, opposite Pymble station on the North Shore line.

Slowly moving up the price range are *Hotel Occidental* (☎ 02-9299 2531), 43 York St, near Circular Quay station ($60) and *Grand Hotel* (☎ 02-9232 3755), 30 Hunter St, near Wynyard station is a one-star Pub-stay hotel where a single costs $70. Another one-star hotel is *Mercantile Hotel* (☎ 02-9247 3570, ⌨ merc@tpg.com.au), 25 George St, The Rocks, which charges $70 for a single, including breakfast.

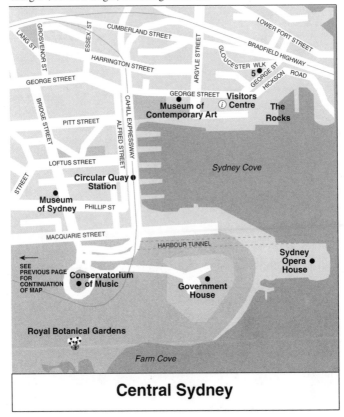

Central Sydney

O'Malley's (☎ 02-9357 2211), 228 William St, near Kings Cross station, charges $80 for an en suite room, including breakfast.

Up-market

Castlereagh Inn (☎ 02-9284 1000, ⌨ castlein@ozemail.com.au), 169 Castlereagh St, a three-star hotel near Town Hall station, charges $105 for an en suite room.

For around $135 you could have a room in *Pacific International Inn* (☎ 02-9211 4311),721 George St, near Central Station. You should expect to pay around $160 at *Wynyard Vista Hotel* (☎ 02-9290 1840), 7 York St, near Wynyard station.

WHERE TO EAT

In Sydney you can enjoy Oriental cuisine equal to any in Hong Kong (and some pretty awful stuff as well). Quality does not always vary in proportion to price and since proprietors and menus frequently change it would be potentially misleading to suggest specific establishments in a book of this sort. Local advice is worth seeking.

Another good indicator is to note how well a restaurant is patronised. Plenty of Chinese people in a Chinese restaurant is usually a fair indication of authenticity and quality. A local guide, *Cheap eats in Sydney,* is published annually and is available from newsagents. In this context 'cheap' means good value for money, not cheap and nasty.

The Chinatown area (the first stop on the Light Rail from Central), the city centre (Town Hall station) and the Rocks (Circular Quay station) abound in good eating places but some are aimed at tourists and prices are therefore upwardly adjusted.

For excellent Greek cuisine try the *Hellenic Club* (☎ 02-9261 4910), 5th Floor, 251 Elizabeth St; visitors are welcome. There are many other ethnic restaurants. Pick up a copy of the guide to cheap eats mentioned above or simply stroll down the streets and make your own selection.

DAY TRIPS FROM SYDNEY

To the South Coast (C 9014)

Consider a trip down the coast line to Nowra and back. Not much of Australia's coast is visible from its railways, but the Illawarra line is an exception, taking the passenger right to the water's edge or along the cliff tops. North of Wollongong a small section of the coast scenery is marred by coal mining, but the natural features still predominate.

Trains leave Sydney for Nowra at more or less hourly intervals (two hourly on mornings and at weekends), from 04.52 on weekdays, 05.44 at weekends, and arrive at Kiama in about 2 hours 20 minutes and Nowra in

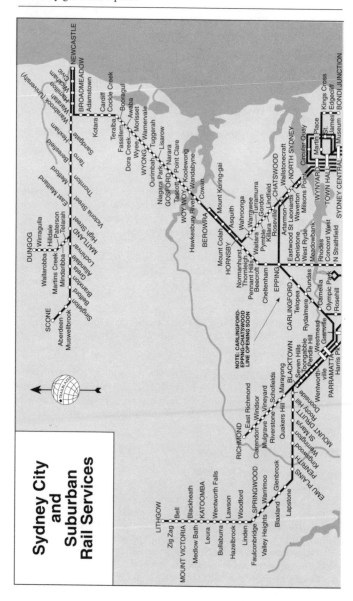

Sydney City
and
Suburban
Rail Services

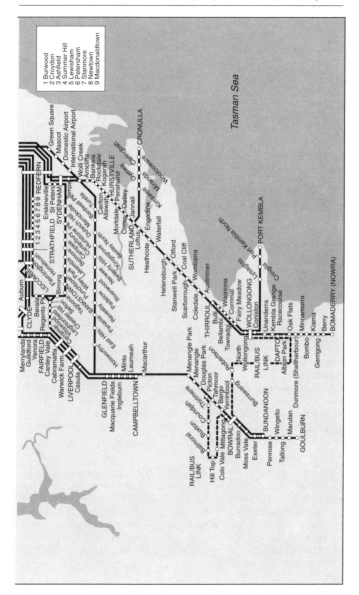

about 2 hours 50 minutes. Return services depart from Nowra just as frequently but at more erratic intervals (varying from 32 to 121 minutes). All trains involve a change between local electric and diesel Endeavour units at Dapto. Last return times from Nowra if you intend catching the Melbourne XPT from Sydney are 16.51 on weekdays, 17.32 on Saturdays, Sundays and public holidays, departures from Kiama are 17.30 and 18.10 respectively. There are much later trains to Sydney itself.

Wollongong, featured in the Australian TV *Aunty Jack* series, gave rise to a 'What's wrong with Wollongong' quip. You'll find out, but be prepared for a surprise. Like all hard-earning industrial towns, Wollongong has a warmth about it that many other places lack. You will feel this even more if you go down the branch to **Port Kembla** where the steelworks are. Port Kembla is not everyone's cup of tea, but have a quick beer and say hello to the friendly locals. The pub (*Steelworks Hotel*, ☎ 02-4274 1049) is a short walk from the station and there is usually a good 30 minutes or so before the local train returns to Wollongong.

A branch line from Unanderra south of Wollongong goes to Moss Vale on the main line south to Melbourne. Until recently a privately-operated train made this a worthwhile detour. A delightful round trip from Sydney was down the coast past Wollongong, up through the rainforest to Moss Vale and back into Sydney via Campbelltown but at the time of writing the regular service operates only as far as Robertson, 22½km short of Moss Vale but there is a special round-trip excursion on Wednesdays. For details contact 3801 Ltd (☎ 1300 65 3801) (see also p255).

There are tempting places to break a journey most of the way from Unanderra, south of Wollongong, to Nowra (Bomaderry), the end of the line. At **Bombo** the beach is just over the track from the station platform. **Kiama** is worth a visit to see the nearby blowhole and Cathedral Rocks. **Berry, the** last stop before Nowra, is another little place with its centre of activity near the station. Visit the antique shop and enjoy good food at the local pub, *Berry Hotel* (☎ 02-4464 1011), Queen St, where rooms cost $45. At **Nowra**, there is time for lunch, a walk round town, and then a choice of trains for your return.

To the Southern Highlands

Frequent suburban electric trains serve Campbelltown, while diesel Endeavour sets of CityRail, plus Xplorer or XPT trains offer a somewhat erratic but roughly hourly service to and from Moss Vale, Goulburn and intermediate stations, with three trains daily continuing to Canberra.

Day trips can easily be made to all destinations from the early morning. The last trains for a same-day return are at 17.15 from Canberra, 19.45 from Goulburn (21.18 on Fridays, Saturdays and public holidays, 18.44 on Sundays), and 20.42 from Moss Vale (plus 22.15 on Fridays and Saturdays) (C 9014, 9021).

To the Blue Mountains

Possibly the most scenic part of the continent, at least of readily accessible places, the Blue Mountains west of Sydney feature towering escarpments, waterfalls, deep bush and scenic lookouts, and can be visited on a coach tour from the principal centre, **Katoomba**, or by bush-walking tracks, a steam railway, cable car and the world's steepest funicular railway (see p257). Katoomba is reached by fast and frequent trains from Sydney (C9014). **Springwood**, with its Norman Lindsay gallery and museum, **Wentworth Falls**, **Leura**, **Blackheath**, and **Mount Victoria** are other convenient stations for access to this National Park.

Just short of the interurban terminus at Lithgow is a tiny platform called **Zigzag**, a request stop and station for the Zigzag Railway (see p260), which operates at weekends. Here you can take a steam train up a private line on the old switchback route which crossed the mountains before they built the present line which pierced the ranges with its ten tunnels. The line climbs from Bottom Points, adjoining the Zigzag platform, to Top Points, then goes on past Mt Sinai through a tunnel to Clarence. From Clarence, you return to the bottom and hail the train for the return to Sydney. From Katoomba and Leura there are other tours such as the Freedom of the Blue Mountains Explorer bus.

To the central west
Sydney–Orange–Wellington–Dubbo (C 9020)

A day trip from Sydney is possible to the central west using the XPT from Sydney at 07.10, returning from Dubbo at 14.10, Wellington 14.49, Orange 15.55 and Bathurst 17.14. This service reaches Sydney at 20.48, just missing the overnight Southern Cross XPT to Melbourne, but passengers can change to it at Strathfield at 20.34. Prior booking for this is essential as the connection is not guaranteed nor even advertised.

To the central coast and Newcastle (C 9014 and local)

There are frequent trains to Mount Kuring-gai and Hawkesbury River (55 minutes), Gosford (72 to 82 minutes) and Wyong (85 to 100 minutes); also to Newcastle at intervals up to 16.12 which arrives in Newcastle at 18.40 (Broadmeadow 18.31). You don't have to go back to Sydney if you are going north overnight because the Brisbane XPT calls at Hornsby at 16.56, Gosford at 17.41 and Broadmeadow at 18.45. There are later trains to the central coast and Newcastle if you intend a longer break of journey by staying overnight.

If travelling south from Sydney that day you will have less time to spare: deadline times to return for the Southern Cross Melbourne XPT on weekdays are 18.02 from Newcastle, 18.12 from Broadmeadow, 19.02 from Wyong, 19.17 from Gosford and 19.42 from Hawkesbury River. Weekend and holiday times are approximately 40 minutes earlier. These connections all involve changing at Strathfield to the Melbourne train. If

❏ **Table 11**
Sydney–Dungog–Gloucester (C 9016, 9017 and local)

Sydney	dep	07.15	11.35	16.24	Gloucester	dep		12.24	17.40
Maitland	dep	09.58	14.18	19.09	Dungog	dep	08.17	13.18	18.34
Dungog	arr	10.42	15.03	19.55	Maitland	arr	09.00	14.01	19.17
Gloucester	arr	11.35	15.58		Sydney	arr	11.38	16.34	21.51

Notes
Daily XPT trains with buffet.
A more frequent service to and from Dungog only, changing at Hamilton from or to Sydney, is available.

you have left your luggage at Sydney and not booked it on the XPT you will have to leave earlier but times vary at weekends so local enquiry is essential.

Day trips further north, to Dungog or Gloucester, can be made using the XPT or local trains changing at Hamilton, but the area north of Maitland and Hunter Valley is better covered by a two-day trip or a break of journey northbound or by making excursions from a base in or near Newcastle; some ideas are offered on pp221-223. The XPT timetable for this area is summarised in Table 11 above.

TWO-DAY AND LONGER TRIPS FROM SYDNEY

A two-day trip from Sydney can take you into the Northern Tablelands of New South Wales or to Moree. Daylight travel is by Xplorer air-conditioned diesel train with buffet and all trains require reservations; for times see C 9018.

The limitations on other possibilities for rail travel in New South Wales depend only on how long you have before going on interstate (or home) from Sydney. It is a good idea to make a provincial town your base for part of the time. Places such as Maitland, Orange, or Goulburn, all rail junctions, will shorten many of your 'away day' trips. If you have to get back to Sydney for an interstate journey, remember the deadlines (see the box below).

❏ **Deadline departures from Sydney:**

13.10	The Ghan to Adelaide and Alice Springs (Sunday)
14.55	Indian Pacific to Adelaide and Perth (Monday and Thursday)
16.24	Brisbane XPT (daily)
20.43	Southern Cross XPT to Melbourne (daily)

Melbourne

ORIENTATION

Melbourne has long been Sydney's arch rival and was Australia's administrative capital before the creation of Canberra. The 64 regular street blocks of its central business district are ringed by the railway, serving the main stations of Spencer St (interstate), Flinders St (for all local lines), Parliament, Central (formerly Museum) and Flagstaff. No part of the city centre is more than ten minutes' walk from one of these stations.

An intricate network of tram routes also links the stations with city centre streets and with most of the inner suburbs. Suburban and outer urban routes penetrate to the outer suburbs and rural hinterland and go around Port Phillip Bay to Geelong in the west and Frankston and Stony Point in the east. Spencer St is reportedly Australia's busiest railway station, and is also the terminal for V/line coach services operating from Melbourne, but Flinders St is in the very heart of the city, adjoining Princes Bridge which crosses the Yarra, linking the southern end of Swanston St with St Kilda Rd.

Batman Avenue runs along the side of the Yarra south of the Flinders St railway yards; on the west of Flinders St to the south of the Yarra is Melbourne's casino, officially the Crown Entertainment Complex, reached on foot or by tram down Market St. The City Circle free tram links Flinders St, Spencer St, Flagstaff, Melbourne Central and Parliament stations.

Information about Melbourne can be obtained from the information booths in Bourke St Mall, City Square and in Rialto observation deck. To book tours and accommodation it is best to go to Victoria Visitor Information Centre (☎ 03-9658 9955), in the old town hall on the corner of Little Collins and Swanston streets.

WHAT TO SEE AND DO

Around Spencer St station

A block east of Spencer St station you can enjoy a panoramic view of Melbourne and Port Phillip Bay from the observation deck on the 55th floor of Rialto Towers, claimed to be the tallest building in Australia (but see Sydney p127). This traditional Sydney/Melbourne rivalry was challenged in the 1970s when there were moves in Brisbane to promote the world's tallest building, not just Australia's. *Up where we belong* was the theme tune, but like the Tower of Babel it never really got off the ground and led to a lot of squabbling.

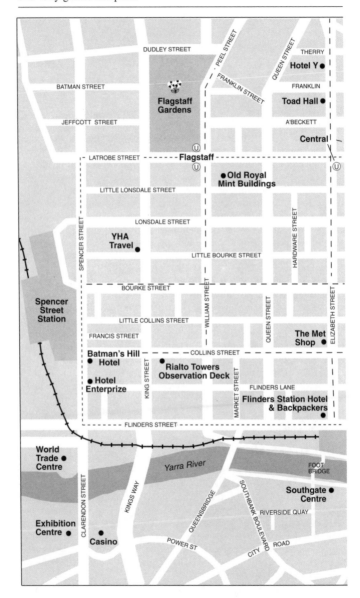

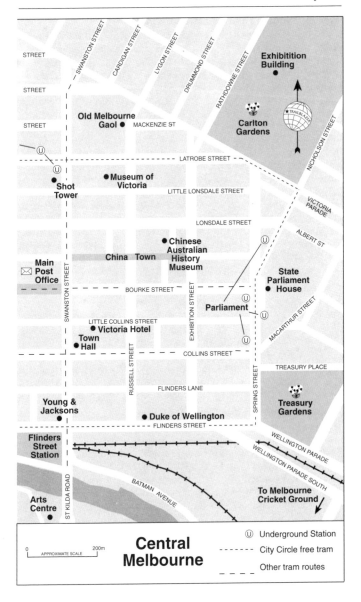

STREET

STREET

STREET

SWANSTON STREET

CARDIGAN STREET

LYGON STREET

DRUMMOND STREET

RATHDOWNE STREET

NICHOLSON STREET

Exhibition Building ●

Old Melbourne Gaol ●   MACKENZIE ST

Carlton Gardens

★ TRAILBLAZER

LATROBE STREET

Ⓤ

Ⓤ

● **Museum of Victoria**

Shot Tower

LITTLE LONSDALE STREET

VICTORIA PARADE

LONSDALE STREET

ALBERT ST

● **Chinese Australian History Museum**

China Town

Ⓤ

Main Post Office ✉

SWANSTON STREET

BOURKE STREET

Ⓤ

Parliament

State Parliament House ●

MACARTHUR STREET

LITTLE COLLINS STREET

● **Victoria Hotel**

Town Hall ●

RUSSELL STREET

EXHIBITION STREET

Ⓤ

Ⓤ

COLLINS STREET

SPRING STREET

TREASURY PLACE

Young & Jacksons ●

FLINDERS LANE

● **Duke of Wellington**

FLINDERS STREET

Treasury Gardens

Flinders Street Station

Young & Jacksons ●

ST KILDA ROAD

BATMAN   AVENUE

WELLINGTON PARADE

WELLINGTON PARADE SOUTH

To Melbourne Cricket Ground ↙

Arts Centre ●

0   200m
APPROXIMATE SCALE

Central Melbourne

Ⓤ Underground Station

- - - - - City Circle free tram

— — — Other tram routes

Around Flinders St and Jolimont stations

Just opposite **Flinders St** station is Young and Jackson's *Prince's Bridge Hotel*, where Lefebvre's famous *Chloe* painting which caused much controversy when first acquired in 1883 is displayed in an upstairs bar.

For nature in a different form, Melbourne's Royal Botanic Gardens, open daily until sunset, boasts the largest plant collection in the Southern hemisphere; any tram down St Kilda Rd from Flinders St will take you there. Sidney Meyer Music Bowl is here, too, where Australia's much-loved group, The Seekers, gave their triumphant homecoming free performance to a record crowd of 220,000 on returning from their world tour in 1967. Also in St Kilda Rd is Australia's largest art collection at the National Gallery, open daily, and the Victorian Arts Centre, Melbourne's answer to the Sydney Opera House. Day tours or performances must be booked well in advance and are not cheap. From the Arts Centre, go along the banks of the Yarra, walk or hire a cycle, or take a ferry boat from Princes Walk (adjoining Batman Avenue) on the northern bank. Walk or take a tram to the east end of Flinders St for a look at Treasury Gardens.

Jolimont station, a little further on, is handy for Melbourne Cricket Ground and nearby Fitzroy Gardens, where Captain Cook's cottage, imported from Yorkshire, honours the discoverer of eastern Australia.

Around Central station

A block to the north-east of Central station, in Russell St, is the Old Melbourne Gaol and Penal Museum, whilst just to the west at the corner of Elizabeth and Lonsdale Sts is the Melbourne Central shopping complex, which encloses the old Shot Tower. A little further afield in Carlton, see the exhibit of Australian ceramics, weaving and hand-made jewellery in the Galaxy of Handicrafts, 99 Cardigan St. A tram up Swanston St will take you there or it is a short walk from Central station. Nearby Lygon St is famous for its ethnic restaurants, coffee bars and boutiques.

Around Parliament and Royal Park stations

See the Museum of Chinese Australian History at 22 Cohen Place, in the heart of Chinatown (Lonsdale and Little Bourke Sts which are close to **Parliament** station), open daily except Tuesdays. For bargain craft wares, try the Meat Market Craft Centre, 42 Courtney St, North Melbourne (by tram along Flemington Rd). Just north again is Royal Park and the Zoological Gardens, traversed by tram route, or by train to **Royal Park** station (13 minutes, C 9023).

WHERE TO STAY

Budget/mid-range

Dorms and rooms are available at both *Flinders Station Hotel & Backpackers* (☎ 03-9620 5100, 🖹 03-9620 5101), 35 Elizabeth St (between Flinders St and Flinders Lane), and *Toad Hall* (☎ 02-9600 9010), 441 Elizabeth St, at the Central station end of Elizabeth St.

A short walk from Central Station, *Hotel Y* (☎ 03-9329 5188), 489 Elizabeth St, is run by the YWCA but is not institutional. It has a variety of accommodation to suit most budgets and is reliably reported to have friendly staff and good food in the attached restaurant.

Pub rooms are available at the *Duke of Wellington* (☎ 03-9650 4984), on the corner of Flinders St and Russell St, one block east of Flinders St station, for $45-$80 including breakfast.

A three-star hotel two blocks from Spencer St station is *Hotel Enterprize* (freecall ☎ 1800 033 451, ☎ 03-9629 6991, 🖥 entrpriz@ozemail.com.au), 44 Spencer St, where you should expect to pay $79 for an en suite room.

Spanning the mid- to up-market range is *Victoria Hotel* (☎ 03-9653 0441), 215 Little Collins St (near Flinders St station); a three-star Flag Hotel where rooms start at $42 and go up to $130.

Up-market
Almost opposite Spencer St station is *Batman's Hill* (☎ 03-9614 6344), 66-70 Spencer St, where prices start from $155. Slightly cheaper but also on Spencer St is *Pacific International Terrace Inn* (☎ 03-9621 3333, 16 Spencer St, where a room costs $124, including breakfast.

Other
With anything more than a couple of days in the Melbourne area it is worth thinking of staying a fair way out of town as accommodation is often cheaper. Geelong, Seymour, Kyneton, Ballan and Ballarat are worth considering as they have reasonably frequent trains to the city. There are evening trains to all the places described in Day trips from Melbourne (see pp144-149), so that stopovers of two or more nights can be made.

WHERE TO EAT

Eating places are almost too numerous to mention, with almost every type of cuisine to choose from. In the central city area, north of Flinders St station, Little Bourke St and St Kilda (the last named readily accessible by tram), there are restaurants, snack bars, brasseries, pubs with counter lunch, coffee houses and milk bars. There is no need to go more than a couple of blocks from any of the inner city stations (Flinders, Spencer or a station on the loop) to find something to match your taste and pocket.

For a unique culinary and travel experience, try the *Colonial Tramcar Restaurant*; for reservations (lunch or dinner), phone ☎ 03-9596 6500 or call at their office, 254 Bay St, Brighton (take a tram or train to North Brighton station). The gastronomic journey starts at National Art Gallery just south of Flinders St railway station.

A train out to Eltham will let you enjoy the fare at award-winning chef *Stephen Mercer's Restaurant* (☎ 03-9431 1015), 732 Main Rd, whilst just opposite Spencer St station the *Jarrah Room* and *Pizza Shoppe* at Hotel Enterprize offer generous helpings of well-prepared and often exotic food at attractive prices.

A DAY'S TRAVEL IN THE SUBURBAN AREA

Even if you are visiting Melbourne for only one day you have time between the arrival of overnight trains from interstate and their departure the same evening to travel all over the suburban area, around the bay to **Frankston** in the east (58 minutes) or to **Geelong** in the west. Geelong is a 60- to 65-minute journey (C 9023) but is not covered by Metcard tickets.

For a pocket tour, take in Flinders St and the underground loop (for city centre sights and shops), St Kilda (for the beach), historic Port Melbourne and **Williamstown** at the mouth of the Yarra in the morning and go out towards the Dandenong Ranges in the afternoon. Williamstown has both Historic and Maritime museums, not to mention a Railway Museum 500m from North Williamstown station.

If races or shows are on, you can go by train to **Newmarket**, the showgrounds or Flemington racecourse. The Royal Melbourne Show is in September and the Melbourne Cup in November, but there are race meetings all year at Flemington.

The picturesque Dandenong Ranges, an hour from Melbourne by electric train to **Upper Ferntree Gully** or **Belgrave** (C 9023), are Melbourne's doorstep national park. Here you can see lyrebirds displaying their plumage, or visit the 40-hectare rhododendron garden at nearby Olinda.

From Belgrave, the Puffing Billy steam train skirts the south of the Dandenongs to **Emerald** and **Gembrook**. Operated by Emerald Tourist Railway Board, the Puffing Billy Railway runs daily except Christmas Day, but on days of total fire ban will be diesel hauled and operate at a reduced service; see p260 for more details.

North of the Dandenongs is **Lilydale** (a good suburban base 50 minutes from the city by frequent suburban train), from where connecting bus No 685 serves Healesville with its sanctuary. Here you can watch kangaroos, koalas, emus, wombats and platypuses in a natural setting.

DAY TRIPS FROM MELBOURNE
Port Phillip Bay
There is a local line to **Stony Point** for the ferry to Phillip Island (summer only) with its penguins. Take the suburban train to Frankston and change there. The ferry is only a few minutes trip.

Local transport services
For those without an Austrailpass, rail/bus/tram passes on the Met can be obtained for parts or the whole of the Melbourne area by the hour or day at very reasonable rates; less than $10 will cover a full day throughout all the zones.

For local train services, fares and timetables visit the Met Shop, 103 Elizabeth St, or call the Met Information Centre on ☎ 131 638 between 07.00 and 21.00 any day.

Trains operate every 10 to 40 minutes depending on the route and time of day or week and trams every 3 to 30 minutes. A useful booklet *Visit Melbourne's Attractions* is available free of charge.

There is a frequent V/line passenger service between Melbourne and **Geelong**, Victoria's second city. Geelong is the main centre for touring the Bellarine Peninsula and parts of the south-west coast as well as being a good 'out of town' base for Melbourne sightseeing. Trains run approximately every hour from Melbourne to Geelong from 05.45 to 23.30 Mondays to Fridays, but the last return train from Geelong is at 21.15. The service is less frequent and extensive at weekends.

To the east – Gippsland
All stations in Gippsland, east of the Melbourne metropolitan area, are within day-return reach of Melbourne but to see the sights of the region two or three days are needed.

The rail system east of Melbourne serves the Latrobe Valley industrial towns of **Moe**, **Morwell** and **Traralgon**, then goes on through **Rosedale** to **Sale** in East Gippsland (C 9029). Another branch used to serve South Gippsland (see p262 for details of the private service replacing part of this route).

For catching the overnight service to Sydney or Adelaide at Melbourne, deadline departures are 16.50 from Sale, 17.25 from Traralgon, 17.47 from Moe and 18.06 from Warragul on weekdays; on Saturdays and Sundays times vary by up to 10 minutes (earlier or later), so check local timetables carefully beforehand.

To the north
The main line from Melbourne to Sydney is also served by V-line intercity trains as far as the border at Albury-Wodonga. For local intercity services see Cooks table 9028. All Melbourne–Albury local trains stop at **Seymour** (70 minutes from Melbourne), **Benalla** (another hour), **Wangaratta** (an hour from Albury) and **Wodonga**, Albury's Victorian twin city; for schedules of local intercity services see C 9028.

A day trip into the Goulburn Valley is another option. Trains go only as far as Shepparton, from where Hoys Coaches connect to **Cobram** on the NSW border (C 9025). Return times if travelling interstate to Adelaide

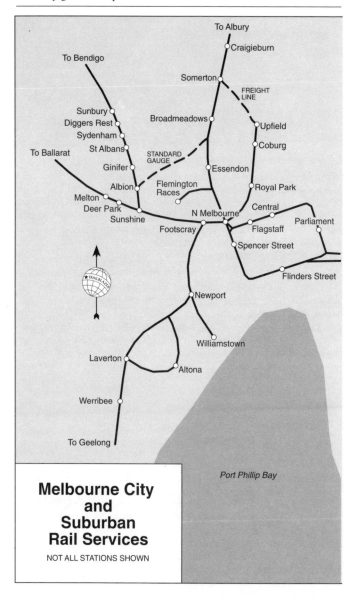

To Albury

Craigieburn

Somerton

FREIGHT LINE

To Bendigo

Sunbury
Diggers Rest
Sydenham
St Albans
Ginifer

Broadmeadows

Upfield

Coburg

To Ballarat

STANDARD GAUGE

Essendon

Royal Park

Albion
Melton
Deer Park
Sunshine

Flemington Races

N Melbourne

Central

Parliament

Footscray

Flagstaff

Spencer Street

Flinders Street

Newport

Williamstown

Laverton

Altona

Werribee

To Geelong

Port Phillip Bay

Melbourne City and Suburban Rail Services

NOT ALL STATIONS SHOWN

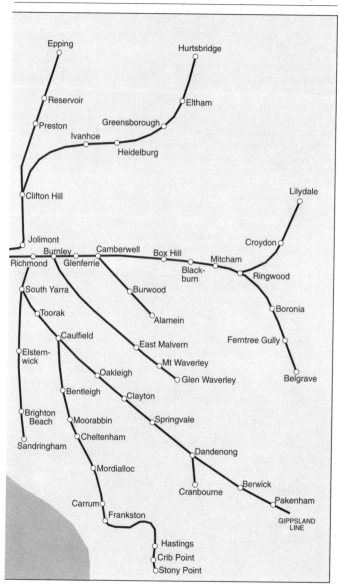

are 16.00 from Albury, 17.19 from Benalla, and 14.55 from Shepparton, in each case rather later on Saturdays and Sundays.

To the west

Warrnambool and places in between there and Geelong such as **Winchelsea**, **Colac**, **Camperdown** and **Terang**, are within day-return distance of Melbourne but if visiting this area a two-day trip, perhaps based on Geelong, gives more opportunities.

If visiting Geelong or the Victorian south-west coast, the last departure to connect with the Southern Cross to Sydney is at 18.25 (Monday to Friday), 18.30 (Saturday) or 17.30 (Sunday). The last train from beyond Geelong (Colac, Camperdown and Warrnambool) is in good time for the Overland or The Ghan to Adelaide at Melbourne, but not the Sydney XPT. Whilst both Adelaide trains stop at Geelong North Shore if booked, there is no convenient connection from Geelong or further west. To avoid a long wait at an empty platform, take a taxi from Geelong to North Shore or take the train on to Melbourne for this connection.

The historic town of **Ballarat**, home of the Ballarat Vintage Tramway (see p260), is an easy day-return trip by local V/line train. The journey takes 1½ hours each way and trains are roughly every 90 minutes from 08.00 to 20.35, slightly less frequently at weekends. Return trains are up to 19.15 except on Saturdays, but if travelling the same day to Sydney the last connections leave Ballarat at 16.20 Monday to Friday and at 17.10 on Sundays. The last train on Saturdays, at 18.00, is in time for the XPT connection.

Bendigo and **Castlemaine,** on the north-western line, are also within day-return distance with trains at roughly the same frequency as those to

---

❏ **Table 12**
Melbourne–Bendigo–Kerang–Swan Hill

		Friday	Sunday	Mon-Thu	Saturday
Melbourne	dep	16.37	17.30	17.42	17.50
Bendigo	dep	18.45	19.36	19.40	19.42
Kerang	arr	20.11	21.02	21.07	21.08
Swan Hill	arr	20.55	21.45	21.50	21.50

		Mon-Sat	Sunday
Swan Hill	dep	07.10	16.40
Kerang	dep	07.49	17.19
Bendigo	arr	09.17	18.47
Melbourne	arr	11.05	20.47

Notes
Great Northern loco-hauled buffet car train, first class and economy.
The Sunday afternoon train from Swan Hill is too late to catch the overnight XPT to Sydney but in time for night trains to Adelaide.

❑ **Deadline Departures**
19.45   The Southern Cross for Sydney which also picks up at Benalla at
         21.38 and Wangaratta at 22.04.
21.30   The Overland to Adelaide which also picks up at Geelong North
         Shore at 22.29. The Ghan, Wednesday only, is an hour later.

Ballarat. The first is at 08.35 from Spencer St, an hour later on Sundays. The last return times from Bendigo are 18.15 on weekdays, 18.50 at weekends, but to catch the XPT for Sydney you need to take the daily 16.20 service; times from Castlemaine are 22 minutes later.

TWO- TO THREE-DAY TRIPS FROM MELBOURNE

Swan Hill and **Kerang** are within striking distance and so is Echuca, the last named only on either a day return on Sunday afternoon or a Friday night to Sunday trip.

Swan Hill has a daily service but one that was designed for Swan Hill rather than Melbourne residents. A summary timetable is given in Table 12 (p148) and features of these destinations and other excursions are described on pp79-80 and p207.

Brisbane

ORIENTATION

Subtropical Brisbane's warmth will greet you as you alight at this northern capital. Founded in the 1830s and now established as Australia's third city, Brisbane has seen rapid urban growth in the last three decades and its straggling suburbs cover an area equal to Greater London. Unlike Sydney and Melbourne, the city is under one administration: its budget is equal to that of the state of Tasmania.

Brisbane's suburban trains are all modern, smooth, well-furnished electric units. The two main stations, Roma St and Central, are in the city centre and within 15 minutes' walk of each other.

A circular inner-city bus route takes the strain out of walking between city centre features (the main strain being having to wait to cross roads at traffic lights) but it takes just about the same time whether you walk or wait for the bus. Another good way to get around is the CityCat ferry service; take a CityCat to South Bank Parklands and Brisbane Convention Centre (these occupy part of the site of the former World Expo 1988); on foot these can be reached in five minutes across Victoria Bridge.

Tourism Brisbane (☎ 07-3221 8411, 🖹 07-3229 5126) has an information office in the City Hall (King George Sq), but for information about accommodation or to make a booking it is best to go to Brisbane Visitors' Accommodation Service (☎ 07-3236 2020), on both levels of the transit centre at Roma St station.

WHAT TO SEE AND DO

Around Roma St and Central stations

Climb up to the Old Windmill observatory on Wickham Terrace, northeast of **Roma St** station, or go down through King George Square and Albert St to Queen St Mall. From the northern end of the Mall take the walkway along the side of Anzac Square or through the square and past the Shrine of Remembrance to the old Central station facade, now the entrance to the Sheraton Hotel (as well as to the station itself).

In the area around **Central** station it is possible to see giant old fig trees, particularly at the bottom end of Creek St and at some other road junctions in the inner suburbs. At Eagle St Pier an outstanding craft market is open every Sunday.

About 300m south of Eagle St Pier is Brisbane Botanic Gardens; the 20-hectare site offers a profusion of sub-tropical flowers and shrubs.

Around South Brisbane and Vulture St stations

South Brisbane station, the first stop from Roma St over the Merivale A-frame bridge, adjoins the Parklands, while right opposite the station is the Cultural Centre with its Performing Arts complex, restaurants and bars. Across the road (by covered walkway) is also Queensland Art Gallery with its fine collection of paintings, sculptures, photographs and prints, and Queensland Museum where the exhibits include dinosaurs and the only surviving World War 1 German tank.

On Sidon St at the east end of the Parklands, near **Vulture St** station (the next station after South Brisbane on the Beenleigh and Cleveland lines), you can see many fine ship models and an old frigate at Queensland Maritime Museum, open on Wednesdays, Saturdays and Sundays from 10.00.

Around Brunswick St and Bowen Hills stations

Less than a kilometre north of Central is **Brunswick St**, the station for colourful Fortitude Valley with its many ethnic restaurants and Brisbane's Chinatown. At the east end of Brunswick St is New Farm Park, with up to 12,000 rose trees in bloom between September and November (as well as avenues of jacaranda and poinciana trees) beside Brisbane River. Visit St John's Cathedral, open daily, where brass-rubbing workshops are held (check times locally). At nearby Spring Hill are many of Brisbane's dozens of art and craft galleries. Near here, too, is the Brisbane Exhibition site – they call it the Ekka. If an exhibition is on, there will be frequent special trains from all city stations, and your rail pass will be honoured.

Within walking distance of **Bowen Hills** station (the next to the north after Brunswick St) in Jordan Tee is Miegunyah, built in 1884 and now a Folk Museum, open Tuesdays, Wednesdays, Saturdays and Sundays from 10.30. Less than a kilometre away is Brisbane's oldest surviving house, Newstead, at the bend of the river in Newstead Park. Look along the river to the wharves in both directions and across to Bulimba Point. Downstream the Gateway Bridge dominates the skyline beyond Hamilton Reach, while the jets loom large overhead on their approach to Brisbane airport.

Just behind the Brekky Creek Hotel in Higgs St is a rare Chinese joss-house (☎ 07-3262 5588 for appointment), built in 1884. It is a one kilo-

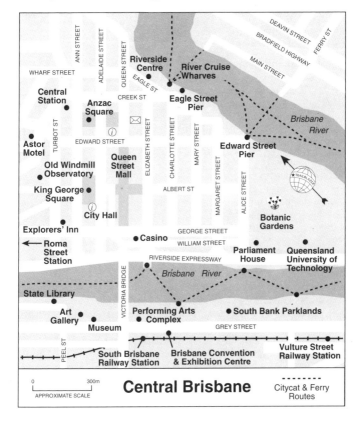

Central Brisbane

Travel in the suburban area
For exploring the Brisbane area by rail various area tickets offer unlimited travel in one day, valid on City Council buses and ferries as well as trains. A Day Rover covers all stations on the Citytrain network after 09.00 on weekdays or all day otherwise. This does not include the interurban routes beyond Beenleigh, Caboolture or Ipswich. For enquiries about Citytrains and buses, phone ☎ 131 230 or 07-3235 5555 or simply call at Roma St or Central station.

The suburban rail system can also take you to the coast at Manly, Lota, or Raby Bay (Ormiston station on the Cleveland line, 50 minutes, C 9015), or south-east to Beenleigh (41 minutes by express, hourly from Roma St or 56 minutes by stopping train every half hour) for the Rum distillery and nearby Lion Park.

metre walk north-east from Bowen Hills station; alternatively you can go back along the riverside from Bretts Wharf on a Citycat.

For the rail enthusiast

There is a railway shop at the eastern end of the station building at South Brisbane, whilst at Ipswich (55 minutes by Citytrain) the Railway Workshops are open to visitors (see p264). The Australian Railway Historical Society (see p263) operates several steam trains in this area. En route to Ipswich you can hardly fail to note the historic Castlemaine Brewery, home of XXXX beer, on the right at Milton station, first after leaving Roma St.

Around Dakabin station

For exotic animals, birds and plants visit Alma Park Zoo and the 13-hectare Tropical Palm Gardens, open daily, just over a kilometre from Dakabin station on the Caboolture line. Some trains have special bus connections to Alma Park – ask for leaflets at Central or Roma St.

WHERE TO STAY

Budget/mid-range

The facilities at **Brisbane Backpackers Resort** (☎ 07-3844 9956 or freecall ☎ 1800 626 452, ▣ brisbanebackpackers@b022.aone.net.au), 110 Vulture St, West End (west of Vulture St station), include a licensed bar, pool, sauna and spa – a five-star backpacker hotel! An en suite single costs $47; dorms are also available. **Palace Backpackers** (☎ 1800 676340), right opposite Central station, is a former Salvation Army citadel, now with a licensed bar. Dorm beds cost from $15, single rooms with communal facilities from $22. **Brisbane City YHA** (☎ 07-3236 1004, ▤ 07-3236 1947, ▣ bnecity@yhaquld.org.au), 392 Upper Roma St, has beds from $17.

A change from rail travel?
Near the airport (there is no rail link yet so you need a taxi or the airport bus) you can see the Southern Cross, the aircraft in which the first solo flight to Australia was made from England in 1928.

River cruises as well as ferries will give you unrivalled views of the city and its bridges, particularly at night. Take a dinner cruise on the Kookaburra Queen (☎ 07-3352 3797 for reservations), a launch trip to Tangalooma on Moreton Island, or a day cruise to Stradbroke if you have a day or more to spare.

Within day-trip reach by coach is the rainforest of Lamington National Park, an unforgettable experience of mountains and gorges, breathtaking vistas, cool dense forests, waterfalls, colourful parrots, rosellas and bower birds and little pademelons. These are marsupials the size of rabbits which hop around unconcerned while you feed the rosellas. Visitors can obtain lunch at *O'Reilly's Guest House*, high in the park.

The best panorama of Brisbane is from the viewpoint on Mount Coot-tha, a short drive from the city centre but unfortunately not connected by public transport. You can make a day of it there, exploring the rainforest, then call for afternoon tea or dinner at the restaurant. There are more lookout points in Brisbane Forest Park, further into the ranges. If you are unable to reach the real thing, there is a simulated rainforest in Mount Coot-tha Botanic Gardens, open daily from 08.00, and served by City Council buses. Australia's largest planetarium is also located there: viewing times should be checked locally.

Equally accessible is Brisbane's most popular tourist spot for overseas visitors, the world famous Lone Pine Sanctuary at Fig Tree Pocket. Open daily, it can be reached by City bus No 445 (except Sundays) or No 430 from the city or from Indooroopilly Interchange (near the station) or by taking a launch from North Quay (☎ 07-3221 0300). Entry is $12.50 for an adult; child and other reductions are available. You can hold a koala, be photographed wearing a snake, feed the kangaroos, wallabies and emus, and see wombats, dingos, sugar gliders and the elusive and unbelievable platypus.

Although it is just over 1km from Brunswick St station, the friendly *Globetrekkers Backpacker Hostel* (☎ 07-3358 1251, 🖳 www.globe-trekkers.net), 35 Balfour St, New Farm (in 'The Valley' off Brunswick St) is worth considering because it offers a pickup service from city railway stations. Dorm beds cost $16 or $90 per week, a twin or double room $36, en suite $40. *Indooroopilly Hotel* (☎ 07-3378 1533), opposite Indooroopilly station, costs from $50 for an en suite room with TV.

A short walk from Roma St station is *Explorers' Inn* (freecall ☎ 1800 623 288, ☎ 07-3211 3488), 63 Turbot St, where an en suite single costs costs $69. *Astor Motel* (☎ 07-3831 9522), Wickham Terrace, is one block west of the upper end of the subway exit of Central station; it is a three-star hotel and charges $89-$95 for rooms with en suite facilities. Another three-star hotel in the same area is *Camelot Inn* (☎ 07-3832 5115), 40 Astor Terrace; rooms start from $97.

Fish terminology
A word of warning: in Australia 'lobster' always means crayfish, 'trout' may mean Coral trout, a choice white-fleshed reef fish but nothing at all like brown or rainbow trout or sea trout, and 'salmon', unless specified as red, can mean a very unexciting greyish fish called Australian salmon and bearing no relationship to the kind known in North America and Europe.

Up-market

Gazebo Hotel (tollfree ☎ 1800 777 789 or ☎ 07-3831 6177), 345 Wickham Terrace, can be reached by city circle bus from Roma St. It is a three-star Flag Hotel which overlooks parklands; the rooms have private balconies and cost $106 including breakfast.

Centra Hotel (☎ 07-3328 2222, 🖥 hotel@brisbane.centra.com.au), at Roma St Transit Centre, was formerly a Travelodge; rooms cost $126.

The *Sheraton* (☎ 07-3835 3535), above Brisbane Central Station, is a five-star hotel with rooms from $181.

WHERE TO EAT

Eagle St wharf area (three blocks down Creek St from Central), Fortitude Valley (Chinatown) adjacent to Brunswick St Station, South Bank Parklands (South Brisbane or Vulture St stations), the City Mall and areas between there and Central Station; also Park Rd Milton (adjacent to the station) and the Toowong station area offer a wide variety of eating places.

Brisbane city centre is well supplied with restaurants. At *Fihelly's Arms Bar*, at the Ann St entrance to Central station, you can enjoy a cheap but nourishing counter lunch while looking at railway memorabilia adorning the walls. Between there and Queen St Mall, and within and around the Mall, are numerous eating places. In the Wintergarden on the Mall try *Fasta Pasta* for attractively priced Italian fare or *Britannia Inn* (formerly at World Expo '88) for British tucker.

You will find other restaurants, rather more up-market, at the Riverside Centre on the edge of the CBD (Central Business District). Walk there or take the city circle bus to Eagle St Wharf, three blocks down Creek St from Central. Fortitude Valley (Chinatown) adjacent to Brunswick St station and South Bank Parklands (South Brisbane or Vulture St stations) are other areas with a plentiful supply of restaurants.

In the Newstead area, visit the famous *Breakfast Creek (Brekky Creek) Hotel*, 2 Kingsford Smith Drive, north of the river, for a beer or big succulent steaks, or try the seafood at the *Breakfast Creek Wharf*.

On the river side of the railway at Milton (turn left out of the subway from the station), Park St is reputed to be Brisbane's latest hangout for the 'cafe latte' set. Handy places for lunch or dinner include *Green Fern café-restaurant* for authentic Asian fare, while just a little further along the road *Arrivederci* means what the name implies. Both are licensed.

DAY TRIPS FROM BRISBANE

To the Coast

Frequent local trains serve **Sandgate** on Bramble Bay and **Shorncliffe** on Moreton Bay, also **Lota** on Waterloo Bay, and **Ormiston** and **Cleveland** on Raby Bay. Journey times vary from 30 to 50 minutes (C 9015). These bayside suburbs are all on part of the greater Moreton Bay and are more in the nature of commuter suburbs than coastal resorts. From Cleveland, Stradbroke Ferries operates a water taxi service to **Stradbroke Island**, with a courtesy bus from the railway station to the ferry terminal, and from Caboolture, 60 minutes by City train, buses connect to **Bribie Island** (40 minutes).

Day trips (or longer) by catamaran to Moreton Island for the Wild Dolphin Resort at Tangalooma can be made from Brisbane's Pinkenba jetty (courtesy buses from Roma St Transit Centre); the fare is $30. Whale-watching cruises are also offered during the migratory season, usually August to October. Prices range from $75 ($40 for under 15s). Whale-watching tours also operate from Redcliffe, 30 minutes from Brisbane by Hornibrook Bus Lines. Details of all such tours and many others can be obtained at the Transit Centre, Roma St station.

The Citytrain network extends to the **Gold Coast**. Half-hourly express trains serve Coomera, Helensvale, Nerang and Robina. Local timetables give full details and reduced fares are available at the weekend.

The **Gold Coast**, of which Surfers Paradise is the heart, is noted for its surf beaches, its mountainous hinterland, sailing on the Broadwater, the many islands, the famous 'meter maids' in the main shopping area, its casino, and its excellent restaurants. Queensland seafoods are a speciality; try Queensland mud crab or Moreton Bay bugs.

The current terminus of the QR Gold Coast Railway at Robina near Mudgeeraba in the Gold Coast hinterland is 7km west of Mermaid Beach, but there are proposals for an extension further south to Coolangatta. The Interurban Multiple-unit trains of the Gold Coast line are capable of 140km/h though start-to-stop speeds are substantially lower. At intermediate stations on the line between Helensvale and Beenleigh there are connecting buses to local attractions such as Dreamworld (see p265) at

---

❏ **Prices in this book – Australian dollars**
Note that all prices quoted in this book are given in Australian dollars unless otherwise indicated. The current exchange rate is Australian $1 to US$0.58 or UK£0.38. For up-to-the-minute rates visit **www.xe.net/currency**.

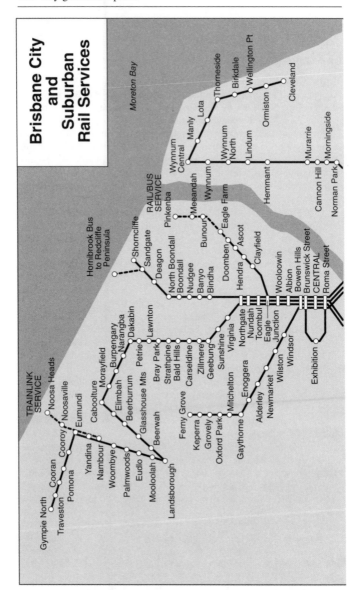

Brisbane City
and
Suburban
Rail Services

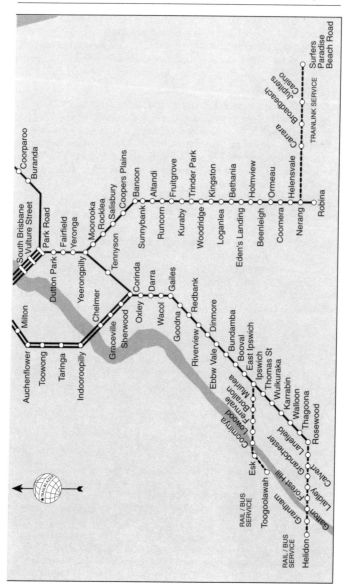

Coomera, a major entertainment park, whilst at Nerang there are connecting buses to and from Surfers Paradise and Broadbeach.

Gold Coast attractions include Seaworld at Main Beach, Warner Bros Movie World at Oxenford, Jupiter's Casino at Broadbeach and Currumbin Wildlife Sanctuary; all are accessible by local Surfside buses.

To the west

Helidon is worth a visit for its mineral springs but apart from the Westlander on two evenings a week, it is now accessible only by bus from Ipswich, although passengers with a rail ticket are allowed a discount. If you don't like natural mineral water there is a pub just opposite the station and a coffee shop a hundred metres down a street of colourful jacaranda trees. Otherwise **Rosewood** is as far west as you can go in a day by rail at the present time.

To the north

Beerwah is the station for Australia Zoo (☎ 07-5494 1134, 🖹 07-5494 8604, 🖳 qreptile@ozemail.com.au), famed internationally for TV's *Crocodile Hunter* series featuring Steve and Terri Irwin. The zoo is open daily except Christmas Day from 08.30 to 16.00, admission is $13; there is a café and shopping facilities, and a courtesy bus will meet the train. The Citytrain Sunshine Coast service runs on average every 95 minutes from 05.34 to 21.23 on weekdays, with slightly fewer runs at weekends. Journey time ranges from 70 minutes (for a through train) to 100 minutes when a change is needed at Caboolture.

Nambour, approximately two hours by QR interurban electric trains, is another good place for a break of journey or day trip, being the gateway to the Sunshine and Sun Coast resorts. A QR Trainlink bus connects with most trains at Nambour for **Noosa** on the Sunshine Coast (C 9015). There

---

❏ **Deadline departures**

Evening deadline departure times from Roma St are:

17.00	The Tilt Train to Bundaberg
18.25	The Spirit of the Outback to Longreach
18.55	The Spirit of the Tropics to Townsville
19.20	The Westlander to Charleville

The Westlander may be joined (with prior booking) at Corinda (19.34); Ipswich (20.03) or Rosewood (20.19), while the North Coast trains may all be joined at Caboolture, Nambour, Cooroy or Gympie North.

Most long-distance trains from Brisbane leave in the morning, including the interstate service to Sydney. This leaves from platform 1. All other long-distance trains leave from platform 10, except the Westlander which leaves from platform 2. You should allow a good ten minutes to cross to platform 10 with your luggage from the suburban platforms or from the coach station. If you are travelling on the Great South Pacific Express you will be escorted to the right platform from your check-in at the Heritage Hotel.

are also connections from **Eumundi**. Sunshine Coast Sunbus services (☎ 131 230) meet most train arrivals and departures at Landsborough for Caloundra and Maroochydore, at Nambour for Buderim, Coolum Beach, Alexandra Headland, Perigian and just about the whole of the Sunshine Coast and at Cooroy for Tewantin and Noosa Heads.

A short bus ride from Nambour will bring you to the Big Pineapple complex where you can buy local products and ride a cane train (see p263) through the pineapple plantation. If your itinerary includes time for a whole day in this area, you do not need to hire a car or take a cab as buses operate roughly hourly between Nambour and Maroochydore and the Sun Coast at Noosa. Worth visiting are the coloured sands of Cooloola National Park and there are many excellent beaches within easy striking distance.

The world's largest ginger factory (☎ 07-5494 1555) is on Pioneer Road, **Yandina**, 8km north of Nambour. It is open daily 08.30 to 16.30 except on certain public holidays; there are ginger and macadamia nut products for sale, a restaurant, gardens, a wildlife enclosure and an internal narrow-gauge cane railway (see p267). Interurban trains of QR serve Yandina, but not frequently (see Table 17, p267).

Cooray and Gympie trains (C 9013, 9015)

Cooroy and **Gympie** are within day-return distance of Brisbane but not conveniently by Citytrain. The former is a small friendly town, its centre adjoining the station, where two pubs and the local RSL club combine to tempt visitors to enjoy a lunch break; for comments on Gympie see p229.

Train services on this part of the North Coast line have been altered several times in the last three years and up-to-date details should be checked locally before travel (C 9013, 9015). The table below is a sum-

❏ Cooroy and Gympie trains		
Monday	Brisbane 08.25	Cooroy 10.56 to 14.50, return arr 17.00 Gympie N 11.39 to 12.07, return arr 14.40
Tuesday	Brisbane 08.25	Cooroy 10.56 to 14.50, return arr 17.00 Gympie N 11.39 to 12.40, return arr 16.10
Wednesday	Brisbane 10.30	Cooroy 12.18 to 14.50, return arr 17.00
Thursday	Brisbane 08.25	Cooroy 10.56 to 14.50, return arr 17.00 Gympie N 11.39 to 12.07, return arr 14.40
Friday	Brisbane 10.30	Cooroy 12.18 to 14.50, return arr 17.00
Saturday	Brisbane 07.30	Cooroy 10.02 to 12.43, return arr 14.40 Gympie N 10.40 to 12.07, return arr 14.40
Sunday	Brisbane 08.25 Brisbane 10.30	Gympie N 11.39 to 16.20, return arr 19.14 Cooroy 12.18 to 16.59, return arr 19.14

mary of day return possibilities as at the time of publication. Most services require prior booking, usually only a day or two in advance. All times for Brisbane in the table (p159) refer to Roma St station. This summary gives the longest (or only) possible time available at the places named on the days indicated, by **day return** travel.

See also Other excursions in the Brisbane area, p263.

Adelaide

ORIENTATION

Adelaide is the City of Light, its site being chosen and original plan drawn by surveyor Colonel William Light in 1836. For a panoramic view of Adelaide go to Light's Vision on Montefiore Hill, just three kilometres north of the central station.

There is a fairly comprehensive network of suburban services, including buses and a tram in the Adelaide area but from long-distance trains you have first to get to a local station. The main city station, on North Terrace, is 3km from the interstate terminal at Keswick; therefore you must first go (a 10-minute walk) to the suburban platform at Keswick. The railway planners have rather overlooked the passengers' need for a direct link between platforms and many of the local trains do not stop at Keswick. Check the times first and consider the expensive option of taking a taxi, or the airport bus (see p101).

Having reached the suburban platform expect to wait up to an hour for a local train. The service is roughly every 30 minutes between 06.20 and 18.50 on weekdays and hourly between 08.00 and 23.00 on Saturdays, Sundays and holidays. You have to walk just as far if you want to catch a city bus. Leave your heavy luggage in a locker at the Great Southern terminal if you are in Adelaide only for the day.

A free booklet *Adelaide and attractions* is published regularly by Countrywide Tourist Promotions P/L, (☎ 08-8232 5433). Numerous half-day, day or longer tours are available by coach from central Adelaide. Adelaide Sightseeing Travel Centre (☎ 08-8231 4144, 🖹 08-8410 2269, 🖳 adelsight@macbbs.com.au and 🖳 www.adelaidesightseeing.com.au) is at 101 Franklin St (the Greyhound terminal).

The South Australian Tourist Commission Travel Centre (☎ 08-8463 4500 or ☎ 1300 655 276), diagonally opposite the city station at 1 King

---

(**Opposite**) **Top**: The Glenelg tram; this is Australia's only remaining inter-urban tramway (see pp165 and 268). **Bottom**: The Brisbane skyline from South Bank.

William St) has maps and information and provides a booking service. It also has details and prices for state-run tours to sights such as Cleland Conservation Park (where you can hold koalas and feed kangaroos), the National Park and beaches, Torrens Gorge, Morialta Falls, and the wineries of the Barossa Valley and the Southern Vales. At Barossa Junction, old railway carriages make an unusual hotel and restaurant complex.

For details of the Barossa Wine Train see p58.

WHAT TO SEE AND DO

Once at the old city station you are in the heart of the town. Immediately adjoining is the new Festival Centre (☎ 08-8216 8600, King William Rd) with its concert halls and theatre, restaurants and plaza. There are hourly guided tours on Mondays to Saturdays from 10am. Take a cruise on the nearby River Torrens to the zoo (☎ 08-8267 3255, Frome Rd), noted for its birds, or try a ride on the O-Bahn guided busway, Australia's first, which runs through some of the parklands of Adelaide's 'green belt'. It passes close to the station, as does a local city centre bus. The O-Bahn, opened in 1986, extends for 12km to Tea Tree Plaza at Modbury and is the longest and fastest guided busway in the world. Service frequency varies from every 15 minutes on Sundays and holidays to one to three minutes at weekday peak; the journey takes 20 minutes.

At the east end of North Terrace the Botanic Gardens features spectacular water lilies. Near the station see the collection of prints, drawings, sculpture, graphic arts, coins and paintings at the Art Gallery of South Australia (☎ 08-8207 7000), and the Australian birds and animals in the South Australian Museum (☎ 08-8207 7500), which also holds the largest collection of Aboriginal artefacts in the world.

Rundle Mall in the centre of the city (one block south from North Terrace) has many attractive restaurants as well as shops. At 5 Rundle Mall is an underground opal mine: there is another at 33 King William St which runs at right angles to the Mall.

Historic Port Adelaide is worth a visit for its shops, Sunday market, boat cruises and museums. Suburban trains serve **Port Adelaide**, **Largs** (for Largs Bay historic village) and **Outer Harbour**.

WHERE TO STAY

Budget/mid-range

Two hostels that are worth trying, even though they are not particularly close to the railway stations, are *Adelaide YHA Hostel* (☎ 08-8223 6007,

---

(**Opposite**) Fremantle, historic gateway port to Western Australia.

Travel in the suburban area
Much of the Adelaide area, including the beach suburbs of Brighton, Seacliffe, Marino, Largs and Outer Harbour, is served by both bus and train. TransAdelaide operates the suburban bus, rail and tram services and Metro tickets are available in several varieties (zonal, multi-trip, day-trip, etc) covering all modes.

A local Day Pass costing a few dollars covers all TransAdelaide suburban buses and trains as well as tram and O-Bahn (see p161) routes, but not the various privately-run buses which also operate in the metropolitan area.

For all public transport enquiries phone ☎ 08-8210 1000 (07.00-20.00) or call at the TransAdelaide Timetable Information Office on the concourse at Adelaide city station, or visit the Passenger Transport Information Centre on the corner of King William and Currie Sts.

08-8223 2888), 290 Gilles St, and *Glenelg Backpackers Resort* (☎ 08-8376 0007, freecall ☎ 1-800066422), 7 Moseley St, which is near the terminus of Glenelg tram. Beds at both start from $15.

There are several hotels within a short walk of the suburban railway station on North Terrace. Among the cheapest is *Austral Hotel* (☎ 08-8223 4660), 205 Rundle St, where rooms cost $25-$35. Both *Ambassadors Hotel* (☎ 08-8231 4331), 107 King William St, and *Princes Arcade Motel* (☎ 08-8231 9524), 262 Hindley St, are two-star places which have rooms from $45.

Also on Hindley St, at No 23, and also with two stars though slightly more expensive is *City Central Motel* (☎ 08-8231 4049); rooms cost $52-59 en suite. *Festival Lodge Motel* (☎ 08-8212 7877), 140 North Terrace, a three-star hotel where rooms cost $69.

In Glenelg, a tram ride from the city centre, *St Vincent Hotel* (☎ 08-8294 4377), 28 Jetty Rd, costs $33/$55 (single/double) or $45/$65 en suite.

Up-market
South Park Hotel (☎ 08-8212 1277), on the corner of South and West Terrace, and about 15 minutes' walk from the interstate platforms at Keswick, is a four-star Flag-choice hotel with views over parkland; rooms start from $119. Another Flag-choice hotel, *Hindley Parkroyal* (☎ 08-8231 5552), 65 Hindley St, is only a block south of the City station; rooms cost from $260.

WHERE TO EAT

There are numerous eating places of varied ethnic styles (including Australian) in Rundle St, Rundle Mall and Hindley St, all within easy walking distance of the city railway station on North Terrace.

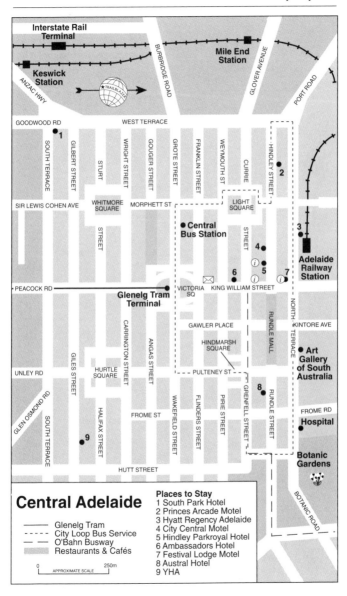

Interstate Rail Terminal

Mile End Station

Keswick Station

ANZAC HWY

★ TRAILBLAZER

BURBRIDGE ROAD

GLOVER AVENUE

PORT ROAD

GOODWOOD RD

WEST TERRACE

● 1

SOUTH TERRACE

GILBERT STREET

STURT

WRIGHT STREET

GOUGER STREET

GROTE STREET

FRANKLIN STREET

WEYMOUTH ST

CURRIE

HINDLEY STREET

● 2

SIR LEWIS COHEN AVE

WHITMORE SQUARE

MORPHETT ST

LIGHT SQUARE

STREET

STREET

● **Central Bus Station**

● 3

● 4

ⓘ

● 5

Adelaide Railway Station

PEACOCK RD

Glenelg Tram Terminal

VICTORIA SQ

✉

● 6

KING WILLIAM STREET

ⓘ

● 7

ⓘ

CARRINGTON STREET

ANGAS STREET

GAWLER PLACE

HINDMARSH SQUARE

RUNDLE MALL

NORTH TERRACE

KINTORE AVE

● **Art Gallery of South Australia**

UNLEY RD

GILES STREET

HURTLE SQUARE

PULTENEY ST

GLEN OSMOND RD

SOUTH TERRACE

HALIFAX STREET

FROME ST

WAKEFIELD STREET

FLINDERS STREET

PIRIE STREET

GRENFELL STREET

RUNDLE STREET

● 8

FROME RD

Hospital

● 9

HUTT STREET

Botanic Gardens

BOTANIC ROAD

Central Adelaide

—— Glenelg Tram
---- City Loop Bus Service
— — O'Bahn Busway
▨ Restaurants & Cafés

0   250m
APPROXIMATE SCALE

Places to Stay
1 South Park Hotel
2 Princes Arcade Motel
3 Hyatt Regency Adelaide
4 City Central Motel
5 Hindley Parkroyal Hotel
6 Ambassadors Hotel
7 Festival Lodge Motel
8 Austral Hotel
9 YHA

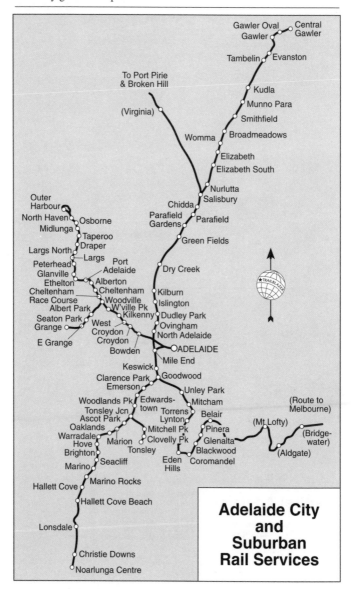

Adelaide City
and
Suburban
Rail Services

❏ **Deadline departures**
From Keswick GSR terminal:
18.30   The Indian Pacific to the west
15.00   The Ghan to Alice Springs
        The Overland, Ghan and Indian Pacific eastbound leave Keswick in the
morning.

DAY TRIPS FROM ADELAIDE

Among the many interesting day or half-day tours from Adelaide is the tram ride to **Glenelg**, about 20-minutes from Victoria Square in the city or from Goodwood, the next station south of Keswick (C 9030). Trams run about every 15 minutes on average. The fare is not covered by the Australpass but will not break you.

The Glenelg tram (see p268) is the only interurban tram-ride left in Australia and Glenelg, at the seaside on Spencer Gulf, is well worth a visit. At Glenelg North you can watch the sea life at Marineland, then stroll along the beach or take a bus to the pier at Grange. Try the nearby *Grange Hotel* (☎ 08-8356 8111) for an evening meal or night-stop, cheaper than in the city and only 22 minutes away by train.

Adelaide is not well situated for day trips much beyond the suburban area, but you can go up into the Mt Lofty ranges, known locally as the Adelaide Hills, by local train as far as **Belair**, 36 minutes, where there is a national park; the entrance immediately adjoins the station. The view of Adelaide's lights from this railway is particularly good and may be enjoyed by travellers on local services. Although the railway continues much further into the ranges, only buses now serve places east of Belair such as Aldgate, Bridgewater and Mount Barker (but see p270).

Perth

ORIENTATION

Perth is Australia's most isolated state capital, with at least 3000km of ocean to the west and about the same amount of desert to the east. Australians refer to residents of Western Australia as 'sandgropers'.

As Saltzman's *Eurail Guide* points out (despite its name the *Eurail Guide* has some coverage of railways worldwide), Perth is known for its 'wide sandy beaches on the Indian Ocean, with good surfing', an apt description. Take the suburban train from Perth City or East Perth to Cottesloe or North Fremantle (C 9037), the latter close to Leighton beach, formerly reached by a footbridge over the incongruous and now abandoned railway yards. Choicer beaches are found north and south, reached by Transperth buses.

East Perth Terminal is not in the town centre, but adjoins the suburban station of East Perth from where local trains will take you to Perth city station (four minutes), right in the heart and adjoining the bus terminal. A free city circle bus runs from here, but many of the sights and places you will want to visit are within easy walking distance.

Western Australia Tourist Centre (☎ 08-9483 1111, freecall ☎ 1300 361351, 🖹 08-9481 0190) has an office, open daily, on the corner of Forrest Place and Wellington St, just opposite the railway station.

WHAT TO SEE AND DO

Visit Hay St Mall, with London Court, a shopping area recreated as a 16th-century English street; the red London double-decker bus parked in the street is your signpost. Round the corner (to the west) in St George's Terrace see the historic cloisters and archway. Walk over Barracks Archway (the bridge over the freeway) and up to the 400-hectare Kings Park for the marvellous display of wild flowers and the view over Perth Water. Look for the old windmill at the southern end of Narrows Bridge, then stroll back past Parliament House, on Harvest Terrace, to the markets in West Perth, where the train will take you back to the city.

North of City station in Beaufort St see the exhibit of large Blue Whale skeletons, meteorites, Aboriginal culture and paintings in the Western Australian Art Gallery, and the old Gaol and Barracks Museum.

On the other side of the railway, Barrack St leads down to Perth Water and the ferry terminal. Look out for the lovely Georgian-style Old Court House in nearby Stirling Gardens, or take the ferry to the popular Rottnest Island resort, 18km offshore; ferries operate five days a week, daily in summer. See p271 for details of the Oliver Hill Railway on the island.

You can also go further afield by train. From City station the suburban system can take you north to **Stirling** (9 minutes), **Whitfords**, (17 minutes), **Joondalup** (23 minutes) or **Currambine** (27 minutes) on Perth's railway where much of the route is in the centre strip of a freeway (C 9037 and local). Or you can go west to **Bayswater** (11 minutes), **Bassendean** (16 minutes, see p270 for details of Bassendean Rail Transport Museum) or **Midland** (25 minutes), where you are near the Swan valley and you can take river cruises or visit the vineyards near Middle Swan. Suburban trains also go south to **Kelmscott** (31 minutes) and **Armadale** (39 minutes) on the south-west line to Bunbury. Transperth buses serve most districts and supplement the rail system; phone ☎ 136 213 for local transport information.

Perhaps the most interesting local excursion when in the Perth area is to go down the coast to the port of **Fremantle** (28 minutes) where the sta-

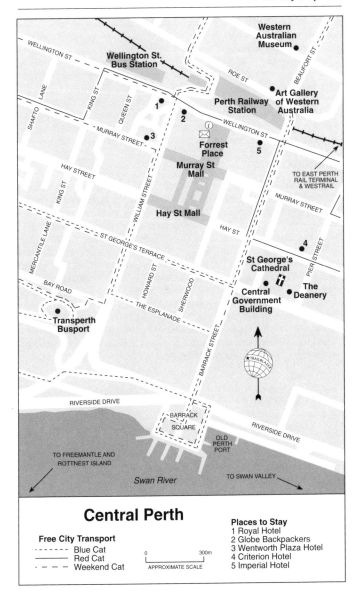

Central Perth

Free City Transport
----- Blue Cat
——— Red Cat
·— — Weekend Cat

0   300m
APPROXIMATE SCALE

Places to Stay
1 Royal Hotel
2 Globe Backpackers
3 Wentworth Plaza Hotel
4 Criterion Hotel
5 Imperial Hotel

tion itself, built in 1906, is a designated historic building. There are frequent suburban trains between 05.20 and midnight Monday to Saturday, or from 06.58 on Sunday (C 9037 and local). This is an easy half-day trip with plenty to see.

Here you can wander down to the harbour and on to the yacht club, home of the boat which took away the Americas Cup for the first time in 135 years (New Zealand has taken it since then). Visit the Maritime Museum and Art Centre and see the great views of the city and harbour from the Round House. Have some fish and chips at *Cicerello's* on the waterside before you return to the station for the trip back to Perth.

WHERE TO STAY

Budget/mid-range

The most convenient hostel for City station is *Globe Backpackers* (☎ 08-9321 4080), 479 Wellington St, which has dorms, single and twin rooms (a single with en suite facilities and continental breakfast costs $27). *Britannia International YHA* (☎ 08-9328 6121, ▤ 08-9227 9784), 253 William St, charges $16 for a bed.

One block west of City station *Royal Hotel* (☎ 08-9324 1510), on the corner of Wellington and William Sts, costs $30-$45. *The Imperial* (☎ 08-9641 1010) offers single and twin rooms from $25 per person and en suite rooms for $40 including continental breakfast.

Bayswater Hotel Motel (☎ 08-9271 7111), Railway Parade, Bayswater (11 minutes on the Midland line) charges $25 for a room or $55-65 for a unit with en suite facilities, whilst at Fremantle there are pub-style hotels reasonably close to the station.

Up-market

The free bus service within the city area makes it relatively easy to get to *Airways City Hotel* (☎ 08-9323 7799), 195 Adelaide Terrace, where rooms cost from $80 for a double, and to *Criterion Hotel* (☎ 08-9235 5155), 560 Hay St, a three-star hotel which charges $95-$115 for a room including breakfast.

Another three-star hotel that is worth considering is *Wentworth Plaza Hotel* (☎ 08-9481 1000, ☎ 1800 355109, ▤ 08-9321 2443), 300 Murray St. It is a short walk from City station; rooms start from $85.

WHERE TO EAT

Numerous eating places of are found at the *Down Under Food Hall*, Hay St Mall and the slightly more up-market *Carillon Arcade Food Hall*. For a good English pub-style meal, the *Moon and Sixpence* is a popular restaurant in Wentworth Plaza Hotel at 300 Murray St.

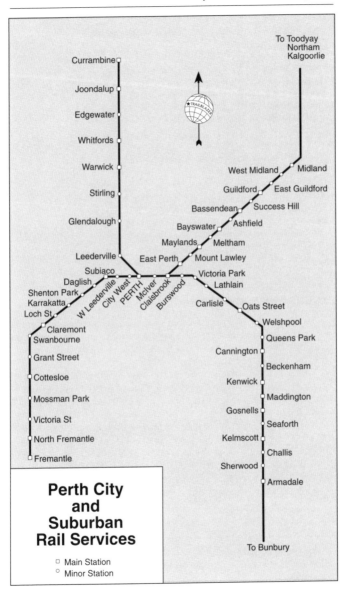

**Perth City
and
Suburban
Rail Services**

▫ Main Station
○ Minor Station

Table 13 Perth–Toodyay–Northam (C 9033 and local)

		Mon/Wed/ Fri/Sun	Tue/Thu	Sun	Mon/Wed Fri	Mon-Fri
East Perth	dep	08.45	09.15	14.50	1540	17.30
Bayswater	dep		a	a		
Midland	dep	09.00	09.40	15.05	15.55	17.45
Toodyay	arr	10.00	10.38	16.05	16.53	18.43
Northam	arr	10.24	11.00	16.29	17.18	19.40

		Mon-Fri	Mon/Wed Fri	Sat	Tue/Thu	Mon	Sun	Wed/Fri
Northam	dep	06.30	13.00	14.17	14.45	19.48	20.10	21.40b
Toodyay	dep	06.50	13.24	14.40	15.05	20.12	20.32	22.00b
Midland	arr	07.50	14.21	15.37	16.00	21.10	21.33	22.55b
Bayswater	arr	c			c			
East Perth	arr	08.10	14.45	16.00	16.20	21.30	21.55	23.20b

Notes:

All trains are one class only. Refreshments are available.

a Calls to take up only
b 10 minutes later on Wednesdays
c Calls to set down only

EXCURSIONS FROM PERTH

Rail excursions beyond the suburban system can be taken either on the south-west line to Bunbury or the main transcontinental route to Kalgoorlie. Transperth services may be extended to **Toodyay**, 93km from Perth Terminal in the attractive Avon Valley.

This would be a pleasant alternative stopping place for a night with accommodation close to the station. Even without an extension of the suburban services, a day return to the city can be achieved through Westrail's Avon Link.

Northam is another possible night-stop, though rather far out at 120km. If visiting Perth on the Great Southern there is ample time for a half-day or overnight excursion to Toodyay or Northam while the Indian Pacific is stabled in Perth. The Indian, by arrangement only, can pick up eastbound or set down westbound at Northam.

Table 13 above summarises the train services on this line.

❏ **Deadline departures**
10.55 from the East Perth Terminal. Allow a good hour to return from Fremantle.

Canberra

ORIENTATION

If your itinerary includes Canberra, or you have time for a two-day trip from Sydney, there are plenty of interesting features to see. Australia's Federal capital is famed for its layout and civic buildings, pedestrian ways and new towns which distinguish it from the unplanned city growth elsewhere.

Canberra railway station is on Wentworth Avenue, Kingston, about 6km from the city centre, so taking a taxi or local bus is recommended.

There is a visitor information centre (☎ 02-6205 0044, 🖹 02-6205 0776) at 330 Northbourne Avenue, Dickson.

WHAT TO SEE AND DO

Lake Burley Griffin (named after the American architect who won the original competition to design this national capital), and its 147-metre water jet (operates 10.00 to 12.00 and 14.00 to 16.00) is worth a visit. Concerts of the 53-bell carillon on Aspen Island are held on Wednesdays and at weekends.

In this national capital city you can see Parliament House (the new and the old), the prime minister's lodge, the various foreign embassies, the National Library (☎ 02-6262 1111, 🖹 02-6257 1703, Parkes Place) with its modern art display, the Academy of Science, the War Memorial and museum (☎ 02-6243 4211, 🖹 02-6243 4473, Anzac Parade, Campbell). An inexpensive tour is offered by ACT Tourist Bureau (☎ 02-6205 0666), located in the Civic Centre.

There are marvellous views from Mt Ainslie, Mt Pleasant and Red Hill Lookout. See the 6000 native Australian plants in the Botanic Gardens, the old locomotive bell in All Saints Anglican church and, if you have time, Tidbinbilla Nature Reserve 39km away or the rather delightful model English village at Cockington Green.

The former Canberra Monaro Express continued south from Canberra past Tuggeranong New Town to Cooma on the edge of the Snowy Mountains, where buses (State Rail operated) connect south to Bombola and have now replaced the train to Cooma itself. Cooma is a gateway to Mt Kosciusko, the highest peak in Australia, where the Perisher SkiTube (p259) takes tourists by funicular railway to the ski slopes of the Snowy Mountains National Park.

See p255 for details of Canberra Railway Museum.

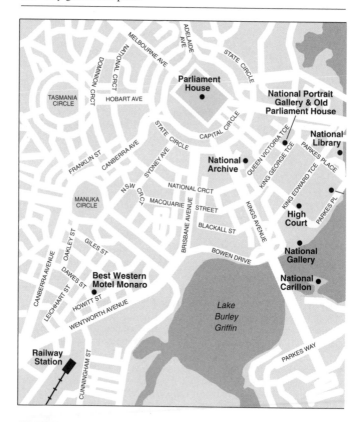

WHERE TO STAY AND EAT

Canberra is not well supplied with convenient hotels, being planned as a government city.

Canberra YHA (☎ 02-6248 9155, 📄 02-6249 1731, 🖥 canberra@yhansw.org.au), 191 Dryandra St, O'Connor, has dorm beds ($18) and double/twin rooms ($24); facilities include self-contained kitchens, a common area and a games area and a pick-up service is provided on request.

If you prefer to be located more centrally, *City Walk Hotel* (☎ 02-6257 0124), 2 Mort St, has basic rooms for $37-42; facilities include a kitchen for self-catering and an Irish-style pub, *King O'Malley's*, serving Guinness. *Kythera Motel* (☎ 02-6248 7611), at 98/100 Northbourne

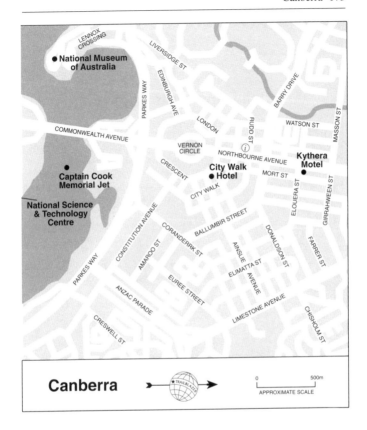

Canberra

0   500m

APPROXIMATE SCALE

Avenue, Braddon, has en suite rooms for $85 and both Italian and Chinese restaurants as well as a swimming pool.

Two places nearer the railway station, which is in Kingston south-east of the city centre, are *Victor Lodge* (☎ 02-6295 7777), 29 Dawes St, which offers accommodation for a variety of budgets starting from $18 and *Motel Monaro* (☎ 02-6295 2111), 27 Dawes St, part of the Best Western chain, where rooms start from $79.

Nearby Queanbeyan, 10 minutes away in NSW with thrice-daily trains and one return bus trip offers viable alternatives. *Queanbeyan Hotel* and the *Sunshine*, *Twin Cities* and *Wallaby* motels are all within a stone's throw of the railway station; for further details contact Queanbeyan Visitor Information Centre (☎ 1800 026192), 1 Farrer Place.

PART 5: ROUTE GUIDES

Using the route guides

The following route guides take the traveller along the routes in one direction following basically the order of Itinerary 6 (pp72-73). Major diversions from that route are suggested where they might be made.

Unless and until some form of automatic global positioning is introduced on trains a rail passenger is unable simply to press a button for a pointer on a screen map to indicate 'you are here'. How then do you find out? There are four ways:

● **1** Check the time and compare it with the timetable (if you have one). On some long-distance services a timetable sheet may be provided on the train.

● **2** Obvious, this one: look out of the window for names of stations, signal boxes or other railway buildings, place names on hotels, garages or other buildings or road signs.

● **3** Look out for line-side distance markers (kilometre posts). These will be little white boards low down close to the track on either side. You need to watch out for them. There should be one every kilometre but there is a problem in that the base point, 0km, may not be the place you started from. Usually but not always it will be a main station and you will not know where it is. Also, as they are intended as identification points for railway operation they may or may not represent the true distance from anywhere because such things as alterations to train workings or yard location and track realignments can change distances.

● **4** Ask the passenger attendant if there is one (and there is nearly always some railway person on board).

Distances where given in the following route guides, are from the starting point of the route described except where stated otherwise. They may simply indicate the length of named sections of the route being described. These are not 'sections' in the railway operation sense. The distances given, though correct, may not correspond to distances shown on kilometre-marker posts.

Places mentioned in the route descriptions that are in the suburban areas of the capital cities are shown on the relevant city and suburban rail services map in Part 4.

Trans Australia route

SYDNEY TO ALICE SPRINGS (VIA ADELAIDE)

Sydney to Lithgow   [Map 1]

(Distances given are from Sydney)
After Strathfield, the busy junction in Sydney's western suburbs, the train passes through Lidcombe, junction for the Olympic Park Sprint shuttle train; Granville, main junction for the south, then the outer suburban and historic town of Parramatta; this is commuter territory. Frequent electric multiple-unit trains (EMUs) serve these and many other intermediate stations but long-distance trains omit most if not all.

    Penrith marks the end of the low-lying urban areas, being less than 30m above sea level. The frequent service to town and **Red Cow Hotel** (☎ 02-4721 2030), over the road from the station, make Penrith a good base for the Sydney area. Leaving Penrith the line crosses the Nepean River, tributary to the Hawkesbury. The next station, Emu Plains, marks the 1 in 60 start of an 82km climb to the line summit at 1092m in the Blue Mountains.

    The short Glenbrook tunnel leads to Lapstone, the first of many popular outer suburban commuter settlements in the mountains. Rugged gorge scenery is visible on the left. The next station, **Glenbrook**, is in the bush but houses can still be seen. Around Blaxland your ears may pop as you reach the 330m (1000ft) contour. A vast expanse of bush is seen on the right and the highway on the left has now crossed to the right. After Warrimoo

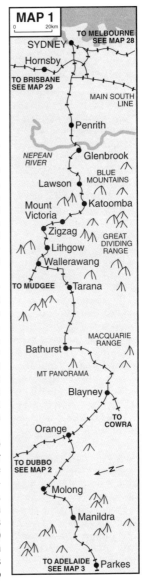

MAP 1

0   20km

TO MELBOURNE
SEE MAP 28

SYDNEY
Hornsby

TO BRISBANE
SEE MAP 29

MAIN SOUTH
LINE

Penrith

NEPEAN
RIVER

Glenbrook

BLUE
MOUNTAINS

Lawson

Mount
Victoria

Katoomba

Zigzag

GREAT
DIVIDING
RANGE

Lithgow

Wallerawang

TO MUDGEE

Tarana

MACQUARIE
RANGE

Bathurst

MT PANORAMA

Blayney

TO
COWRA

Orange

TO DUBBO
SEE MAP 2

Molong

Manildra

TO ADELAIDE
SEE MAP 3

Parkes

and Valley Heights the gradient steepens to 1 in 33 and the curves become tighter and more frequent. Speeds here, even for express commuter EMUs, fall to an average of less than 60km/h.

After Faulconbridge is a vast panorama of tree-covered plateau and wooded ravines on both sides of the line. It is best to be in the lounge or dining car on the Indian Pacific or Ghan for this part of the trip so that you can see out both sides at once. Look out of the window in the direction where the sun is behind you if it is morning or evening time.

Lawson appears as a little village, with a pub opposite the station. Approaching Bullaburra the panorama widens out to the north-west but for the most dramatic views keep looking out on the south side.

After Wentworth Falls and Leura comes **Katoomba**, 1000m above sea level, near the top of the range on the edge of the Megalong Valley. This is an ideal place to stay for a night or more. It is a stopping place for the XPT but not the long-distance interstate services. *Gearins Hotel* (☎ 02-4782 4395, 233 Gt Western Highway), Katoomba's oldest, is just behind the station on the north side and offers good clean accommodation at very reasonable rates ($25 single with shared facilities). There are many attractions in Katoomba – the skyway cable car and the world's steepest incline railway (see p257) but even if you stop for only an hour or two (say between the XPT and an interurban train) you can visit Kingsford Smith Park just across the road past *Metropole Guest House* (☎ 02-4782 2417) which is almost opposite the station entrance. In this lovely quiet wooded area a walk of even 50m in either direction will take you into a different world; with the call of the birds and the scent of the trees you really know you are in the mountains.

Around and beyond Katoomba are great views over the gorges. Mount Victoria, terminus and depot for many of the commuter services, is the base town for visits to the famous Jenolan Caves. Between here and the little station of Bell is the line's summit, after which the descent begins on the very edge of a ravine, with ten tunnels in quick succession. Between tunnels 4 and 5 you have a brief glimpse of daylight as the train crosses a short bridge over a deep gorge between high walls of bare rock.

Descending towards Lithgow look out, above you to the left, for the viaducts of the Zigzag railway, the original route by which the trains crossed the range. Coming from the east you will see them first on the left, then right, because of the curvature of the route. Now a tourist line, with steam, the Zigzag railway can be reached by road or by local train from Lithgow or Sydney. **Zigzag** is a request stop on the CityRail Blue Mountain service during the hours when the Zigzag railway is operating (see p260).

Lithgow, 156km from Sydney, is the first stop of the Indian Pacific and The Ghan. It also marks the end of the CityRail electric service and is an important railway motive-power depot.

Lithgow to Orange [Map 1]

Wallerawang (171km), the junction for the currently disused (but on promise of re-opening) Mudgee line, is conspicuous for its large power station seen north of the track. Further west, Rydal and **Tarana** are request stops for the XPT; the latter is a passing place with a loop line. In this area, particularly on the curves east of Tarana, you may notice double tracking but one line of this section is disused, abandoned and rusting. 12-chain curves abound and you will feel them.

On the downhill run into **Bathurst** (240km) you should see, ahead beyond the town to the south-west, Mt Panorama, scene of the Bathurst 1000 Motor Race held annually in October and November. Bathurst, the first inland city to be developed by Europeans, is proud of its old buildings, most of which can be seen on a walking tour. See the humble cottage where former prime minister Ben Chifley lived and the steam engine he drove as a railway employee.

Leaving Bathurst the train begins to climb again. After passing through George's Plains the gradient steepens to 1 in 40 and there are more 12-chain curves which keep the speed well down. Just west of the disused but repainted station of Newbridge comes an unscheduled halt (as far as the passenger is aware). At the lineside is a board saying 'replace electric train staff', marking the entry into a double track section. This lasts as far as **Blayney**, junction for the currently unused link through **Cowra** (see p257 for details about Lachlan Valley Railway) and Young to the main south line, but which is expected to re-open.

Orange (322km), birthplace of poet AB 'Banjo' Patterson, who wrote the words of Australia's unofficial anthem *Waltzing Matilda*, is the next stop; from here the Central West XPT turns north for Wellington and Dubbo and the Broken Hill 'outback' service rests for the night. These trains use Orange main station but the Indian Pacific and Ghan call only at Orange East Fork (see p125).

Orange, named after the Prince of Orange, is an excellent centre for exploring the Canobolas country (not a Greek name as it may sound but formed from two Aboriginal words – Coona and booloo meaning two peaks). The mountain of that name, some 14km south-west of the city, is an extinct volcano and is the highest point between the Blue Mountains and the Indian Ocean.

Hotel Canobolas (☎ 02-6362 2444, Summer St) has rooms from $30 and is round the corner from the station, as are the restful civic park, the post office, and the new library and regional gallery. Call at the Visitors Centre (☎ 02-6361 5226, on Byng St) for information on a walking tour of the historic buildings. Coach tours of the surrounding area coordinate with the arrival and departure of the XPT train; phone ☎ 02-6362 4822 for information.

Orange to Dubbo (140km)

The branch to the north is part of a line which formerly penetrated far into the outback of New South Wales and was the route of a train called the Far West Express. Its route included what must have been another of the longest straight rail lines in the world, 186km without a curve, half as long again as the longest in the USA. At one time it was proposed that this route be extended across the border to link with Queensland outback lines and thence on to the Northern Territory. 'Back of Bourke' is an Australian euphemism for the real outback, but now only buses contracted to Countrylink go beyond Dubbo, either north to Bourke, Brewarrina and Lightning Ridge or west as an alternative service to Broken Hill.

The station at **Stuart Town** is the first call for the XPT after Orange. Scene of a former gold rush and immortalised by Banjo Patterson's poem *The man from Ironbark* (its former name) this is a place where the casual prospector can still readily find a little 'colour' in a pan. The next stop, **Wellington**, is near Mount Arthur and the Wellington caves are within 9km of the town.

Geurie, 23km north of Wellington and the last stop before Dubbo, is a small town with some interesting antique and craft shops.

In **Dubbo** the well-preserved old Gaol is in Macquarie St in the town centre, a few blocks' west from the station and round the corner from the police station – so watch your step! Open daily from 09.00 to 16.30 ($5 admission) the Gaol features a self-guided tour and also has a souvenir shop. Almost opposite, on Macquarie St, is *Amaroo Hotel*, (☎ 02-6892 3533) one of NSW's Pubstay hotels, with clean accommodation and an absolutely first-class bistro with a good wine list; try the Scotch fillet if you like a large, tender steak; rooms from $50 en suite including breakfast. Other pubs, motels and hostels abound, ranging from *Backpackers* (☎ 02-6882 0922, 87 Brisbane St) which charges from $14 to *Zoofari Lodge* (☎ 1800 676308) at $180; that price includes free entry to the zoo and all meals. Western Plains Zoo is at Victoria Park, 5km south-west of town.

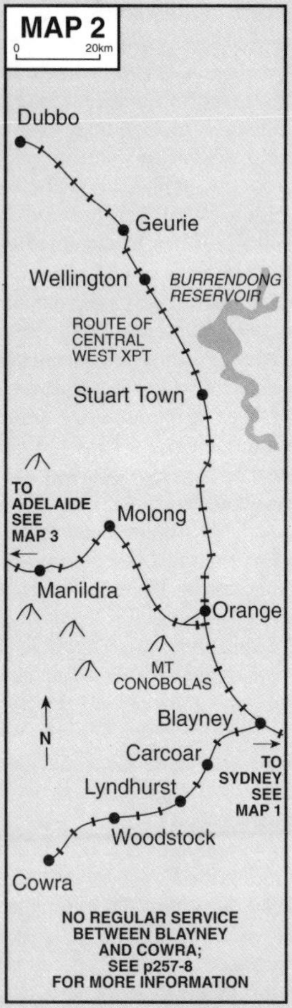

MAP 2

0   20km

Dubbo

Geurie

Wellington

BURRENDONG
RESERVOIR

ROUTE OF
CENTRAL
WEST XPT

Stuart Town

TO
ADELAIDE
SEE
MAP 3

Molong

Manildra

Orange

MT
CONOBOLAS

Blayney

N

Carcoar

TO
SYDNEY
SEE
MAP 1

Lyndhurst

Woodstock

Cowra

NO REGULAR SERVICE
BETWEEN BLAYNEY
AND COWRA;
SEE p257-8
FOR MORE INFORMATION

Orange to Broken Hill (802km) [Maps 1, 3, 4 and 5]

Formerly named Bushman's, **Parkes**, the first stop west of Orange, was renamed in 1873 after Sir Henry Parkes, five times premier of New South Wales and popularly regarded as the 'father' of Federation. Parkes was and still is an important railway junction. For many years the changing station for passengers to or from Broken Hill on the famous Silver City Comet, it is now reached by Great Southern trains at around midnight. The Broken Hill weekly service called during daylight hours and then only in the westbound direction. The town centre is just over half a kilometre from the station. About as far again to the north-east is Memorial Hill lookout, while 21km north of town is the famous Commonwealth Scientific and Industrial Research Organisation (CSIRO) radio telescope, open to visitors daily.

Condobolin, 547km from Sydney on the banks of the Lachlan River, is another place visited by most trains only in the wee small hours but if planning to take a break there, *Railway Hotel* (☎ 02-6895 2650) conveniently and logically adjoins the station. Between 1898 and 1927 Condobolin was the western terminus of the NSW Western Main railway line.

Grain silos, along with great mounds of grain covered with tarpaulins and possibly a few sandhills are among the features in a fairly flat landscape you may see by moonlight if awake on this part of the journey. By day in the distance you may see what appear to be sheets of water – such mirages are common in this part of the country due to the heat and flatness. During the night the interstate trains pass through **Eubalong West**, **Ivanhoe** and **Darnick**, usually without stopping except

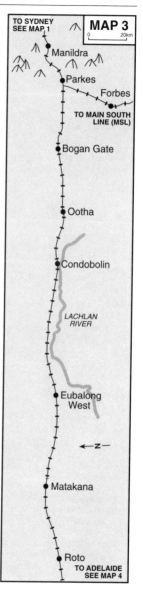

MAP 3

TO SYDNEY SEE MAP 1

0   20km

Manildra

Parkes

Forbes

TO MAIN SOUTH LINE (MSL)

Bogan Gate

Ootha

Condobolin

LACHLAN RIVER

Eubalong West

←–z–

Matakana

Roto

TO ADELAIDE SEE MAP 4

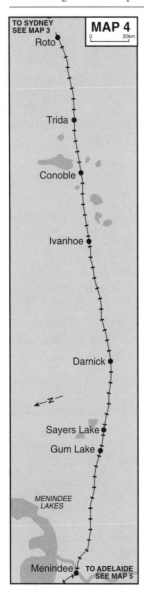

MAP 4

0   20km

TO SYDNEY
SEE MAP 3

Roto

Trida

Conoble

Ivanhoe

Darnick

Sayers Lake

Gum Lake

MENINDEE
LAKES

Menindee   TO ADELAIDE
                      SEE MAP 5

perhaps at Ivanhoe, but these are regular stops for the daytime Broken Hill train. Another stop is likely around an hour after Darnick when it crosses the east-bound Indian Pacific.

Travelling west on the Indian Pacific or Ghan you may see kangaroos and emus in the early dawn before or after you approach **Menindee** across the Darling River. The Menindee lakes, close by on the south side past the station, contain more water than Sydney Harbour.

Broken Hill (The Barrier City)

You reach Broken Hill around breakfast time on the Indian but earlier on The Ghan (evening if on the 'outback' train and in the afternoon on the Indian or Ghan returning east). The schedules of the Indian Pacific allow an hour or more before the train continues and a coach tour is available for $15. If exploring on your own, note the 30-minute time zone adjustment here, so beware. Check the departure time with the station master or train manager. Broken Hill follows Central Australian Time, half an hour earlier than the Eastern time of the rest of New South Wales.

But Broken Hill deserves more than a one-hour visit: it is worth breaking your journey to stay the night. Unfortunately this may involve up to a three-day break between trains. The range of options is summarised in Table 4 on p78.

Being built over rich deposits of silver, lead and zinc, Broken Hill is rich in mining (and railway) history and boasts some of the finest vernacular architecture of the period. Do not fail to look at the magnificent old *Palace Hotel* (☎ 08-8088 1699, single $28, double en suite $48), with its iron verandah, and ask proprietor Mario about the painting on the ceiling.

You can also visit without charge the wonderful Musicians' Club, opposite the railway station at 276 Crystal St; the saxophone chandelier in the entrance lobby is unique. See the collection of coins, minerals, shells and Aboriginal artefacts at Carlton Gardens and Art Gallery, and the restored Afghan Mosque, once used by the camel drivers imported to carry supplies through the region. If you would like an underground tour, you can visit the original Broken Hill Proprietary (BHP) mine, don a helmet with miner's lamp and descend in the original cage to the levels where first were worked what are among the richest ore deposits of silver lead and zinc in the world. Delprat's Underground Tours (☎ 08-8088 1604) operate weekdays at 10.30 and on Saturdays at 14.00.

Old timers will tell you that workers in the mines have an easy time of it nowadays. If they do, it is due in large measure to their predecessors who fought hard for the gains now enjoyed. Broken Hill workers were among the pioneers of collective bargaining and other social and industrial issues.

The Broken Hill Company itself, now known as the Big Australian, no longer owns the mines but the Barrier Industrial Council, a grouping of trade unions which once more or less ran the town, is still around. Trades Hall in Blende St is worth a visit to learn something of the Hill's industrial history. The main road from NSW Western Plains to Adelaide running through Broken Hill is called the Barrier Highway, but within the city this and most other roads are named after minerals.

Broken Hill Transport Museum (see p255) has a fine mineral collection as well as railway items. For details of other

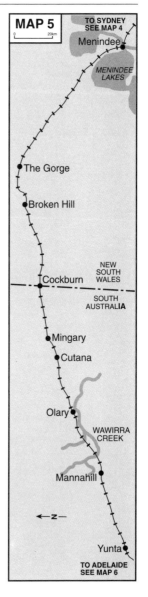

MAP 5

0   20km

TO SYDNEY
SEE MAP 4

Menindee

MENINDEE
LAKES

The Gorge

Broken Hill

NEW
SOUTH
WALES

Cockburn

SOUTH
AUSTRALIA

Mingary

Cutana

Olary

WAWIRRA
CREEK

Mannahill

←—N—

Yunta

TO ADELAIDE
SEE MAP 6

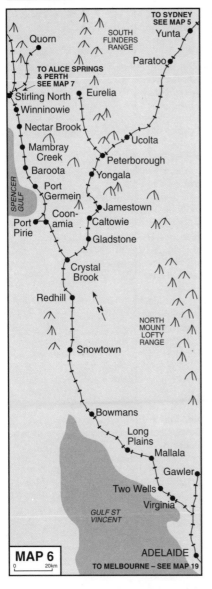

things to see, tours, free local maps etc contact Broken Hill Visitor Information Centre (☎ 08-8087 6077, 🖷 08-8088 5209, 🖳 tourist@pcpro. net.au).

Scenic air tours operate from Broken Hill to nearby places of interest such as the diggings of the world's only source of black opals at White Cliffs. Trips are also possible to Kinchega National Park and several outback stations.

Twenty-three kilometres north-west of Broken Hill lies the restored ghost town of Silverton and further afield at Mootwingee, 132km to the north-east, are Aboriginal rock carvings. You will learn perhaps just as much, but not see it all, by simply spending some time in the bar of one of this industrial town's many old hotels and talking to its warm and friendly people.

The oldest of these hotels, licensed since 1886, is **West Darling Motor Hotel** (☎ 08-8087 2691) at the corner of Argent and Oxide streets. It offers a variety of accommodation, attractive prices and good tucker; a useful adjunct for travellers is a fully-equipped laundromat.

Broken Hill to Gladstone [Maps 5 and 6]

Not long after leaving Broken Hill the train crosses the border into South Australia at **Cockburn**, 48km from Broken Hill.

For the next 147km from here to Crystal Brook there are traces of the old Silverton Tramway alongside the track. Before 1969 this narrow-gauge line was the only link between Broken Hill and Port Pirie on the South Australian network. On this 'tramway' eight-coupled steam locomotives capable of hauling a thousand tonnes ran up a 1 in 100 gradient, a real railway by any standard! As the late C Hamilton Ellis observed, 'A tramway is simply a form of railway and the term is ambiguous ... freely used to describe lines laid along streets, lines laid over the countryside, lines worked by horses, steam or electricity.' Conversely, the world's largest electric trams in fact operated on a railway named as such: the Swansea and Mumbles Railway in Wales.

Olary started life in the 1880s to service the road and railway but little is left other than the pub and general store. The train does not stop.

Peterborough, like its English counterpart, is important in railway history, because it is where three rail gauges met and passengers from Broken Hill formerly joined the train to Adelaide. Unlike Peterborough on Britain's East Coast Main Line, South Australia's Peterborough is now barely a whistle stop, but for enthusiasts there is an operating steam railway and museum (see p270).

Jamestown, a former junction with the South Australian broad-gauge system, is now acknowledged only by a slowing down as the train glides through the old station, now a National Trust museum. The surrounding country is noted for the Euro – not the currency of Europe, but the name of a thick-haired hill-dwelling cousin of the kangaroo, also known as the wallaroo.

At **Gladstone**, rail buffs have a rare treat: in the yards on the right are triple-gauge tracks of four parallel rails and a complicated system of points and crossings. Three gauges, standard, Irish (1600 mm) and narrow (1067 mm) met here; all were operational until well into the 1970s.

Gladstone is a centre for the wheat trade in this area and a request stop on the Indian Pacific. Look out on the left after Gladstone for the remnants of the former narrow-gauge railway between there and Port Pirie.

Crystal Brook to Adelaide (195km) [Map 6]

At **Crystal Brook** the trains now leave the Sydney–Perth direct route for a diversion to Adelaide, which replaced Port Pirie as the turning point after the link to Adelaide was standardised. En route to Adelaide's outer northern suburbs the line passes through rich South Australian farming country with Spencer Gulf to the right and the Mt Lofty ranges to the left.

After Adelaide, the Indian Pacific and The Ghan from Sydney now retrace 195km of their route; this happens in both directions. Refreshed by the break in South Australia's capital city, you may now have time to notice things you may have missed on the inward journey. After leaving Adelaide's Keswick terminal note on the right the lines to the original station, now the suburban terminal. See the way the edge of the city stands out behind a 'green wedge' on the right as you continue north to the planned suburb of Salisbury and past a Royal Australian Air Force base. You may see some camels in enclosed paddocks, a reminder of earlier transport on the north–south route. A few are still around but many escaped into the wild and roam the Central Australian desert. Packs of wild camels are seen nowhere else in the world, but some are now collected and farmed; eye fillet of camel is worth tasting.

Adelaide to Port Augusta [Maps 6 and 7]

After leaving the Adelaide environs the train passes through **Bowmans**, at the head of Gulf St Vincent, **Snowtown**, a major junction in narrow-gauge days and former stop, and Crystal Brook, where the line rejoins the Broken Hill–Port Pirie route.

Coonamia is now the station for **Port Pirie**, the latter being reached by railway bus (about 3km). The town itself is worth visiting to see the former station's long platform and, down the main street, the original station preserved as a museum. Port Pirie boasts the largest lead-smelting plant in the world; you can see its tall chimney to the left after leaving Coonamia. Little tubes of smelter slag containing traces of lead, silver, zinc and gold can be purchased in town. Port Pirie was formerly a compulsory stop on the TransAustralian route where three rail gauges met.

Between Port Pirie and Port Augusta, Spencer Gulf is close on the left and the attractive Flinders Ranges are on the right. At **Port Germein** you may see on the left the 4km-long timber jetty, relic of the days when the tall ships crowded this former busy port.

Four kilometres before Port Augusta is **Stirling North**, junction for the old route to Alice Springs via Quorn and Marree. The part between Stirling North and Woolshed Flat, a little west of Quorn has recently been re-opened by the Pichi Richi tourist railway (see p268). Stirling North is also the junction for the later

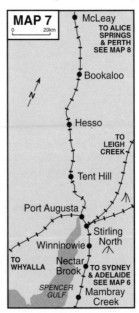

MAP 7
0   20km

McLeay
TO ALICE
SPRINGS
& PERTH
SEE MAP 8

Bookaloo

N

Hesso

TO
LEIGH
CREEK

Tent Hill

Port Augusta

Stirling
North

Winninowie

TO
WHYALLA

Nectar
Brook

TO SYDNEY
& ADELAIDE
SEE MAP 6

SPENCER
GULF

Mambray
Creek

standard-gauge route to Marree, followed by The Ghan until 1980 with a change to narrow gauge for the last 870km to Alice Springs. That line now ends at Leigh Creek coal mine, 245km from Stirling North.

Port Augusta at the head of Spencer Gulf holds an important place in Australia's railway history, being a major operating and workshop centre of the former Commonwealth Railways. It is still an important railway centre and worth a visit even though most trains now call only in the early hours or late at night.

Port Augusta to Alice Springs (1243km) [Maps 7, 8, 9, 10 and 11]

At Spencer Junction, a major goods yard 3km beyond Port Augusta, is a 73km branch to **Whyalla**. This branch line was approved for construction by the former Commonwealth Railways before 1970 and opened with great pomp and circumstance. By 1973 a daily passenger service from Port Augusta was in operation, using railcars and with a self-serve buffet, but it was withdrawn, then re-opened, then withdrawn again. Since 1979 only goods trains have remained.

West of Port Augusta the train winds its way at night through numerous sand hills and past salt pans and scrub forests, an eerie scene by moonlight if you happen to be awake. A brief stop may be made at **Pimba** but this is best looked for on an eastbound journey on the Indian Pacific when in late evening off to the left you may catch a glimpse of the disused rail branch to **Woomera**, 6km to the north, site of a Defence Department rocket-testing range. The name is an Aboriginal word for a throwing stick.

The train calls at **Tarcoola** (412km from Port Augusta) in the early hours but

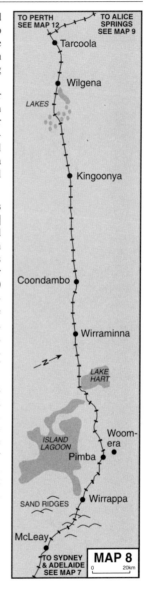

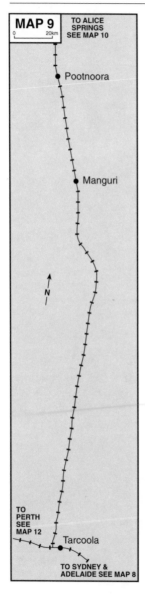

MAP 9

TO ALICE
SPRINGS
SEE MAP 10

0   20km

Pootnoora

Manguri

N

TO
PERTH
SEE
MAP 12

Tarcoola

TO SYDNEY &
ADELAIDE SEE MAP 8

in the evening on the way back east. Tarcoola has the only hotel (see below) between Port Augusta and Kalgoorlie, 1277km further west. The town is named after a horse that won the Melbourne Cup in 1893 and until very recently there was an annual horse race here on which there were reputedly no bets and no-one knew which horse won. To get the real feel of being in the middle of nowhere, step down from the train and breathe the pure air of the outback. The sky will be brilliant with stars. Before sunset you may· already have seen the stars shining against the brilliant red sky. Dawn will be similar, golden red above the brown earth all around.

Note that to stop off at Tarcoola it is important always to telephone the hotel first (*Wilgena Hotel*, ☎ 08-8672 2042). Remember this is literally in the middle of nowhere and people do not normally just turn up. If you fail to notify people in advance you may not even be allowed off the train. Provided you are expected, you will be welcomed and the hotel will be able to confirm your onward booking and check its arrival time.

Tarcoola is where The Ghan diverts from the TransAustralian route to reach Alice Springs, replacing the original route from Port Augusta at Stirling North through Quorn and Marree. **Manguri**, most likely noticed in the late evening on the return journey, is the stop for nearby Coober Pedy, famous for opals, where the daytime temperatures are so high that many inhabitants live underground.

Highlights of the line between Tarcoola and Alice Springs include the crossing of the Northern Territory border just south of Kulgera. You may see the signboard first thing in the morning or in the evening on the return journey. Then around 40km north of **Kulgera** look out on the right for the **Iron Man**, a monument to the railway workers who built the new line and where the Alice used to stop for photographs. This impressionistic sculpture of twisted steel rails and concrete created by the builders of the line marks the site of the millionth sleeper to be laid on this track, built in 1980 to replace the old flood-prone line.

Further on you are unlikely to miss the 15-span bridge over the **Finke River**; this follows a course millions of years old and although usually fairly dry, it can become a raging torrent after heavy winter rain. Finke river crossing is about the nearest place on the railway to Ayers Rock; it's only about 90km to the bus stop at Erldunda Resort and then less than a three-hour ride! The sheer size of Australia is brought home on a journey like this.

Approaching Alice Springs the train passes through the Heavitree Gap in the MacDonnell ranges, outcrops of special interest to geologists. **Todd River** is also close by east of the track.

Alice Springs (the Red Centre)

Alice Springs, capital of the Red Centre, is the current railhead and gateway to the Northern Territory.

By any standards Alice Springs, or simply The Alice as Australians say, must be regarded as part of the Australian Outback. It certainly looked like it in the film *A Town like Alice* although the scenes were mostly shot in Broken Hill and Silverton in western New South Wales. The Alice is over 650km as the crow flies from any town with a population of more than 20,000 (and even that is Mount Isa in far western Queensland). It is located in the very centre of the continent, nearly a

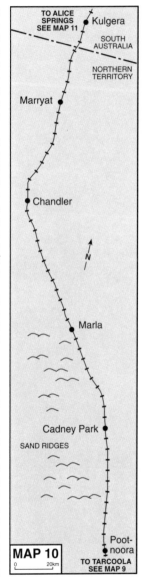

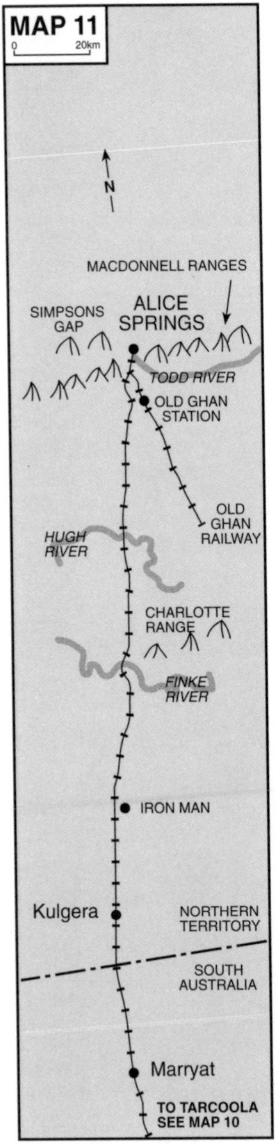

MAP 11
0   20km

N

MACDONNELL RANGES

SIMPSONS GAP   ALICE SPRINGS

TODD RIVER

OLD GHAN STATION

OLD GHAN RAILWAY

HUGH RIVER

CHARLOTTE RANGE

FINKE RIVER

IRON MAN

Kulgera   NORTHERN TERRITORY

SOUTH AUSTRALIA

Marryat

TO TARCOOLA SEE MAP 10

thousand kilometres from the nearest reach of the sea.

Even if you are on an out-and-back trip with only a few hours to spare there is still time to mooch around town. You can do a walking tour of the town centre in an hour or so; see the Aviation museum, the School of the Air, the Panorama 'Guth' and the Old Gaol, or walk up to Anzac Hill Lookout to view the surroundings. You have time for a couple of beers or a counter lunch in one of the excellent restaurants, where you may sample some of the more unusual meats found in the Northern Territory, like camel, buffalo, crocodile, emu and kangaroo. Eye fillet of camel is superb, whilst roo steaks are fat free, as tasty as venison, and low in cholesterol; try *Alice's Restaurant* in Todd Mall (also known as Scotty's Bar) for lunch.

A short way north of the town is the old Telegraph Station, site of the original Alice Springs and well worth a visit. If staying overnight you can visit the Casino, or try a buffalo steak with witchetty grub dressing in the *Overlander Steakhouse* at 72 Hartley St. If you have a car and would like a good lunch with wine *Chateau Hornsby winery*, 14 kilometres east of the city is worth visiting; it is the only winery in the Territory, whose waters come from artesian bores. For something completely different, you can indulge in an afternoon camel safari followed by a barbecue, or you can go out on a bush-tucker excursion to watch boomerang throwing, Aboriginal dancing and eat witchetty grubs live.

Coach tours and regular flights from Alice Springs serve all the surrounding natural attractions including Uluru and Katatjuta (formerly Ayers Rock and the Olgas), the MacDonnell Ranges and

Kings Canyon; Uluru is six hours by coach. If time permits, stay at Yulara, its modern township; there is everything from a Sheraton hotel to camping sites; you can listen to an Aboriginal folk group and learn how not to play a didgeridoo, or you can take a three-day bus pass from Ayers Rock Touring Company for conducted tours of the Rock and the Olgas. The Red Centre is not quite the traditional outback, but it is not to be missed.

An unusual bus service, the Alice Wanderer, offers a 70-minute tour of major attractions around the city, with commentary, including the Old Telegraph Station, the old Ghan train (p271), Anzac Hill and many others; the fare is $20 and it starts from Todd Mall in the city centre. The journey may be broken at any stop so the tour can be made to last a whole day.

If you are fortunate enough to be in Alice Springs at the right time of year, around the first Saturday in October, you may have an opportunity to witness its unique boat race, the Henley-on-Todd Regatta. Held in the dry bed of the Todd River, with contestants carrying their boats, this had to be cancelled in 1994. The reason it couldn't be run? The river was full of water!

TARCOOLA TO PERTH (ACROSS THE NULLARBOR)

Tarcoola to Cook (410km)   [Maps 12 and 13]
West from Tarcoola the landscape begins to change. Around **Wynbring** the track enters an area characterised by long sand ridges, which are the principal landscape feature for the next hour or so. This is the edge of the Great Victoria Desert which stretches 1000km to the north-west.

Barton, which the eastbound train passes around breakfast time, is one of a number of former railway settlements along the route named after former prime ministers of which Barton was the first; he was sworn in on 1 January 1901, the day of Federation. Barton is also close to an important Aboriginal ceremonial area.

Near **Ooldea** (pronounced Oolday) is the only natural source of water on the Nullarbor, believed to come from an underground river over 400km away to the north. Ooldea is where the construction teams building the line met in 1917. To the north, not long after Ooldea, you may see a vehi-

---

The way to the west – watch your time!
There are time changes between South and Western Australia. The train timetable follows the correct time, whether Central (CST) as in Adelaide or Western (WST) which, subject to the one hour adjustment when summer time applies in South Australia, is normally 1½ hours different; train time may not be the same. To even out the change and avoid things like having two meals only a couple of hours apart, the train operates in its own internal time zone and the conductor will tell you what time it is. Any clocks on the train will usually be wrong, as will your watch!

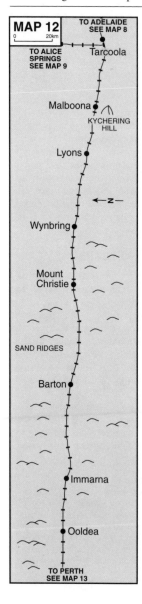

MAP 12

0   20km

TO ADELAIDE
SEE MAP 8

TO ALICE
SPRINGS
SEE MAP 9

Tarcoola

Malboona

KYCHERING
HILL

Lyons

←Z→

Wynbring

Mount
Christie

SAND RIDGES

Barton

Immarna

Ooldea

TO PERTH
SEE MAP 13

cle coming towards the track in a cloud of dust; the vehicle will cross the track at the next siding, **Watson**. This could be from Maralinga, 40km away on the low ridge to the north, the long-guarded site of a once-thriving township of scientists and service personnel. Maralinga (meaning 'thunder') is a place of shame. In 1956/7 a series of atomic bomb tests was carried out by Britain. Australian, Canadian and British soldiers were used as guinea pigs, entering the area just after a blast. Although the site was finally cleared of radiation hazard and rehabilitated on 1 March 2000 some personnel are still awaiting compensation, as are survivors from the unknown number of Aborigines then living in the locality. These literally did not count as far as officialdom was concerned (see p98).

You will notice that vegetation has now virtually completely disappeared. So have curves; if you were allowed to look out of the door of the train you would see that the line is straight as far as the eye can see. The Indian Pacific has now entered the longest straight line of railway in the whole world and there will be no more curves for at least the next six hours.

The long straight starts 705.6km from Port Augusta and 293km from Tarcoola and it extends for the next 477.6km, ending just before **Nurina**. Most of this whole day on the train will be spent riding smoothly across the Nullarbor Plain.

This would be a good time to get your 'train legs' if you started the journey in Perth, but if you came from the east you would be well adjusted by now. The only walking you need to do is backwards and forwards along the corridor to and from the toilet, lounge or dining car. You can stretch your legs a bit further at the next stop, Cook.

Cook

Around mid-morning, in either direction, the train will stop at Cook, where you put your watch back again (or forward if returning east). Cook (Queen City of the Nullarbor) is known among other things for its jail cells. These now adjoin the station; one for males and one for females, and they look very much like the little tin sheds people used to have at the bottom of the garden before the advent of piped sewage disposal. Cook until recently also had a hospital, but with such a small population (a few dozen at most) it was hard to keep enough patients (let alone doctors and nurses, one would imagine). Travellers were therefore invited to 'go crook at Cook' – the Australian colloquial for getting sick.

The resident population is now only three but they will still ply you with souvenirs when the train stops there for half an hour or more, as it usually does. Like souvenirs everywhere, not all will have been made in Cook. The Cook interlude is a good time to get out and stretch your legs, but don't forget to look along the track. You won't see a longer stretch of straight line anywhere. If you are able to look along the straight at night towards the headlights of an oncoming train, it is an unbelievably long time before it reaches you – but this would be possible only if your train is running extremely late, or you are travelling in the truck drivers' carriage of a freight train.

Cook to Kalgoorlie (867km)
[Maps 13, 14, 15 and 16]

Approaching the small siding of **Deakin**, about 139km from Cook, the train crosses the South Australia/Western Australia border. This, like other lineside features, is likely to be announced, but look out for

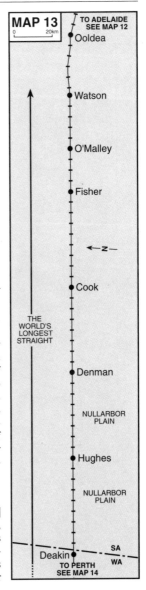

MAP 13
0   20km

TO ADELAIDE
SEE MAP 12

Ooldea

Watson

O'Malley

Fisher

←—z—

Cook

THE WORLD'S LONGEST STRAIGHT

Denman

NULLARBOR PLAIN

Hughes

NULLARBOR PLAIN

Deakin

SA
WA

TO PERTH
SEE MAP 14

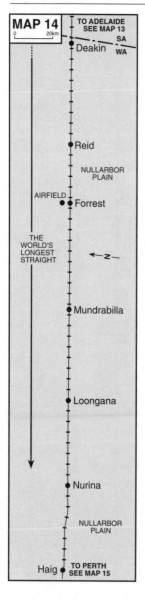

MAP 14
0   20km

TO ADELAIDE
SEE MAP 13

Deakin   SA
          WA

Reid

NULLARBOR PLAIN

AIRFIELD
● ● Forrest

THE WORLD'S LONGEST STRAIGHT

← z —

Mundrabilla

Loongana

Nurina

NULLARBOR PLAIN

Haig   TO PERTH SEE MAP 15

the welcoming hoarding at the lineside. Perched on top you may see a wedge-tailed eagle, the Indian Pacific's logo. To watch these mighty birds swoop down on seemingly invisible prey is an experience long remembered.

Around lunchtime going west or waking-up time travelling eastwards from Perth the train passes or may stop to allow another train to cross at **Forrest**. The name is that of a former Australian prime minister; nothing to do with trees, being in the middle of the Nullarbor – Null Arbor, the plain with no trees (Latin, not Aboriginal, as is sometimes thought). Forrest is noted for its international standard airfield, used during World War II and occasionally more recently as an emergency alternative to Perth.

Loongana is the last station before the end of the long straight. This was a watering stop in steam train days. It is noted for its stalactite caves which hold some of the earliest evidence of human settlement in Australia.

Rawlinna, the next stopping place going west, was noted for its social club, which boasted the largest car park in the world – space for a million cars at least: north, east and west from the club the empty car park reaches to the horizon and beyond – the Nullarbor plain. Apart from the station, the club and the railway rest house, there is not a tree or building in sight.

Zanthus, 169km further on was once a major stop for trains like the Tea and Sugar supply train, which in 1983 waited

(**Opposite**) **Top**: On the world's longest straight (the Nullarbor Plain). **Bottom**: The Indian Pacific stops at Cook (see p191) where you are invited to go crook. With the hospital now closed this is no longer good advice.

there for over three hours while the residents would do their weekly shopping, but the next scheduled stop for the Indian Pacific is not until Kalgoorlie.

Kalgoorlie (The Golden City)

Kalgoorlie, rich in history and present-day interest, is the evening stop of the Indian Pacific. The current schedules allow plenty of time to look around and there is much to see. A coach tour is an optional extra for passengers but many find it interesting enough to walk around on their own.

Kalgoorlie should be a prime choice for a stopover of even two or three days to appreciate its real atmosphere; Itinerary 6 (pp72-73) gives the option of a night-stop. There are comfortable historic hotels where you can stay the night (such as *The Palace*, *Exchange*, *The Old Australia*), some just opposite the station. There's another kind of accommodation in Hay St, to your right from the station; not very prepossessing externally, but it is said to include the very best in personal comfort. Coach tour guides will be sure to point it out but be warned – a night there will not appeal to all and it is very expensive.

More gold has been won in Kalgoorlie than anywhere else on earth and if in Kalgoorlie for even just as long as the train waits, follow Paddy Hannan's golden footsteps to his monument; he was the bloke who discovered gold in this area. You can also see the old brewery bearing his name, a historic building but, alas, no longer producing the pale amber fluid. If

(**Opposite**) The SteamRanger (see p269) which until 1996 steamed out of Adelaide. The SteamRanger Tourist Railway now operates between Mount Barker and Victor Harbor.

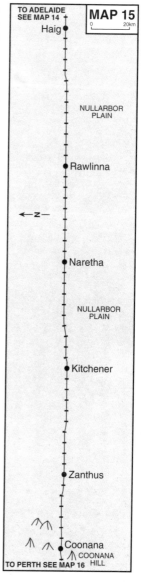

TO ADELAIDE
SEE MAP 14

MAP 15

0   20km

Haig

NULLARBOR
PLAIN

Rawlinna

←N—

Naretha

NULLARBOR
PLAIN

Kitchener

Zanthus

Coonana
COONANA
HILL

TO PERTH SEE MAP 16

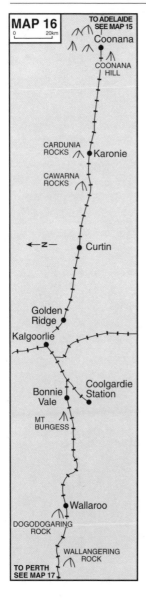

MAP 16
0   20km

TO ADELAIDE
SEE MAP 15

Coonana

COONANA
HILL

CARDUNIA
ROCKS   Karonie

CAWARNA
ROCKS

←–z–→   Curtin

Golden
Ridge
Kalgoorlie

Bonnie
Vale   Coolgardie
Station

MT
BURGESS

Wallaroo

DOGODOGARING
ROCK

WALLANGERING
ROCK

TO PERTH
SEE MAP 17

staying a day or more, visit the Museum of the Goldfields (open 10.30-12.30, 14.30-16.30), Boulder and the 'Rattler' train on the Golden Mile (see p270), Hainault gold mine and the lookout. The tourist bureau (☎ 08-9021 1966), in Hannan St, four blocks from the station, is open daily though at varying times.

While waiting for your train to depart you may see a freight train thundering by on an outside track. These mostly ignore Kalgoorlie, having their own stations at Parkeston (National Rail) 5km to the east and at West Kalgoorlie (Westrail) on the other side.

Kalgoorlie station has other features of interest. Notice the standpipes for watering the passenger trains; there are enough for a train of around 20 coaches. Some of the longest passenger trains ever put together ran on this route, when floods caused delays which resulted in the running of combined Indian Pacific/ TransAustralian sets. There are historical notes about the railways of this area in the booking hall and you might be interested to learn that Kalgoorlie boasts the longest railway platform in Australia still in use (526.5m), which you will know about if you try walking its length with your heavy luggage! Actually, the *Guinness Book of Rail Facts and Feats* states that Perth Terminal main platform is 762m. Someone has it wrong!

Some 40km from Kalgoorlie and 14km south of **Bonnie Vale** railway station is historic **Coolgardie**, well worth a visit if you are staying in the Goldfields region for a day or two.

Kalgoorlie to Perth (655km)
[Maps 16, 17 and 18]
Most of the line between Kalgoorlie and Perth can be viewed in daylight on the

return journey, or from the Westrail Prospector train in either direction. The views are similar on both sides of the train, but with slightly more of interest on the north.

Vast lakes and salt pans around **Koolyanobbing** are visible on the north side, as well as great mounds of salt at the lineside. Look out also for the vermin proof fence, a historic and famous feature of Australian outback regions which like so many other attempts to curb nature, was not a howling success.

Southern Cross is a busy town where in the southern springtime the surrounding area is ablaze with wild flowers. Named after the constellation featured on the Australian flag and vividly displayed in the night sky of the outback.

Merredin is an important junction on the West Australian narrow-gauge rail system and, like Southern Cross, an optional stop for the Indian Pacific.

If travelling west on the Indian Pacific, you will probably be asleep most of this part of the journey, and probably not notice **Cunderdin**, **Meckering**, or **Grass Valley**, optional stops only for the Prospector. Meckering was the scene of one of Australia's worst earthquakes, which devastated the town in 1968. A low escarpment which it created is visible in the area.

You should notice **Northam** if you're awake a few hours before the final approach to Western Australia's capital city. On the banks of the Avon River, Northam is noted for its white swans – these may be familiar to visitors from northern Europe but are rare in Western Australia, home of the famous Black Swan. If breaking the journey here, the **Transcontinental Tavern**, (☎ 08-9622 5746) just left of the station, offers cheap

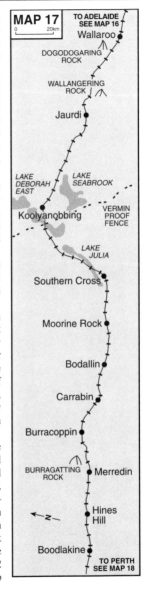

MAP 17
0   20km

TO ADELAIDE
SEE MAP 16

Wallaroo

DOGODOGARING
ROCK

WALLANGERING
ROCK

Jaurdi

LAKE
DEBORAH
EAST

LAKE
SEABROOK

Koolyanobbing

VERMIN
PROOF
FENCE

LAKE
JULIA

Southern Cross

Moorine Rock

Bodallin

Carrabin

Burracoppin

BURRAGATTING
ROCK

Merredin

Hines
Hill

Boodlakine

TO PERTH
SEE MAP 18

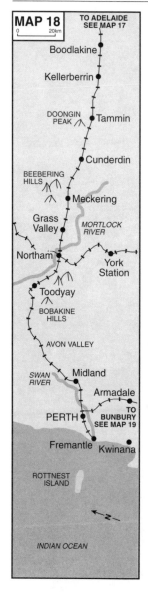

MAP 18
0   20km

TO ADELAIDE
SEE MAP 17

Boodlakine

Kellerberrin

DOONGIN
PEAK
Tammin

Cunderdin

BEEBERING
HILLS
Meckering

Grass
Valley

MORTLOCK
RIVER

Northam
York
Station

Toodyay
BOBAKINE
HILLS

AVON VALLEY

SWAN
RIVER
Midland

Armadale

PERTH
TO
BUNBURY
SEE MAP 19

Fremantle Kwinana

ROTTNEST
ISLAND

INDIAN OCEAN

($20) pub-type accommodation with a friendly host. For a breakfast snack, try the refreshment room at the station.

Look out after Northam for the picturesque and pleasantly-winding Avon valley with its brightly-coloured parrots and flocks of black cockatoos. Rail buffs will be interested in the combined-gauge track between Perth and Northam; standard and 1067mm (3ft 6in) gauge together. **Toodyay**, a regular stop for the Prospector and the express commuter service, the Avon Link, would be another good place for a night stopover.

Notes on Perth appear on pp165-170.

Perth to Bunbury　　　　　[Map 19]
Instead of staying in or around Perth, a pleasant day trip by rail takes you 181km south down to Bunbury. Commercial development, however, seems to be the main feature in the first 15km or so of the line south from Perth City station; the line is shared by Transperth electric trains as far as **Armadale**, 30km, where transfer can be made to the Australind service.

Mundijong, junction for a disused branch to **Jarrahdale**, is the nearest station to Jarrahdale National Park. Jarrah is one of the tallest of the Eucalypts, producing hard durable timber, logged extensively in this area.

At **Pinjarra**, 87km, the Hotham Valley Tourist Railway (see p271) runs to **Dwellingup** in the Darling Range east of the coastal plain.

Harvey is the centre of a fruit-growing and popular bushwalking area, close to Yalgorup National Park. Around this area and generally north of Bunbury the country is full of wild flowers. You can hardly miss them even without taking one of the special wildflower bus tours put on by Westrail.

Bunbury is now the most southerly terminus of the passenger rail system in Western Australia, although the line through Donnybrook to Bridgetown, some 102km further south was briefly re-opened in 1995 for an experimental weekend extension to the Australind service. Bunbury is on the Indian Ocean. Worth seeing are the basalt rock formations on the beach, the many historic buildings like *Rose Inn* near the old station (try a counter meal there). Commercial redevelopment unfortunately displaced Bunbury station to Wollaston, about 2km away, but a free bus service connects with the trains. See p270 for details of Boyanup Transport Museum.

South-eastern Australia

ADELAIDE TO MELBOURNE

Adelaide to Murray Bridge [Map 20]
(Note: distances given are from Keswick but may not correspond to present kilometre posts at the lineside owing to route realignment.)

The Adelaide–Melbourne line has never been noted for speed; the first 50km out of Adelaide reveal why. Minutes after leaving Keswick terminal the track swings east away from the coastal suburban lines to climb into the Mt Lofty ranges, known in this area as Adelaide Hills. At Torrens Park (9km) the line swings south-west bringing the coastline of Gulf St Vincent into view ahead. It then curves through 180°, climbing all the way up to Belair, 18km, which marks the present-day end of the TransAdelaide system. Suburban trains formerly continued a further 12km through the ranges past Mount Lofty and Aldgate to Bridgewater. This was a conditional stop

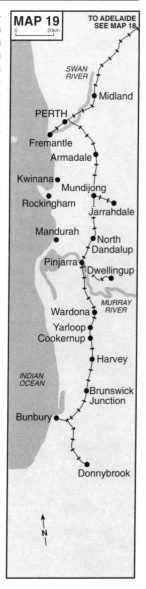

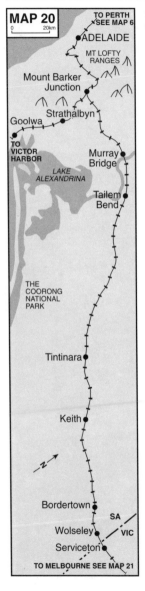

MAP 20
0   20km

TO PERTH
SEE MAP 6

ADELAIDE

MT LOFTY
RANGES

Mount Barker
Junction

Strathalbyn

Goolwa

TO
VICTOR
HARBOR

Murray
Bridge

LAKE
ALEXANDRINA

Tailem
Bend

THE
COORONG
NATIONAL
PARK

Tintinara

Keith

Bordertown

SA

Wolseley   VIC

Serviceton

TO MELBOURNE SEE MAP 21

for the Overland as well as for the then existing Mount Gambier Bluebird trains.

After Bridgewater the next places of interest are **Mount Barker Junction** (the northern end of the privately-run SteamRanger branch to Victor Harbor, see p269) and Nairne (52km), one of South Australia's oldest settlements.

The eastbound Melbourne Ghan, leaving Adelaide at 10.15, and now the rescheduled Overland, make it possible to see the whole Adelaide–Melbourne route by train in daylight for the first time in more than 20 years. Before its introduction late in 1998, most of the then 774km-journey was by night. Passengers could look back on the lights of the city (Adelaide or Melbourne depending on the direction) as the trip commenced and then wake to greet the dawn among the hills around Ballan in Victoria eastbound, or the Adelaide Hills of the Mt Lofty ranges westbound.

Still today, westbound on the Overland or The Ghan, passengers wake to an early morning crossing of the Murray and after climbing again up to Mount Barker Junction, the rail route winds down through the national park area of the Mt Lofty ranges between Bridgewater and Adelaide, giving views on the final approach to Adelaide over Gulf St Vincent.

Murray Bridge to Bordertown
[Map 20]

Just beyond Murray Bridge station (93km) the eastbound train crosses the 576m-long Murray Bridge, over the Murray. This crossing is 40km from the entry of Australia's greatest river system into Lake Alexandrina from which it flows into the Southern Ocean. East of the Murray lies **Tailem Bend** (117km), junction for some of South Australia's remaining broad-gauge lines. From here branches ran north to the Riverland irrigation districts around Berri and Renmark, major wine and fruit-producing areas. The present railhead is at Loxton, 159km from Tailem Bend, but passenger trains have not used this line since the early 1970s. Another branch still runs through to join the Victorian system at Pinnaroo but passenger trains had been replaced by buses even before 1970.

Tintinara (208km) and **Keith** (245km) are former stops on the Overland and were also served by the Mount Gambier Bluebird railcar until the latter's controversial withdrawal in the spate of rail closures in the 1970s. Now served only by V/line's Speedlink bus between Adelaide and Melbourne, these little towns are full of history.

Bordertown (290km) was never in fact on the South Australia/Victoria border which is 19km further east. Although originating in the 1850s as a gold-mining camp, Bordertown's main claim to fame is probably as the birthplace of RJ Hawke, former Australian trade union leader and one of its best-known prime ministers (from 1983 to 1991).

Bordertown to Nhill   [Map 21]
Wolseley (304km), originally named Tatiara which was the Aboriginal name for the district, meaning 'good country', is the junction for the currently disused Mount Gambier line.

Serviceton (312km from Keswick, 462km from Melbourne by the original route through Bacchus Marsh and Ballarat) was the scene of arguments between smugglers and customs in the days before the border had been accurately surveyed. The 1889 station building, classified (listed) by the National Trust, is

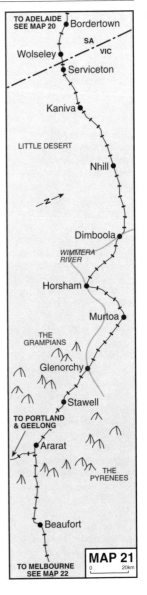

TO ADELAIDE
SEE MAP 20   Bordertown

SA
Wolseley   VIC

Serviceton

Kaniva

LITTLE DESERT

Nhill

Dimboola

WIMMERA
RIVER

Horsham

Murtoa

THE
GRAMPIANS

Glenorchy

Stawell

TO PORTLAND
& GEELONG

Ararat

THE
PYRENEES

Beaufort

MAP 21
0   20km
TO MELBOURNE
SEE MAP 22

built over former dungeons and doubles as *Serviceton Hotel*. **Kaniva**, (335km) was in the same disputed territory in the 1880s. It is also gateway to the area known as The Little Desert.

   Nhill, 374km from Keswick and 400km from Melbourne on the old route has three distinctions; it is exactly halfway between Melbourne and Adelaide on the Western Highway, it claims to have the largest single-bin grain silo in the Southern hemisphere and it was the first Victorian country town to have electric street lighting.

Nhill to Geelong [Maps 21 and 22]

(Note: From here on, kilometre distances are to Melbourne via Cressy, the new route taken by the Overland and Melbourne Ghan.) Distance figures quoted in the GSR *Journey Guide Book for The Ghan* may not all correspond with official route kilometres quoted here.

   Dimboola, 423km from Melbourne via Cressy and 412km from Keswick, is one of the few remaining stops on this route. It was reached by the railway in 1882 and was the terminus of the last V/line passenger train to run west of Ballarat, the Wimmera Limited. Wimmera is the name of the surrounding district, noted for waterfowl. Dimboola dates from the 1840s and acquired a certain fame from a satirical play of that name first staged in Melbourne in 1969.

   Horsham, 388km, regional capital of the Wimmera and on the banks of the Wimmera River, hosts conventions and sporting meetings. It is the birthplace of Kevin Magee, famed in the motorcycle-racing world. Wimmera wool factory is open from 10.00 to 16.00 almost every day of the year.

   Murtoa, 359km, considered the centre of Victoria's wheat district is a small town, with a population of about 1000, on the edge of Lake Marma.

   Although the GSR booklet about The Ghan mentions Stawell, the timetable sheet on the train does not; it is 15km after Deep Lead Loop (317km) for which the timetable gives 17.01 as the passing time. Accessible now only by V/line coach from Horsham or Ararat (C 9090a), **Stawell's** attractions include a unique chiming clock on the town hall tower, a 'world in miniature' and the winding Gold Reef Mall. This has been a good centre from which to explore Grampians National Park since the former railway to Fyans Creek, the heart of this scenic area, was abandoned. The Grampians are clearly visible here to the south from the eastbound train.

   Ararat, 265km by marker post but in fact closer to 272km, is the junction of the standard and broad gauge. It is 563km from Keswick and 211km from Melbourne on the old route. Ararat station adjoins the town centre. From here until 1981, Australia's then fastest train served Hamilton, **the** wool capital of the world and a good centre for a Western

Victoria stay. Hamilton is now served by bus from Ballarat (2¼ hours, C 9117), or from Terang or Warrnambool on the West Coast Railway (1 hour 40 minutes, C 9027 and local).

Maroona, 250km, is a junction where the line to Melbourne via Geelong swings east from the Hamilton and Portland branch which is now used only by goods trains.

You can watch out for Nerrin Nerrin (211km), Pura Pura (202km) and **Vite Vite** (192km) but these former stations will be hard to find. A passing loop should enable the vigilant to locate Vite Vite.

After the Berrybank loop (156km) the train runs downhill for about 5km to the crossing of the Hamilton Highway. About 8km south of the line from here as the train approaches **Cressy** (150km) is one of Victoria's largest salt lakes, Lake Corangamite. Cressy was once an important rail junction, the east-west line being crossed by a north-south link between Ballarat and Colac on the West Coast line. That route was abandoned in November 1953 and passenger trains have not served Cressy on the Geelong–Ararat route for longer still, the last train being a car goods train in January 1952.

The standard-gauge line from Adelaide to Melbourne joins the Victorian broad-gauge route from Victoria's west coast at **Geelong North Shore**, (72km) where a new platform was constructed in 1999. The various authorities argued for four years over who should pay for this since the interstate line was standardised. Although Geelong is Victoria's second city there is nothing much at North Shore; if leaving the train there it might be wise to have a taxi waiting; not all local trains stop at North Shore and there could be as much as two hours wait for a connection

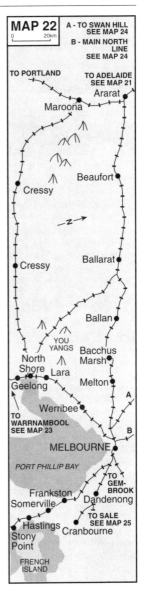

Geelong to Melbourne [Map 22]

North of Geelong is a major industrial area. Geelong itself is a pleasant and busy city with a throbbing nightlife. At Corio, the station after Geelong North Shore, Australia's own whisky was produced for a while. Very popular (it was cheaper than imported Scotch) in the 1960s it is rarely heard of today.

The hills to the left seen north of **Lara** (58km) are the You Yangs, of volcanic origin and a designated national park, rich in wildlife, particularly birds, koalas and kangaroos.

Werribee (32km) marks the start of Melbourne's suburban system. Bayside Trains operate the Met services from here right round the bay to Frankston. The route between here and Melbourne is marked by the wharves and industry which are mostly on this side of Port Phillip Bay. At Newport (11km), a junction of suburban passenger and goods lines, you are barely 20 minutes from Spencer St, so be ready to leave the train. On the Bay side of the train are Newport Railway Workshops (see p262) and ahead to the right you should see Melbourne's Westgate Bridge which carries a freeway over the Yarra.

For information on Melbourne see pp139-149.

Coastal and inland routes in Victoria

MELBOURNE TO BALLARAT [Map 22]

Sunshine (13km), in the inner western suburbs, was for many years the transfer station for passengers from Adelaide joining the daylight train to Sydney, the western line to Ballarat being the original interstate route.

Deer Park, Rockbank and **Melton** are in commuter territory though not served by The Met system as such. V/line passenger trains offer a service that is just enough to make work or shopping trips to Melbourne attractive. **Bacchus Marsh** (51km) on the Werribee River is the terminus for most commuter services on this line. The marsh itself was drained long ago and now produces vegetables.

The route west to Ballarat features a steep climb towards **Ballan** half an hour to an hour after leaving Melbourne Spencer St station, with views back over the lights of the city, specially impressive at night-time.

Ballarat (119km), one of Victoria's major regional cities, reeks with history. South-east of the town is the site of the Eureka Stockade of 1854 where Peter Lawler, later a member of parliament, led the miners in a revolt against government licensing policies.

The white on blue Eureka flag still symbolises this successful insurrection which led to the institution of the 'Miners' Right', an official licence to dig for gold. Attractions of Ballarat include the vintage tramway and museum (see p260), many historic buildings, Sovereign Hill (a recreated mining settlement where you can pan for gold) and the railway station; the station is a particularly fine building with arched roof, old-fashioned level-crossing gates, signal cabin and gantry, classics of industrial archaeology.

The Begonia Festival is held in early March, and there is also the Yellowglen Winery, specialising in *méthode Champenoise* sparkling dry wine of fine quality. The station is conveniently located in the heart of the city.

GEELONG TO WARRNAMBOOL
[Map 23]

(Distances quoted are from Melbourne Spencer St except where stated.)

Geelong (73km) is the starting point for the West Coast Railway proper. South Geelong is a commuter station serving the suburbs less than 2km away. West Coast trains do not stop here.

Winchelsea (114km) on the Barwon River has an unenviable claim to a place in history; rabbits were first imported into Australia here. To the south are the Otway Ranges. Fifteen kilometres beyond Winchelsea the railway swings across the adjoining highway to the small township of Birregurra (134km) at which only some trains stop. A 90° curve brings the line back to cross the highway again at Warncoort (the station is long gone).

The next station is **Colac** (153km) on the lake of that name; Lake Colac is the largest freshwater lake in Victoria. Colac Botanic Gardens are on the foreshore and the lake is a popular swimming and boating area. The town centre is close to the station on the north.

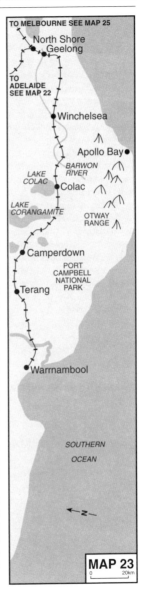

TO MELBOURNE SEE MAP 25

North Shore
Geelong

TO ADELAIDE SEE MAP 22

Winchelsea

Apollo Bay

BARWON RIVER

LAKE COLAC

Colac

LAKE CORANGAMITE

OTWAY RANGE

Camperdown

PORT CAMPBELL NATIONAL PARK

Terang

Warrnambool

SOUTHERN OCEAN

N

MAP 23
0   20km

The rich agricultural country around here is part of a vast basalt plain. Crater lakes abound. Pirron Yallock (168km) is at the southern tip of Lake Corangamite, the largest in Victoria and three times as salty as sea water. The station here no longer exists.

Camperdown (198km) is surrounded by crater lakes. The main street has a shaded avenue of English elms and is dominated by an imposing clock tower. Dry stone walls bounding paddocks around Camperdown are reminiscent of north England. They were in fact built by Scottish and Irish immigrants and dug well into the ground to stop the spread of the rabbit pest. Vain hope!

Terang (221km) is a rich dairying centre; Glenormiston Agricultural College is open to visitors.

Warrnambool (267km), marks the end of the passenger line operated by West Coast Railway. It features safe wide surf beaches and a look-out from which, during winter (June to October), the rare southern right whales can be seen coming in to calve in the sheltered waters. Flagstaff Hill Maritime Museum, seen on the right as the train approaches the station, recreates the days of sail. The nearby historic fishing village of Port Fairy (29km), Hopkins Falls (14km) and Tower Hill Reserve – a tour through an extinct volcano – are among the other attractions which the tourist information centre (☎ 03-5564 7837) in Raglan Parade will tell you all about; it is open daily.

West Coast Railway organises several such tours, mostly of one day but also overnight at weekends. These cover, among other attractions, the Twelve Apostles and 'London Bridge' on the Great Ocean Road, and a visit to Logans Beach where whales are most likely to be seen close by in season.

MELBOURNE TO SWAN HILL AND ECHUCA (C9032) [Map 24]

St Albans (19km) is the northern terminus of the Met's Hillside trains, although there is some inter-availability of ticketing in that Metcards can be used on V/line trains to Sunbury. *St Albans Hotel* (☎ 03-9366 2066) adjoining the station currently has no residential accommodation but is a good spot to break a journey for a counter lunch. The line from here to Bendigo was built between 1858 and 1862 and was one of the most expensive country railways built in Australia, being double track with easy curves and gradients (none steeper than 1 in 50), stone bridges and station buildings, a line of the highest engineering standard almost worthy of an engineer such as IK Brunel of Britain's Great Western fame.

Sydenham (24km) and Diggers Rest (33km) are the nearest stations to Organ Pipes National Park, which contains a wall of basalt columns somewhat reminiscent of the Giants' Causeway in Antrim, Northern Ireland.

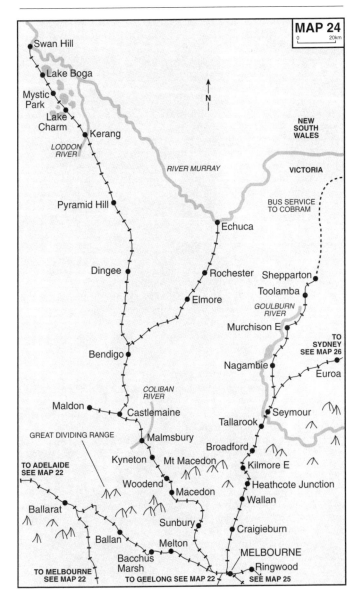

MAP 24

0   20km

Swan Hill

Lake Boga

Mystic Park

Lake Charm

Kerang

LODDON RIVER

RIVER MURRAY

NEW SOUTH WALES

VICTORIA

Pyramid Hill

BUS SERVICE TO COBRAM

Echuca

Dingee

Rochester

Shepparton

Toolamba

Elmore

GOULBURN RIVER

Murchison E

Bendigo

Nagambie

Euroa

TO SYDNEY SEE MAP 26

COLIBAN RIVER

Maldon

Castlemaine

Seymour

Tallarook

GREAT DIVIDING RANGE

Malmsbury

Broadford

Kyneton

Mt Macedon

Kilmore E

TO ADELAIDE SEE MAP 22

Woodend

Heathcote Junction

Macedon

Wallan

Ballarat

Sunbury

Craigieburn

Ballan

Melton

MELBOURNE

Bacchus Marsh

Ringwood

TO MELBOURNE SEE MAP 22

TO GEELONG SEE MAP 22

SEE MAP 25

Sunbury (38km), reputedly the place where test cricket's ashes were created, marks the start of the climb up over the Dividing Range with a 1 in 50 gradient for the first 2km after the little platform at Rupertswood (39.5km). This is possibly the only remaining stop on an Australian main line exclusively for school students, serving the Salesian Catholic College there. Look out for the superb old stone buildings of Rupertswood situated in park-like grounds on the right 1½km north of Sunbury. The foundations were laid in 1874 and Rupertswood is on the Victorian Heritage Register.

Climbing steadily through Clarkefield (50km), Riddell's Creek (57km), Gisborne (64km) and **Macedon** (70km) the line reaches the summit at 580m above sea level just before **Woodend** (78km), from where connecting coaches run to Trentham, Daylesford and Ballarat.

Mt Macedon, a 1013m-high extinct volcano and a forest park, is clearly seen about 10km off to the right, whilst about 7km north-east of Woodend station is Hanging Rock, scene of the ill-fated picnic. It is said to be worth the climb for the view alone.

Malmsbury (102km) is heralded by a magnificent bluestone viaduct by which the railway crosses the Coliban River.

A steep descent leads into **Castlemaine** (125km), now the last station before Bendigo. In the railway yard left of the track is a historic preserved signal box and behind that an old pub, *Railway Hotel*. Castlemaine is full of railway and other history. It is the junction for the old railway to Maldon (see p261), opened in 1884, closed in 1976 but since restored by a preservation society formed that same year. In contrast to the several 'recreated' historic townships, Maldon is a living example of a small mining town of the last century, where an enlightened local council maintains strict control of all new building. Castlemaine rock (a peppermint sweet, not a geological feature) is still manufactured here. It gave its red and yellow colours to the cans of a now well-known beer of the same name, Castlemaine XXXX, first produced here at Fitzgerald's Brewery, but now at Milton Brewery in Queensland.

The former stations of Kangaroo Flat and Golden Square herald the approach to **Bendigo** (162km). Scene of a gold rush in 1851, this city has a wealth of Australian history, perhaps typified by its magnificently opulent Shamrock Hotel. The original Chinese joss house is worth a visit. Take a ride on the tram (see p261), visit the pottery and climb to the top of the Central Deborah Mine. If waiting here between trains or on a day trip, *Café Spiral* just down the road from the station on the right is handy for a good lunch.

Large mullock heaps are a reminder of the 1852 gold rush which was the start of Eaglehawk (170km). Now a suburb of Bendigo, it is the junction of freight lines to Robinvale and Sea Lake on which the last passenger trains ran in the late 1970s.

Pyramid (249km), station for Pyramid Hill, featuring a pyramid-shaped hill of white granite. Stud farms and merino sheep are the mainstay of the area. *Victoria Hotel* (☎ 03-5455 7391) adjoins the station.

Kerang (289km) on the Loddon River borders an area of wetlands where protected migratory ibis and other birds come to breed. Sir John Gorton, Australian prime minister 1968-71, was a former Shire councillor here.

Lake Charm, **Mystic Park** and **Lake Boga** (307, 317 and 330km) are no longer passenger stops but the lakes and features of this area are clearly visible from passing trains. Caravans fringe the water line and the lakes are popular holiday and recreational areas for swimming, boating and fishing, and on Lake Boga, water skiing, wind surfing and the like. During World War II Lake Boga was an RAAF flying-boat base. A restored Catalina commemorates those days.

Swan Hill (345km), population around 9000, is a major market centre for this part of the Murray River irrigation area. Its attractions include the recreated Pioneer Settlement on Horseshoe Bend which features the largest paddle steamer to operate on the Murray. River cruises at Swan Hill operate daily between 10.30 and 14.30.

There are numerous restaurants, a military museum, and historic homesteads. *White Swan Hotel* (☎ 03-5032 2761, 182 Campbell St), a block and a half ahead, then right, from the station, offers comfortable cheap accommodation (rooms $25 to $40), has a good restaurant which is open till late and an Irish Bar, *Paddy Curran's*, where they serve real draught Guinness. Fridays and Saturdays are music nights and can be noisy.

Bendigo to Echuca [Map 24]

Leaving the Swan Hill line at North Bendigo Junction, the rail route to Echuca is almost straight and not far from level. It descends very gradually from over 200m to less than 100m in 86km, a mean gradient of about 1 in 1000. Despite such easy conditions, the average speed is markedly lower than the preceding run to Bendigo, possibly because the track saw no passenger trains for nearly 20 years from 1978.

Elmore (207km from Melbourne) and **Rochester** (223km) are the only intermediate stops before Echuca. At both places the town centre, pubs, banks and shops are opposite the railway station.

Echuca (233km) was the location for the TV series *All the Rivers Run*. Established as a working steam port in 1865, Echuca was the first port on the Murray to be reached by rail and is full of history. Numerous hotels, souvenir shops, wine-tasting places etc are in and around the historic port area. See the old wharves of massive red gum logs, the historic buildings, and the art and craft shop. You could also take a river cruise on a paddle steamer or visit Tisdall's winery. *Pastoral Hotel* (☎ 03-5482

1812), with motel accommodation, is opposite the railway station, which is a short walk from the town centre and port area, passing the visitor information centre on the way. The railway formerly shared right of way with the road across the bridge to Moama and Deniliquin in NSW, where passenger trains used to go.

At the time of writing, trains serve Echuca only on Friday and Sunday but this is likely to improve. Meanwhile there are bus connections to Echuca from Bendigo and from Murchison East on the rail line to Shepparton.

SEYMOUR TO SHEPPARTON (AND COBRAM)   [Map 24]

Seymour (99km from Melbourne on the Victorian broad-gauge route through Essendon) is the effective junction for the Goulburn Valley line, though the actual rail junction is at **Mangalore**, 10km further north. Seymour is a good place for a break of journey, the station adjoining the middle of the main street, with shops, pubs, accommodation etc right opposite. Cross the railway line by the subway at the south end of the platform so that you don't get run over by the train!

Nagambie (126km) adjoins the lake of that name, one of five in this part of the Goulburn Valley, rich in fauna and flora and catering to a wide range of water activities. Among the attractions of this area are several wineries, including some of Australia's best known. The railway station is on the edge of town, about 700m from the Central Business District (CBD) which is itself on the edge of the lake.

Murchison, on the Goulburn river, was established in 1840 and is the oldest town in the region. In 1969 an unusual meteorite with a cell-like organic structure crashed in fragments around the town. Murchison has another claim to fame, boasting the largest plane tree in the world. The River Bank Gardens, Strawberry Farm, Longleat Winery and *Gallery Tea Rooms* are among Murchison's other attractions for the visitor. The station (147km) is at Murchison East, 2km from town.

Toolamba (166km) is no longer a passenger station but was formerly the junction for the Murchison–Echuca line on which passenger services were withdrawn in the 1980s.

Mooroopna, 26km north of Murchison East, might be regarded as a suburb of Shepparton. This is the heart of the fruit-growing area. The Ardmona cannery, a name well known in Australia for tinned fruit, adjoins the railway station just south of the town centre.

Shepparton (182km) is home of the Shepparton Preserving Company (SPC) and famed for its SPC tinned fruit. This is also a vegetable growing area and the major city of the Goulburn Valley. The Visitors Centre (☎ 03-5831 4400 or 1800 808 839, 🖹 5822 2311) is at Victoria Park Lake, Wyndham St.

Cobram is about an hour's ride by Hoys coach from Shepparton, and if on a day trip from Melbourne, an interesting alternative to spending several hours in Shepparton. The coach passes Numurkah and Strathmerton en route. At Cobram, the *pub* at the corner of Main St and Station St, opposite the station, offers a good Chinese counter lunch and the chance of friendly conversation with the locals, many of them ex-railway workers.

MELBOURNE TO THE DANDENONGS
[Map 25]

The Dandenong ranges are accessible from Melbourne by the Hillside trains of the Met system as far as Lilydale, Ferntree Gully and Belgrave. **Belgrave** is the western terminus of the narrow-gauge Emerald Tourist Railway, popularly known as the Puffing Billy Railway (see p260), to Menzies Creek, Lakeside, **Emerald**, Cockatoo and **Gembrook**. The timetable and a detailed route map are available to passengers on this 25km scenic route; the information given is not repeated here. The line penetrates deep into the Dandenongs with many twists and turns, much of it in forest country. The large lake to the south between Menzies Creek and Emerald is Cardinia Creek Reservoir of the Melbourne and Metropolitan Board of Works.

There is a refreshment room and toilets at Belgrave Puffing Billy station, refreshment trolleys at Menzies Creek and other stops on the line. Opposite Gembrook station is *Ranges Hotel* (☎ 03-5968 1220); Gembrook also has tea rooms, craft shops, a motor museum and a working pottery. Rambles through the forest and organised tours are available and there is a souvenir kiosk with refreshments on the station.

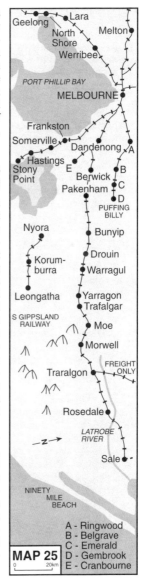

MAP 25

A - Ringwood
B - Belgrave
C - Emerald
D - Gembrook
E - Cranbourne

MELBOURNE TO SALE (GIPPSLAND LINE)   [Map 25]

The first stop from Melbourne's Spencer St on the Gippsland line is Flinders St (1.2km), for long the main hub of the suburban rail network. Gippsland trains call here to pick up only, as they do also at Caulfield (12km) and **Dandenong** (31km); the latter is an industrial suburb which bears little relationship to the Dandenong Ranges, 18km to the north.

Pakenham (58km) is the terminus of the suburban system. Among interesting places between here and the next major station, Warragul, are Nar-Nar-Goon (66km), believed to be an Aboriginal word for the koala, Garfield (75km), named not after the cartoon cat but an American president who was murdered, and **Bunyip** (79km), on the river of that name. Bunyip is the name of a legendary water-dwelling, man-eating monster believed to have inhabited the area. After Bunyip comes Longwarry (83km), then **Drouin** (92km), a major centre for locally produced gourmet foods and site of one of the largest milk-processing plants in Australia.

Between Longwarry and Warragul gradients of up to 1 in 50 flank the summit of this otherwise fairly level route. Recognisable by the way the 'down' and 'up' lines diverge just after Drouin station, the 'down' track reaches 19m higher than the 'up', at 167m above sea level.

Warragul (100km) is a major station, once the junction for a branch up into the hills of the Dividing Range. For long after the branch line closed in 1958 a board on the station announced 'Change here for the Noojee line'.

The major towns in the Latrobe Valley in Gippsland are Moe, Morwell and Traralgon. **Moe** (130km) is the main residential centre for the brown coal-mining area, where the site of a former town, Yallourn, was 'resumed' for coal mining. Moe is also the junction for the former narrow-gauge Moe–Walhalla branch, part of which has been restored (p262).

Morwell (144km), a centre for the dairying industry, is best known for its open-cut mine, producing around 15 million tonnes of coal annually, and group of power stations of which Hazelwood is the largest in Victoria. Morwell power station is also a briquette factory; coal briquettes have been one of the principal traffics on the railway for many years.

Traralgon (158km) is an industrial town but with a pleasant and quiet main street near the railway station. It is the junction for the freight-only line through Maffra to Bairnsdale in East Gippsland.

Rosedale (180km) on the Latrobe River is a quiet pleasant town; it is the gateway to Holey Plains State Park and the last station before the current line terminus at Sale (206km). **Sale** is the administrative centre for Bass Strait oil, which is treated and stabilised at nearby Longford. It is also a gateway to the Gippsland Lakes and Victoria's Ninety Mile Beach stretching from Seaspray to Lakes Entrance.

Melbourne to Sydney and branches

MELBOURNE TO BENALLA   [Maps 24 and 26]

The broad-gauge and standard-gauge lines follow different routes for the first half-hour of the journey north from Melbourne. The shortest route is the broad-gauge line through Essendon (10km) used by V/line, Hoys and Met services. The standard-gauge line, after swinging over the Essendon route on a flyover in the first two kilometres, runs west to Sunshine where a platform allowed connection with the Overland from Adelaide in its broad-gauge days.

Just beyond Sunshine at Albion (15km) the new route swings east to cross the Essendon route by another flyover south of Broadmeadows (17km via Essendon, 28km via Sunshine). In Assisted Passage days migrants arriving at Port Melbourne were first taken to an army camp at Broadmeadows via a short spur line just north of the station. Tullamarine airport is close by to the west. North from Broadmeadows the two lines run more or less parallel but with fewer platforms serving the newer line.

Suburban (Met) services terminate at Broadmeadows. V/line outer urban trains run as far as Seymour (99km via Sunshine) serving up to eight further stations as the line climbs through the tail end of the Great Dividing Range. The summit of 349m is reached 5km after **Wallan** (47km) at **Heathcote Junction**; the 60km branch to Heathcote itself closed in 1968. Further on as the line descends towards the Goulburn Valley is **Tallarook** where a former branch led east beside the Goulburn River into the hills around Lake Eildon, serving the townships of Yea, Alexandra and Mansfield. The first named of these was the site of the long-running Australian TV series *Bellbird* which occasionally featured a railcar at Yea station (renamed Bellbird for the occasion).

Comments on Seymour have already been made (see p208); it is a stopping place for all the broad-gauge trains. There is a platform for the standard gauge but this is used only in an emergency. The next stop for most V/line trains is Avenel (116km), named after a village in Gloucestershire, England, and the town where bushranger Edward (Ned) Kelly went to school. All V/line trains then call at **Euroa** (151km), a small town in a pastoral area around Seven Creeks, famed as the place where the Kelly gang successfully raided a bank in 1878. This event is re-enacted annually. Few trains stop at **Violet Town**, 169km, which is more a village than a town with a population of only 590. In season, fresh blueberries are plentiful here.

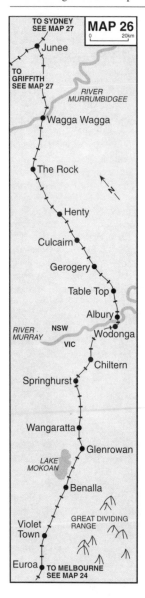

MAP 26

0   20km

TO SYDNEY
SEE MAP 27

Junee

TO GRIFFITH
SEE MAP 27

RIVER MURRUMBIDGEE

Wagga Wagga

The Rock

Henty

Culcairn

Gerogery

Table Top

Albury

RIVER MURRAY   NSW   Wodonga
                VIC

Chiltern

Springhurst

Wangaratta

Glenrowan

LAKE MOKOAN

Benalla

Violet Town   GREAT DIVIDING RANGE

Euroa   TO MELBOURNE
SEE MAP 24

Seymour, Benalla and Wangaratta are gateways to the Goulburn Valley on the west and the mountains (the Victorian Alps) on the east. The valley can be reached by Hoys Coaches' train from Seymour (p208) or bus from Benalla but the Alps only by bus or hired transport.

Benalla (195km) is a major stop, being formerly a junction for a connecting line through Yarrawonga on the River Murray to Oaklands in NSW. The standard-gauge line has a short platform down in a cutting just east of the station forecourt – not easy to find if you do not know where it is and the quiet XPT may not even be heard approaching until it arrives. So if breaking a journey here, be in good time for the connection.

The town centre of Benalla, with a bakery, eating places, banks, a well-stocked second-hand bookshop, and Benalla Gardens park adjoining Lake Benalla on Broken River, is about $^{1}/_{2}$km east of the station. Opposite the station is **Victoria Hotel** (☎ 03-5762 2045) and 100m or so down the road to the right is **North-Eastern Hotel** (☎ 03-5762 3252), with excellent food and motel-style accommodation at very modest rates.

BENALLA TO ALBURY/WODONGA
[Map 26]

Most of the way from Benalla to the state border the railway appears to be double track, but in fact it consists of two single parallel lines, broad gauge on the left, standard on the right; it is flanked by the Hume Highway. Lake Mokoan is the large watery swamp on the west just north of Benalla. Between Benalla and Wangaratta it has been known for the train to be held up by a character with an upturned bucket covering his head and armed with pistols; this might have been for real long ago but any such events nowadays are only re-enactments (usually at weekends). This meant the train had reached **Glenrowan**, famous in Australian history as the haunt of bushranger Ned Kelly; trains no longer stop nor are passengers robbed at gunpoint. To visit Glenrowan two connecting bus services operate to and from Wangaratta on Wednesdays only. A V/line Melbourne to Albury bus also calls there at 17.10 on Fridays (local timetable).

Wangaratta, on the Ovens River, has a standard-gauge platform somewhat hidden like that at Benalla, and the town is similarly slightly distanced from the railway. Also like Benalla it has a *North-Eastern Hotel* (☎ 03-5721 3741) near the station. The town's economy is dominated by textiles, two woollen mills being the main source of employment. The branch railway to Myrtleford and Bright up in the Victorian Alps no longer exists but V/line coaches connect with trains daily and a 1½ to 2½ hour trip can have the visitor within striking distance of Mt Buffalo or Mt Bogong in the heart of the Great Dividing Range.

Chiltern, 37km beyond Wangaratta, is a quiet remnant of a once thriving gold-rush town.

The 'Twin Town' of Albury/Wodonga is the largest urban centre on Australia's mightiest river, the Murray, and was nominated a planned growth centre in the 1970s. Here the Victorian railway meets up with the NSW system. In years past passengers had to change trains, usually in the early hours of the morning. All trains on the standard gauge now run right through, but you can break the journey at Albury by taking a V/line intercity service for the Melbourne–Albury section and the NSW XPT between Albury and Sydney. **Wodonga** has its own railway station; 3km further on the line crosses the river and border for the last kilometre into Albury on the NSW side.

Albury is 307km from Melbourne by V/line, 318km on standard gauge via Sunshine and 646km from Sydney, although the latter depends not only on which route is followed through Sydney's suburbs but on whether the 'up' or 'down' line is followed. The former, from Albury to Sydney, is 3km shorter than the down line. This shows how kilometre posts on the lineside can be rather misleading.

Albury is a centre for tours of the historical gold towns, river centres, wineries, and the snowfields of north-eastern Victoria. Attractions include Albury's fine railway station, Hume Weir (for trout fishing), historic

---

Ettamogah

A magazine, *Australia Post,* featured a cartoon about the goings-on around a ramshackle bush pub called Ettamogah; a real-life replica may be seen at Ettamogah, a former station 9km north of Albury. The name is alleged to be Aboriginal for 'let's have a drink'. Copies of the same crazy building (drinks can be obtained at all) are found in other places in Australia.

Beechworth and Yackandandah, and the many wineries around Rutherglen. There is a free bus tour of Albury/Wodonga and coach tours operate to the surrounding places of interest.

ALBURY/WODONGA TO JUNEE   [Map 26]

Culcairn enjoys Australia's largest artesian water supply and is also shire capital of what is often called Morgan Country, another example of the grudging respect still held in Australia for bushrangers of the past among whom Mad Dan Morgan was one of the most notorious and brutal. The heritage-classified *Hotel Culcairn* (☎ 03-6029 8501) adjoins Culcairn railway station.

At **Henty** note the curiously-named *Doodle Cooma Arms Hotel* (☎ 02-6929 3013) adjoining the station; Doodle Cooma was Henty's original name but it was changed to avoid confusion with Cooma in the Snowy Mountains. Henty has a memorial to Sergeant Smythe, a policeman shot and killed by Mad Dog Morgan just west of the town in 1864.

The Rock is a small township named after a 360m-high rocky out-crop which stands above the surrounding plain about one to two kilometres west of the railway approaching the station. Originally called Hanging Rock, its name was changed to avoid confusion (see p206); the rock itself is a nature reserve and a popular recreation area.

Wagga Wagga is part of the Riverina agricultural area and the largest inland city in NSW with a population approaching 40,000. It boasts Australia's only inland surf lifesaving club beside its beach on the Murrumbidgee River and is also known for Charles Sturt University which has its own winery and a viticulture course in its curriculum. The station is handy for hotels and restaurants, being at the southern end of Bayliss St, the main street. The city's name is usually shortened to Wagga, pronounced Wogga; Wagga means crow in Aboriginal language and there are many crows in the area. Wagga is also a major air force and military base.

Immediately north of Wagga station the railway crosses a series of six viaducts over the river. After passing the now abandoned stations of

---

A record-breaking line

Between Albury and Wagga Wagga are racetrack sections of line where the former Riverina XPT twice broke the Australian train speed record; in 1981 at 183km/h and again on 18 September 1992 when it reached 193km/h. For several years from 1985, when the XPT regularly stopped at the intermediate stations of Culcairn, Henty and The Rock, Australia held a place in the *Railway Gazette* World Speed League (p118). The normal running speeds on this part of the route were 110 to 160km/h yet only a few years earlier trains had to slow down to exchange 'tokens' between sections.

These stations are all now mere request stops.

Bomen and Harefield the line reaches **Junee**, an important junction and railway town past and present.

The town centre with hotels and shops is just outside the station. There is a railway refreshment room with a tourist information centre. The railway roundhouse with 47 repair bays and a large turntable is to the left of the line on the approach from the south. Although the roundhouse was closed in 1993 it has been partly re-opened for use by the private rail company Austrac and it remains a monument of industrial archaeology and is open also as a museum.

Much of Junee's glory lies in the past, thanks to misguided economic rationalism but it is still important as a regional office for Freightcorp, as a train control centre and a crew changeover station. For many years it was one of the only stops (unadvertised because it was used for essential

---

Junee – from the foreword to *Traincatcher*

'Recently I did one of my Sunday morning programs at the town of Junee, in of all places, the railway refreshment rooms. The RRRs are still there, but the local baker now runs the rooms, not to service the trains, but for the people of Junee.

I was reminded of the glory of the age of steam, and the days of rail. Families came to town on Saturday night to watch the trains come and go – The Albury Mail, The Riverina Express and many others. You could stay at the Hotel, upstairs from the refreshment rooms.

Yes, Junee was a Railway Town, and apart from the station it had the 'Roundhouse' where up to 150 men and apprentices – fitters, boiler makers – worked repairing the rolling stock.

While we were there (on the Saturday actually) an XPT whose brakes had jammed was pulled into a siding at Junee. The engine had a 'flat tyre' as it's called, a flat spot caused by the brakes jamming.

In the old days, that is up until 1993 when the 'Roundhouse' closed, that engine could have been repaired right there. Now all repairs, even the most basic like changing a fuse, have to go to Sydney. That XPT was towed at 20km/h to Sydney. And that's progress? No, that's stupidity.'

Ian McNamara of ABC Australia All Over in the foreword of *Traincatcher* by Colin Taylor. IPL Books, Sydney and Wellington, 1996.

'... the refreshment room at Junee... Macca talked about that, and I have a little bit of empathy for that because my Dad was the stationmaster at Junee for many years in the days, the great old days of the railways when the refreshment rooms were open and you charged in off the train and spilt your coffee on the platform, trying to catch the train. It was blowing the whistle, with guys like Trevor Campbell up front driving – or his Dad, driving the train, and all those great days of yesteryear.'

Vince O'Rourke, Chief Executive of QR at the launch of *Traincatcher*, 16 April 1996 at Roma St Station, Brisbane

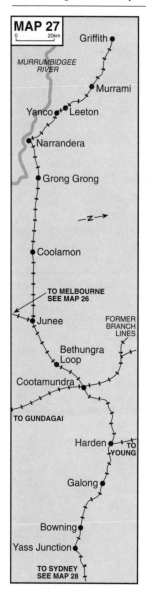

MAP 27
0   20km

Griffith

MURRUMBIDGEE RIVER

Murrami

Yanco   Leeton

Narrandera

Grong Grong

—z—>

Coolamon

TO MELBOURNE
SEE MAP 26

Junee

FORMER BRANCH LINES

Bethungra Loop

Cootamundra

TO GUNDAGAI

Harden   TO YOUNG

Galong

Bowning

Yass Junction

TO SYDNEY
SEE MAP 28

railway purposes only) on the supposedly non-stop Melbourne–Sydney Southern Aurora express. It is the junction where the once-weekly Griffith train is turned to enter the branch line formerly served by 10 weekly trains including the Riverina Express.

JUNEE TO GRIFFITH   [Map 27]

Branching from Junee, the train to Griffith first stops at **Coolamon** (37km from Junee), a delightful small town in turkey-breeding country. A general air of prosperity seems matched by the appearance of the freshly painted station facing the main street, with its waiting room reopened in 1996 when the trains returned.

Not all the former stations have enjoyed the new lease of life experienced by Coolamon. Thirty-nine kilometres beyond Coolamon lies **Grong Grong**, yet another of those double-barrelled place names of Aboriginal origin.

Grong Grong is best known to motorists as the place where the adjoining Newell Highway from the Victorian border to Queensland makes a sharp 90° turn to the north.

Narrandera is one of the oldest settlements in the Riverina. First developed in the 1850s, it grew in importance 30 years later as the railways arrived, first from Melbourne, then from Sydney, adding to its strategic position as a river port.

More recent products of the area are goat mohair and ostriches (for meat, skin and feathers). Narrandera boasts a Royal Doulton fountain, of which there are only two worldwide.

Yanco is no longer a passenger station but remains a junction for the truncated Hay branch of the railway.

Leeton is the administrative centre of the surrounding Murrumbidgee irrigation districts. Fruit and wine growing are important here; it is the home of the Letona tinned-fruit cannery and Quelch citrus-juice factory. Sheep's milk is another speciality.

Griffith, the largest centre in NSW west of Wagga, is regarded as the centre of Australia's wine and food country, the Riverina. Originally the home of the Wiradjuri tribe, it soon became the domain of squatters following in the wake of explorers Oxley and Sturt. Irrigation from the Murrumbidgee River since 1913 stimulated its growth and the original town plan was the work of American architect Walter Burley Griffin, well known as the designer of Canberra but perhaps less so as architect for a large number of incinerators in various parts of the country.

Italian migrants and their descendants give the area its justifiable reputation for good food and wine. There are plenty of wineries to visit and restaurants to enjoy the region's produce. The area produces 15 per cent of Australia's wine and 90 per cent of its rice as well as 70 per cent of NSW's wine and citrus fruit. Pioneer Park open-air museum is just over 1km north of the railway station,; the station is right in the town centre one street north of the main street, Banna Avenue. The museum, which adjoins Rotary Lookout above the town, commemorates the life and times of early pioneers and is one among many attractions for the visitor. Accommodation ranges from luxury motel units to shearer's quarters at *Pioneer Park* (☎ 02-6962 4196). The information centre (☎ 02-6962 4145) is just 200m from the station.

JUNEE TO GOULBURN   [Maps 27 and 28]

Between Junee and Cootamundra watch out for the **Bethungra loop**, where the northbound line describes a complete circle to overcome the gradient while the line south follows a more direct route.

Cootamundra is the junction for a cross-country route to Parkes on the main west line from Sydney, sometimes used by interstate trains when engineering work or other factors affect the usual route. It is also a junction for other branches on which the passenger trains have been replaced by buses, such as Gundagai (famous for its dog on the tucker box and the song 'The Road to Gundagai') and Wyalong. It was Cootamundra's position as a main junction that turned it from a small village to an important town in the late 1800s. It is now a main rail/bus interchange. Hotels and other town centre features are within 200m of the station. A graceful wattle tree takes its name from Cootamundra, while a restored nursing home in Adams St commemorates the birth here of Australia's cricketing great, Sir Donald Bradman, in 1908.

After Cootamundra, the Melbourne–Sydney mainline passes **Harden**, from where State Rail bus services replaced trains in 1983 on the former

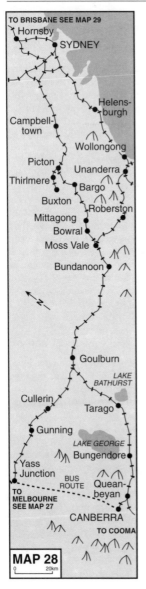

TO BRISBANE SEE MAP 29
Hornsby
SYDNEY
Helensburgh
Campbelltown
Wollongong
Picton
Unanderra
Thirlmere
Bargo
Buxton
Roberston
Mittagong
Bowral
Moss Vale
Bundanoon
Goulburn
LAKE BATHURST
Cullerin
Tarago
Gunning
LAKE GEORGE
Bungendore
Yass Junction
BUS ROUTE
Queanbeyan
TO MELBOURNE SEE MAP 27
CANBERRA
TO COOMA
MAP 28
0   20km

branch through the fruit country of Young and Cowra to the western mainline at Blayney. For reasons known only to anonymous bureaucrats the connection has since been moved back to Cootamundra, making the bus journey longer. The town of Harden is seemingly inexplicably also known as Murrumburrah, but the Readers Digest *Illustrated Guide to Australian Places* gives a fascinating account of how it happened, largely to do with the coming of the railway in 1877.

Yass Junction offers an alternative link to Canberra, for rail passengers from Victoria or the Riverina, by changing to the connecting Countrylink bus instead of continuing to the rail junction at Goulburn. Yass Town is a little over 3km away, the branch railway long disused. **Gunning**, more a farming village than a town, is a request stop for the daylight Melbourne XPT. After leaving Gunning the track climbs steadily up through curves of down to 280m radius (14 chain) towards the former station of **Cullerin**, the highest point on the line at 256m, before descending more gradually through Breadalbane (also now closed) to the junction for Canberra.

GOULBURN TO SYDNEY [Map 28]

After Goulburn the mainline descends from the Southern Highlands through **Moss Vale**, a pleasant little destination for a day trip from Sydney or a break of journey. Bus connections from here provide a link to the Illawarra district at Wollongong (see p220).

On the left of the track at the request stop of **Mittagong** (just after **Bowral**, another request stop) look out for the original line of the Great Southern Railway of 1867 which descends from the

Goulburn to Canberra [Map 28]

At Goulburn (or more accurately at Joppa Junction 6km earlier coming from the south) the line for Canberra and the Southern Highlands branches off from the main south line. Goulburn is an important railway centre and terminus for CityRail's interurban Endeavour services from Sydney. It is also served by Countrylink Xplorer trains to Canberra. Goulburn began life as a garrison town for guarding convicts: it has since become an important farming and pastoral centre. Its several claims to fame include being the last town in the British Empire to become a city through Royal Letters Patent and having the only pre-Federation brewery still operating. Goulburn jail is one of the most conspicuous features on the east of the town; travelling towards Sydney, look out to your left for it after leaving Goulburn station.

Features of the Canberra route include **Lake Bathurst**, on the east near the first stop, **Tarago**, the much larger but frequently dried-up **Lake George** on the west approaching **Bungendore** and the scenic Molonglo Gorge, on the right after Bungendore.

The former Canberra Monaro Express divided at **Queanbeyan**, the main part continuing south to Cooma on the edge of the Snowy Mountains.

Cooma and places further south are now served by Countrylink coaches from Canberra station. Queanbeyan town centre, unlike that of Canberra, is close to the station, making it a handy base for exploration of the region including the federal capital itself. See p258 for details of Michelago Tourist Railway.

Queanbeyan is in New South Wales. So is Canberra geographically but not politically, being in a separate enclave known as the ACT (Australian Capital Territory).

Canberra, the end of the line, is Australia's national capital, although Sydney is the largest urban area. Notes on what to see and do in Canberra are on pp171-173.

highlands more directly than the present mainline built in 1919. The former line proved too steep for most trains (1 in 30 as against 1 in 75 maximum for the new line). NSW Rail Transport Museum at Thirlmere (see p259) operates trains on part of this old route from the southern end at **Picton**.

Campbelltown, a modern planned new town, marks the beginning of the greater Sydney area and from here on in (or rather from Macarthur, a more recent purely suburban station 2km south), the line is shared by electric multiple-unit trains of various shapes but all double deck.

Mainline trains into Sydney from Campbelltown can and do follow different routes, either via East Hills, the newest and shortest, or via Sefton Park, the most general in recent years, or via Granville, the longest. By either of the older routes, a stop may be made at Strathfield, sometimes making connections with trains to or from the north and west possible.

Notes on 'the big smoke' (an affectionate if rather derogatory name for Sydney) appear on pp126-138.

Sydney to Nowra: The Illawarra Line
This is a suburban/outer urban route which until a decade or so ago offered an alternative route for the first part of a rail journey to the south, since trains connected from **Unanderra** to **Moss Vale**. Major places on the route are mentioned on pp133-136 and p255.

Between **Oatley** and **Como**, look out for the attractive waterside area of George's River to the east. The Sydney suburbs virtually disappear or become lost in the bush not long after **Sutherland** (25km). **Waterfall** marks the northern edge of the scenic winding route through bushland which continues through **Helensburgh**, **Otford** and **Stanwell Park**. The route then swings along the coast, winding among forested cliffs and tunnels and bays on the edge of the Pacific north and south of **Coalcliff**, the only ugly spot, but fortunately very briefly glimpsed. There is a great view over to Port Kembla after Coalcliff tunnel and another view of the coast, close to, at Scarborough. After **Wollongong** (p136) the line climbs higher and generally a little further from the sea, but descends again right to the beach at **Bombo**. Before the terminus at **Nowra** (also called Bomaderry) the train stops at **Kiama** and **Berry** where a break of journey or turnaround is worthwhile.

Sydney to northern NSW and Brisbane

SYDNEY TO NEWCASTLE   [Map 29]

(Distances given are from Sydney via Strathfield)

Climbing north out of Strathfield in Sydney's western suburbs and once clear of the northern suburbs beyond **Hornsby** (30 minutes after leaving Sydney), the trains follow the edge of Ku-ring-gai Chase National Park (on the right) through Berowra and **Cowan**, then descend steeply through the Boronia tunnels until the waters of the Hawkesbury River come into view (on the left and right as you cross the bridge). Delightful forest and lake scenery of Brisbane Water National Park flank the line (mostly on the right) from **Hawkesbury River** (57km) to **Gosford** (81km), a useful turning point for a day trip. Just north of the bridge over the Hawkesbury the line curves along the west shore of Mullet Creek. For many years the old lady who lived in a small cottage between the railway and the water would wave to the passing train. The Woy Woy tunnel which follows, 13km south of Gosford, will be of interest to rail fans. Look out for the oyster beds in the waters of this area (and try some in a local restaurant when you return to Sydney!). Oysters are a favourite seafood and are plentiful on Australia's eastern seaboard.

Some surprisingly fast running will be experienced on the far from straight track north from Gosford through **Wyong** and **Morisset**.

Broadmeadow (two hours from Sydney) is the junction for Newcastle, a coal port and the birthplace of Australia's railways (see p109). This is the gateway to Hunter Valley, one of Australia's premier wine regions west of Maitland. Perhaps incongruously, coal is also a feature of Hunter Valley, particularly around Newcastle and Maitland, and heavy coal trains can be observed on the freight lines paralleling the route between Broadmeadow and Maitland.

Here also is one of the straightest and fastest parts of the main North Coast line, on which the XPT will quickly achieve and maintain its permitted maximum of 160km/h; at one time the train conductor would proudly announce 'The train is now travelling at 100 miles an hour'. Slow to fully adapt to metric measurement, everyone on board understood but the news appeared to frighten some older passengers and the practice ceased.

NEWCASTLE TO MAITLAND
[Map 29]

Newcastle, terminus of the electric interurban services from Sydney, is a coal town, but has maritime, local history and shell museums and an art gallery. Nearby Hamilton, first stop on the spur line to Newcastle and where you change trains for the locals to Maitland, is an attractive place for a break of journey, being regarded as Newcastle's 'Sunset Strip' or 'Bondi', a major night activity spot offering an impressive selection of good, mostly ethnic, restaurants as well as cheap hotel accommodation all within a stone's throw of the railway station.

Maitland, 31km west of Newcastle and 193km from Sydney, is a historic town with a thriving city centre just north

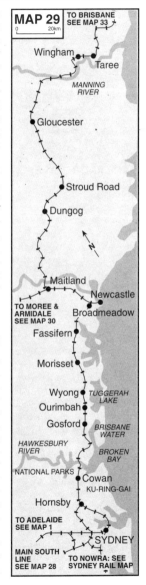

of the station. Visit the Grossman House Historical Museum, just past the pubs north of the station forecourt. From Maitland you could take a taxi to the Pokolbin wine district, 31km away. North Coast and Tableland trains go direct to Maitland from Sydney and the Brisbane XPT leaves there at 19.09 so make sure your taxi is booked for the return in time if you are continuing north.

However, the Hunter Valley wine-growing area is also served by the stations at Branxton, Singleton and Muswellbrook, reached by Citytrain Endeavour services on the Hunter Valley route or by Countrylink Tableland Xplorers, branching from the North Coast line just beyond Maitland.

MAITLAND TO WERRIS CREEK (218km)   [Map 30]

Branxton, just east of Singleton, is the nearest station for the Pokolbin vineyard district but the local train service is vestigial and there are no reasonable connections with buses. Cessnock is the major centre but passenger trains ceased running there over 20 years ago.

Most big names in Australian wine are in this area, between Rothbury and Bellbird, 10 to 16km south of the railway. Most wineries are open every day of the week. There are holiday cabins, a wine village and motel-type units where, if in a hired car, you can stay the night to sober up before going back to the train. Whether visiting the Hunter vineyards by taxi, hired car or public transport, an overnight stop is recommended since rail and bus schedules are not conducive to a quick visit. See p256 for details of Hunter Valley Railway Museum.

Singleton, where the railway crosses the Hunter River, has a long history being one of the oldest towns in the state and a varied economic base: vegetable and fruit growing, viticulture, timber milling, an army base and tourism all contributing. The railway station itself is one of particular interest while the giant Liddell power station with its 132m-high cooling towers and 10km-long conveyor belt is a reminder that Singleton is the state's main producer of opencast coal.

Muswellbrook is 96km beyond Maitland. The town centre is just north of Muswellbrook station on the New England Highway. This is a good centre for visiting the wineries of the Upper Hunter Valley, of which the nearest, Queldinburg, open seven days a week, is less than 2km away, and there are pubs to stay in immediately opposite the station. Muswellbrook has a colourful display of jacarandas in bloom in the last two months of the year. It is the junction for a freight and mineral line inland to Gulgong.

A further 26km brings the train to **Scone**, a town associated with horses and noted for breeding because of the many studs in the area. There is a Thoroughbred Carnival in May, a Polo Carnival in July and a Bushmans

Carnival in November. The early European settlers were Scots, hence the name from the original crowning place of Scottish kings. Scone is the current limit of the Hunter Valley local Endeavour diesel train services.

Some 17km north of Scone, on the right you should see Mt Wingen, the burning mountain, in which a coal seam well below the surface has been burning for thousands of years. Wingen station no longer exists but here the uphill gradient steepens as the line climbs through Murulla towards **Murrurundi**, which lies in a narrow valley in the Liverpool Range. Like many places inland from Australia's east coast Murrurundi's growth was spurred on in the 19th century when for a time it was the railhead. Bushranger Ben Hall spent his childhood here.

A further steepening of the gradient with many twists and turns brings the line to the summit of this section at **Ardglen**, 632m above sea level, just after the short Ardglen tunnel through the Liverpool Range.

Willow Tree is the next station after a downhill run of 12km and then comes **Quirindi**. The origin of the name and its original spelling are matters of debate. Like Muswellbrook, Quirindi has hotels and pubs opposite the station and a wealth of jacaranda trees.

Werris Creek is a railway junction where the Tableland Xplorer divides, the front half going north-west to Moree and the rear north to Armidale. Another branch, freight and grain only, goes 190km west to Merrygoen. The station is heritage listed, and on the remnant of a loop line south-west of the station may be seen what appears to be a locomotive graveyard.

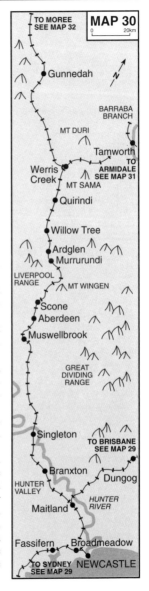

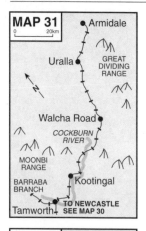

MAP 31
0   20km
Armidale
Uralla
GREAT DIVIDING RANGE
Walcha Road
COCKBURN RIVER
MOONBI RANGE
BARRABA BRANCH
Kootingal
Tamworth
TO NEWCASTLE SEE MAP 30

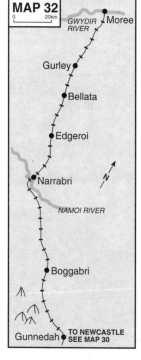

MAP 32
0   20km
GWYDIR RIVER
Moree
Gurley
Bellata
Edgeroi
Narrabri
NAMOI RIVER
Boggabri
Gunnedah
TO NEWCASTLE SEE MAP 30

WERRIS CREEK TO ARMIDALE
[Maps 30 and 31]

Tamworth, 455km from Sydney, is famous for its country music festival held over 11 days in January. Historic buildings, galleries, friendly family pubs and surrounding bush walks are other features. *Tamworth Hotel* (☎ 02-6766 2923) is opposite the station.

After the small station of **Kootingal** the track goes along the west side of the attractive valley of the Cockburn River, climbing steeply after about 13km through successive curves to cross the Moonbi Range near Walcha Road. **Walcha Road** is the station without a town; there is nowhere to go unless you have arranged transport. The town is 20km to the east on the other side of the Great Dividing Range. The 1106m line summit is 15km beyond Walcha Road where the line crosses to the eastern side of the range. Pleasant rolling country heralds the approach to Armidale from the south. **Uralla**, the last intermediate stop was the final resting place of the bushranger, Thunderbolt.

Armidale holds a people's market in the mall on the last Sunday of each month. Worth visiting too is the Folk Museum on Faulkner St. Follow Barney St east from the station to reach the town centre but it is a long way.

To reach most of the hotels in Armidale it is worth taking a taxi; *Wicklow Hotel* (☎ 02-6772 2421, close to Beardy St Mall in the town centre) has

(**Opposite**): The train on the Kuranda Scenic Railway (see p249) crossing Stoney Creek bridge, north Queensland.

comfortable rooms at under $20, making the taxi ride affordable. Armidale Visitors' Centre (☎ 02-6772 4655, 🖥 02-6771 4486) is nearby at 82 Marsh St.

On returning south by train, be in the buffet car early for breakfast, particularly if you want a bacon sandwich because they are very popular.

WERRIS CREEK TO MOREE
[Maps 30 and 32]

Gunnedah, **Boggabri** and **Narrabri** are the main stations on this route. These, and others no longer open, are marked by grain silos: wheat is a major crop and Gunnedah is one of the largest centres in Australia for wheat and stock sales. From here the line follows the Namoi River, with the Nandewar Range away to the east after Boggabri. Narrabri is the junction for the line to Walgett, mainly used by wheat trains.

At **Moree** on the Gwydir River there are hotels close to the station. Take your swimming togs (cozzie, bathers): no visitor to Moree should miss an early morning bathe in the spa pool just a block or two away from the station.

Moree water comes from underground, the Great Artesian Basin. The song *We are Australian* featured by The Seekers refers to 'the black soil of the plain': Moree is in the middle of it, one of the most fertile areas in the country. Cotton has in recent years overtaken wheat and wool as the major product of the region.

(**Opposite**) **Top**: Views of rainforest and the Pacific Ocean from the Skyrail. **Bottom**: The terminal of the scenic railway in Kuranda with the Skyrail terminal in the background.

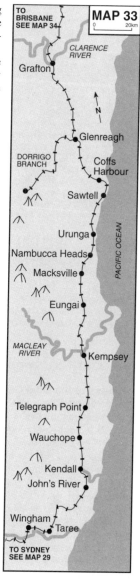

Why the railway?
Prior to Federation there was no greater achievement for the local
member for a bush electorate than to get a railway line – or two or
three – cutting across his constituency. And they tried and vied with all their
might.

It's not hard to see why railways were so popular. The same year as the
decision to extend the line to Werris Creek was made, the Hon Thomas Dangar,
on his way to Sydney to that very session of parliament, had to cross the
Breeza Plains by coach.

It was a foul autumn night, raining fiercely, and the road was an inter-
minable bog. The horses knocked up time and time again. As they floundered
across the plain, the wind strengthened to gale force and eventually the horses
lost their footing, breaking the pole and releasing the team from the coach.

Armed with lamps and tomahawks, Mr Dangar and the driver searched for
a sapling to repair the broken pole, while the other passengers searched in the
dark for the horses.

Cold, wet, mud splattered, bedraggled and far too late to catch the train,
the travellers arrived at the railhead – then at Willow Tree.

Such a journey was not uncommon and the mania for the railway had its
roots in people's experience of the alternatives.

Rail was not just quicker, it was far quicker. It was not just cheaper but
immensely cheaper. Not just safe and more comfortable but unbelievably so.

And rail was the great technological wonder of the age. It was fashionable
to be fascinated by railways.

From *Werris Creek railway station Conservation Management plan* by J Carr
and J Perry, published in *This Month in New England Country* in December 1999
and reproduced here by kind permission of This Month Publications Pty Ltd.

THE NORTH COAST ROUTE (MAITLAND TO BRISBANE)

Maitland to the Gold Coast   [Maps 29, 33 and 34]
(Distances given are from Sydney)

After **Maitland**, 193km, a good place to break the journey for a night-
stop, the North Coast line swings away from the valley and curves northwards among bush-covered hills between **Dungog** (245km) and **Taree**
(379km); Taree is the connecting point for a Countrylink bus service on
an alternative route from Newcastle via the coast and Great Lakes district.

On the right side, if travelling in daytime, you should catch glimpses
of the coastal lakes north of Johns River (418km) and of the Pacific
Ocean, north of **Macksville** (552km), especially at **Urunga** (581km).

Most of the scenery on this part of the line is pleasant and varied, with
numerous creeks, plantations and small settlements. It is well worth
breaking a journey in this area at one of the intermediate stations of
Nambucca Heads (565km), Urunga, Raleigh (586km) or **Sawtell**
(601km).

Coffs Harbour, (608km), self-named capital of 'the Banana Republic' (due to the many plantations in the locality), is noted for the beauty of its coastal scenery, its rich hinterland and magnificent beaches. North of Coffs Harbour the track climbs at a steady 1 in 80 through numerous curves and a series of short tunnels to a minor summit (just over 100 metres) at Landrigan's loop. Rail buffs should watch a few kilometres further on for the historic Dorrigo branch to the left at **Glenreagh** (652km), on the left about 35 minutes north of Coffs Harbour.

Grafton City (696km), terminus of the Grafton XPT and built on both sides of the Clarence River, is noted for its colourful jacaranda trees, smothering the roads and footpaths in season with their beautiful blue-purple blossoms. The Grafton Jacaranda Celebration takes place around October/November.

Casino (805km) is where the line into Queensland breaks from the NSW North Coast route which here veers right to the coast. Two decades ago passengers for the coast had to change trains. Later, a motorail service, the Gold Coast Motorail Express, ran direct from Sydney. This is now the route of the Murwillumbah XPT, without car-carrying facilities.

The first stop on this branch is at **Lismore** (836km) on a narrow flood plain at the confluence of two creeks, prone to flooding in the wet season. This part of northern New South Wales is noted for its lush green pastures. Lismore is the main dairying centre of NSW, while 30km north is the small town of Nimbin, which acquired widespread fame in 1974 and since then as a haven for alternative lifestyles, on which its residents, now second generation, have capitalised and it has become quite a tourist centre.

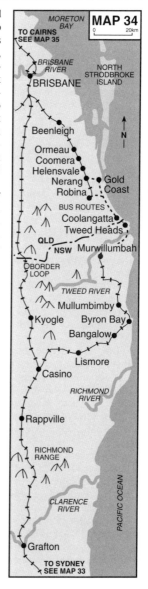

Byron Bay is the furthest point east on Australian railways and is a popular surfing resort. In fact nearby Cape Byron is the furthest point east on
the mainland of Australia. You will see the surfies with their multi-
coloured boards, sun-bleached hair and bronzed skin. A break of journey
here is worthwhile (see p82).

Approaching **Murwillumbah**, the end of the passenger line, an
extinct volcano, Mt Warning, stands out on the west above the farmlands
of the Tweed River valley. There is a convenient *pub* for a meal and a
drink over the road and about 100m east of Murwillumbah station. A connecting bus provides a link to the QR station at **Robina**, or to Beenleigh
or Brisbane. Buses also connect to Surfers Paradise on the Gold Coast.

Notes on the **Gold Coast** appear on p157.

Casino to Brisbane   [Map 34]

Between **Kyogle** (834km) and Tamrookum (909km) the railway passes
through the magnificent border ranges, timber and mist covered with
small waterfalls, bridges and rivers. If travelling in summer on the XPT
from NSW direct to Brisbane, look out in the early morning for the Border
loop. This is of interest because of its spiral tunnels by which the differences in altitude crossing the NSW/Queensland border ranges are overcome.

Throughout the whole border-range crossing of 23km the train nego-
tiates a series of 241m (12 chain) reverse curves on a constant 1 in 66
compensated gradient and traverses five tunnels. The first, spiral No 1, is
38km north of Kyogle, then comes spiral No 2 and the summit within the
next 3km.

The former Border Loop station is at the 271m summit, immediately
followed by the border tunnel and two more tunnels a few kilometres
north. Set in wild country, the border loop area is only accessible, apart
from the railway, by an unsealed gravel road. Before the advent of the
XPT it was best viewed in the morning mists from the northbound
Brisbane Limited but is now best seen from the southbound XPT or the
Great South Pacific Express in either direction about an hour out from
Brisbane.

Rail enthusiasts may note the dual- and combined-gauge track on the
right between Rocklea and the city (after the branch from the Gold Coast
joins the interstate line). At Yeerongpilly, 8km from Roma St, local Gold
Coast trains are likely to swing over onto combined-gauge track west of
the suburban lines.

Approaching Brisbane you will see the city centre on the right as you
pass through South Brisbane station to cross the Merivale Bridge. In the
foreground just before South Brisbane are the South Bank Parklands,
developed on the site of the 1988 World Expo while on the other side of
the track is Brisbane Convention Centre.

The Sunshine route: Brisbane to Cairns

BRISBANE TO BUNDABERG
[Map 35]

Going north from Brisbane the first stop is **Caboolture** which marks the end of the Citytrain intensive suburban network, although outer urban services continue further north. North of Caboolture look out for the **Glasshouse Mountains**, curious volcanic peaks so named by Captain James Cook on 17 May 1770. They are to the left ahead about 21km after leaving Caboolture following a section where very fast running is noticeable after leaving the comparative congestion of suburbia. There are pineapple farms in the foreground.

Most trains stop at **Landsborough** (82km from Brisbane), from where local buses (not covered by rail tickets) serve the southern end of the Sunshine Coast. **Nambour** (104km) is the transfer station for QR bus links to the coast; details are given on pp158-9.

After **Yandina** (112km), a local stop just north of Nambour, there is a long slow climb up the Eumundi Ranges, past **Cooroy** and Pomona to the old gold-mining town of Gympie. In **Pomona** note the old cinema in the town street on the right, whilst on the west of the track appears the distinctive shape of Mt Tiboorbargan, popular with hill climbers. The walking track to the top is clearly visible from the train.

The main station at Gympie is now **Gympie North**, 173km from Brisbane

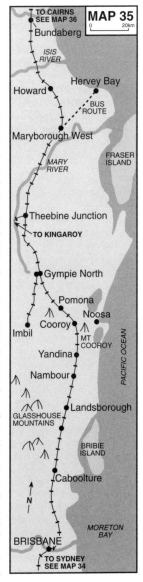

and some 3km from town, which replaced the original station when this part of the North Coast line was electrified and realigned in 1989. A bus link (covered by your ticket) connects with all trains and serves the old station at the north end of the town centre. From here Mary Valley Railway (see p266) operates to **Imbil**.

Although Gympie itself is by-passed by the realigned North Coast line glimpses of the town may be seen on the left before Gympie North. Gympie is a friendly town, full of historic relics. They hold an annual show in late May and a Gold Rush week in mid-October. Local fruits, orange and pineapple, are plentiful and cheap. Gympie is worth a day trip from Brisbane or a break of journey en route to north Queensland. However, the train service is limited and better suited to an overnight stay in Gympie.

The next stop is **Maryborough West**, 262km, the station for Fraser Island. QR operates the Trainlink bus service to Maryborough and Hervey Bay, connecting with the Tilt Train and Spirit of Capricorn. Maryborough, established in 1843, is one of Queensland's oldest cities with many historic buildings and traditional Queensland homes.

Hervey Bay, one of the world's best places to view migrating humpback whales between August and October, is 40-45 minutes by connecting bus from Maryborough West station and is the ferry embarkation point for the nearby World Heritage site Fraser Island, the world's largest sand island covering 16,300 square kilometres.

After Maryborough there follows some fast running, with possibly a conditional stop at **Howard**, before reaching **Bundaberg**, heart of sugarland and home of Queensland's famous rum. If you want to see how they make it, and to taste it, an overnight break of journey is necessary with trains mostly calling at Bundaberg early afternoon northbound and midmorning southbound. However, on four days of the week, Mondays, and Thursdays to Saturdays inclusive, there is the option of a 14-hour break on a southbound journey if you take the midnight sleeper for the return journey to Brisbane.

Bundaberg is also famous for whale watching. Tour packages are available covering arrival and departure transfers, two- or three-nights' accommodation, breakfasts and lunch and cruises to Platypus Bay off Fraser Island and Lady Musgrave Island in the coral reefs of the Capricorn group. Tour prices, not including rail fare, are from $205 per person twin share at three-star hotels.

Over the road from the station *Federal Hotel* offers excellent pub tucker at very moderate prices. Next door is *Matilda Motel* (☎ 07-4151 4717) with excellent moderately-priced single and twin units, while two blocks further down Bourbong St is *Grand Central Bar & Grill* (☎ 07-4151 2441) with clean bedrooms and good pub tucker. There is also a tourist information centre (freecall ☎ 1800 060 499) on Bourbong St.

BUNDABERG TO ROCKHAMPTON
[Map 36]

On leaving Bundaberg the train swings over the wide Burnett river, from which, looking back to the east you should see the whale mural covering the flank of a large building in the town centre. At North Bundaberg the railway runs for a short distance along the street. The next stop, except for the Queenslander, is **Miriam Vale**, a beef cattle and tobacco-producing area.

Gladstone, reached on most northbound services in the evening, bustles with railway activity. It is a colourful town, with its juxtaposition of massive industrial development and a small boat harbour in a beautiful natural setting of tree-clothed hills. Break your journey at Gladstone and take a cab up to the vantage point on Round Hill. The coal terminals, as modern as any in the world, and the railway marshalling yards set in undulating bushland at **Callemondah Yard** (see p265) just north of the river present a most unusual picture.

Further north there may be a stop at **Mount Larcom**, centre of a dairy cattle producing area, which is a pleasant place for a stopover.

Most northbound trains reach **Rockhampton** (see also p266) in the evening. This is the first stop north of the Tropic of Capricorn. If new to Queensland, this is a place to get out of the train and stretch your legs. You will probably feel its warmth even at night. There is up to half an hour's break here but the station is a 10-minute walk from town so there is not enough time to look around unless changing trains; this is now readily possible since the advent of the Tilt Train. On leaving Rockhampton sta-

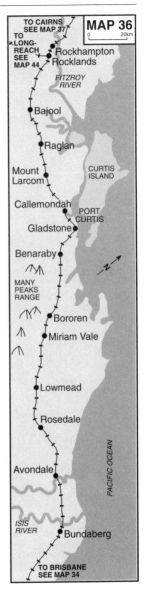

MAP 36
0   20km

TO CAIRNS
SEE MAP 37
TO
LONG-
REACH
SEE
MAP 44

Rockhampton
Rocklands
FITZROY
RIVER

Bajool

Raglan

Mount
Larcom

CURTIS
ISLAND

Callemondah

PORT
CURTIS

Gladstone

Benaraby

MANY
PEAKS
RANGE

Bororen

Miriam Vale

Lowmead

Rosedale

PACIFIC OCEAN

Avondale

ISIS
RIVER

Bundaberg

TO BRISBANE
SEE MAP 34

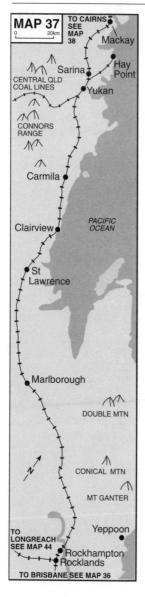

MAP 37
0   20km

TO CAIRNS
SEE MAP 38

Mackay

CENTRAL QLD
COAL LINES

Sarina

Hay Point

Yukan

CONNORS
RANGE

Carmila

PACIFIC
OCEAN

Clairview

St
Lawrence

Marlborough

DOUBLE MTN

CONICAL MTN

MT GANTER

Yeppoon

TO
LONGREACH
SEE MAP 44

Rockhampton
Rocklands

TO BRISBANE SEE MAP 36

tion the line curves west to run along the middle of one of the main town streets, flanked by motor cars and pedestrians, before swinging across the Fitzroy River to continue northwards.

ROCKHAMPTON TO PROSERPINE
[Maps 37 and 38]

To see by daylight the parts of the coast route normally traversed by night necessitates taking the Spirit of the Tropics train between Rockhampton and Townsville.

St Lawrence, 173km north of Rockhampton, is a stopping place usually seen only at night, except from the Spirit of the Tropics. Nearby **Clairview** is one of only two places on this route where the Pacific Ocean is seen from the train; the other is north of Townsville at Cardwell.

Sarina is an important railway junction where the electrified line from the central Queensland coalfields crosses the north coast line to Hay Point coal terminal. There is also a large distillery, but only for industrial alcohol.

Mackay, on the Pioneer River, is a sugar-exporting port with the largest bulk sugar terminal in the world. You may see the burning cane fields light up the sky after harvest, though different harvesting methods have largely transcended this feature and in 1999 it was outlawed for environmental reasons, though it can still be seen.

Proserpine is a major tourism centre. It is also only a short bus ride away from Shute Harbour in Conway National Park and is gateway to the tropical islands of Hayman, Daydream, Hamilton, Lindeman and South Molle in the Whitsundays. But sugar is important too; there is a close up of the sugar mill and its sidings on the right going north on leaving the station.

Mackay and Proserpine are good places from which to visit parts of the Barrier Reef and the tropical islands, but unfortunately they are visited by most passenger trains only in the very early hours (or late in the evening southbound).

PROSERPINE TO TOWNSVILLE (256km)   [Maps 38 and 39]

Bowen, on the Don River and a centre for fruit (it's famous for its mangoes), is 65km north of Proserpine, although the station at New Bowen is some way from town. From there on you are in sugar-cane country most of the way.

Home Hill is 100km further north. Between the twin towns of Home Hill and **Ayr** the train crosses the Burdekin River, the mightiest of the Queensland rivers east of the Great Dividing Range. Rice cultivation is a recent venture in this area.

About 20 minutes after leaving Ayr the train crosses the Haughton River, renowned among the angling fraternity for its barramundi. On the left you may notice a large building named *Giru International Hotel* (☎ 07-4782 9166); if your itinerary allows a break here, hosts Doug and Karen will make sure you have a memorable stay in this lovely example of a typical Aussie country pub. The train stops at **Giru** only by prior booking.

Wild birds including the dancing brolga or native companion are a feature of the marshy flats north of Giru approaching **Cromarty**, half an hour or so before the train starts its slow crawl alongside the main road into Townsville.

Townsville is Queensland's fourth city. Here you have time to look briefly around town and get used to the tropical heat. Flinders Mall, the town's commercial centre, is to your right on leaving the

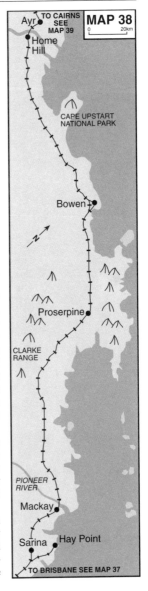

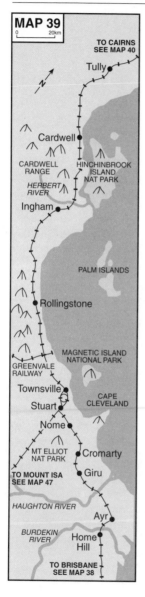

MAP 39

0   20km

TO CAIRNS
SEE MAP 40

Tully

Cardwell

CARDWELL
RANGE

HINCHINBROOK
ISLAND
NAT PARK

HERBERT
RIVER

Ingham

PALM ISLANDS

Rollingstone

MAGNETIC ISLAND
NATIONAL PARK

GREENVALE
RAILWAY

Townsville

Stuart

CAPE
CLEVELAND

Nome

MT ELLIOT
NAT PARK

Cromarty

TO MOUNT ISA
SEE MAP 47

Giru

HAUGHTON RIVER

Ayr

BURDEKIN
RIVER

Home
Hill

TO BRISBANE
SEE MAP 38

station. You first cross a small park and look up towards Castle Hill, a pink granite peak which towers over the city. Then turn round and observe the station building itself, historically the terminus of the former Great Northern Railway and looking very much the part.

Just to the right from near the end of Flinders Mall you will find Ross River, dotted with a myriad of small boats. The quayside is lined by an excellent restaurant and bar complex; you have ample time to visit **Tim's Surf 'n' Turf** if changing at Townsville for the train to Mount Isa. Steaks of unbelievable size, with accompaniments, cost less than $15 while a dozen oysters cost as little as $6.90. You would pay that for half a dozen in most restaurants.

For a cheap place to stay ($20 single) and also good for tucker, try **Great Northern Hotel** (☎ 07-4771 6191, 500 Flinders St), just opposite the station. At weekends (when the restaurant is closed), ask for John's Beef Stuff, a nourishing stew at only $2 a bowl. Counter meals at **Newmarket** on the other side of the road are also good, and on Sundays the Mall is turned into a busy open-air market.

Half-day city bus tours are operated by Ansett Pioneer in Hanran St just east of Townsville station. There are day cruises to the outer Barrier Reef but for around $10 you can enjoy an hour or two among the marine wonders of Reefworld just off The Strand, or take a ferry from Hayles Wharf on Ross Creek over to nearby Magnetic Island.

TOWNSVILLE TO CAIRNS (340km)
[Maps 39 and 40]

Once past Townsville's northern industrial suburbs, the next stop 108km is

Ingham on the Herbert River, original home of the 'Pub with No Beer', made famous the world over in Gordon Parsons' ballad. This was a local hotel which American servicemen were reputed to have drunk dry during World War II. There is a rival claim: at Taylors Arm, 26km from Macksville on the NSW North Coast mainline, the Cosmopolitan Hotel claims this title but Ingham is right on the railway and an easier place to visit – if you go for pubs with no beer. In general, Australians don't.

In any case, the historic pub is no more. *Station Hotel*, just over the road at the southern end of Ingham railway station, is cool and more convenient, serving excellent homemade pies (as well as beer) if you decide to stop there for lunch. Here, as at many places on this route, narrow-gauge cane lines cross the roads and the railway, and you may see cane trains even longer than the Sunlander on their way to the mill.

There is a brief glimpse of the coast 53km further north at **Cardwell**. You should also see some of the many islands on parts of this route. Hinchinbrook Island National Park is particularly prominent, appearing as a mountain range on the seaward side of the railway. The scenery is mostly excellent on both sides: the coast is on the right going north, but a recent scar is the controversial development of the Port Hinchinbrook resort near Cardwell which is plainly visible from the train.

Tully, a major sugar centre, has Australia's highest annual rainfall of 4267mm (68 inches). A stop of around 10 minutes is usually made here; this is useful for smokers.

North of Tully the train passes slowly through lush sugar-cane fields amid tree-

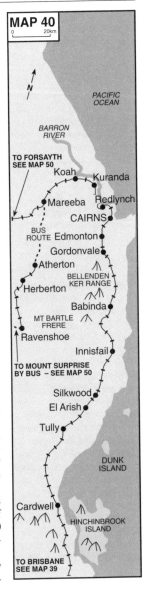

MAP 40

0   20km

N

PACIFIC OCEAN

BARRON RIVER

TO FORSAYTH SEE MAP 50

Koah   Kuranda

Mareeba   Redlynch

CAIRNS

BUS ROUTE   Edmonton

Gordonvale

Atherton

BELLENDEN KER RANGE

Herberton

Babinda

MT BARTLE FRERE

Ravenshoe

Innisfail

TO MOUNT SURPRISE BY BUS – SEE MAP 50

Silkwood

El Arish

Tully

DUNK ISLAND

Cardwell

HINCHINBROOK ISLAND

TO BRISBANE SEE MAP 39

clothed mountains, including Mt Bartle Frere on the left, Queensland's highest peak in the Bellenden Ker Range, north of Innisfail near the little town of Babinda.

Innisfail, 253km north of Townsville in sugar-cane country, is set between the ranges and the sea and is noted for its Chinese temple and Pioneers' monument. Nerada tea plantation, several miles inland, was Australia's first venture into this crop, is now well established and successful. Palmerston National Park is further inland on the road to Millaa Millaa and Ravenshoe on the Atherton Tableland.

Babinda, 59km short of Cairns, is among the places where a stopover can be recommended. It features a nature reserve, The Boulders, where a small river plunges among rocks, scene of both legend and tragedy some years ago when a foolhardy swimmer ignored the warnings. Keep to the excellent deep pool where it is safe.

Closer to Cairns, at **Gordonvale** (32 minutes by train), set among canefields and backed by rainforest, Mulgrave Mill is open for inspection tours even if the Mulgrave Rambler steam train (see p266) is not taking its scenic 15km narrow-gauge rail trip to Orchid Valley.

CAIRNS

Originally known as Trinity Inlet, Cairns is the essence and heart of north Queensland. Warm and extrovert, it is a thriving town with a population of close on 60,000, a major centre of game fishing, and gateway to the Barrier Reef and the Atherton Tableland. The visitor information centre is on Wharf St adjoining the Ocean Liner Terminal. A free booklet with maps and other tourist information is published by Mil and Annette Clay (☎ 07-4034 1825, 🖹 4034 1930 or 🖳 mil@internetnorth.com.au). Attractions of Cairns include the harbour with the marlin jetty and sailing club, the surrounding cane fields and exciting hinterland of misty mountains and tropical rain forest. There are many excellent restaurants and eating places ranging from the really cheap to the very expensive, the latter being particularly noted for seafood. And of course, the easily accessible islands of the Barrier Reef, including Green Island with its underwater observatory. Cairns has many fine hotels, but within reach by rail or bus are smaller places where accommodation can be cheaper; Redlynch, Kuranda, Edmonton, Gordonvale and Babinda.

For a convenient night-stop try **Grand Hotel** (☎ 07-4051 1007) at the corner of Shields and McLeod Sts, close to Cairns Station (a short walk through Cairns Central, a shopping-centre complex). The hotel opened in 1928 just after Cairns was first connected to Brisbane by rail. Music, singing and dancing, in the now famous **Crocodile Bar**, are a feature of most nights. The hotel boasts an 11m-carved wooden crocodile as the main bar; this was carved, in the bar, from north Queensland yellow siris timber by a Papua New Guinean master carver, Ekielus Kambae. Rooms are cheap, breakfasts are included, and the dining-room menu features hearty Queensland tucker including 800g rump steaks and the chance to sample crocodile and kangaroo.

Around Cairns

Despite all the attractions of Cairns itself, it would be almost unforgivable to visit this area and fail to make the rail trip to **Kuranda**. A round trip from Cairns takes three hours, not counting time spent in Kuranda, but Kuranda is also worth an overnight stop. Depending on which train you join for the return trip, there will be time to visit the markets, the *Top Pub* for a good lunch, or the *Bottom Pub* for a cold beer or a bottle of Kuranda Hotel-Motel claret; don't believe everything it says on the label – it's a fine drop and if it knocks you over, you can stay the night in a comfortable motel room there (*Kuranda Hotel-Motel* ☎ 07-4093 7206).

Cairns is a useful base for other local trips, by train, coach, launch or hired car. A day trip to one of the islands on the Great Barrier Reef is easily undertaken from Cairns if you have a whole day there. Full-day coach tours are available to Atherton Tableland, with its crater lakes, orchid gardens and waterfalls; or to Cape Tribulation and Mossman Gorge.

On the north Queensland coast Ballyhooley Express (see p263) is the name of a train on the Mossman Mill sugar-cane railway at Port Douglas north of Cairns. The Queensland cane-line network of so-called tramways extends over 1600km north to south, with over 3000km of track route, much of it interconnected. Its obvious tourist potential is capable of much greater development.

Narrow-gauge railways similar to the cane lines operate at two of Queensland's island resorts, Hayman and Brampton (see p264), to bring visitors from the ferries to the motel.

Referring to sugar-cane lines as tramways and their trains as trams can lead to some curious concepts. In Nambour a sign in the main street warns of 'tram crossing'. A visitor seeking public transport waited ages for a tram until he learned the truth!

Routes in outback Queensland

BRISBANE TO CHARLEVILLE

Brisbane to Toowoomba [Map 41]

At Roma St the Westlander, alone among QR's Traveltrain fleet, leaves not from the main long-distance platform No 10, but from a platform at the other side of the station, closer to the interstate platform, since the

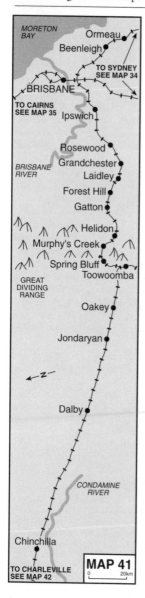

western line exits in the same direction as the line going south. The latter swings away across Brisbane River whilst the western line of four tracks, the main western 'up' and 'down' lines and the adjacent suburban lines, follow the north bank of the river past the Castlemaine XXXX brewery at Milton, through Toowong to cross the river seven or eight minutes after leaving Brisbane at Indooroopilly.

Toowong is the modal interchange for Queensland University; shuttle buses operate from just over the road from the station and opposite the station is *Royal*

The Westlander – survival of the fittest

The Westlander is possibly the most threatened of all QR's major inland air-conditioned services, but it has survived in spite of the worst efforts of government commissions, economic rationalists, treasury 'razor gangs' and the efforts of rival transport operators.

The Westlander's non-air-conditioned cousin, the Dirranbandi Mail described in earlier editions of this book, was the first victim of the branch line closure mania when it hit Queensland in earnest in the early 1990s. That the Westlander still survives, despite the truncation of its route, relocations of a major station, alterations to timetable and days of running, as well as the withdrawal of booking facilities from country stations, is something of a testimony to the determination of country people to hold on to their tangible links with the rest of the world, of which the railway is one of the most symbolic and well-loved.

By travelling on a train like the Westlander you become part of a clan, identifying yourself with local interests and learning about a way of life that is a far cry from the suburban rat race that is now all too typical of the Australia most people know.

Exchange Hotel, a favourite watering place for students after lectures and exams. At Indooroopilly the river is crossed by four bridges side by side, two double-track rail, one for cyclists and one for road traffic, the latter noted for its entry towers and a road surface which seems to be almost constantly under repair.

The river is seen again on the right approaching **Ipswich**, some 45 minutes after leaving Brisbane. From here the first railway in Queensland ran to Grandchester, or Bigge's Camp as it was then called, 31km further on and just past the end of the electrified suburban system recently extended to Rosewood; **Rosewood** and **Grandchester** are request stops for the Westlander. West of Grandchester the train climbs the ranges towards Toowoomba, a long, winding deviation while the highway climbs much more steeply on a shorter but less scenic route. In the Little Liverpool ranges is one of the oldest tunnels and the longest single-bore tunnel on Australian railways. There are good views to the south and east; the best side for viewing is the left going west, however on the westbound journey it will be dark and you will probably be concentrating on having a meal in the grill buffet car. You can see this part of the ranges by day from the eastbound Westlander.

Helidon, at the foot of the main (Great Dividing) range, is a pleasant little town famous for its spa waters and a good place to break the journey. **Spring Bluff**, a picturesque little station right in the middle of the ranges, is always winning the competition for the best-kept station and is worthy of a look on the return trip when its profusion of flower beds is evident on both sides of the track. In late September during Toowoomba's Festival there are usually special 'Carnival of Flowers' excursions to Spring Bluff from Toowoomba.

Toowoomba, Queensland's third city and the garden city of the Darling Downs, sits atop the Dividing Range escarpment. It is well worth

Warwick

Once gateway to the south by rail on the former 'main line', Warwick is 94km south of Toowoomba and can be reached only on an excursion or by freight train or McCafferty's bus. It is the outlet for the fruit-growing area of Queensland's 'Granite Belt'.

For many years the Sydney Express followed the NSW Tableland route as far north as Wallangarra, where the station still stands, junction of the Queensland and New South Wales systems, about five hours south of Warwick by freight train. Orchards, wineries and scenic lookouts in these granite ranges are worth visiting. **Inglewood**, which the Dirranbandi passenger train used to reach in the early hours, was the junction for Queensland's own Texas, a small border town once served by regular freight trains but an early victim of the closures of the last decade. **Dirranbandi** was the end of the south-western line, served now only by twice weekly freight trains. There are not even any substitute buses offered west of Warwick in place of the former mail train.

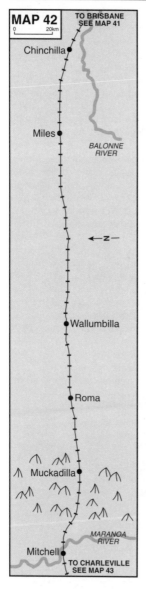

MAP 42

0   20km

TO BRISBANE
SEE MAP 41

Chinchilla

Miles

BALONNE
RIVER

←—z—

Wallumbilla

Roma

Muckadilla

MARANOA
RIVER

Mitchell

TO CHARLEVILLE
SEE MAP 43

a break of journey. Not only has it excellent restaurants and a pleasant climate, it is a colourful town proud of its trees and flowers. On the edge of the escarpment is a great view out across the ranges towards Brisbane. The *station refreshment room* is a relic of gracious living of the past. You will still get silver service, a tablecloth, and a very substantial meal for a ridiculously reasonable price, but unfortunately in the most recent change to the Westlander's itinerary, the Toowoomba stop is either early morning or late at night and the refreshment room traditional lunch is at midday.

Toowoomba to Charleville
[Maps 42, 43 and 44]

There are many places of great interest, historically and otherwise at **Oakey**, **Jondaryan**, **Dalby**, **Chinchilla** and **Miles**, all on the rail line through the fertile Darling Downs west of Toowoomba – but all unfortunately served by train in either direction only in the middle of the night, and Jondaryan no longer even a stopping place.

McCafferty's coaches (C9073 and local) greatly increase the accessibility of these places, especially if you have a joint QR/McCafferty's Pass (see p32). Jondaryan Woolshed is a must if stopping in this area because you can see shearing and other aspects of rural life.

En route to the current terminus of the Westlander at Charleville, is a stop in the early dawn (or late evening on the return) at **Roma**, a flourishing grazing town, centre for gemstones and home of Bassetts winery, long known for its rich Sauternes-style white wines.

Further on are Mitchell and Morven, both worth a visit and linked by bus as well as rail services (C 9012, 9073).

Mitchell, on the banks of the Maranoa River, was named after Sir Thomas Mitchell, explorer and surveyor-general of NSW.

The late Frank Forde, who enjoyed the quaint distinction of being Australia's shortest-serving prime minister (one week only) was born here. Well-loved by all who knew him, Forde was deputy prime minister for many years and represented Australia at the inaugural meeting of the United Nations.

The tourist information centre (☎ 07-4623 1133, 🖷 07-4623 1145) is in Kenniff Courthouse. **Morven** has a historical museum and a *pub* just over the road from the station.

This part of the route is noteworthy for the intriguing names of small siding stops, some of which have almost a poetic quality; **Muckadilla**, **Womalilla**, **Amboola**, **Mungallala**, **Dulbydilla**, **Angellala**, **Sommariva** and **Arabella**; most if not all are of Aboriginal origin.

Charleville

Heart of Queensland's mulga (small acacia) country and second-largest outback town in the state, Charleville is where the train now turns around but formerly divided in two, one part going further west to **Quilpie**. Passengers on the Quilpie portion of the train, for many years consisting of a single coach and known locally and affectionately as the 'Flying Flea', faced five hours rolling uncertainly along the slender track which itself almost disappears – they call it 'two wires in the grass'.

In the main street of Quilpie a road sign tells you how far it is to places further west. If you can face the long bus ride go to the end of the line in Quilpie station yard and look out west. This is the nearest

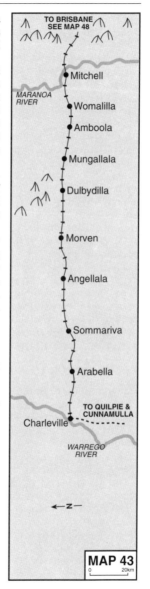

TO BRISBANE
SEE MAP 48

● Mitchell

MARANOA RIVER

● Womalilla

● Amboola

● Mungallala

● Dulbydilla

● Morven

● Angellala

● Sommariva

● Arabella

TO QUILPIE &
CUNNAMULLA

Charleville ●

WARREGO RIVER

←–z–

MAP 43
0   20km

you can get on Australia's rail network to Birdsville, that remotest of all outback settlements, famous for its annual races and the four-wheel drive Birdsville Track down to South Australia. If you intend to stay the night out west, be sure to pack some mosquito repellent; you'll need it.

The other branch from Charleville leads to **Cunnamulla**. Both Quilpie and Cunnamulla are served by connecting buses on charter to Queensland Rail and covered by the Austrail and QR rail passes. There is time for a quick out and back trip with about half an hour in either place while the train turns around and is cleaned and watered in Charleville, but you can spend a little longer and get a good taste of life out west by stopping off instead at one of the smaller places en route such as Wyandra, Cooladdi (Aboriginal for 'Black Duck'), or Cheepie ('Whistling Duck').

You will feel the heat if wandering far from the pub or road house in this area in the middle of the day. Don't walk too far: the ground is full of tiny, prickly, grass-like shrubs. Go back and have a drink before the bus returns. On the other hand, if you wait with the train in Charleville there is much of interest by just taking a walk up the main street.

In *Hotel Corones* (☎ 07-4654 1022) on the right you will find souvenirs of the major floods which inundated the town a few years ago but, although you may see thunder clouds piling up in the afternoon sky, drought is more of an experience in this sunburnt outback country than floods. When there has been 'good' rain, the land can be green here: at other times it is burned bronze. Charleville Information Centre (☎ 07-4654 3052, 🖹 07-4654 1960) is just up the road from the station.

The Westlander runs twice weekly: to stay overnight in the far south-west means spending either two or five days between trains.

ROCKHAMPTON TO WINTON

Rockhampton to Barcaldine   [Maps 44, 45 and 46]
Other inland long-distance trips by air-conditioned train are from Rockhampton and from Townsville. The Spirit of the Outback from 'Rocky' actually starts its journey at Brisbane's Roma St, covering the North Coast sector overnight and in the morning turning to make its leisurely way west through the Bowen Basin coalfields to Longreach, 'border to the far outback'.

At Rockhampton the locomotive changes ends, or a new one is attached and the train retraces its route for 5¹/₂km to **Rocklands**, where it leaves the North Coast mainline for Gracemere on the electrified Midland line.

In times of severe flooding affecting Rockhampton and particularly the low-lying parts of the track between there and Rocklands, passenger trains may use the Gracemere diversion (as all coal trains do) to by-pass Rocky and detour inland via the central Queensland electrified coal lines.

The Spirit of the Outback's next major stop, after negotiating the coastal ranges between **Kabra** and **Duaringa**, is **Bluff**, a major staging post for the coal trains which run almost hourly through this section and where three or more may often be seen together in the four passing 'roads' of the station yard.

Blackwater, a tad further west, is where the mine branches start to peel off the main midland route, south to Laleham and Koorilgah, north to Curragh and at Rangal south again to Boorgoon and Kinrola. Blackwater is a mining town, somewhat famous, or notorious, in Australia's political history as the place where the locals showed a prominent politician, then Federal Treasurer, in no uncertain terms what they thought of his bright idea to tax miners' free housing, a move as unpopular as taking away miners' free coal in Britain or depriving sailors of their rum ration!

At **Burngrove**, made conspicuous by a major electricity substation for the power to the overhead catenaries, the main coal line swings north through Bowen Basin. After passing German Creek it joins other coal lines from Blair Athol, Riverside and Goonyella at Copabella, before winding back down the ranges to the loading terminal at **Hay Point**, south of Mackay, crossing the main coast line at **Yukan**.

The major town between Rockhampton and Longreach is **Emerald**, noted and named for the gemstones mined in the area. The station is on the south side of the main street and is handy for hotels, shops and other amenities. While the train stops (usually for at least 15 minutes) there is time to nip in to one of the *pubs* opposite the railway station for a quick glass of beer or to buy an ice cream at the shop,

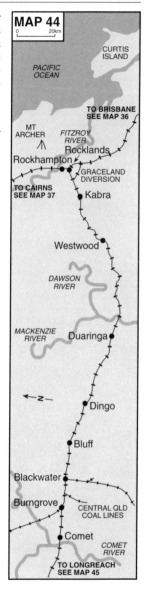

MAP 44

0   20km

CURTIS ISLAND

PACIFIC OCEAN

TO BRISBANE SEE MAP 36

MT ARCHER

FITZROY RIVER

Rocklands

Rockhampton

GRACELAND DIVERSION

TO CAIRNS SEE MAP 37

Kabra

Westwood

DAWSON RIVER

MACKENZIE RIVER

Duaringa

←z→

Dingo

Bluff

Blackwater

Burngrove

CENTRAL QLD COAL LINES

Comet

COMET RIVER

TO LONGREACH SEE MAP 45

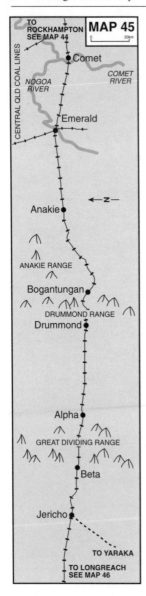

MAP 45

TO ROCKHAMPTON
SEE MAP 44

CENTRAL QLD COAL LINES

Comet

NOGOA RIVER

COMET RIVER

Emerald

Anakie

ANAKIE RANGE

Bogantungan

DRUMMOND RANGE

Drummond

Alpha

GREAT DIVIDING RANGE

Beta

Jericho

TO YARAKA

TO LONGREACH
SEE MAP 46

also opposite the station; this confection is highly regarded locally. But warn the conductor if leaving the train and intending to reboard; passengers have been known to be left behind and forced to beg a lift from local police to catch up with the train further west.

Anakie, nothing to do with lawlessness, is a place name taken from the Aboriginal for 'twin peaks'. The largest sapphire field in the world is here and it is where, in 1935, the 'Star of Queensland' black star sapphire was discovered; this is now kept at the Smithsonian Institute in Washington.

After a brief stop at **Bogantungan**, the climb into the Drummond Range begins; the journey is full of sharp curves which means you can look out of the window from anywhere in the train to see either the locomotive end or the rear or both, curving one way or the other. The curves are as tight as 80m (four chain) radius and the track, which has been climbing steadily for the preceding 26km, steepens to an average 1 in 70 for the 13km up to Hannan's Gap from where it descends at just under 1 in 100 to the tiny station named **Drummond**. The route here is being gradually re-aligned. On the first part of the climb you can see the formation of the original route.

Shortly after Drummond comes **Alpha**, a small settlement but (relative to the scale of things out west) a reasonably important railway centre, where freight trains are marshalled and train staff vans are attached or detached.

Trains for the remote **Yaraka** branch (see p267) may start or finish here, unless at Emerald further back, and they enter and leave the branch at **Jericho**, a slightly larger settlement 55km further west. Between Alpha and Jericho the only other station now operative is Beta; presumably they knew no more letters of the Greek alphabet after that.

At **Barcaldine**, 'Garden City of the West', see the Tree of Knowledge just outside the railway station in Oak St. The Australian Labor Party was founded here after the Shearers' strike of 1891, of which Barcaldine was the centre. The Australian Workers' Heritage Centre ($5 entry, open daily 09.00 to 17.00) commemorates the role of workers in Australian social and political history. Barcaldine also has a folk museum and good outback-style *hotels* where a counter tea and a bed can be obtained at very reasonable cost.

If staying the night is not on your agenda, there is just time to see and photograph the tree while the train pauses at the station. The tourist information centre (☎ 07-4651 1724, 🖹 07-4651 1120) is on Oak St.

Barcaldine to Winton   [Map 46]
Between Barcaldine and Longreach you will be offered high tea in the train's dining car (see p53).

At the risk of missing high tea, but with compensations, you may decide to curtail the trip at **Ilfracombe**, or break the journey there for a few days. Developed from a railway construction camp on part of Wellshot sheep station (the biggest in the region with 400,000 sheep on 6000 square kilometres) the town now has a small open-air museum (Ilfracombe Folk Museum)

Wellshot Hotel (☎ 07-4658 2106) is a 'must' on any tour of outback Queensland. It has cheap unit accommodation and offers meals; features of the bar would captivate any visitor even if the pub had no beer!

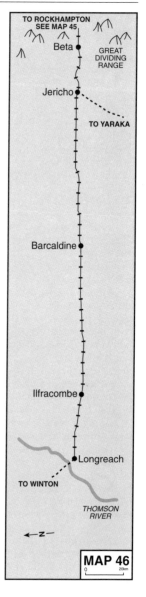

At **Longreach**, visit the early Qantas hangar and the Stockman's Hall of Fame. Australia's own airline, Qantas (Queensland and Northern Territory Air Service) was based in Longreach from 1921 to 1930 and the hangar is preserved as a heritage feature. Excellent meals and cheap accommodation can readily be found in Longreach.

The historic ***Commercial Hotel*** (☎ 07-0658 1677, 🖹 07-0658 1798) housed the original Cobb & Co stagecoach booking office. Rebuilt after a disastrous fire, it is just one block away from the station in Eagle St (the station master will point the way) and has motel-style units at under $50 a night. Longreach also has modern motels with all the amenities and even a night club. It is a place in which it is worth staying more than the one night you would have if returning by the train on which you arrive. The tourist information centre (☎ 07-4658 3555, 🖹 07-4658 3733), open daily, is at Qantas Park.

From Longreach station, Alan and Suzie Smith's Outback Aussie Tours offer excursions to Winton and beyond; phone freecall ☎ 1800 810510 for details. Since the withdrawal of passenger trains between Longreach and Winton, Queensland Rail has charter buses which connect with the arrival and departure of trains, although allowing less time in Winton than there is in Longreach, unless the return journey is postponed to the next of the twice-weekly services.

Winton, a major sheep and cattle centre, is the birthplace of Qantas (the airline) and the song *Waltzing Matilda*; the latter is based on a story about a swagman who stole a sheep and jumped into the Combo Waterhole, 145km from Winton, to escape the police. Written by 'Banjo' Patterson, a visiting solicitor who was staying at nearby Dagworth cattle station a few years later, in 1895, it was first publicly sung in Winton's North Gregory Hotel (☎ 07-4657 1375).

An enthralling account of events connected with the origin of this song, Australia's folk 'anthem', is given in the book *Matilda my Darling* by Nigel Krauth in which, incredibly, the publishers were not allowed to include the words known by heart and loved by all Australians, because some American person or body has apparently acquired the copyright.

Visit the Waltzing Matilda Centre (☎ 07-4657 1466, 🖹 07-4657 1886 or 🖳 matildapronet.net.au) in the main street, 10 minutes from the station, for a journey into history. With $80 and time to spare you could hire a car to see the dinosaur tracks 111km south of town at Lark's Quarry Environmental Park on the Jundah road. Winton's water supply comes from boreholes over a kilometre deep and has a temperature close to boiling point.

The original rail link to Winton was from Hughenden on the QR Great Northern line, and this is now the only way it can be reached by rail, though not without difficulty (see p86). Reinstatement of a regular passenger train service is being actively sought.

TOWNSVILLE TO MOUNT ISA
[Maps 47, 48 and 49]

The Inlander links Townsville and Mount Isa, through Hughenden and such romantic places as Charters Towers, Julia Creek and Cloncurry, not to mention Nonda. One of Queensland's first fully air-conditioned trains, the Inlander first ran in 1953.

At **Charters Towers**, population 10,000, you are back in gold-rush history. Legacies of past glories include more National Trust buildings than anywhere else in Queensland. Seen from the top of Towers Hill and worth a visit, is the Venus Gold Battery, a stamping mill restored by the National Trust. See also the old German Church in Ann St, or simply visit one of the old pubs of which there were 80 in the town's heyday. Gold was discovered here by accident in 1871. The soldier poet known as Breaker Morant lived here during the subsequent gold rush when the population was 30,000.

Hughenden is a place you are only likely to visit by rail en route to or from Winton (see p86), unless joining or leaving a train at a rather isolated station in the middle of the night has irresistible appeal. Many freight trains bypass the station, but stop for brake tests and crew changes on sidings on an avoiding loop to the west. Porcupine Gorge National Park is 63km to the north, while at the Visitor Information Centre and Dinosaur Display (☎ 07-4741 1021) in Gray St, the exhibits include a life-size replica of Australia's own bird-footed dinosaur Muttaburrasaurus, relics of which were found at Muttaburra between here and Longreach.

Richmond is a small town (population 800) approximately midway between Townsville and Mount Isa by road and on

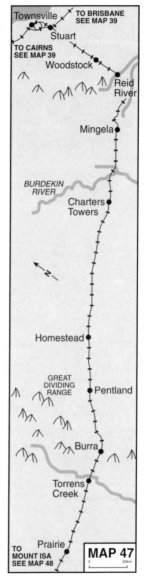

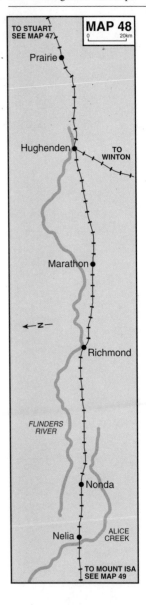

MAP 48

TO STUART
SEE MAP 47

0   20km

Prairie

Hughenden

TO WINTON

Marathon

←─Z─

Richmond

FLINDERS RIVER

Nonda

Nelia

ALICE CREEK

TO MOUNT ISA
SEE MAP 49

the banks of Queensland's longest river, the Flinders. It is described as the heart of the ancient inland sea, and the Marine Fossil Museum (☎ 07-4741 3429), with its rare or unique examples found locally at **Marathon**, which is 48km or about 45 minutes on the train before Richmond, invites the visitor to 'step back 100 million years'. See Australia's best-preserved dinosaur fossil and the 'moon rocks' of limestone displayed at Lions Park.

An hour or more before Julia Creek going west, or 40 minutes or so after midnight going east, the train stops at **Nonda**, a depot for railway freight and mineral train crews which still boasts a station master and a waiting room with refreshments (a soft drink slot machine). Cartoon postcards, obtainable at the station, cynically advertise it as 'Nonda by the Sea'.

Julia Creek, described as being in the middle of nowhere, is reached either in early morning or late at night on the Inlander. This small outback town features in Scyld Berry's book *Train to Julia Creek*, representing to his mind 'the end of a journey in search of the spirit of Australia'.

Cloncurry, known as The Curry, boasts the remains of the 'Great Australian' copper mine of 1867. See also the Cloister of Plaques in Uhr St, site of the Flying Doctor's first base in 1928. Tourist information is available from the Council Chambers, Scarr St. Cloncurry is the junction for the disused Kajabbi branch and a good place to break the journey if intending to take the bus to Normanton and the Gulf Country. Cloncurry also has links with Qantas, Australia's airline which, it is asserted, was 'conceived in Cloncurry, born in Winton and grew up in Longreach'.

Between Cloncurry and Mount Isa the scenery is particularly rugged. On your left you may see wandering camels, one of which was said to be a customer at the pub nearby at **Duchess**, where a brief stop may be made by the Inlander.

Mount Isa, the largest city in the world (by area 40,977 sq km or 15,822 square miles), is roughly twice the size of Wales but with only a fraction of the population, about 25,000. This is an industrial complex which looks almost incongruous in the middle of nowhere. You will be acutely aware of the giant chimneys, but don't miss the Underground Museum in Shackleton St. A nearby lookout offers a good view of the city and mine.

There are many tours available here if your stay is longer than it takes the train to be turned and refurbished. This includes a full 24 hours if you arrive on the Wednesday train from the east. Tours range from the two-hour Mount Isa Explorer covering the world's largest silver, lead and zinc mine to the three-day/two-night all-inclusive Lawn Hill and Riversleigh Safari, visiting world heritage Riversleigh fossil fields and Lawn Hill National Park. Try the Riversleigh Centre (☎ 07-4749 1555, 🖹 07-4743 6296, 🖳 riversleigh@tpgi. com.au) at Centenary Park, or contact Campbell's Tours & Safaris (☎ 07-4743 2006, 🖹 07-4743 6903 or freecall ☎ 1800 242 329) before leaving Townsville on the Mount Isa train.

KURANDA SCENIC RAILWAY

Only 33km long, the Kuranda railway line first runs for 12km along the flat coastal strip north of Cairns to Redlynch,

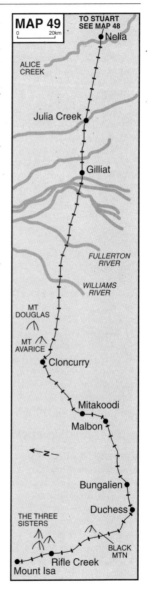

MAP 49

TO STUART
SEE MAP 48

0   20km

Nelia

ALICE
CREEK

Julia Creek

Gilliat

FULLERTON
RIVER

WILLIAMS
RIVER

MT
DOUGLAS

MT
AVARICE

Cloncurry

Mitakoodi

Malbon

← N →

Bungalien

Duchess

THE THREE
SISTERS

BLACK
MTN

Rifle Creek
Mount Isa

where the climb up the coastal ranges really begins. Redlynch came to notice during World War II when it was the site of the largest field hospital in the Southern hemisphere. Before the war some of the cars on this train had sideways seating arranged like a grandstand for better viewing, but facing out from one side of the train only. The cars were converted for ambulance use during the war but the unusual seating was never restored – and no need! There are great views on both sides.

In the next 19km the line rises 318 metres up the side of the Barron River Gorge, first negotiating a horseshoe bend to the right, the Jungara loop, then a series of tight curves and 15 tunnels. The opening up of this rail route into the hinterland in 1891 gave Cairns the edge over its former rivals, Port Douglas and Geraldton (since named Innisfail). First surveyed in 1882, the line took nearly 10 years to construct and enormous difficulties were faced by the workers. A small booklet on the line's history, and including a map, is available to passengers on booking.

Mostly clinging to the edge of a 45-degree slope the line then enters Stoney Creek station, now merely a passing loop but where the train stops to ensure the line ahead is clear. Stoney Creek is crossed by a trestle bridge on another tight bend, almost in the spray of the waterfall. Next, after curving round the bluff past a rock column known as Robbs Monument, the line comes out above the wide amphitheatre above Barron Falls, where the train stops for passengers to look out at the view and take photos. These falls are somewhat disappointing except in heavy rain, because most of the water has been diverted for hydro-electric power.

Kuranda is famous for its railway station, which is like a botanical garden, for the *Bottom Pub* (Kuranda Hotel-Motel see p237) where you can meet some of the locals, for the craft markets (open on Wednesdays, Thursdays, Fridays and Sundays) a hundred metres or so up the main street past the *Top Pub*, and just beyond, the noctarium and butterfly sanctuary. Close to the station on the lower side is the river, while on the higher side just past the pub is the Skyrail terminal.

MAREEBA TO FORSAYTH

Mareeba to Almaden   [Map 50]
Mareeba, the Aboriginal name for 'meeting of the waters' (the Barron and Granite rivers), is a former stopping place of Cobb's coaches and a centre for timber and tobacco. The sawmill yard to the right of the station is worth a look.

The town centre adjoins the station. *Highlander* (formerly Dunlop's) *Hotel*, just over the road, has a reputation for offering the 'best tucker in town'. Mareeba is a useful base for an excursion through tobacco country to Dimbulah or coach trips south into the Atherton Tableland. Mareeba rodeo is held every July in nearby Kerribee Park. A granite gorge, west of the town, has boulders the size of eight-storey buildings.

The railways west of Mareeba in north Queensland were built by the Chillagoe Railway & Mining Co. The Chillagoe line to the then copper mines was completed in 1901 and the Etheridge Railway to Forsayth goldfields in 1911. The whole lot was taken over by the government of Queensland eight years later when mining declined.

The opening of one of the world's most remarkable natural wonders, the Lava Tubes at Undara (see p253), has helped to bring new life to this almost forgotten remnant of a once thriving railway system, where in the old days the Cairns Express was pride of the line and drivers were fined if it ran late.

Chewko, 12km beyond Mareeba was once the major tobacco-growing area in Australia. The Chewko Range is part of the Great Dividing Range; from here on the creeks flow to the west. Watch out beyond Chewko for Arriga Junction, where a new line serves a sugar mill opened in 1998.

Tabacum, from the Latin *nicotina tabacum*, is appropriately named.

Dimbulah is the first comparatively major settlement after Mareeba. It was originally the junction for the line to Mount Mulligan, scene of Queensland's worst mine disaster in 1921. It is an important local centre for fruit and vegetable produce. Conveniently *Junction Hotel* (☎ 07-4093 5206) is opposite the station.

Near **Boonmoo** you will hardly miss Mt Pinnacle on the right ahead. This leads to Cape Horn where, in the gorge on the right, is Australia's shortest telegraph pole. The story has it that you can see the Pacific Ocean, 100km to the east, through

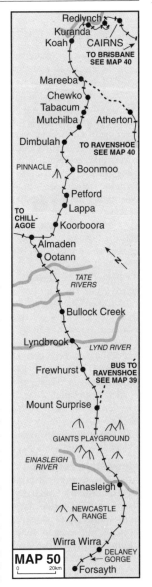

a gap in the ranges but you would need to know the exact spot or spend a fair while in the area to prove it.

Petford boasts a shop and a post office. It is also the site of a work camp for troubled youths which, during 1999, was a source of controversy in the media. The train crew will tell you more if you ask.

At **Lappa**, short for its original name Lappa Lappa, you will note a siding on the left, a remnant of the former branch to Mount Garnet. In the old days this was a railway refreshment stop. The disused pub is still occupied and maintained privately by the owners as a historic feature. Passengers are welcome to enjoy a drink at the bar – but it is strictly BYO.

Almaden or **Alma Den**, also known as Cow Town (you will soon see why) is the last junction on the line and the current overnight stopping place for the westbound Savannahlander. *Railway Hotel*, over the road from the station, takes guests but most opt for the bus connection to the old mining town of **Chillagoe**, 33km to the north along a very rough unsealed track.

Chillagoe is conspicuous with its old smelter chimney; until 1999 it was fired once a year by the locals as a memorial to the past. In the town centre there are two hotels to choose from, *Black Cockatoo* (☎ 07-4094 7168) and *Post Office* (☎ 07-4094 7119), and there is also *Eco-Lodge* (☎ 07-4094 7119, 37 Queen St) on the northern edge of town; a connecting coach serves them all on request. There is time here to visit the Royal Arch Cave National Park or one of the other caves close to town, or the Balancing Rock, the old smelters or marble quarries (the quality matches that from Carrara in Italy). The museum is specially worthy of a visit, where among other things you can learn something of Queensland politics of the past. For information and tour guidance contact the Ranger (☎ 07-4094 7163, 🖹 07-4094 7213) or Queensland Department of Environment and Heritage in Cairns (☎ 07-4051 9811).

The re-opening of the 28½km rail line to Chillagoe is not out of the question. If you travel on the Savannahlander, write to support it. Politics have a lot to with railway openings and closures. People power can, in the end, defeat economic rationalist ideology, as the history of this whole route has demonstrated more than once.

Almaden to Forsayth [Map 50]

After Almaden the route meanders among the hills and creeks, through **Ootann**, **Bullock Creek**, **Lyndbrook** (a former railway staff station in the 'Last Great Train Ride' days), to Fossilbrook Creek where at one time the train would stop to allow passengers to take a dip. The freshwater crocodiles did not seem to mind. After passing **Frewhurst** the train reaches **Mount Surprise** where there is a welcome half-hour break in which to visit one of the two cafés or the pub for lunch. In offering meat pies the landlord may ask whether you want cat or kangaroo. Don't be afraid; you will not be poisoned. Mount Surprise is the overnight stop on the return journey when there is the option of transferring to a bus for a visit to the nearby Undara Lava Tubes, an outstanding system of volcanically-formed caves, believed to be around 200,000 years old but only recently rediscovered. The Lava Tubes are visited by full day, half-day or two-hour tours from *Lava Lodge*, where accommodation is available ranging from tents to berths in railway sleeping cars; for further details and bookings phone ☎ 07-4097 1411.

At Junction Creek, after leaving Mount Surprise, the line cuts through one of the main lava flows. Between Mount Surprise and the next stop, **Einasleigh**, the train wanders through an area known locally as the Giants' Playground. Huge boulders are balanced on the top of rugged crags and you wonder how they got there. Shortly before Einasleigh is the crossing of the Einasleigh River, one of the most photographed and fascinating on the line. The train may stop here for a short while. The line curves and dips down to the bridge and in periods of heavy rain the rails can be under water.

Einasleigh was formerly a copper-mining town and gold was also found in the river. The Kidston Gold Mine, 40km south, is among the top gold-producing mines in Australia. There is a break here in order to visit the pub, the remains of the old town hall (so they tell you) which until blown down in the late 90s in a violent storm was known as Einasleigh's very own 'leaning tower'. Passengers can also visit the adjoining gorge of the Copperfield River; if breaking the journey to stay the night, a dip in its deep pool between the rocks is an exhilarating experience. The freshwater crocs are said to be harmless unless provoked or disturbed while mating.

The train crew will point out various other features and there will be some surprise stops during the final 66km across the Newcastle Range to Forsayth, the end of the line. **Wirra Wirra** is the only intermediate station. On the approach to **Forsayth** the line twists its way along the side of Delaney River Gorge; the shrieking of the wheels on the tight curves announcing its approach to the townsfolk waiting to greet its arrival. *Goldfields Hotel* (☎ 07-4062 5374) is across the road from the station at Forsayth. On the same side as the station you will see one of the diesel mechanical locomotives similar to those used to haul the trains until well into the 1980s.

PART 6: FOR THE ENTHUSIAST

For the enthusiast

This section is obviously misnamed. Of course **all** railways are of interest to enthusiasts, but some are perhaps of more interest than others. This chapter therefore deals with historic, preserved and unusual railways with which Australia abounds.

Travel centres and enquiry offices operated by the various rail systems at the main stations have information on private railways in their area and also on special excursions which are run quite frequently by the Australian Railway Historical Society (ARHS) and other societies, often on lines normally used only for freight or primary produce such as wheat, wool, pineapples etc. An excellent and comprehensive guide to private and preserved railways for the whole of Australia, is published by the NSW Division of ARHS as *Guide to Australian Heritage Trains and Railway Museums*. The 7th edition should be obtainable from most specialist railway bookshops, eg the Railfan Shop in Flinders Lane, Melbourne, or direct from the publishers, ARHS New South Wales Division (☎/🖹 02-9699 1714), 67 Renwick St, Redfern, NSW 2016.

Previous editions of *Australia by Rail* offered an outline itinerary for those rail enthusiasts or any other tourists who might wish to experience some of the best of such railways without spending unnecessary time finding out what there is, where it is, when it operates and how to get there. Most enthusiasts prefer to work out their own itinerary, so in this edition the former itinerary has been replaced with details, state by state, of some of the major rail museums and operating historic or unusual railways; the name of the nearest regular station and, where necessary, the distance or journey time from there to the item of interest as well as advice on how to get to that station (and back) from the nearest major centre are provided. Details of operating times, fares etc should be checked carefully before travel.

As with preserved and private railways the world over, some are now unfortunately totally disconnected from the rest of the system and can only be reached by private transport. Particularly saddening in recent times has been the isolation of the former South Australian railways broad-gauge Mount Barker Junction–Victor Harbor branch from the Adelaide suburban network by the conversion to standard gauge of the Adelaide–Melbourne line east of Belair. This prevents the former loco-hauled SteamRanger (see p269) making a full day-return trip from Adelaide up over the Mt Lofty Ranges which, at 264km each way, was the longest tourist rail route in Australia and one of the most scenic.

NEW SOUTH WALES INCLUDING CANBERRA

3801 Limited and the Cockatoo Run

A circular tour at $89 including a gourmet lunch is offered by 3801 Limited. Leaving Sydney Central at 10.30 on Wednesdays, the diesel-hauled 'Long Lunch Train' of restored and renovated carriages climbs into the Southern Highlands as far as Moss Vale where it stops for an hour's lunch break while the locomotive shunts to the other end for the descent to the coast at Wollongong. Passing through Robertson, home of the famous pig in the film *Babe,* the train reaches Summit Tank, where there is a break to allow passengers to walk to the lookout above Lake Illawarra. The line then descends through virgin rainforest to Unanderra where it joins the coast route back to Sydney, due in at 18.05.

The Cockatoo run between Port Kembla, Unanderra and Robertson only (not connecting to Moss Vale) operates on Tuesdays, Thursdays, Saturdays, Sundays and some public holidays (except Christmas Day), while excursions further afield hauled by steam locomotive 3801 operate at weekends. For bookings and details of specials phone ☎ 1300 65 3801 or call at Wollongong Tourism Office (☎ 02-4228 0300) or any Countrylink travel centre. The nearest stations for the Cockatoo run are Port Kembla and Unanderra, both on CityRail's south coast line.

Broken Hill Transport Museum

Located in the former Sulphide St station of Silverton Tramway, opposite the tourist information centre at the corner of Blende and Bromide Sts, this museum is open daily from 10.00 to 15.00. The static display includes one of the large 4-8-2 steam locos formerly used on the Silverton Tramway and cars from the old Silver City Comet diesel express.

The museum is an easy walk from Broken Hill station, which is served by the Indian Pacific from Sydney or Adelaide twice weekly or The Ghan once weekly. On other days the only access to Broken Hill is by coach to and from the XPT at Dubbo (an $8^1/_2$-hour bus journey connecting with a $6^1/_2$-hour train journey!) or by Hazelton Air Services. For rail connections see the summary on p78 (Table 4).

Canberra Railway Museum

The museum (☎ 02-6239 6707/6295 7909), ARHS, Geijera Place, Kingston, near Canberra station is open at weekends and on public holidays.

Dorrigo Steam Railway and Museum

This museum claims to have the largest collection of railway vehicles in the Southern hemisphere, including 54 locomotives and over 300 other rolling stock items. There are plans to operate steam-hauled tourist trains on the 70km former State Rail branch which joins the main North Coast line at Glenreagh, 43km south of Grafton, but at the time of writing this service is yet to commence and the museum is not open to the public; phone ☎ 02-6657 2176 for further information.

Some vehicles may be seen at Glenreagh on the NSW main North Coast line but this is no longer a stop for mainline trains nor is there a feeder bus service as originally provided when the XPT first replaced the loco-hauled North Coast trains. The sidings at Glenreagh may be observed, if the trains are on time, on the right side of the southbound Grafton XPT at about 07.15 or the southbound Brisbane XPT just after noon or on the left from the northbound Murwillumbah XPT around 16.20.

Hunter Valley

Hunter Valley is the scene of some of Australia's earliest railways (horse-drawn tramways carried coal to Newcastle as long ago as 1827) and, like northern England's Tyneside after which so many of its places are named, it is a fascinating area for the industrial archaeologist as well as the rail enthusiast.

Places of particular interest include Newcastle, Maitland, Morpeth, Hexham, East Greta, Rothbury and Kurri Kurri but, with some exceptions, the major attractions are not readily accessible by public transport. In April, the annual Hunter Valley Steamfest (PO Box 351, Maitland NSW 2320, ☎ 02-4933 2611) is based on Maitland, from where tours by rail and road take in most places of interest.

● **Hunter Valley Railway Museum** The museum (☎ 02-4933 1923, 🖹 02-4933 9923, 🖳 hvrtmuseum@hotmail.com), PO Box 37, Branxton NSW 2335, is at the former Rothbury Colliery, 5km by private line from Branxton which is 10km west of Maitland on the main north line. It has a large collection of NSW passenger carriages, including some complete sets. Steam-hauled trains operate from time to time from Branxton, eg during the Steamfest in April.

Frequent electric trains link Sydney with Newcastle. A regular Endeavour diesel service links Newcastle with the Hunter Valley.

Branxton services are shown in Table 14 on p257.

● **Richmond Vale Railway** This railway, in Kurri Kurri, operates steam trains on the first three Sundays of each month over 4km of line between Richmond Main and Pelaw Main collieries (a route on which steam-

---

(**Opposite**) **Top**: The Ballyhooley express, a 12-tonne diesel loco which hauls period carriages on 3km of the narrow-gauge Mossman Central Mill sugar-cane line (see p263). **Bottom**: The SteamRanger (see p269) approaching Victor Harbor.

❏ **Table 14**
Sydney–Newcastle–Branxton (C 9016 and local)

		Mon-Fri	Mon-Fri	Mon-Fri	Mon-Fri	Sat/Sun	Sat/Sun
Sydney	dep	23.17a	05.41b	13.17c	15.12c		15.17c
Newcastle	dep	03.15	08.07	15.54	17.39	03.54	17.44
Maitland	dep	03.50	08.51	16.29	18.14	04.36	18.19
Branxton	arr	04.09	09.10	16.48	18.33	04.55	18.38

Branxton–Newcastle–Sydney (C 9016 and local)

Branxton	dep	07.07	11.03	19.43	21.28	07.48	21.51
Maitland	arr	07.32	11.24	20.04	21.49	08.09	22.13
Newcastle	arr	08.06	11.58	20.29	22.30	08.43	22.47
Sydney	arr	10.21c	15.10c	23.10c	02.11d	11.10c	02.11d

Notes
Local air-conditioned trains – no catering
a departs previous day, change at Hamilton
b change at Broadmeadow
c change at Hamilton
d arrives next day, change at Hamilton.

hauled coal trains regularly operated until as late as 1987). For further details write to PO Box 224, Kurri Kurri, NSW 2327 or phone ☎ 02-4937 5344. Frequent local buses, operated by Rover coaches (☎ 02-49901699), run between Kurri Kurri and Maitland.

Katoomba Scenic Railway

A 1219mm-gauge railway which was built to serve a coal mine, this 0.45km (¼ mile) incline railway is the steepest in the world with a maximum gradient of 128 per cent (1 in 0.78). The frequent service operates daily between 09.00 and 16.50; the return fare is $3.60. The railway is reached by bus from opposite Carrington Hotel outside Katoomba station, or by a 2.5km walk. The top station (where the trip starts) adjoins the Katoomba Skyway terminal, the descent gives magnificent views of Blue Mountain scenery and the bottom station gives access to walking tracks in Jamieson Valley.

Katoomba station, 110km west of Sydney, is served by frequent interurban EMUs from Central (C 9014 and local).

Lachlan Valley Railway, Cowra

The museum and depot at Cowra is reached by Countrylink XPT and coach connection via Bathurst on the western line from Sydney Central.

(**Opposite**) The Ipswich Workshops (see p264), Queensland, are the only railway workshops in Australia that have been operating since the 1860s. Queensland Rail's heritage fleet of steam locos are restored here.

Trains operate to various points along the Harden–Cowra–Blayney line at weekends, once or twice monthly; phone ☎ 02-9809 2021 or 🖹 02-6341 3599 for timetables, fares and bookings.

Although Countrylink trains call at Blayney, the 'connecting' buses to or from Cowra (a 70-minute journey) miss the train by just a few minutes in each direction: one of those seemingly deliberate non-connections some railway systems achieve so effortlessly! But a night-stop in Blayney can avoid an extra 35 minutes of bus travel from Bathurst.

Metro Monorail, Sydney

Metro Monorail, of the straddle type, circles the central area of the city and the Darling Harbour complex.

The nearest CityRail station is Town Hall (three minutes from Central), just one street block away. A day pass costs $6 and the complete circuit takes just over 10 minutes, trains running every few minutes. A trip on the monorail is an excellent way to get a snapshot of Sydney's many attractions.

Michelago Tourist Railway, Queanbeyan

This railway usually operates on the first and third Sunday of each month over 50km of the former Queanbeyan–Cooma–Bombala branch of State Rail. A scenic route commencing with a 1 in 40 climb and affording views of Tuggeranong, one of Canberra's satellite new towns.

Excursion trains operate to scenic Molonglo Gorge and various centres in the Southern Highlands. Dinner and dinner/dance excursions are among a variety of temptations offered. Details and bookings from ARHS Tours (☎ 02-6239 6707 or ☎ 02-6295 7909), PO Box 112, Civic Square, ACT 2608. Queanbeyan station is reached by Countrylink's Xplorer services from Sydney or Canberra.

Table 15 below summarises the connecting service.

❏ **Table 15**

Sydney–Queanbeyan–Canberra (Countrylink) (C 9021)

Train No		619	621	623
Sydney	dep	07.05	11.44	18.14
Queanbeyan	arr	10.58	15.35	22.05
Canberra	arr	11.15	15.50	22.21

Canberra–Queanbeyan–Sydney (Countrylink) (C 9021)

Train No		620	622	624
Canberra	dep	06.45	12.15	17.15
Queanbeyan	arr	06.53	12.23	17.23
Sydney	arr	10.55	16.24	21.26

Notes All trains are air-conditioned, have refreshment facilities, require reservations and operate daily.

NSW Rail Transport Museum, Thirlmere

Whatever Dorrigo Museum may claim, NSW Rail Transport Museum (☎ 02-9744 9999 or ☎ 02-4681 8001), at Thirlmere, is regarded as Australia's largest and includes an operating steam-hauled service on Sundays, holiday Mondays and on Wednesdays in school holidays. These connect with frequent CityRail electric trains at Picton on the main south line, 82km from Sydney, while Thirlmere itself can be reached by connecting private bus from Picton. Trains run from Picton to Buxton (13.8km) on the route of the steeply-graded original south mainline (it is a steady 1 in 40 most of the way from Picton to Thirlmere).

The museum is open daily (except on Good Friday and Christmas Day). Admission costs $6, the train ride is $8, with reductions for pensioners and students.

Perisher Skitube Railway (C 9019)

An 8.6km standard gauge on Voll Rack system, electric, offering a 12-minute journey mostly every 20 minutes (less frequent in the off-ski season) from Thredbo (Bullocks Terminal) to Perisher Valley, 70 per cent of the route being in tunnel; for further details phone ☎ 02-6456 2010. Reputed to have the widest rail-passenger vehicles in the world, it is also the world's fastest rack railway at 40km/h and Australia's highest railway reaching an altitude of 1900m.

Bus connections by Greyhound, twice daily from Canberra (Jolimont bus station), take 3 hours 10 minutes. The Skitube return fare is $25.

Powerhouse Museum, Sydney

A museum of transport and technology (☎ 02-9217 0111), including rail exhibits, open daily from 10.00 to 17.00, admission costs $8. Located in Harris St, Ultimo, and linked to the city by the metro monorail (Haymarket Station).

Sydney Tramway Museum, Loftus, and Sutherland Tourist Tramway

The tram terminus is just south of Sutherland station, and the museum (open on Wednesdays, Sundays and public holidays) adjoins Loftus station. The tram operates on the former 2km Royal National Park branch of State Rail.

Served by frequent electric trains, it is a 36-minute journey from Sydney Central to Loftus. An adult all-day ticket ($10) covers the museum and the tram route; for details phone ☎ 02-9542 3646.

❏ **Prices in this book – Australian dollars**
Note that all prices quoted in this book are given in Australian dollars unless otherwise indicated. The current exchange rate is Australian $1 to US$0.58 or UK£0.38. For up-to-the-minute rates visit **www.xe.net/currency**.

Zigzag Railway, Lithgow

Steam trains and vintage railmotors on 7.5km of the historic Blue Mountains former zigzag route, one of the engineering wonders of the 19th century, now converted to 1067mm gauge.

The service operates throughout the year (except on Christmas Day) from around 09.00 to 18.00. The full return trip from Bottom Points to Clarence takes 1½ to 2 hours and costs $10. Zigzag is a request stop on the regular Sydney–Lithgow interurban services (C 9014 and local). The 08.02 train from Sydney Central is the recommended connection. For further details phone ☎ 02-6353 1795, ▤ 02-6353 1801 or for recorded information ☎ 02-6351 4826.

VICTORIA

Ballarat Vintage Tramway

Ballarat Vintage Tramway (☎ 03-5334 1580), 1.3km through Botanic Gardens, is part of Ballarat's original tramway system which opened in 1887 and closed in 1971.

The tramway is open from around noon on Saturdays, Sundays and holidays and can be reached by bus No 15 from Post Office Corner near the railway station, itself a historic monument. Ballarat is 119km from Melbourne Spencer St and is reached by a fairly frequent V/line train service taking about 90 minutes (C 9031).

Puffing Billy Railway, Belgrave

The Puffing Billy Preservation Society (☎ 03-9754 6800, ▤ 03-9754 2513, ✉ pbr@pbr.org.au), part of a statutory body known as the Emerald Tourist Railway Board, operates this narrow-gauge (762mm or 2 ft 6 in) branch of the former Victorian Railways (VR) system.

The pioneer and best known of Australia's preserved railways, it was extended in 1998 deep into the Dandenong Ranges to the original terminus at Gembrook, 24km from Belgrave. Mostly operated by steam, such as a 2-6-2 Prairie Tank, and manned by volunteers, trains run at least twice daily except on Christmas Day. The adult return fare Belgrave–Gembrook (4½ hours) is $26.

Shorter trips may be made, eg to Menzies Creek, where the Society has a steam museum, to Lakeside (two hours), or to Emerald. There are luncheon and afternoon tea specials on some days, while a night train with licensed dining car is available for special bookings or when advertised. Access by frequent suburban train from Flinders St or Spencer St, Melbourne, to Belgrave, 70 minutes (C 9023), Information leaflets are available at Spencer St station and Belgrave. *Ranges Hotel* (☎ 03-5968 1220), opposite the station in Gembrook, is convenient for an overnight stay or a lunch break.

Bellarine Peninsula Railway, Queenscliffe–Drysdale

The 16km remnant of the former Geelong–Queenscliffe branch is reached by frequent trains from Melbourne to Geelong (60 minutes, C 9023) with a connecting bus to Queenscliffe.

The railway operates on Sundays and public holidays with additional days during school holiday periods.

The adult return fare is $9. For detailed timings and days of operation, phone ☎ 03-5258 2069.

Bendigo trams

The trams go through the city centre, within walking distance of Bendigo station, passing historic buildings, the old tram depot and Central Deborah gold mine.

The service runs from 10.00 daily except Christmas Day; a travelling restaurant tram operates throughout the day on Fridays and Saturdays. For further details phone ☎ 03-5443-8117. Bendigo is 162km from Melbourne and is served by regular V/line trains (C 9032).

Castlemaine and Maldon Railway

This runs on Sundays and most holidays, except during total fire bans, on 8km of the former Victorian Railways branch. Maldon station is a National Trust listed building and the town itself is subject to special preservation policies.

The fare is $10; for details phone ☎ 03-5475 2966 on operating days, or ☎ 03-5475 2598, 🗎 03-5475 1427 at other times, or email 🖳 cmr@castlemaine.net.au.

Castlemaine, 16km from Maldon and 125km from Melbourne on the Bendigo line, is the nearest station, from where there is a very limited bus service (C 9032).

Central Highlands Tourist Railway, Daylesford

Central Highlands Tourist Railway (☎ 03-5348 3503 or ☎ 03-5348 3927) operates on a partly-restored 1600mm-gauge branch line between Daylesford and Karlsruhe.

Ex-VR vintage railmotors operate on Sundays hourly between 10.00 and 14.45 and on Saturday evenings. Daylesford railway station in Raglan St is 125km from Melbourne, reached by V/line train and bus, changing at Woodend, a two-hour journey overall.

There is no bus service on Sunday until the evening, so prospective travellers on this railway must stay overnight on Saturday in Daylesford if relying on public transport (C 9032).

South Gippsland Railway, Korumburra

One of Australia's newest steam railways (also operates diesel railcars from South Australia and a diesel electric railmotor ex-Victorian Railways) has brought passenger services back to the twice-closed South Gippsland line between Nyora and Leongatha, up to 80 kilometres of route.

The line normally operates every Sunday, with extra days in December and January. All trains have refreshments, but no alcohol. Evening trips may include a 'sausage sizzle' and charter trips may be arranged.

Current timetables are obtainable from major V/line stations in the Gippsland area, such as Traralgon, or by phoning ☎ 03-5658 1111, 🗎 03-5658 1511 or freecall ☎ 1800 630 704.

The return fare to Leongatha is $16. Korumburra station is a 2 to 2¹/₂ hour journey by V/line coach from Melbourne or Dandenong (C 9023, 9096).

The Vintage Train

Based at Newport Workshops, Melbourne (not a museum), Steamrail Victoria operates heritage steam-, diesel- and electric-hauled day and overnight train tours throughout Victoria. Steamrail has the largest collection of operational heritage locomotives and rolling stock in Victoria, dating back to the 19th century.

For further information phone ☎ 03-9397 1953 or visit 💻 www.steamrail.com.au.

Yarra Valley Tourist Railway

Trains operate half-hourly every Sunday and on public holidays over 9.5km of the former VR Healesville branch from Yarra Glen, north of Lilydale, current terminus of the Melbourne Met system; phone ☎ 03-5962 2490 for further details; the railway can be reached by frequent suburban electric trains from Melbourne to Lilydale (a 55-minute journey), thence by private bus to Healesville (32 minutes).

West Coast Railway

Not merely a preserved, enthusiast or tourist railway except in the sense that its founders in 1993 'preserved' a service that otherwise would have been abandoned, that its directors, Gary McDonald and Don Gibson, are clearly rail enthusiasts and that its trains attract tourists; the West Coast Railway is unique in Australia in that its regular motive power includes steam: a 4-6-4 Hudson R711 express passenger locomotive built by the North British Co for Victorian Railways in the early 1950s and an antique Y112 0-6-0 from 1889. For details of regular services see p57 (C 9027).

Walhalla Goldfields Railway

Walhalla is 44km north of Moe in Gippsland and two hours drive east from Melbourne. Even though the railway cannot be reached by public transport mention must be made of the 42km narrow-gauge (762mm) line operated by Victorian Railways between 1910 and 1954 through spectacular mountain scenery, which is being progressively restored by an enthusiast group, the Walhalla Goldfields Railway Inc. At the time of writing, three trips are made on Saturdays between Thompson and Happy Creek, with four on Sundays. The line is expected to be extended to Walhalla itself in 2001. For further information phone ☎ 03-9513 3969 or check the website 🖳 www.comu.net.au\wgr.

QUEENSLAND

Ballyhooley Express, Port Douglas, north Queensland

A commuter service of period carriages hauled by a 12-tonne diesel loco on 3km of the narrow-gauge (610mm) Mossman Central Mill sugar-cane line between Marina Mirage station and St. Crispin's in Port Douglas; a 15-minute journey including two intermediate stops with five departures each day; booking is not required.

For further details phone the mill at ☎ 07-4098 1400. Coral Coaches operates a regular bus service between Cairns, Mossman (1 hour 20 minutes) and Port Douglas (1 hour 50 minutes).

Big Pineapple Railway, Nambour

A miniature rail circuit of pineapple plantations, built on the lines of sugar cane railways. The railway features a steep climb on a reverse curve and is situated 6.4km south of Nambour on the Bruce Highway, 10 minutes by frequent local buses from Nambour railway station.

Nambour is 1 hour 40 minutes by electric train from Brisbane, with an average of 12 trains a day each way (C 9013 and local). The Moreton Central Sugar Mill also operates cane trains which may be seen crossing streets in the town.

Brisbane Tramway Museum, Ferny Grove

This is an operating electric tramway and museum (☎ 07-3351 1776) 500m from the railway station on Brisbane suburban electric line, 25 min-

---

Other excursions in the Brisbane area

In the Brisbane area there are frequent excursions operated by the ARHS and by Trainaway Tours. These are well advertised at local stations and tourist agencies and frequently cover routes not served by regular trains. The rolling stock includes vintage carriages and motive power is usually steam, including such locomotives as the Class 10 0-4-2 locomotive No 6 built by Nelson & Co in 1865 and a magnificent restored Beyer Garratt 4-8-2+2-8-4 built in Manchester in 1949.

Excursions are also operated by Swanbank Railway near Ipswich (vintage steam train) and at the Rosewood Railway Museum at Cabanda. Unfortunately, both are accessible only by private transport, despite the existence of rail track from the nearest stations, Bundamba and Rosewood, both on the Brisbane Citytrain network.

utes from Central station. It is open on Sundays from 12.30 to 16.00 and admission costs $5 for adults.

QR Railway Workshops, Ipswich

A unique heritage attraction is The Workshops, North Ipswich, the only Australian rail workshops from the 1860s still operating. A two-hour walking tour offers a fascinating insight into the bygone era of steam. It's the working world of steam, where QR's heritage fleet of steam locomotives undergo restoration.

Site tours are offered every Wednesday at 10.30 and 13.30; group tours other days by arrangement. Lunch is available in the heritage-listed Workers' Canteen. Take the Westside bus direct from Ipswich station. Bookings to Ipswich Tourism (☎ 07-3281 0555).

Brampton Island Railway

This line runs from the jetty to the resort on Brampton Island, reached by launch from Mackay, but the railway station is somewhat distant from the jetty. There is a similar railway at Hayman Island Resort in the Whitsunday Islands near Proserpine, which is perhaps more accessible, involving a 45-minute bus ride from Proserpine station to Shute Harbour, followed by a short sea crossing. Proserpine Mill, close to the station is a major centre for Queensland cane-train activity. Table 16 below shows how to get to Proserpine.

❏ **Table 16**
Brisbane–Proserpine–Townsville C 9013

		Tue/Thu/Sat	Sun	Wed/Sun
Brisbane	dep	08.25a	08.25b	18.55c
		Wed/Fri/Sun	Mon	Thu/Mon
Proserpine	arr	03.56	03.56	13.45
Proserpine	dep	04.01	04.01	13.50
Townsville	arr	08.20	08.20	18.05

Townsville–Proserpine–Brisbane C 9013

		Tue/Fri	Tue	Mon/Thu/Sat
Townsville	dep	08.00c	15.15b	15.45a
Proserpine	arr	12.15	19.25	20.03
Proserpine	dep	12.20	19.30	20.08
		Wed/Sat	Wed	Tue/Fri/Sun
Brisbane	arr	06.20	15.10	16.10

Notes
QR air-conditioned services with dining, buffet and sleeping cars.
This table does not include the Great South Pacific Express.
a Sunlander
b Queenslander
c Spirit of the Tropics

Callemondah Yard, Gladstone

Gladstone is full of railway interest, both in the layout of the tracks through, around and behind the town, in the variety of trains you will encounter and in the almost constant activity.

At Callemondah Yard, 5km north of Gladstone station, is a vast complex of sidings, where electric and diesel locos are assigned their respective tasks. From Callemondah, the catenaries reach north and west to Emerald and, via the Bowen Basin coalfields, to Hay Point on the coast; also south to Brisbane, while diesel-operated routes strike inland to the mines of the Callide and Dawson valleys.

Gladstone is worth a break of journey for the enthusiast, but much may be observed merely passing through. The Sunlander and other long-distance trains pass Gladstone but the best viewing is in daylight on the all-electric Tilt Train (C 9013).

Dreamworld, Coomera

On the Pacific Highway, west of Gold Coast city, the Dreamworld complex includes a 3km railway at 610mm-gauge with ex-Canefield locomotives. Local buses meet QR Citytrains Gold Coast expresses at Coomera Station. The trains take one hour from Brisbane and run hourly from early morning till nearly midnight (half hourly on Saturdays and Sundays).

Dreamworld is open daily except Christmas Day. Admission to the park includes other features and shows.

Durandur Railway and Museum, Woodford

A 610mm-gauge railway which operates on Sundays only on 1km of trackbed of the former Wamuran–Kilcoy branch at Woodford, 24km west of Caboolture. Caboolture is 50 minutes by a half-hourly service from Central station, Brisbane, on the regular Citytrain network, but a taxi or hired car may be needed from there. Phone ☎ 07-3265 6834 or 07-5496 6470 for further information and to make a booking.

Dee River Railway, Mount Morgan

What might have been the slowest passenger train in the world (Thangool–Rockhampton, 178km at an overall mean speed of 11.25km/h), ran on this line in central Queensland until the mid-1980s. Among the few still operational remnants of the former Callide Valley branch of QR from Kabra Junction to Thangool is the ARHS-operated 3.5km railway between historic Mount Morgan and Cattle Creek siding. Four bridges and a tunnel, plus Mount Morgan's imposing railway station building, are features of the route. The complex is open daily and trains operate from 10.00 on Saturdays and Sundays, with group specials on request. For more details phone ☎ 07-4938 2312.

Mount Morgan can be reached by Young's bus service from Rockhampton, 38km to the north-east.

The Gulflander, Savannahlander and Kuranda Scenic Railway

These are a 'must' for every rail enthusiast, not to mention the everyday tourist, and are covered on pp54-55, pp88-90 and pp249-253).

Mary Valley Heritage Railway, Gympie

Steam-hauled trains, every Sunday, and railmotors, on Sundays and Tuesdays, depart Gympie for Kandanga (29.5km) and Imbil (39.6km) on the former Brooloo line along the Mary Valley. The timetable allows a break for lunch in Kandanga or Imbil, or time to visit the museum in Kandanga. The adult return fare is $25; further details available from ☎ 07-5482 2750, 🖷 5482 7622 or 🖳 www.cooloola.org.au/mvhr/. Gympie station is reached by QR courtesy bus connecting with interurban and Traveltrains at Gympie North but timetables favour a Gympie nightstop.

The Mulgrave Rambler, Gordonvale

Until recently operated only as a charter train or by excursions advertised locally, this cane line is the most accessible of all since the station immediately adjoins QR Gordonvale station, 22km south of Cairns and a regular stop for the Sunlander. Hauled by the Nelson, a restored Fowler 0-4-2 oil-fired steam loco, the route circles Mulgrave Mill, then passes canefields, river and rainforest to Orchid Valley where tropical plants, entertainment and refreshments are among the attractions. When the trains ran, a connecting coach was provided from Cairns. The Mill management has recently abandoned the Rambler activity but, as with so many things, public demand and encouragement from tourist bodies may induce a change of attitude. Phone ☎ 07-4043 3333 or North Queensland Tourism on ☎ 07-4051 3588 and tell them you want to travel on it.

RAILCo, Ravenshoe

The Ravenshoe-Atherton Insteam Locomotion Company, to give it its full title, operates mid-week, weekend and holiday services on the 22km Atherton–Herberton section of the former QR Atherton Tablelands branch, south of Mareeba. The route includes a 7km climb at 1 in 33 through the ranges. The company also operates a weekend and holiday service over the southern 7km of the former branch from Ravenshoe to Queensland's highest railway station at Tumoulin, 965m above sea level. Phone ☎ 07-4097 6698 for information.

Atherton and Ravenshoe are accessible from Cairns or Kuranda (see p237) by Coral Coaches Cairns–Karumba service (C 9070).

Rockhampton

Rockhampton, 630km and seven hours by train from Brisbane, is the northern limit of the QR electrified mainline and terminus of the Tilt Train intercity service, a place of great interest to rail enthusiasts (C 9013).

Most long-distance trains stop at least 25 minutes in Rockhampton, where there is time to explore the station environs. Just beyond the station the railway goes along the middle of a public street before swinging north across the river. Near the station is the original roundhouse, built in 1915 with a central turntable serving 52 locomotive bays, and other historic buildings. If changing trains or staying overnight a visit to the Central District Train Control Centre at Rocky (always learn what the locals call it) is a must, but you would have to ask permission – see Rockhampton's station master and tell him you've heard so much about it you want to tell your people back home. As they say, flattery will get you everywhere.

Other Rockhampton railway attractions include the Archer Park Railway Museum and Rockhampton Steam Tramway.

Buderim Ginger Factory, Yandina

There is a 1km loop railway of 610mm-gauge at this factory, about 200m walk from the station. A day-return trip from Brisbane is only possible on Mondays to Fridays and allows barely 40 minutes at Yandina, but the Tewantin bus service connects with four interurban trains at Nambour each weekday and with three on Saturdays and Sundays, the times varying. It is worth staying a night; *Yandina Hotel* (☎ 07-5446 7341) provides pub-style accommodation and adjoins the station.

Table 17 below summarises the Yandina train services.

Yaraka branch, QR

The Yaraka branch is one of only three in Queensland at the time of writing on which scheduled goods trains still, at least notionally, carry 'passenger accommodation'; the others being the Kingaroy branch and the Hughenden–Winton line.

Any such accommodation is most likely to consist of a grey-painted crew van and not only may the train not run to time (or at all); it may not carry any such accommodation. Enthusiasts should therefore check not only the most up-to-date timetables (C9011 for Yaraka via Jericho, C9008 for Hughenden–Winton) but also enquire from the appropriate district headquarters of Queensland Rail a few days before commencing travel.

❏ **Table 17**
Brisbane–Yandina (local)

		Mon-Fri	Daily
Brisbane	dep	12.07	17.33
Yandina	arr	14.17	19.32

Yandina–Brisbane (local)

		Mon-Fri	Sat	Mon-Fri	Sun
Yandina	dep	06.53	07.22	15.00	16.53
Brisbane	arr	08.44	09.15	17.00	19.02

Notes
Times are from Roma St but all trains call at Central

Trains on such lines, although timetabled, tend to run only according to customer requirements; you would not want to get off the comfortable Spirit of the Outback only to find that week's Yaraka 'mixed' would not be running. The station master's office at Emerald (☎ 07-4983 8351) should be contacted for details of running times and necessary ticketing.

The Yaraka branch extends for 271km from Jericho on the Rockhampton–Longreach line. Just under halfway along is Blackall, where shearer Jackie Howe hand-sheared 321 sheep in one day. At Blackall is the 'Black Stump' in the grounds of the state school: the only problem being almost every state in Australia claims its own black stump. But Blackall does have a 225-million-year-old fossil tree stump in Shamrock St.

Hughenden to Winton is 212km, while Kingaroy is 131km from Theebine, itself 34km from Gympie North, the nearest regular passenger station on the North Coast line. Although these branches commence at mainline junctions, connections in the normal sense of the word are usually non-existent and departure and arrival times tend to be at unattractive hours.

SOUTH AUSTRALIA

St Kilda Tramway Museum

A museum and 2km operating tram track to the seafront, which is best reached by taxi from Salisbury station on the suburban system (Gawler line, C 9030). The museum is open from 13.00 to 17.00 on Sundays and most public holidays.

Glenelg Tramway

A frequent and daily service on the 11km former private railway from central Adelaide (Victoria Square, 1km from City station) to the seaside suburb of Glenelg.

To avoid the walk or local bus, take a local TransAdelaide Belair or Noarlunga train from City station or from the Keswick suburban platforms to Goodwood, near to which the tram route intersects the railway route (C 9030).

Pichi Richi Railway, Quorn

Narrow gauge (1067mm), mostly steam, (including a steam motor coach, the Coffee Pot), this was part of the original Great Northern Railway intended to link Port Augusta with Darwin. It was at Quorn that the Great Northern Express to Oodnadatta was first nicknamed the Afghan Express, later shortened to become the legendary Ghan.

Historic trains, which consist of former SAR or Commonwealth Railway heritage vehicles, run from Quorn between April and November. Steam is currently scheduled for runs to Stirling North (33km) every

Saturday from April to October and every Wednesday from July to October. The adult return fare is $48 and the return journey takes four hours.

Additional services, steam or vintage railcar, run to Woolshed Flat (16.5km) on nominated days and in holiday periods between April and November. The adult return fare is $26 and the return journey time is approximately two hours. For bookings phone/fax ☎/▤ 08-8658 1109, for recorded information phone ☎ 08-8395 2566, or phone Pichi Richi Railway society's secretary on ☎ 08-8276 6232. The postal address is Railway station, Railway Terrace, Quorn, SA 5433. Workshop/museum tours (☎ 08-8352 5230) can also be arranged.

Quorn is accessible from Port Augusta, a major stop on the route of the Indian Pacific and The Ghan. Stateliner buses operate three days a week (Sundays, Wednesdays and Fridays, returning Sundays, Thursdays and Fridays, a 40-minute journey) but overnight stays in both Port Augusta and Quorn would usually need to be taken into account by those wishing to travel on the railway. There are also local buses to Stirling North but travellers wishing to join the trains there should first contact Pichi Richi Railway society for up-to-date advice, as connections are doubtful.

SteamRanger, Goolwa

The SteamRanger depot which formerly adjoined Dry Creek station on the Adelaide suburban network had to be relocated in 1996 following standardisation of the Adelaide–Melbourne line. The new depot is at Mount Barker, about 5km from Mount Barker Junction.

The SteamRanger Tourist Railway (1600mm) now operates between Mount Barker Junction, Mount Barker, Goolwa and Victor Harbor. A variety of services are available, mostly on Sundays, but not on days of total fire ban. These include the **Highlander** from Mount Barker to Philcox Hill summit, then back down the Mt Lofty ranges to Strathalbyn and back, the **Southern Encounter** from Mount Barker down to Victor Harbor and back, and the **Cockle Train** between Goolwa and Victor Harbor, sometimes diesel hauled or consisting of one of Adelaide's historic 'Red Hen' railcars. A buffet car is usually attached to the main services, which are likely to be hauled by ex-SAR 4-8-4 semi-streamlined locomotive No 520.

At Goolwa a boat trip on the lower reaches of the Murray may be offered and at Victor Harbor there is a horse-drawn tram ride to Granite Island on Encounter Bay. The adult fares range from $5 (return Mount Barker Junction) to $38 full round trip. The rolling stock includes vintage compartment coaches with a tavern car. Details from SteamRanger (☎ 08-8391 1223, ▤ 08-8391 1933, ▣ www.steamranger.org.au), Box 960, Mount Barker, SA 5251.

The only public transport access to Mount Barker is by Hills Transit buses from Adelaide via Aldgate, Bridgewater (both also on the railway but with closed stations) and historic Hahndorf. These run several times daily, phone ☎ 08-8339 1191 for information. On Sundays a bus tour connects with the Cockle Train service; for details phone ☎ 08-8332 1401.

A private train is to start running between Adelaide and Tailem Bend on Sundays, connecting with the SteamRanger service at Mount Barker. For details phone SteamRanger or S Morritz on ☎ 08-8531 1552.

Steamtown, Peterborough

Excursions are operated over the southern part of the Peterborough–Quorn 1067mm railway, between Peterborough and Orroroo or Eurelia, 57km, usually on Sundays and holiday weekends between Easter and October. The adult return fare to Orroroo is $25, Eurelia $35. For other details and bookings phone ☎ 08-8651 3566, ☎ 08-8212 1505 or, after hours, ☎ 08-8522 1394. The triple-gauge roundhouse at Peterborough is National Trust classified. Peterborough is a conditional stop on the Indian Pacific.

WESTERN AUSTRALIA

Bassendean Rail Transport Museum

Bassendean Rail Transport Museum (☎ 08-9279 7189), 136 Railway Parade, is an ARHS railway museum which is 400m north of Ashfield station, on Perth's suburban system (Midland line). It is open on Sundays and public holidays from 13.00 to 17.00.

Bennett Brook Railway

Bennett Brook Railway (☎ 08-9249 3861) is 8km north of Perth, a 5.7km long 610mm-gauge loop line through bushland, linking items of railway interest in Whiteman Park. It operates from 11.00 to 17.00 on Sundays and 11.00 to 16.00 Wednesdays to Saturdays. The Whiteman Park Tramway Museum, including a 4km standard-gauge electric tramway, is part of the park complex. Access is by taxi from Guildford station on the Transperth suburban system (Midland line C 9037 and local).

Boyanup Transport Museum

Home of the historic steam locomotive the Leschenault Lady and other relics. Diesel trips are operated within the museum yard. Boyanup station is 18km from Bunbury; access is by Westrail coach from Bunbury station or Brunswick Junction, both served by the Australind service from Perth. Boyanup is halfway between Bunbury and Donnybrook on the Western Highway (C 9036, 9134); phone ☎ 08-9731 5250 for further information.

Golden Mile Railway, Boulder

A 7km narrow-gauge (1067 mm) loop line, linking Boulder, Golden Gate and Trafalgar. Trains depart Boulder station at 10.00 daily with an extra service on Sundays and public and school holidays; the adult fare is $9. For details phone (mobile phone) ☎ 0407 387883, or enquire at Kalgoorlie Tourist Bureau (☎ 08-9021 1966. Kalgoorlie is on the Sydney–Perth TransAustralian rail route served by both the Indian Pacific and the Prospector from Perth (655 km). The Goldenlines bus service operates between Kalgoorlie and Boulder (5km) daily except Sunday.

Hotham Valley Tourist Railway and Etmilyn Forest Tramway

Hotham Valley Tourist Railway operates steam trains on the 24km Pinjarra–Dwellingup line, with connections from Perth City (80km) by Westrail's Australind. Trains depart Pinjarra at 11.00 on Wednesdays between April and November and a through train, the Dwellingup Forest Ranger, runs from Perth City on selected Saturdays and Sundays between May and October for an eight-hour round trip.

Etmilyn Forest Tramway operates on Tuesdays, Thursdays and weekends including holiday Mondays, with tour bus connections from Perth. Hotham Valley Railway also operates steam and diesel excursions on other routes within Western Australia. For further details and bookings phone ☎ 08-9221 4444, ☎ 08-9421 1908 or ☎ 08-9531 1133, 🖹 08-9221 3065 and 🖳 hvtr@easymail.com.au.

Oliver Hill Railway, Rottnest Island

A re-built military railway (☎ 08-9222 5600), 8.5km long, links the old jetty to the Oliver Hill gun batteries. Four trains run daily from Settlement Station, Kingstown, at 10.30, 11.30, 12.45 and 14.00, the round trip taking two hours. The adult fare ($9) includes a tour of the gun emplacements. The island is accessible by ferry from Perth and Fremantle and by airbus.

NORTHERN TERRITORY

The Old Ghan

The Ghan Preservation Society operates a four or five days a week service, between April and October, over 26km from MacDonnell Siding, Alice Springs, to Ewaninga Sidings on the original Marree–Alice Springs narrow-gauge line; the adult return fare (a one-hour trip) is $15. Trains carry refreshments and an evening dinner trip is operated every Friday night.

For further details, times and bookings phone the society on ☎ 08-8955 5047, or Central Australian Tourism on ☎ 08-8951 8555 or freecall ☎ 1800 621 336. Alice Wanderer bus services from the town centre call at the siding regularly during the day.

TASMANIA

There are no mainline passenger railways in Tasmania, so access to any private or preserved railways has to be by other forms of transport. The railways listed below, which include actual train travel, are particularly worth visiting.

Derwent Valley Railway, New Norfolk
This railway runs tours, usually monthly on Sundays, on the scenic Derwent Valley line from New Norfolk station, 38km north-west of Hobart to Mt Field National Park and Maydena. New Norfolk is 55 minutes by bus from Hobart. For further information phone ☎ 03-6281 1946.

Don River Railway
The Van Dieman Light Railway Society Inc operates a 4km, 1067mm-gauge branch railway, which was closed in 1963 and restored in 1971. Steam-hauled vintage trains run alongside Don River to Coles Beach, 3.5km west of Devonport. Trains operate from 09.00 to 16.00 daily except on Christmas Day and Good Friday. There is also a museum. On selected dates, special trains venture onto the mainline system. For further details contact the Tasmanian Visitor Information Network (☎ 03-6230 8235) or Don Museum (☎ 03-6424 6335).

Ida Bay Railway, Lune River
This is Tasmania's longest-running 610mm-gauge railway; it is 6.8km in length and is 113km south of Hobart on the Huon Highway. Services are operated several times daily on various dates throughout the year. Hobart coaches run on weekdays to Dover (a one-hour journey), from where Ida Bay is a further 20km. For further information phone ☎ 03-6223 5893.

Tasmanian Transport Museum, Glenorchy
This museum can be reached by northern suburbs bus from Hobart. It is open on Saturdays, Sundays and public holidays and entry includes short (0.5km) rides on the track of the former Hobart–Launceston mainline. For further information phone ☎ 03-6272 7721.

Wee Georgie Wood Steam Railway, Tullah
About 1.8km of the former tramway from Farrell to the silver-mining centre of Tullah on Tasmania's west coast has been restored and steam trains operate on alternate Sundays between September and Easter. For details, contact the Tasmanian Visitor Information Network (☎ 03-6230 8235).

The Abt Rack Railway, Strahan
The latest news is that the historic and dramatic rail route through the gorge of King River between Queenstown and Strahan, which was closed in 1963 after 67 years serving the mines of Mount Lyell, is being restored as a tourist project. Trains are expected to be running by September 2001. For details, contact the Tasmanian Visitor Information Network (☎ 03-6230 8235).

Envoi

Perhaps you lose yourself somewhere in the heart of Australia, in the bush, in the vast emptiness of the Nullarbor, the lush greenery of the tropical rainforest, the sun and surf of Australia's miles of golden beaches or the bustling brashness of the major cities. Maybe you are just caught up with the excitement of a party, the 'footy', the fever of the Melbourne Cup when all Australia stands still, or you succumb to the rich variety of food, from witchetty grub soup to mud crab, from king prawns to barbecued Western beef steak, or you are busy 'looking at' (as the wine buffs say) the fine Australian wines – the golden yellow of Coonawarra Chardonnay or the rich ruby purple of the Hunter Valley reds with, so they say, the flavour of a well-worn saddle (it may not sound very appealing until you taste it). Or you are enchanted by the wildlife, the myriad of brightly coloured birds, the possums and the wallabies, not to mention the crocodiles and snakes which are best seen from a protected position.

You may even just be taken by the people, the friendliness, mateship and trusting attitude you meet in so many places, especially in small towns and in the bush, or when travelling, or in a pub. Even in major cities a person can buy a drink at the bar and leave the change on the counter while attending to a call of nature or some other matter. That pile of change, reserved for the next drink, will remain untouched. To violate it would provoke outrage. And in a pub, especially in the outback and in provincial towns, you will hear stories in abundance, tall tales and true ones – the latter often the strangest. Too true, mate, don't you worry about that!

You could even be listening to our radio programmes, such as the ABC's 'Australia all Over', on which you will hear similar stories of the outback and ballads of the bush, or tales of trains, old and new.

The story is told of a retired railwayman in Italy who lived the rest of his life on the trains: he had a free gold pass. I suspect that some Australians are more than a little that way inclined. Travelling across the Nullarbor, up the Queensland coast or in the outback you will meet people who do the trip every year on their pensioner pass, some to visit relatives, some just for a holiday, and some just because it has grown into them.

For whatever reason, or for none you can put a finger on, some places will make you want to linger, will draw you back, and if you go there by rail in the first place you can probably go there again. You can see much of the country and feel its spirit without ever going far from a railway or spending much more time out of a train than it takes to wait for the next one – but remember that this may not be until the following day, or week!

So have a good trip, stay awhile, and come again. See ya!

APPENDIX A: BIBLIOGRAPHY

General guidebooks have already been mentioned. There are more detailed guides for specific areas, eg the Thomas Cook Travellers series: *Sydney and New South Wales*. Lonely Planet has guides covering *New South Wales & Australian Capital Territory*, *Victoria*, *Queensland*, *South Australia*, *Western Australia*, *Northern Territory*, *Outback Australia* and *Tasmania*. Suggestions for further reading are:

GENERAL

Blainey, Geoffrey *The Tyranny of Distance*, Sun Books, Melbourne 1966

Culotta, Nino *They're a Weird Mob*, Ure-Smith, Sydney, 1957

Gilbert, Kevin *Because a White Man'll Never Do It*, Angus & Robertson, 1973

Hughes, Robert *The Fatal Shore*, Pan Books, London, 1988

Keesing, Nancy (Ed) *History of the Australian gold rushes*, Angus & Robertson, Australian Classics Edition, 1971.

Krauth, Nigel *Matilda my Darling* Allen & Unwin, Sydney, 1983

McNamara, Ian *Australia All Over*, ABC Enterprises, Sydney, 1992

Maris, Hyllus and Borg, Sonia *Women of the Sun*, Penguin Books Australia Ltd, 1985

Neidje, Bill *Story about Feeling*, Magabala Books, Broome, WA, 1989

Readers Digest *Book of Australian Facts 1992*

RAIL TRAVEL

Berry, Scyld *Train to Julia Creek, A Journey to the Heart of Australia*, Hodder & Stoughton, London, 1985

Bromby, Robin (Ed) *Australian Rail Companion*, Sherbrooke Sutherland, Sydney, 1989

Dennis, Anthony and Rayner, Michael *Ticket to Ride: A Rail Journey Around Australia* Simon & Schuster, Australia 1989

Kennedy, Ludovic *A Book of Railway Journeys, An Anthology*, Great Britain, Fontana/Collins, 1981

Taylor, Colin *Great Rail Non-Journeys of Australia*, University of Queensland Press, Brisbane, 1986

Taylor, Colin *Traincatcher* IPL Books, Wellington NZ, 1996

Whitelock, Derek *Gone on The Ghan (and other great railway journeys of Australia)* Savvas Publishing, Adelaide, 1986

AUSTRALIAN RAILWAY HISTORY AND SPECIALIST BOOKS

Adam Smith, Patsy *When we Rode the Rails*, J M Dent, Melbourne, 1983

Belbin, Phil and Burke, David *Changing Trains*, North Ryde, Methuen Australia, 1982

Bromby, Robin *The Country Railway in Australia* Cromarty Press, Sydney, 1983

Bromby, Robin *Rails to the Top End*, Cromarty Press, Sydney, 1987

Churchman, Geoffrey B *Railway Electrification in Australia and New Zealand*, IPL Books, Sydney & Wellington, 1995

Daddow, Viv *The Puffing Pioneers and Queensland's Railway Builders*, University of Queensland Press, Brisbane, 1975

Ellis, R F *Rails to the Tableland*, ARHS, Brisbane, 1976

Gunn, John *Along Parallel lines, A History of the Railways of New South Wales 1850-1986*, Melbourne University Press, 1989

Kerr, John *Triumph of Narrow Gauge, A History of Queensland Railways* Boolarong Publications, Brisbane 1990

APPENDIX B: AUSTRALIAN ENGLISH

Some expressions which are common in Strine (Australian English) may be unfamiliar to the visitor. More commonly-used examples are:

arvo	afternoon
barbie	barbecue
bathers	swimming costume (especially in Victoria and Tasmania)
bewdy	excellent! well done!
black stump	fabled remains of a tree marking the farthest outback
blue	fierce argument, fight, bad mistake
bushranger	highwayman, bandit
BYO	bring your own (usually drinks, as at a café or restaurant)
chips (bag of)	packet of potato crisps
chunder	vomit
cozzie	swimming costume (especially in NSW)
cowboy	reckless driver (especially of truck)
crook	sick, ill, off-colour
drapes	curtains
doona	duvet
dunny	toilet (originally outside as in bush dwellings)
esky	portable ice-box
go bush	leave civilisation
hoon	dangerously foolish young person
lollies	sweets, candies
mozzie	mosquito
mullock	mining refuse, muck
Pom	English person
road house	outback transport café-cum-pub, sometimes with accommodation
sanger	sandwich
see ya (later)	goodbye
she'll be right	don't worry
snags	sausages
soft drink	pop, lemonade or any fizzy non-alcoholic drink
strides	trousers
stubbie	375ml bottle of beer
sunnies	sunglasses
the bush	outback, woodland, remote country and by extension the population of such areas
tinnie or coldie	can or stubbie of cold beer
togs	bathing costume, sports clothes
troppo	foolish, affected by the heat
tucker	food
ute	small motor truck
witchetty grub	an edible wood-boring caterpillar
Woop Woop	any unnamed remote outback town (derogatory)
wowser	person who disapproves of drink, dancing, fun
wowserism	having a wowser attitude
yakka	manual work

APPENDIX C: GLOSSARY

12-chain curve a curve of 241m radius. Railway people still use chains when describing curve radii just as nautical people use knots for wind and vessel speeds rather than km/h.

broad gauge rail line of greater than standard gauge (qv)

car goods goods train with a passenger van

catenaries the wires carrying power on an electrified railway

combined gauge rail line of three or more rails combining two or more different gauges

consist (as a noun) the composition or make-up of a train

eight-coupled (steam locomotives) locomotive with eight driving wheels (four axles)

electric multiple unit trainset of electric-powered carriages which may be coupled to others of the same kind

HST High Speed Train (British Rail)

Irish gauge 1600mm (5ft 3in) between rails

mixed train train consisting of passenger coaches and goods wagons

motive power depot glorified large-scale engine shed

narrow gauge railway line of less than standard gauge (qv)

rake a string of carriages or other vehicles forming the trailing part of a train (ie other than the locomotive or power unit)

reverse curve compound left/right curve

roundhouse large engine shed with a turntable in the middle

standard gauge railway line 1435mm (4ft 8½in) between rails

TGV Train à grande Vitesse – the French high-speed trains

through train a train which goes from an origin or to a destination which is beyond or off the normal route of services on a particular line; similarly 'through carriage' and 'through service'.

token small container enclosing authority to proceed on single-track section

trainset a train (usually passenger) of fixed consist

triple gauge rail track consisting of four rails combining three different gauges ie 1067mm, 1435mm and 1600mm

XPT the express passenger train of New South Wales based on the British InterCity 125 HST

APPENDIX D: BUS/RAIL CONNECTIONS

IN NEW SOUTH WALES
Narrandera and Griffith from **Wagga Wagga** (C 9107)
Gundagai and Tumut from **Cootamundra** (C 9106, 9110)
Griffith, Hay and Mildura (Vic) from **Cootamundra**
Echuca (Vic) from **Albury** via Tocumwal (C 9126)
Cooma and Bombola from **Canberra** (C 9120 and local)
Thredbo (for Mt Blue Cow) from Canberra (C 9098)
Mudgee from **Lithgow** (C 9088)
Cobar and Bourke from **Dubbo** (C 9097 and 9110)
Cowra from **Orange** (C 9104)
Forbes and Eugowra from **Orange** and **Parkes** (C 9104 and local)
Oberon from **Mount Victoria** (local)
Cooma, Bega and Eden from **Goulburn** and **Canberra**
Glen Innes and Tenterfield from **Armidale** (C 9074)

In addition, railway buses provide potentially useful cross-country links between some of the railway routes, as follows:

Cootamundra (Main South line) to Condobolin (Western mainline) (C 9106)
Cootamundra to Orange and Bathurst (Western mainline) (C 9104)
Cootamundra to Dubbo (Central west line) (C 9104)
Dubbo (Central west line) to Parkes and Broken Hill (Western main line) (C 9076, 9110)
Yass Junction (Main South line) to Canberra (C 9102)
Wagga Wagga (Main South line) to Griffith (C 9107)
Grafton City (North Coast mainline) to Moree (Northwest) (C 9091)

IN VICTORIA
Echuca from Bendigo (C 9076)
Bairnsdale and Orbost from **Sale**.(Gippsland line) (C 9120)
Balranald (NSW), Robinvale and Euston (NSW) from **Swan Hill** (C 9105)
Maldon and Maryborough from **Castlemaine** (V/line local timetable)
Daylesford from **Woodend** (Bendigo line) (V/line local timetable)
Portland and Mount Gambier (South Australia) from **Warrnambool**. (C 9121)

Rail-operated coaches provide useful links between some rail routes:
Echuca to Shepparton (V/line local timetable)
Benalla (NE interstate line) to Shepparton (Goulburn Valley) (C 9076, 9126)
Echuca to Murchison East (Goulburn Valley) (V/line local timetable)
Echuca to Kerang (C 9126)
Ballarat (Western line) to Camperdown and Warrnambool (WCR) (local)
Ballarat to Bendigo (C 9119)
Ballarat to Castlemaine (Bendigo line) (C 9119 and local)
Ballarat to Geelong (C 9119)
Cranbourne (The Met) to Nyora (South Gippsland railway) (local)

IN QUEENSLAND
The buses are private, but mostly operated by McCafferty's, a Toowoomba-based company with an office in Roma St Transit Centre, Brisbane. A QR/McCafferty's Road/Rail Pass is available for journeys entirely within Queensland (see p32).

● **1**   A bus runs daily between Barcaldine (Midland line) and Charleville (Western line) via Blackall (Yaraka branch) at 18.10 to reach Charleville at 23.35, returning at 03.55 to arrive in Barcaldine at 09.45 (C 9073). An alternative northbound service returns from Morven (Western line) at 17.10, reaching Barcaldine at 22.35.

● **2**   Buses leave Cloncurry (Mount Isa line) daily for Winton and Longreach (Midland line) at 09.30, arriving in Longreach at 16.10. The return service from Longreach is at 11.00, arriving in Cloncurry at 17.30 (C 9073).

● **3**   Buses leave Mackay (main north line) daily for Emerald (Midland line) at 08.00, arriving at 14.00. The return service leaves Emerald at 13.00, arriving in Mackay at 18.25 (C 9080).

● **4**   There are indirect coach links between Mount Isa (Queensland) and Alice Springs by McCafferty's and Greyhound services. The timetables are complicated but may be summarised as follows (C 9075, 9125):

A daily Greyhound coach from Mount Isa at 10.30, with a five-hour evening wait for a connection at Tennant Creek (NT), arrives in Alice Springs at 05.30 the next day. A McCafferty's daily coach leaves Mount Isa at 19.45 for Tennant Creek, arriving at 02.50 the next day with a four times weekly connection to Alice Springs at 03.30, arriving at 09.30. On Mondays and Thursdays this connects with the train from Townsville at Mount Isa and with The Ghan at Alice Springs.

Returning, the Greyhound coach departs Alice Springs daily at 17.15 with a midnight connection in Tennant Creek, to reach Mount Isa at 07.45 the next day. McCafferty's daily coach leaves Tennant Creek at 23.00 arriving Mount Isa at 06.40 with a connection from Alice Springs at 16.15 four days a week. The Tuesday and Friday departures from Alice Springs connect with The Ghan and the Thursday and Sunday departures connect at Mount Isa with the Inlander to Townsville.

● **5**   Coral Coaches and other connections between Cloncurry, the Gulf Country, Mareeba and Cairns were summarised on pp75, 89 and 90, Itinerary 7 and Table 10.

INDEX

Trans-Siberian Handbook *Bryn Thomas*
432 pages, 50 maps, 32 colour photos
ISBN 1 873756 42 9, *5th edition*, £11.99, US$19.95
First edition short-listed for the **Thomas Cook Guidebook
Awards**. Fifth edition of the most popular guide to the world's
longest rail journey. How to arrange a trip, plus a km-by-km guide
to the Trans-Siberian, Trans-Manchurian and Trans-Mongolian
routes. Fully updated and expanded to include extra information
on travelling independently in Russia.
'The Trans-Siberian Handbook is a must.' **The Sunday Times**
'Definitive guide' **Condé Nast Traveler**

❏ OTHER GUIDES FROM TRAILBLAZER PUBLICATIONS

Adventure Motorcycling Handbook	4th edn Nov 2000
Asia Overland – A Route & Planning Guide	1st edn out now
Azerbaijan (with Georgia)	2nd edn mid 2001
The Blues Highway – New Orleans to Chicago	1st edn mid 2001
China by Rail	1st edn out now
Inca Trail, Cuzco & Machu Picchu	1st edn out now
Indian Ashram Guide	1st edn early 2001
Istanbul to Cairo Overland	1st edn out now
Japan by Rail	1st edn mid 2001
Land's End to John o'Groats	1st edn Dec 2001
Mexico's Yucatan & the Ruta Maya	1st edn mid 2001
Norway's Arctic Highway	1st edn Dec 2001
Tibet Overland – mountain biking & jeep touring	1st edn early 2001
Siberian BAM Guide – rail, rivers & road	2nd edn Dec 2000
Silk Route by Rail	2nd edn out now
Sahara Overland – a route & planning guide	1st edn out now
Sahara Abenteuerhandbuch (German edition)	1st edn early 2001
Ski Canada – where to ski and snowboard	1st edn out now
Trans-Siberian Handbook	5th edn Dec 2000
Trans-Canada Rail Guide	2nd edn out now
Trekking in the Annapurna Region	3rd edn out now
Trekking in the Everest Region	3rd edn out now
Trekking in Langtang, Gosainkund & Helambu	1st edn out now
Trekking in Corsica	1st edn Dec 2001
Trekking in the Dolomites	1st edn Dec 2000
Trekking in Ladakh	2nd edn out now
Trekking in Morocco	1st edn out now
Trekking in the Pyrenees	1st edn out now
Vietnam by Rail	1st edn Dec 2000

For more information about Trailblazer and our expanding range of guides,
for where to find your nearest stockist, for guidebook updates
or for credit card mail order sales (post free worldwide) visit our Web site:

www.trailblazer-guides.com

ROUTE GUIDES FOR THE ADVENTUROUS TRAVELLER

Trans-Canada Rail Guide *Melissa Graham*
240 pages, 31 maps, 24 colour photos
ISBN 1 873756 39 9, *2nd edition*, £10.99, US$16.95
Expanded 2nd edition now includes Calgary city guide. Comprehensive guide to Canada's trans-continental railroad. Covers the entire route from coast to coast. What to see and where to stay in the cities along the line, with information for all budgets.
*Invaluable – **The Daily Telegraph***

China by Rail *Douglas Streatfeild-James*
384 pages, 54 maps, 30 colour photos
ISBN 1 873756 15 1, *1st edition*, £11.95, US$17.95
The guide to China for rail travellers. Most visitors use the comprehensive rail system to get around. This guide takes in all the main attractions, with full details of where to stay and where to eat – for all budgets. Beijing, Hong Kong and 32 towns covered in detail.

Japan by Rail *Ramsey Zarifeh*
256 pages, 40 maps, 30 colour photos
ISBN 1 873756 23 2, *1st edition*, £11.99, US$18.95
With a Japan Railpass, travelling around this country can be surprisingly good value. This guide includes detailed route and planning information, where to stay, where to eat and the most interesting places to stop off along the way. Includes rail maps and town plans.

Vietnam by Rail *Tess Read*
256 pages, 45 maps, 30 colour photos
ISBN 1 873756 44 5, *1st edition*, £10.99, US$18.95
The 'Reunification Express' railway links the north and south and is the most popular way to travel the country. Includes a history of Vietnam's railways, and a detailed route guide with 12 strip maps. Plus comprehensive guides to 24 towns and cities.

Silk Route by Rail *Dominic Streatfeild-James*
320 pages, 37 maps, 30 colour photos
ISBN 1 873756 14 3, *2nd edition*, £10.95, US$17.95
First edition short-listed for the **Thomas Cook Guidebook Awards**. Covers the railway line which follows the old Silk Route. It's possible to travel by rail from Moscow via the Central Asian cities of Samarkand and Tashkent across western China to Beijing. Includes guides to 17 cities along the way.

Siberian BAM Guide – rail, rivers & road
Athol Yates and *Nicholas Zvegintzov*
416 pages, 20 colour photos, 50 B&W photos
ISBN 1 873756 18 6, *2nd edition*, £13.99, US$23.95
Comprehensive guide to the BAM Zone in NE Siberia. Includes a detailed guide to the 3400-km Baikal Amur Mainline (BAM) railway which traverses east Siberia from the Pacific Ocean to Lake Baikal. Detailed information on how to take the train and where to go in the BAM Zone. Plus Lena River routes.
'...an encyclopaedic companion.' **The Independent**